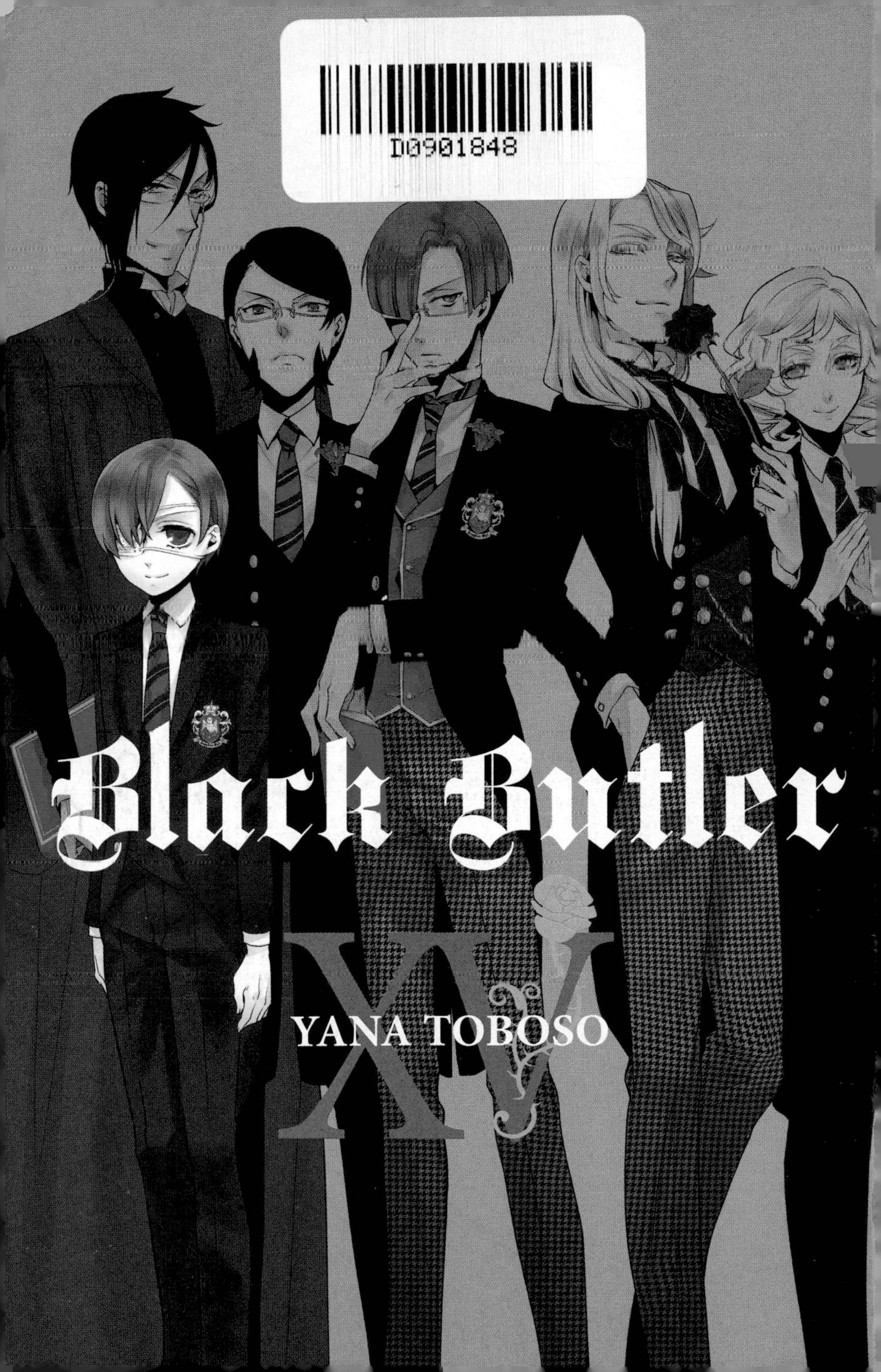
Black Butler
XV
YANA TOBOSO

Contents

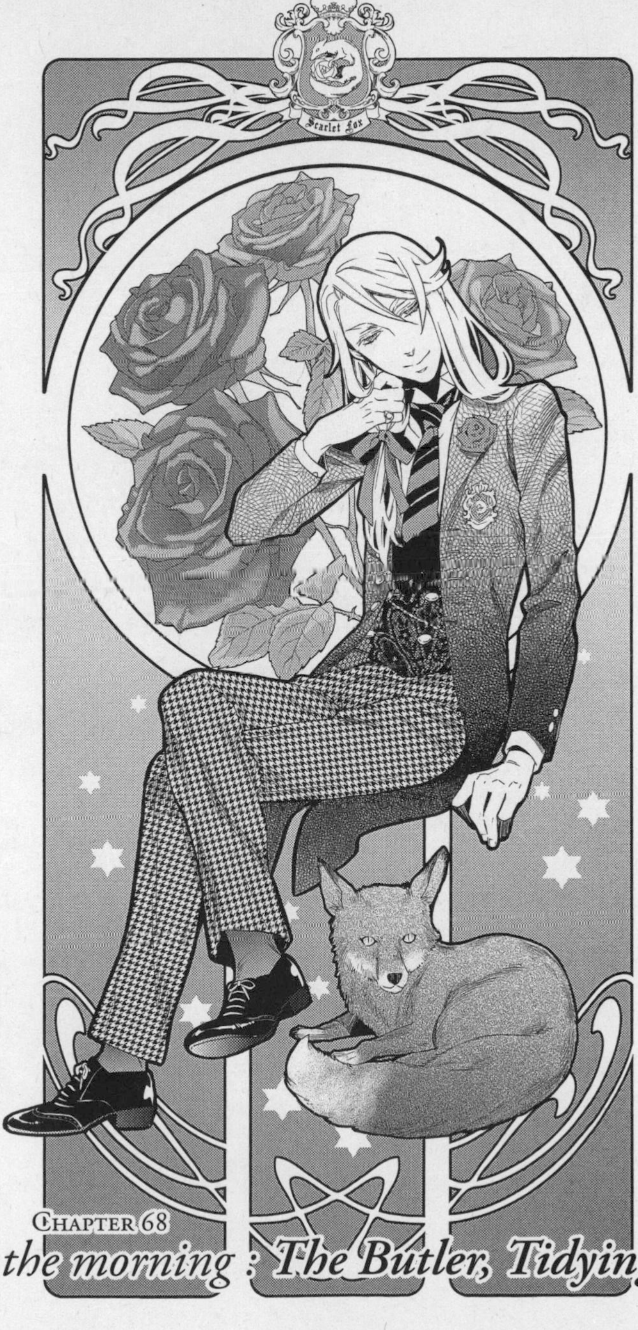
Scarlet Fox

CHAPTER 68

In the morning : The Butler, Tidying Up

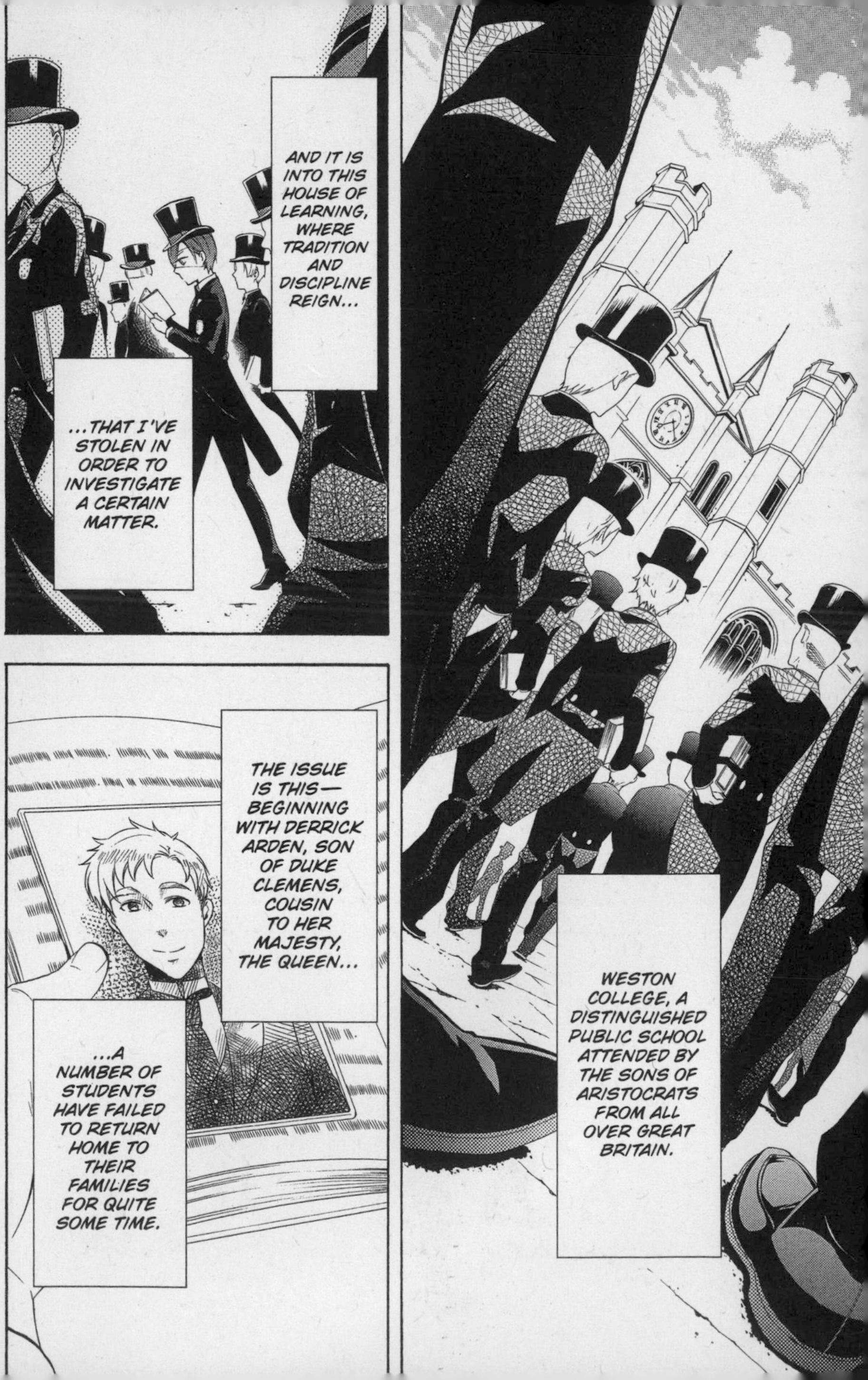
WESTON COLLEGE, A DISTINGUISHED PUBLIC SCHOOL ATTENDED BY THE SONS OF ARISTOCRATS FROM ALL OVER GREAT BRITAIN.
AND IT IS INTO THIS HOUSE OF LEARNING, WHERE TRADITION AND DISCIPLINE REIGN...
...THAT I'VE STOLEN IN ORDER TO INVESTIGATE A CERTAIN MATTER.
THE ISSUE IS THIS—BEGINNING WITH DERRICK ARDEN, SON OF DUKE CLEMENS, COUSIN TO HER MAJESTY, THE QUEEN...
...A NUMBER OF STUDENTS HAVE FAILED TO RETURN HOME TO THEIR FAMILIES FOR QUITE SOME TIME.

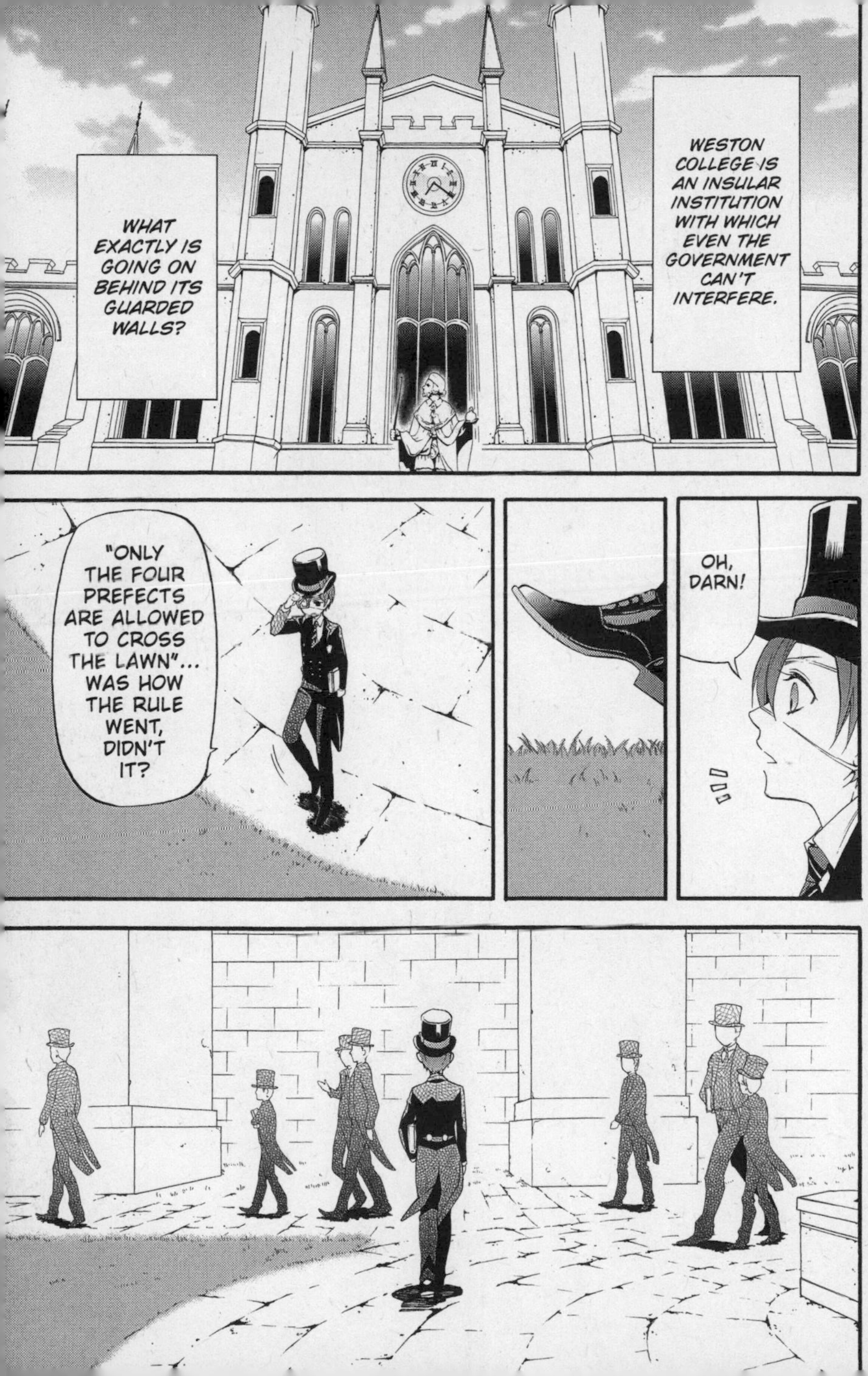
WESTON COLLEGE IS AN INSULAR INSTITUTION WITH WHICH EVEN THE GOVERNMENT CAN'T INTERFERE.
WHAT EXACTLY IS GOING ON BEHIND ITS GUARDED WALLS?
OH, DARN!
"ONLY THE FOUR PREFECTS ARE ALLOWED TO CROSS THE LAWN"... WAS HOW THE RULE WENT, DIDN'T IT?

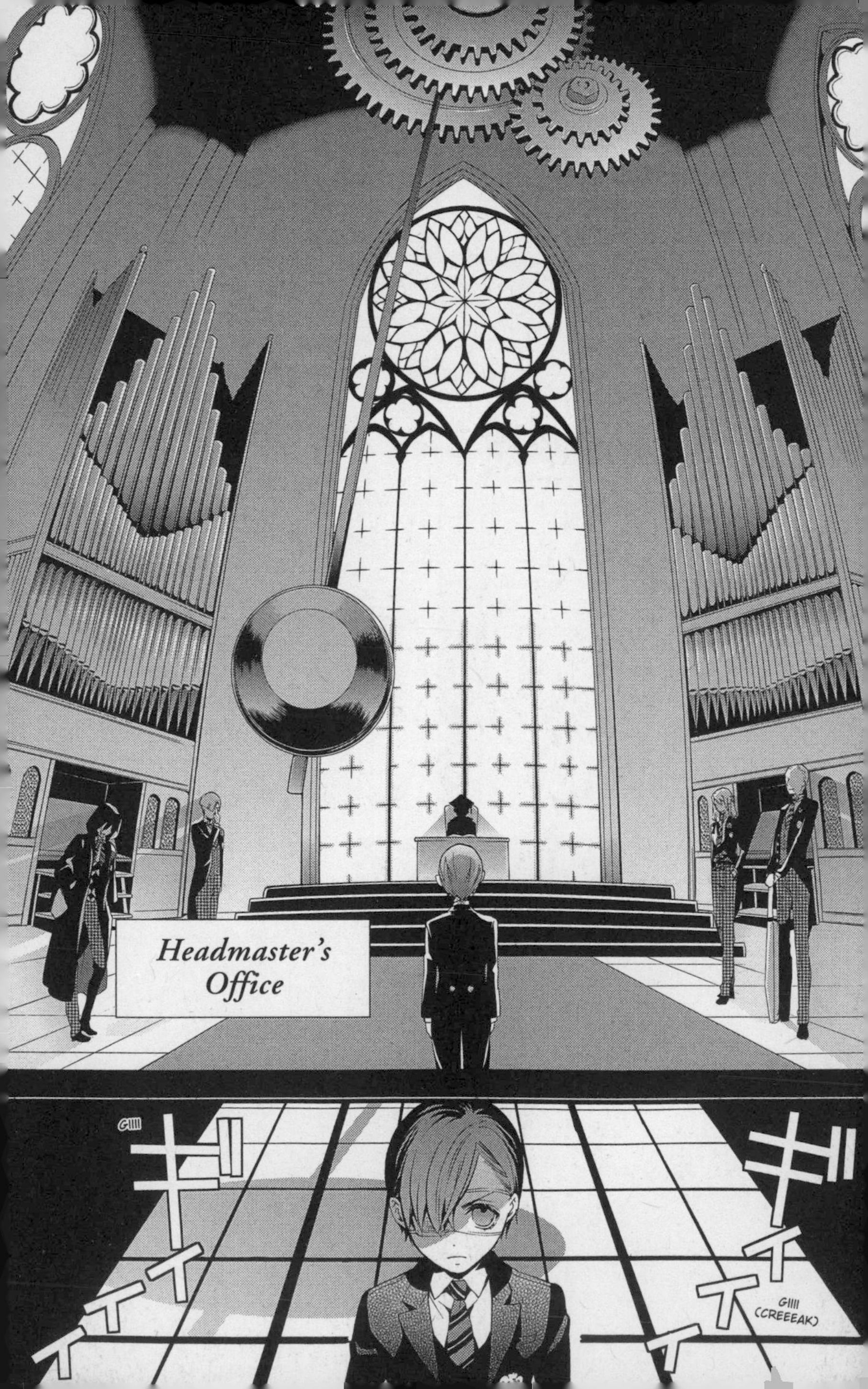
Headmaster's Office
GIIII
(CREEEAK)
GIIII

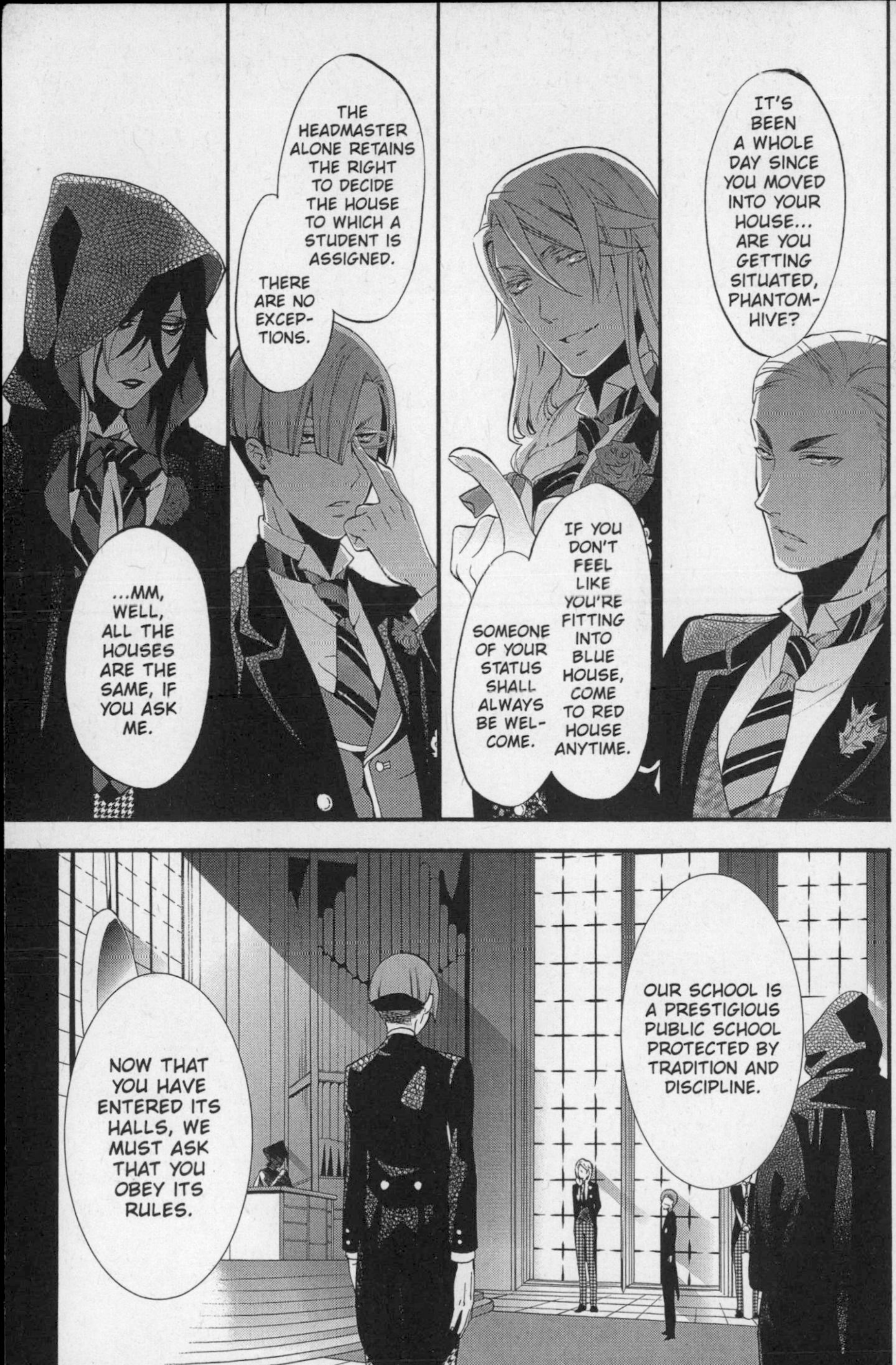
IT'S BEEN A WHOLE DAY SINCE YOU MOVED INTO YOUR HOUSE... ARE YOU GETTING SITUATED, PHANTOM-HIVE?
IF YOU DON'T FEEL LIKE YOU'RE FITTING INTO BLUE HOUSE, COME TO RED HOUSE ANYTIME.
SOMEONE OF YOUR STATUS SHALL ALWAYS BE WEL-COME.
THE HEADMASTER ALONE RETAINS THE RIGHT TO DECIDE THE HOUSE TO WHICH A STUDENT IS ASSIGNED.
THERE ARE NO EXCEP-TIONS.
...MM, WELL, ALL THE HOUSES ARE THE SAME, IF YOU ASK ME.
OUR SCHOOL IS A PRESTIGIOUS PUBLIC SCHOOL PROTECTED BY TRADITION AND DISCIPLINE.
NOW THAT YOU HAVE ENTERED ITS HALLS, WE MUST ASK THAT YOU OBEY ITS RULES.

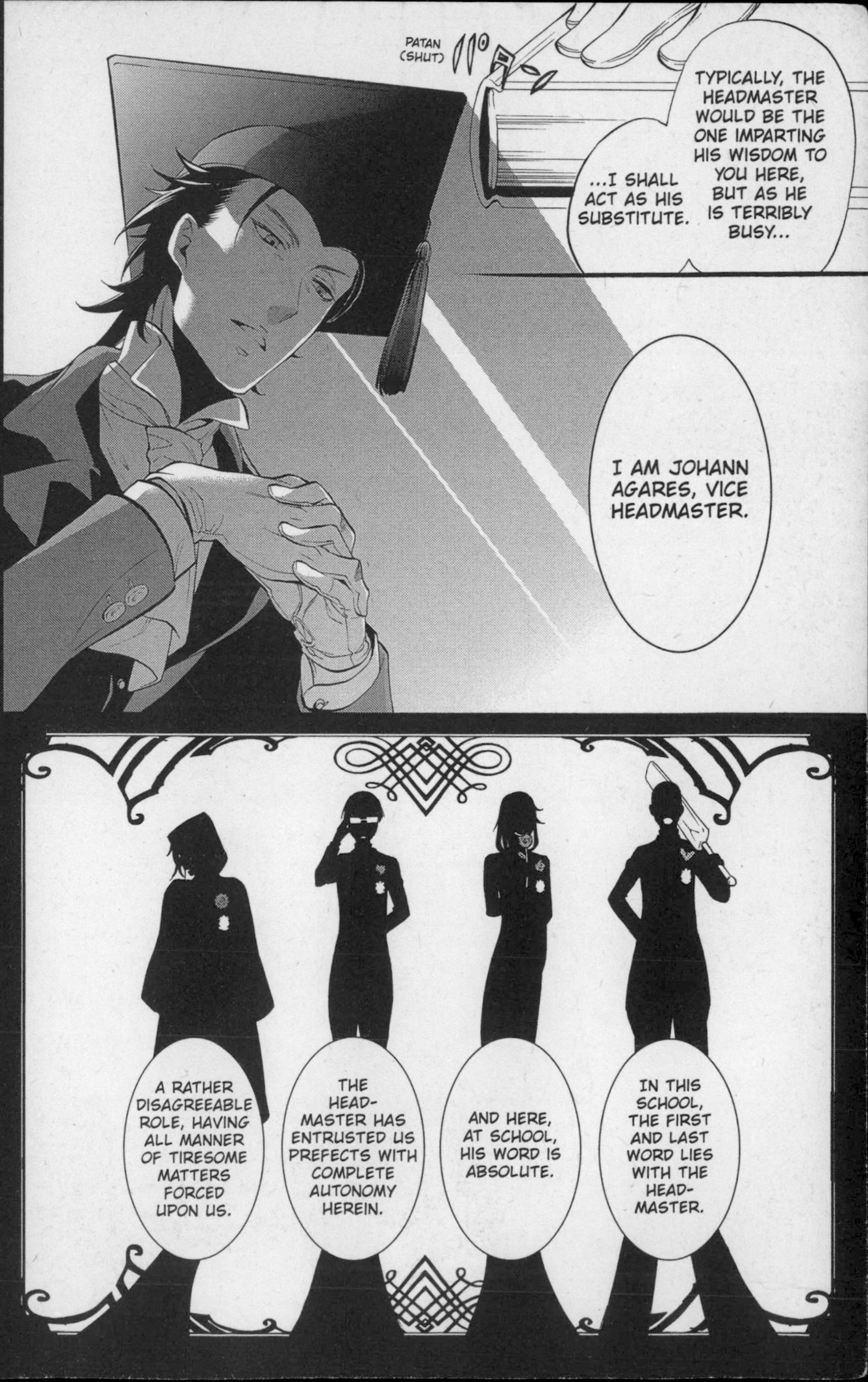
PATAN (SHUT)
TYPICALLY, THE HEADMASTER WOULD BE THE ONE IMPARTING HIS WISDOM TO YOU HERE, BUT AS HE IS TERRIBLY BUSY...
...I SHALL ACT AS HIS SUBSTITUTE.
I AM JOHANN AGARES, VICE HEADMASTER.
IN THIS SCHOOL, THE FIRST AND LAST WORD LIES WITH THE HEAD-MASTER.
AND HERE, AT SCHOOL, HIS WORD IS ABSOLUTE.
THE HEAD-MASTER HAS ENTRUSTED US PREFECTS WITH COMPLETE AUTONOMY HEREIN.
A RATHER DISAGREEABLE ROLE, HAVING ALL MANNER OF TIRESOME MATTERS FORCED UPON US.

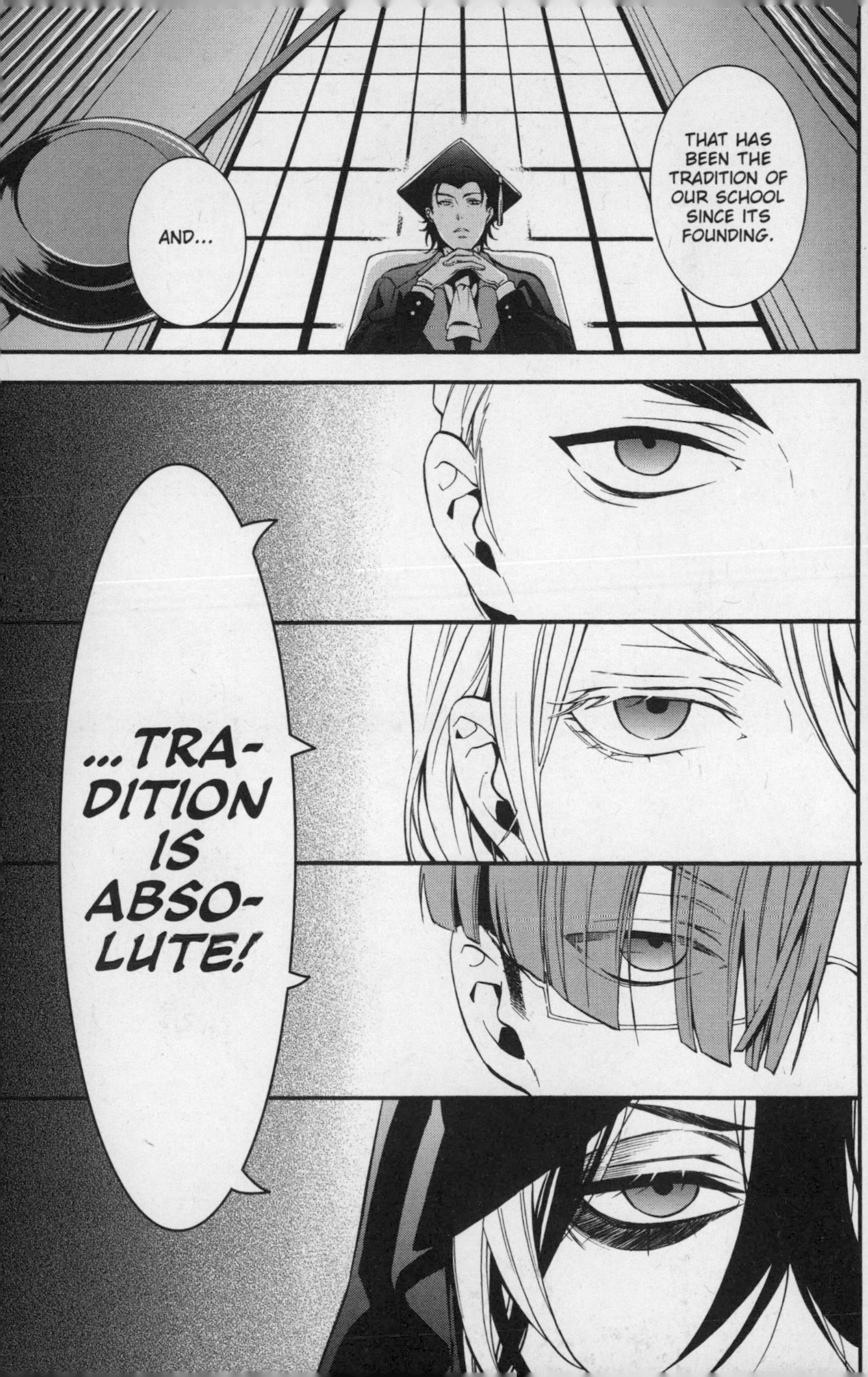
THAT HAS BEEN THE TRADITION OF OUR SCHOOL SINCE ITS FOUNDING.
AND...
...TRADITION IS ABSOLUTE!

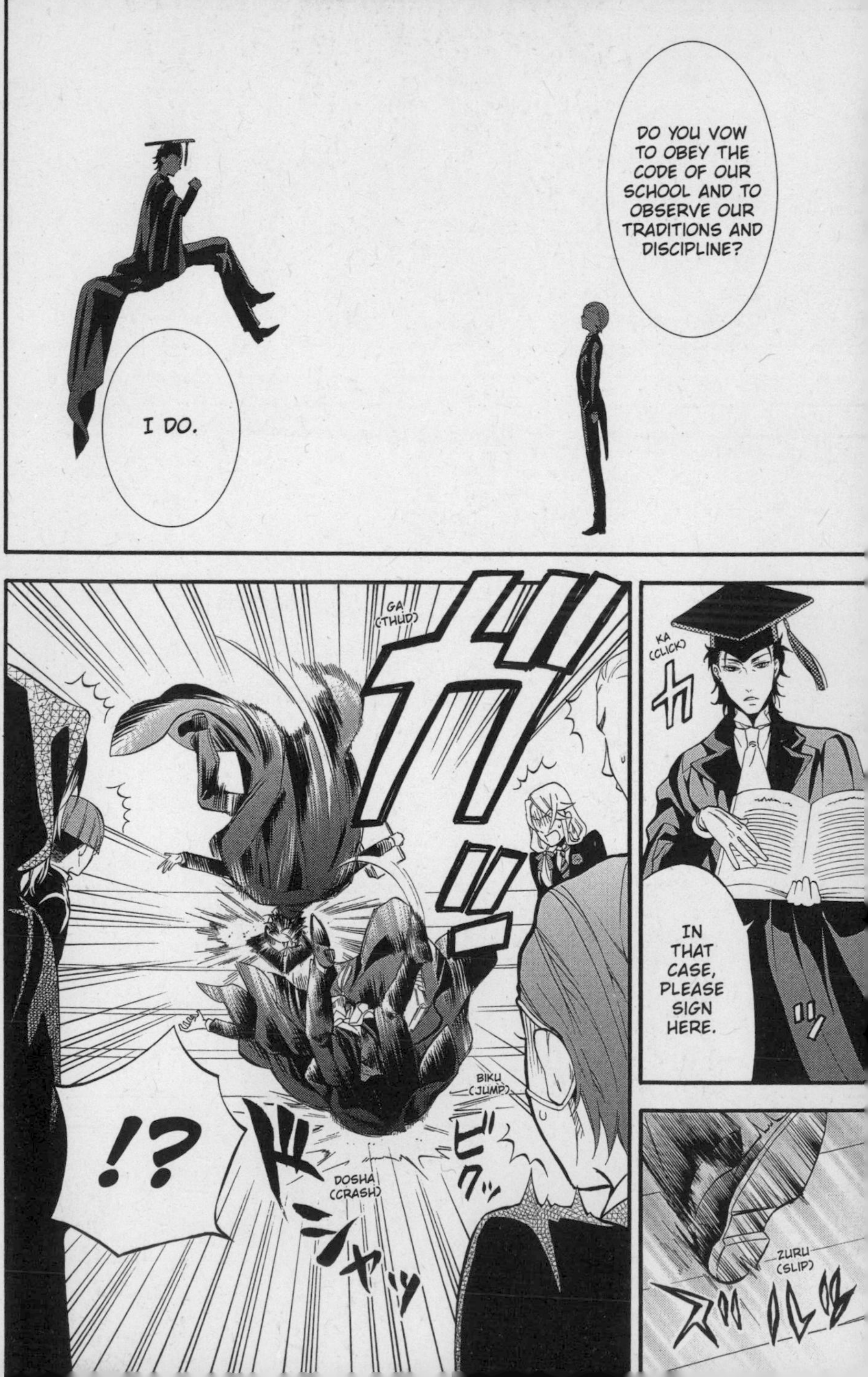
DO YOU VOW TO OBEY THE CODE OF OUR SCHOOL AND TO OBSERVE OUR TRADITIONS AND DISCIPLINE?
I DO.
KA (CLICK)
IN THAT CASE, PLEASE SIGN HERE.
ZURU (SLIP)
GA (THUD)
BIKU (JUMP)
DOSHA (CRASH)
!?

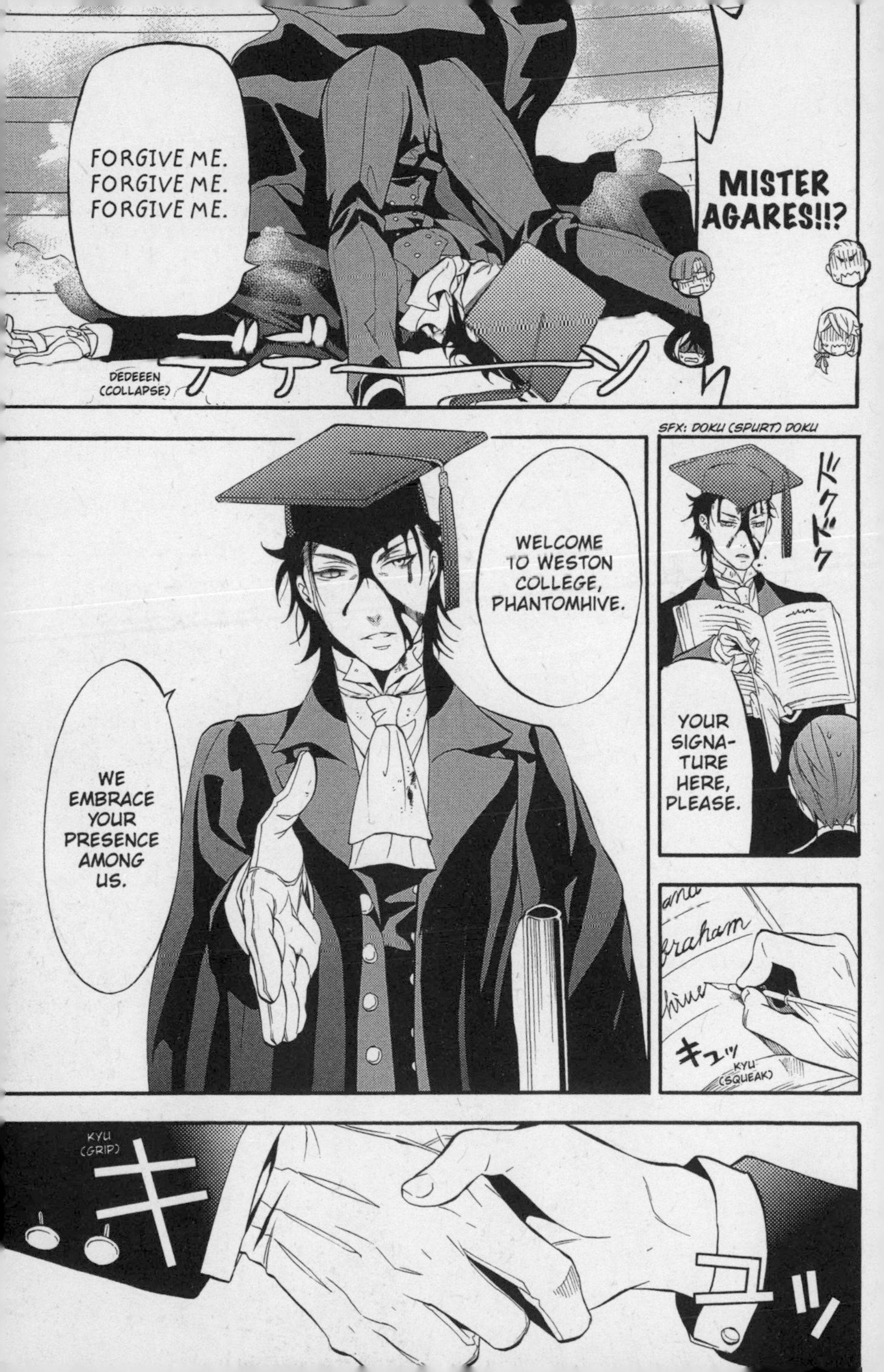
MISTER AGARES!!?
FORGIVE ME. FORGIVE ME. FORGIVE ME.
DEDEEN (COLLAPSE)
SFX: DOKU (SPURT) DOKU
ドクドク
YOUR SIGNATURE HERE, PLEASE.
キュッ
KYU (SQUEAK)
WELCOME TO WESTON COLLEGE, PHANTOMHIVE.
WE EMBRACE YOUR PRESENCE AMONG US.
KYU (GRIP)
キュッ

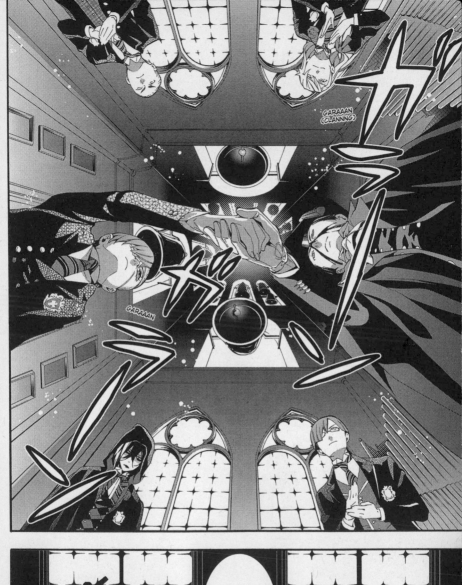

GARAAAN
(CLANNNG)

GARAAAN

MAY YOU ENJOY YOUR SCHOOL LIFE HERE.

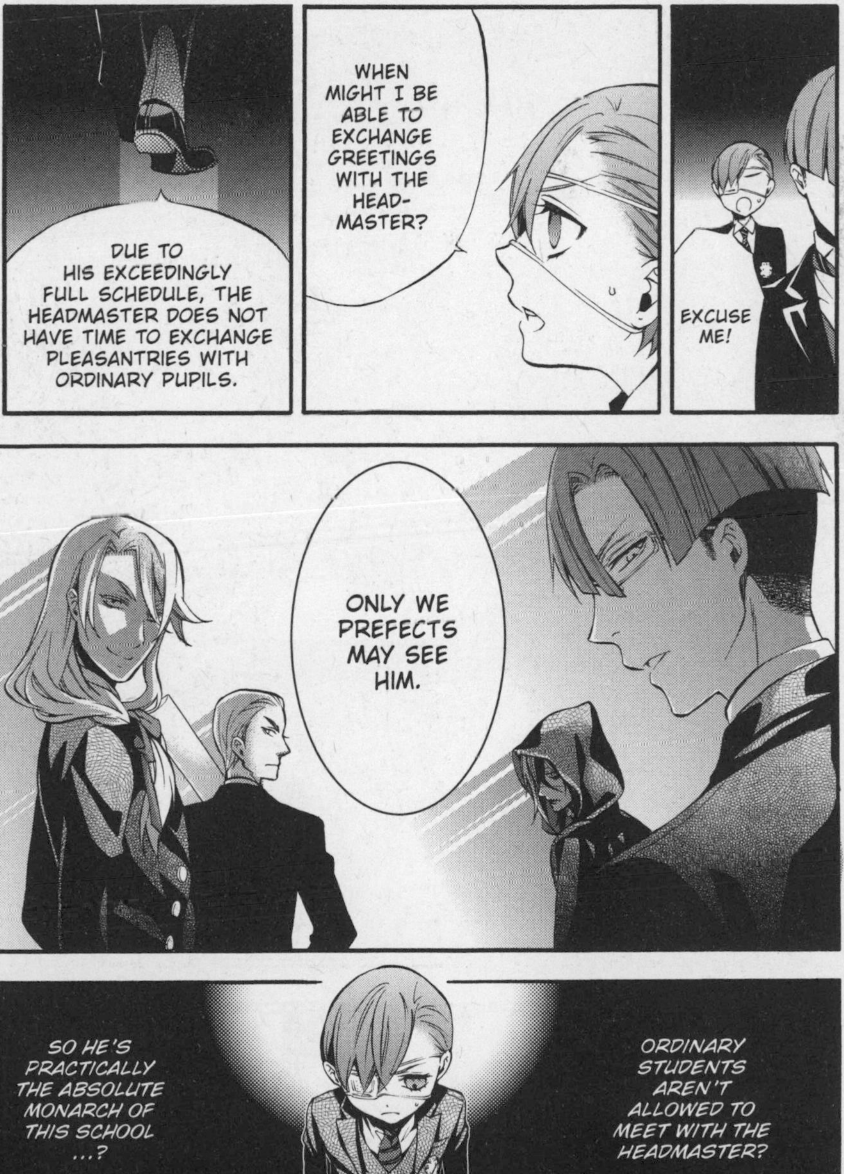
EXCUSE ME!
WHEN MIGHT I BE ABLE TO EXCHANGE GREETINGS WITH THE HEAD-MASTER?
DUE TO HIS EXCEEDINGLY FULL SCHEDULE, THE HEADMASTER DOES NOT HAVE TIME TO EXCHANGE PLEASANTRIES WITH ORDINARY PUPILS.
ONLY WE PREFECTS MAY SEE HIM.
ORDINARY STUDENTS AREN'T ALLOWED TO MEET WITH THE HEADMASTER?
SO HE'S PRACTICALLY THE ABSOLUTE MONARCH OF THIS SCHOOL ...?

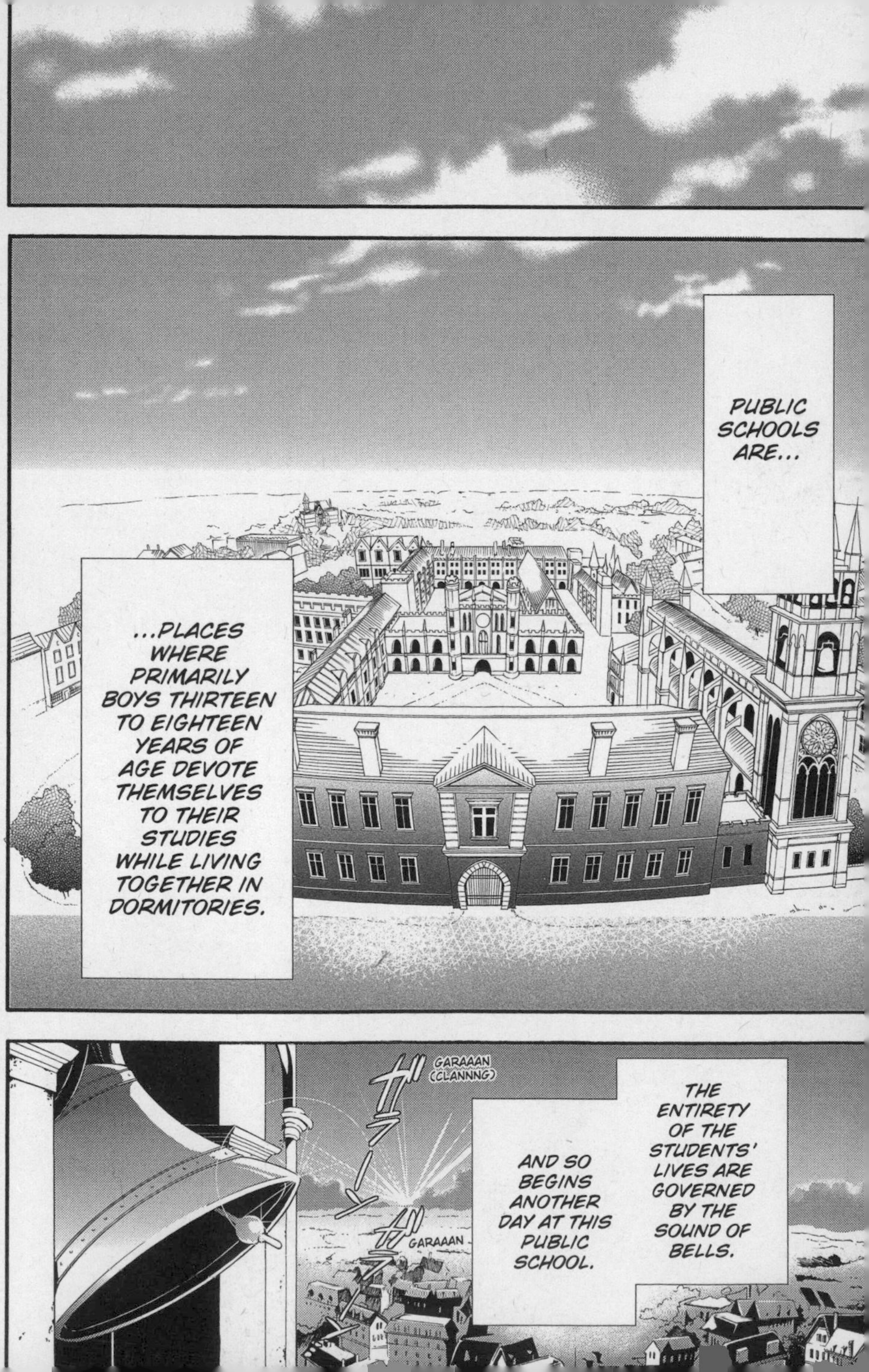
PUBLIC SCHOOLS ARE...
...PLACES WHERE PRIMARILY BOYS THIRTEEN TO EIGHTEEN YEARS OF AGE DEVOTE THEMSELVES TO THEIR STUDIES WHILE LIVING TOGETHER IN DORMITORIES.
THE ENTIRETY OF THE STUDENTS' LIVES ARE GOVERNED BY THE SOUND OF BELLS.
AND SO BEGINS ANOTHER DAY AT THIS PUBLIC SCHOOL.
GARAAAN (CLANNNG)
GARAAAN

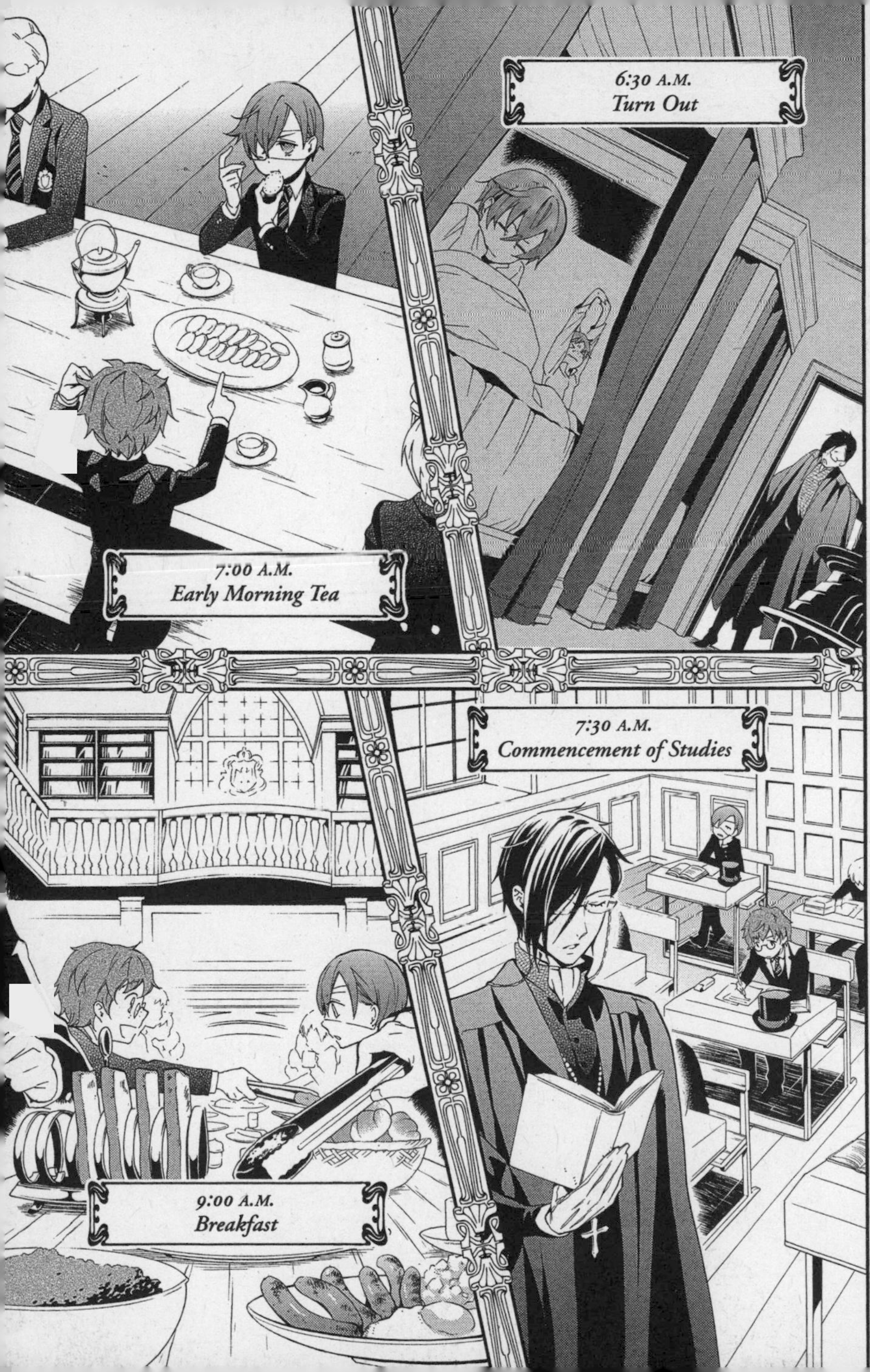
6:30 A.M.
Turn Out
7:00 A.M.
Early Morning Tea
7:30 A.M.
Commencement of Studies
9:00 A.M.
Breakfast

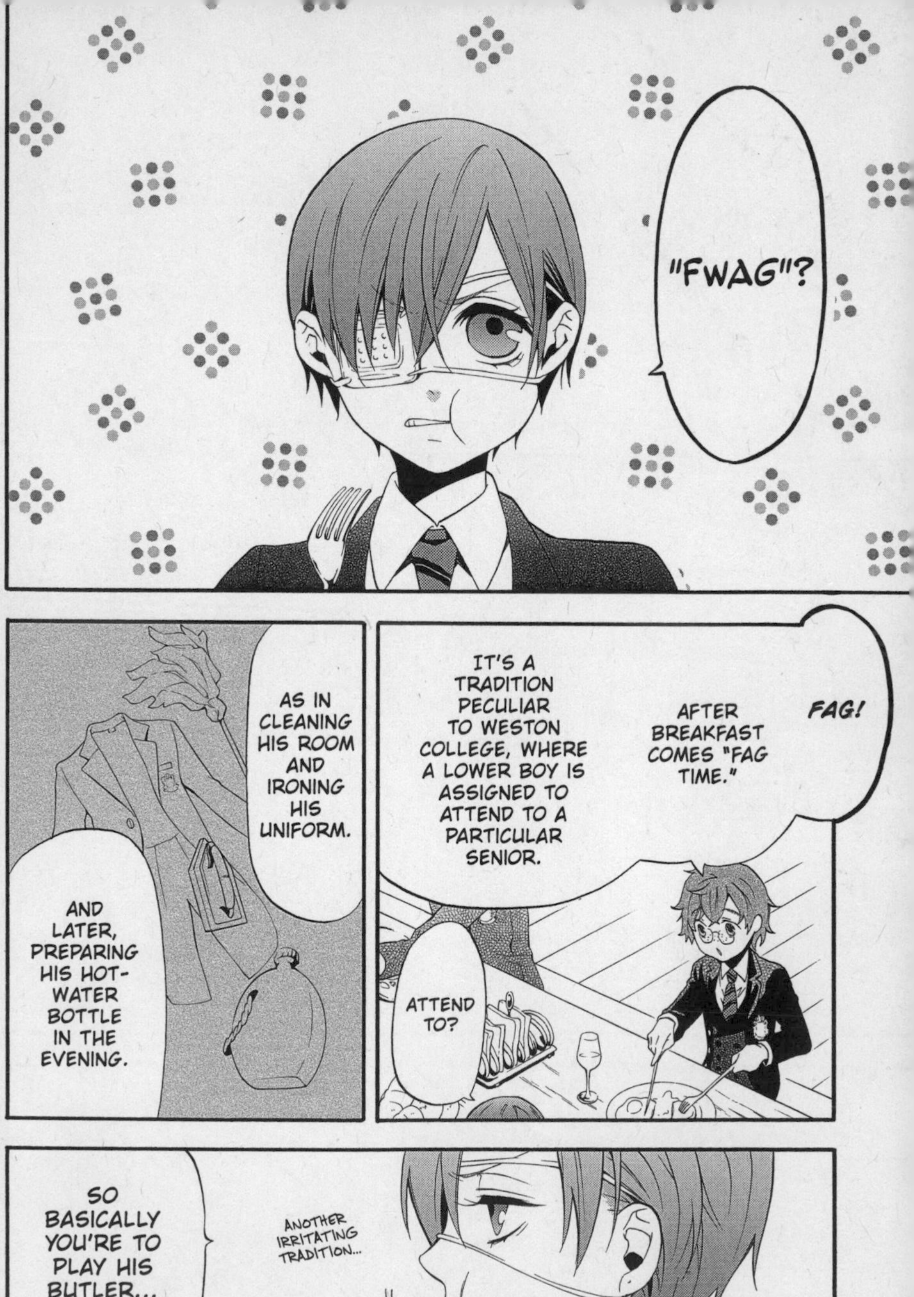
"FWAG"?
FAG!
AFTER BREAKFAST COMES "FAG TIME."
IT'S A TRADITION PECULIAR TO WESTON COLLEGE, WHERE A LOWER BOY IS ASSIGNED TO ATTEND TO A PARTICULAR SENIOR.
ATTEND TO?
AS IN CLEANING HIS ROOM AND IRONING HIS UNIFORM.
AND LATER, PREPARING HIS HOT-WATER BOTTLE IN THE EVENING.
SO BASICALLY YOU'RE TO PLAY HIS BUTLER...
ANOTHER IRRITATING TRADITION...

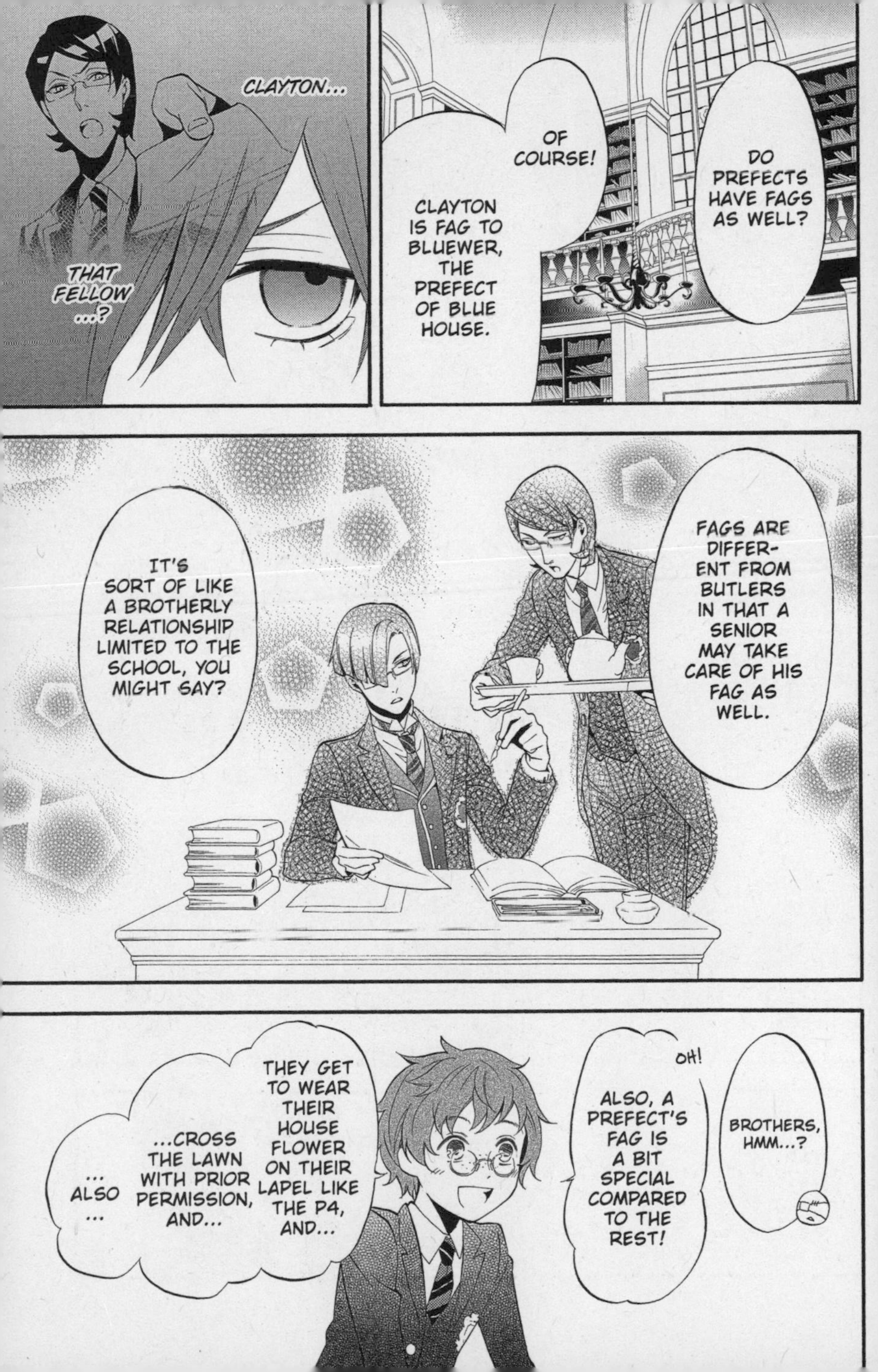
DO PREFECTS HAVE FAGS AS WELL?
OF COURSE!
CLAYTON IS FAG TO BLUEWER, THE PREFECT OF BLUE HOUSE.
CLAYTON...
THAT FELLOW ...?
FAGS ARE DIFFERENT FROM BUTLERS IN THAT A SENIOR MAY TAKE CARE OF HIS FAG AS WELL.
IT'S SORT OF LIKE A BROTHERLY RELATIONSHIP LIMITED TO THE SCHOOL, YOU MIGHT SAY?
BROTHERS, HMM...?
OH!
ALSO, A PREFECT'S FAG IS A BIT SPECIAL COMPARED TO THE REST!
THEY GET TO WEAR THEIR HOUSE FLOWER ON THEIR LAPEL LIKE THE P4, AND...
...CROSS THE LAWN WITH PRIOR PERMISSION, AND...
... ALSO ...

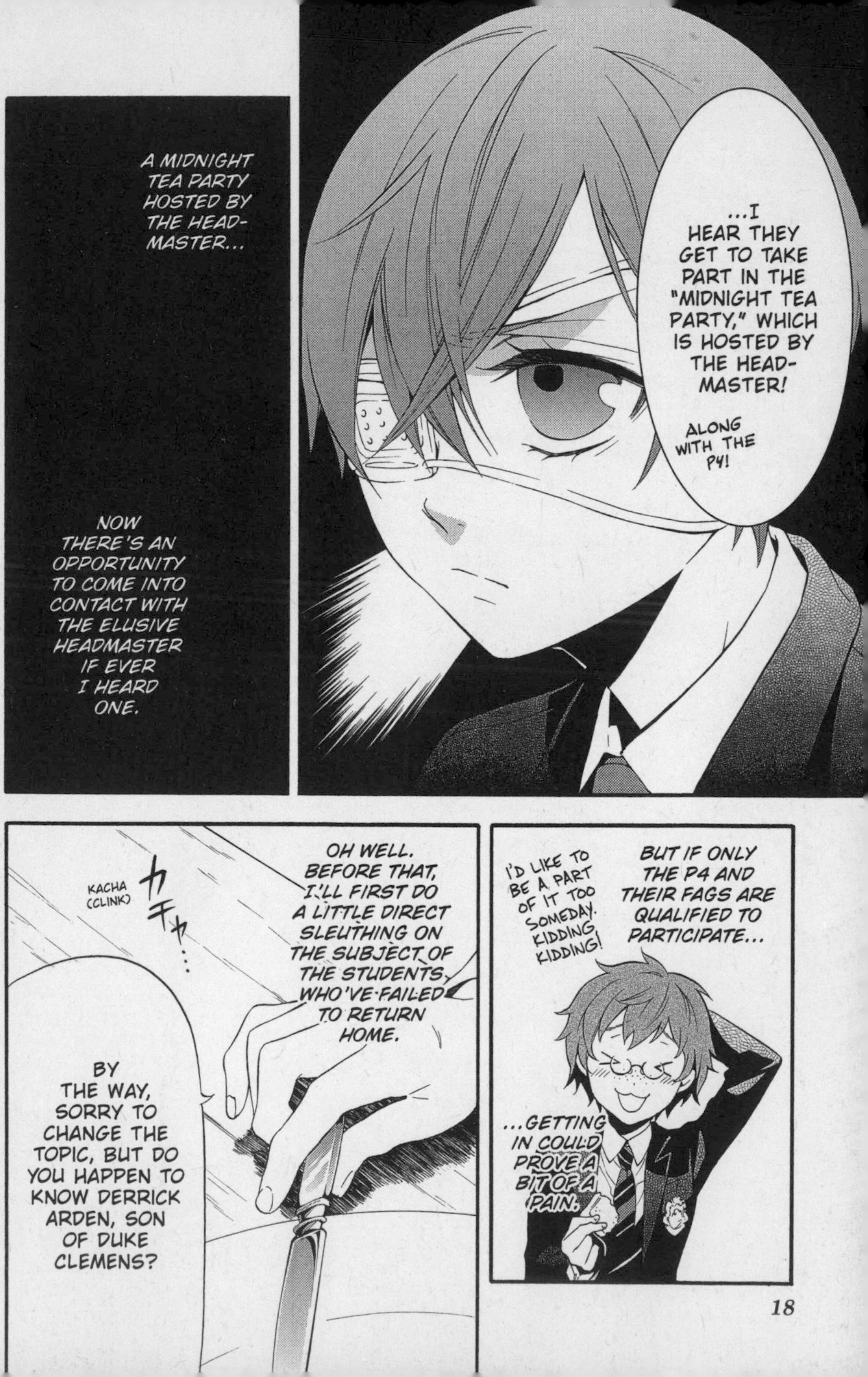
...I HEAR THEY GET TO TAKE PART IN THE "MIDNIGHT TEA PARTY," WHICH IS HOSTED BY THE HEAD-MASTER!
ALONG WITH THE P4!
A MIDNIGHT TEA PARTY HOSTED BY THE HEAD-MASTER...
NOW THERE'S AN OPPORTUNITY TO COME INTO CONTACT WITH THE ELUSIVE HEADMASTER IF EVER I HEARD ONE.
BUT IF ONLY THE P4 AND THEIR FAGS ARE QUALIFIED TO PARTICIPATE...
I'D LIKE TO BE A PART OF IT TOO SOMEDAY. KIDDING KIDDING!
...GETTING IN COULD PROVE A BIT OF A PAIN.
OH WELL. BEFORE THAT, I'LL FIRST DO A LITTLE DIRECT SLEUTHING ON THE SUBJECT OF THE STUDENTS WHO'VE FAILED TO RETURN HOME.
KACHA (CLINK)
カチャ…
BY THE WAY, SORRY TO CHANGE THE TOPIC, BUT DO YOU HAPPEN TO KNOW DERRICK ARDEN, SON OF DUKE CLEMENS?

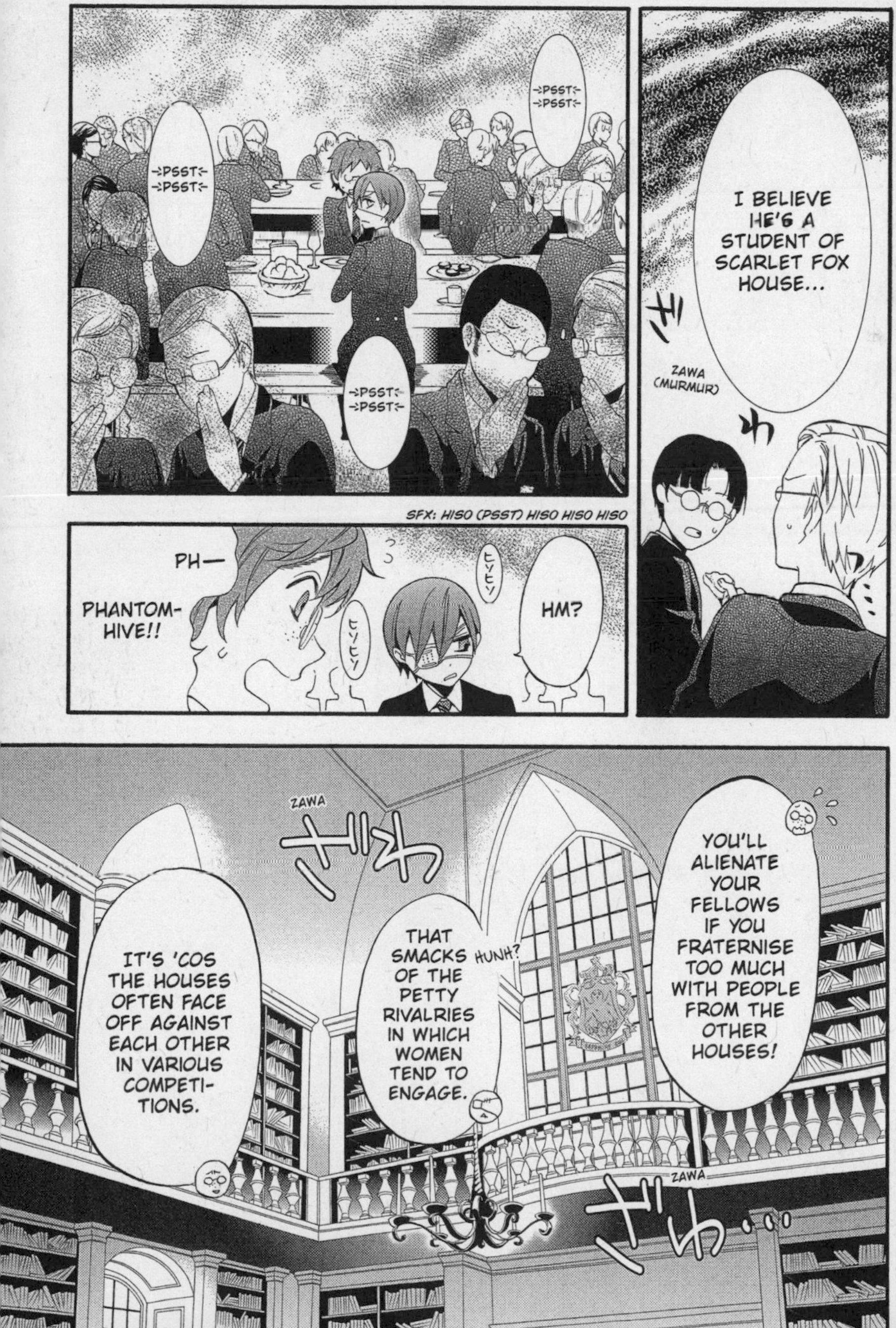
I BELIEVE HE'S A STUDENT OF SCARLET FOX HOUSE...
ZAWA (MURMUR)
-PSST- -PSST-
-PSST- -PSST-
-PSST- -PSST-
SFX: HISO (PSST) HISO HISO HISO
HM?
ヒソヒソ
ヒソヒソ
PH— PHANTOM-HIVE!!
YOU'LL ALIENATE YOUR FELLOWS IF YOU FRATERNISE TOO MUCH WITH PEOPLE FROM THE OTHER HOUSES!
ZAWA
HUNH?
THAT SMACKS OF THE PETTY RIVALRIES IN WHICH WOMEN TEND TO ENGAGE.
IT'S 'COS THE HOUSES OFTEN FACE OFF AGAINST EACH OTHER IN VARIOUS COMPETI-TIONS.
ZAWA

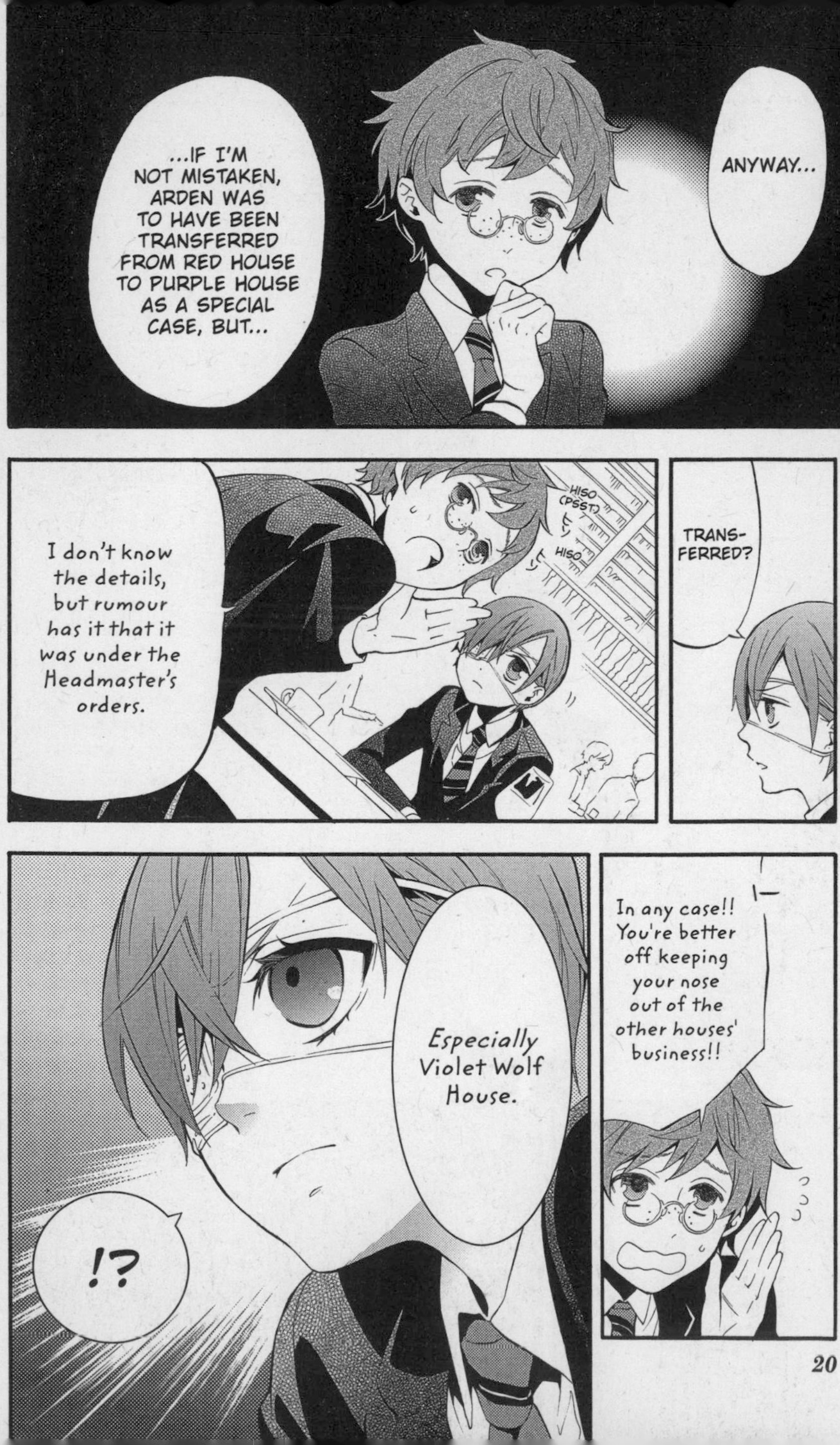
ANYWAY...
...IF I'M NOT MISTAKEN, ARDEN WAS TO HAVE BEEN TRANSFERRED FROM RED HOUSE TO PURPLE HOUSE AS A SPECIAL CASE, BUT...
TRANS-FERRED?
HISO (PSST)
HISO
I don't know the details, but rumour has it that it was under the Headmaster's orders.
In any case!! You're better off keeping your nose out of the other houses' business!!
Especially Violet Wolf House.
!?

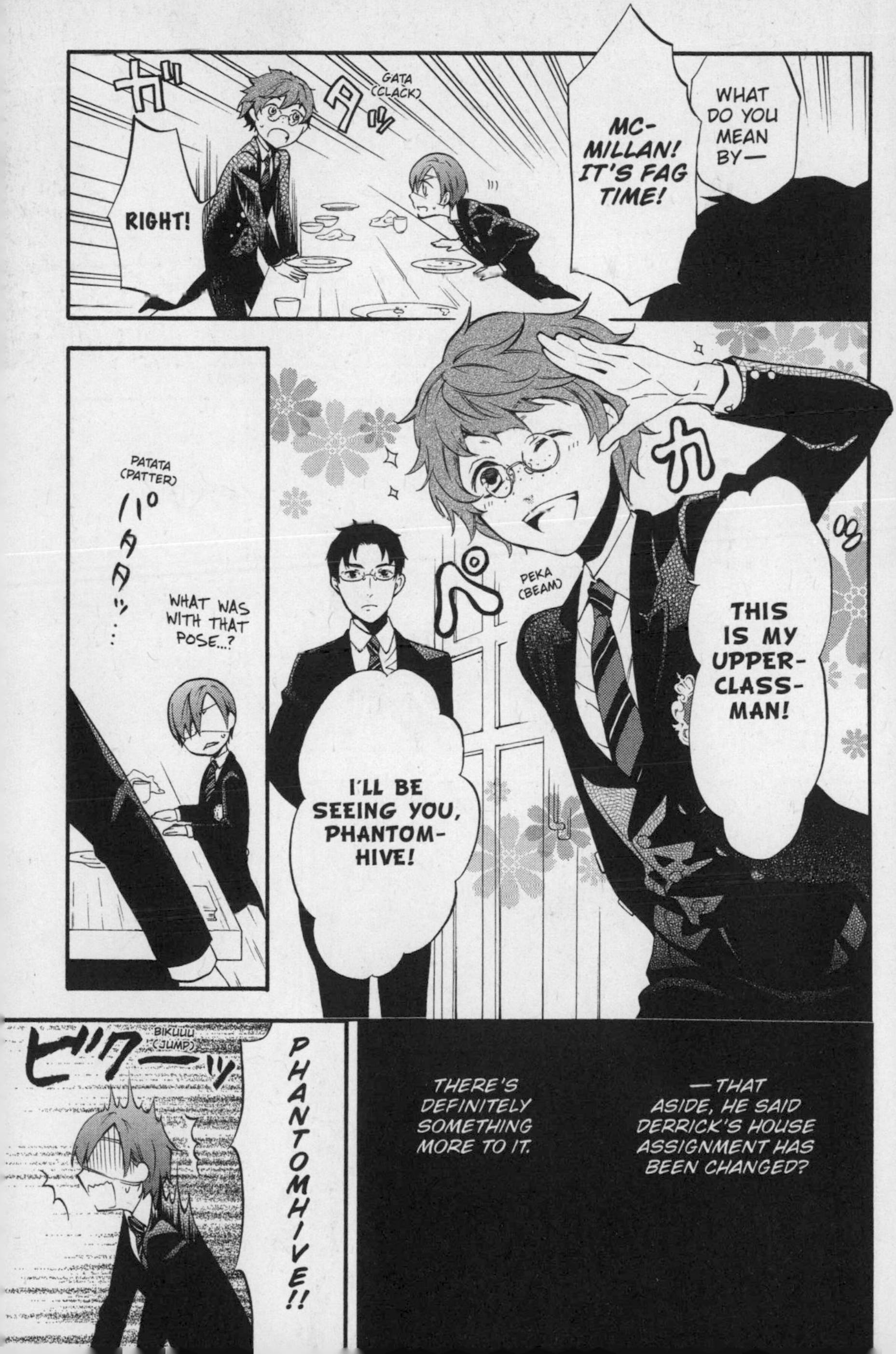
WHAT DO YOU MEAN BY—
MC-MILLAN! IT'S FAG TIME!
GATA (CLACK)
RIGHT!
THIS IS MY UPPER-CLASS-MAN!
PEKA (BEAM)
I'LL BE SEEING YOU, PHANTOM-HIVE!
PATATA (PATTER)
WHAT WAS WITH THAT POSE...?
—THAT ASIDE, HE SAID DERRICK'S HOUSE ASSIGNMENT HAS BEEN CHANGED?
THERE'S DEFINITELY SOMETHING MORE TO IT.
PHANTOMHIVE!!
BIKUUU (JUMP)

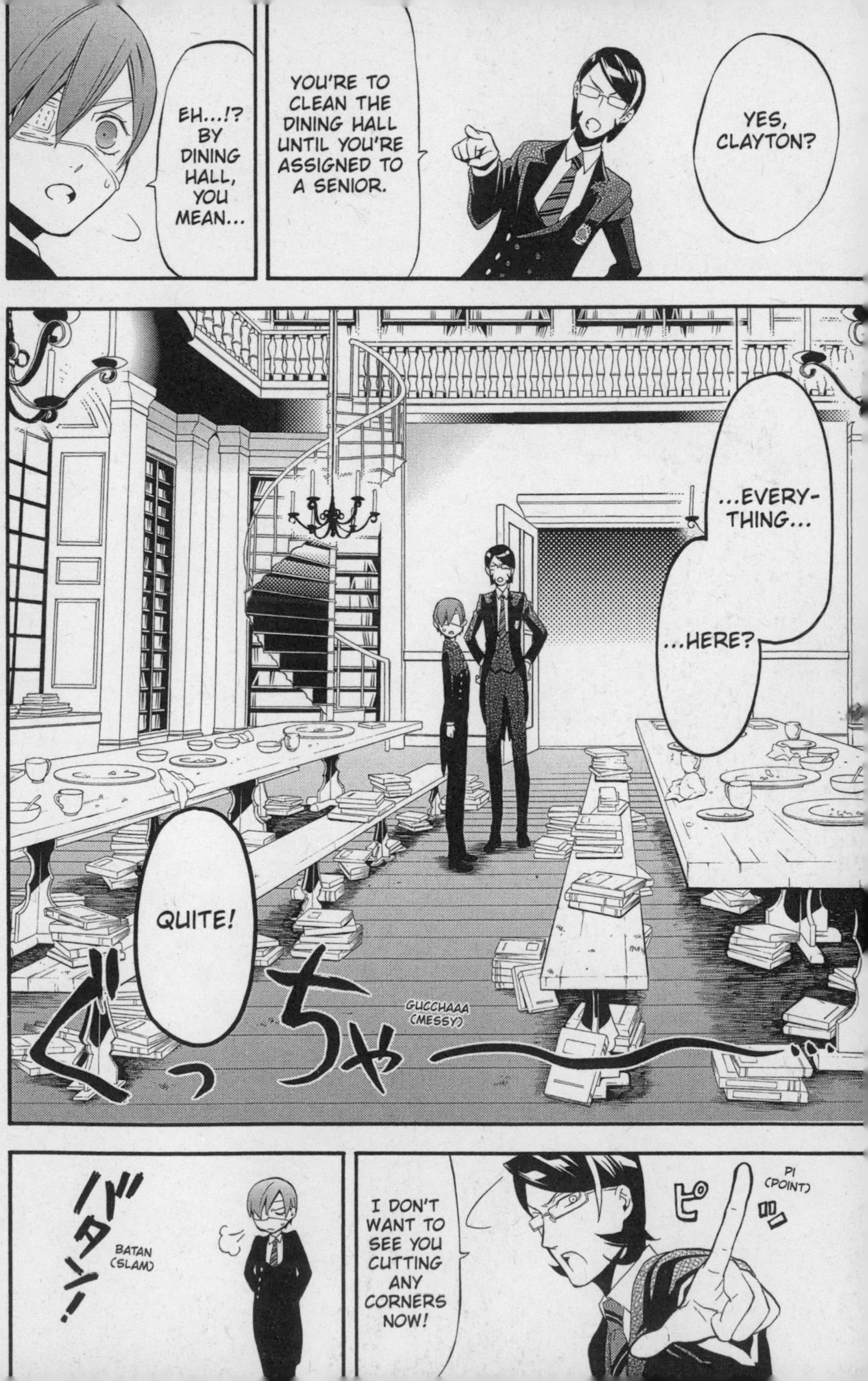
YES, CLAYTON?
YOU'RE TO CLEAN THE DINING HALL UNTIL YOU'RE ASSIGNED TO A SENIOR.
EH...!? BY DINING HALL, YOU MEAN...
...EVERYTHING...
...HERE?
QUITE!
GUCCHAAA (MESSY)
PI (POINT)
I DON'T WANT TO SEE YOU CUTTING ANY CORNERS NOW!
BATAN (SLAM)

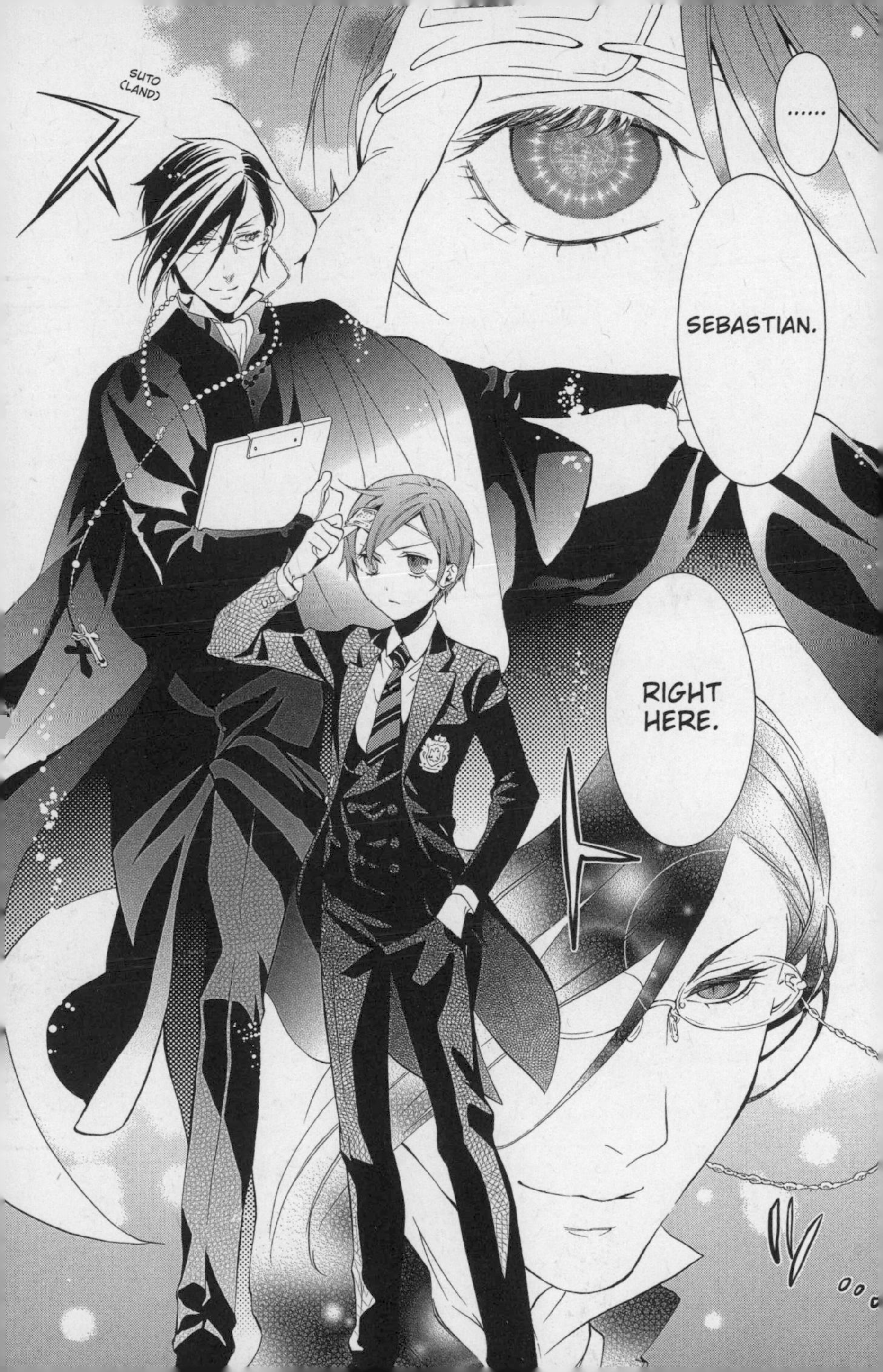
......
SUTO (LAND)
SEBASTIAN.
RIGHT HERE.

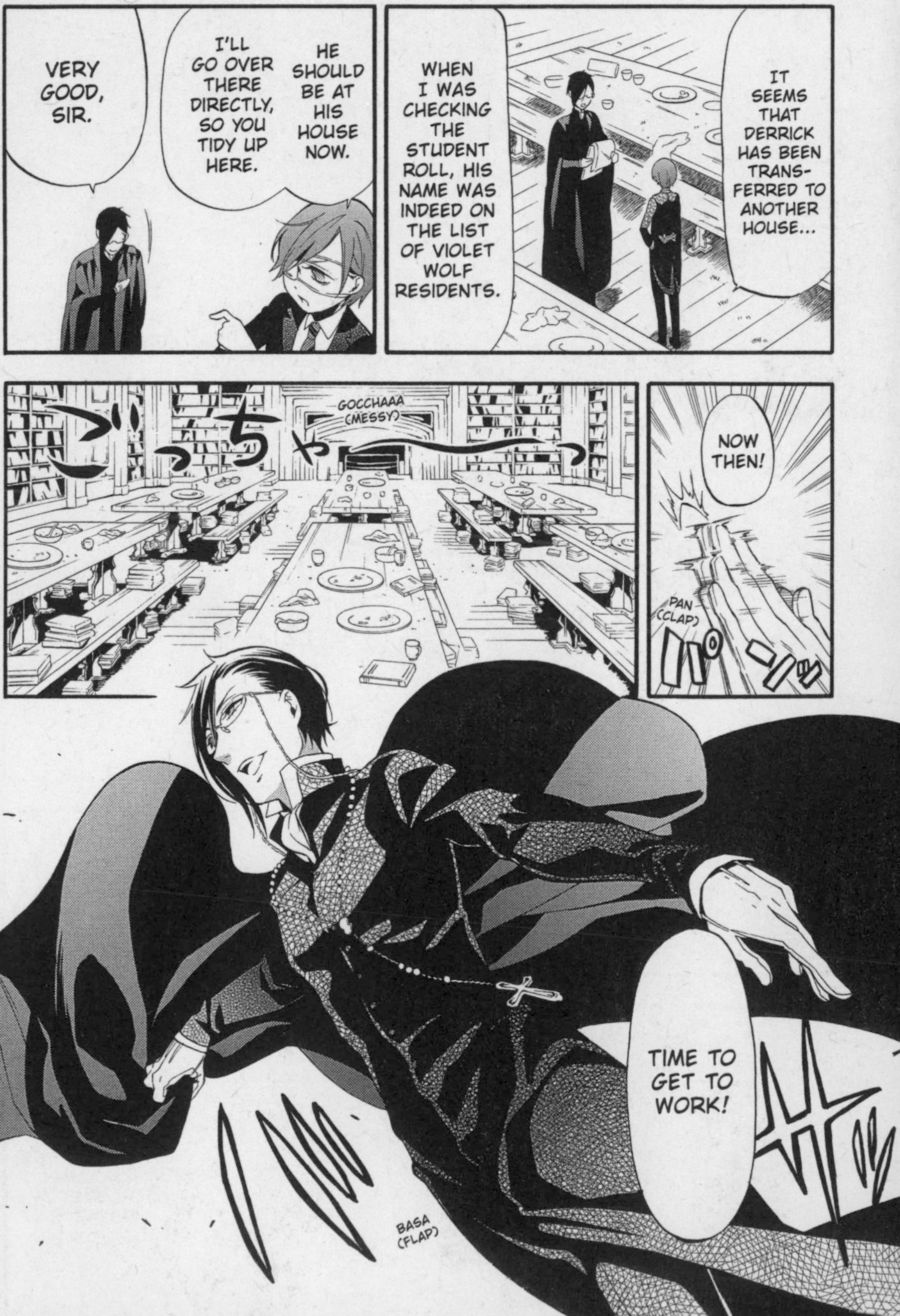
IT SEEMS THAT DERRICK HAS BEEN TRANS-FERRED TO ANOTHER HOUSE...
WHEN I WAS CHECKING THE STUDENT ROLL, HIS NAME WAS INDEED ON THE LIST OF VIOLET WOLF RESIDENTS.
HE SHOULD BE AT HIS HOUSE NOW.
I'LL GO OVER THERE DIRECTLY, SO YOU TIDY UP HERE.
VERY GOOD, SIR.
NOW THEN!
PAN (CLAP)
GOCCHAAA (MESSY)
TIME TO GET TO WORK!
BASA (FLAP)

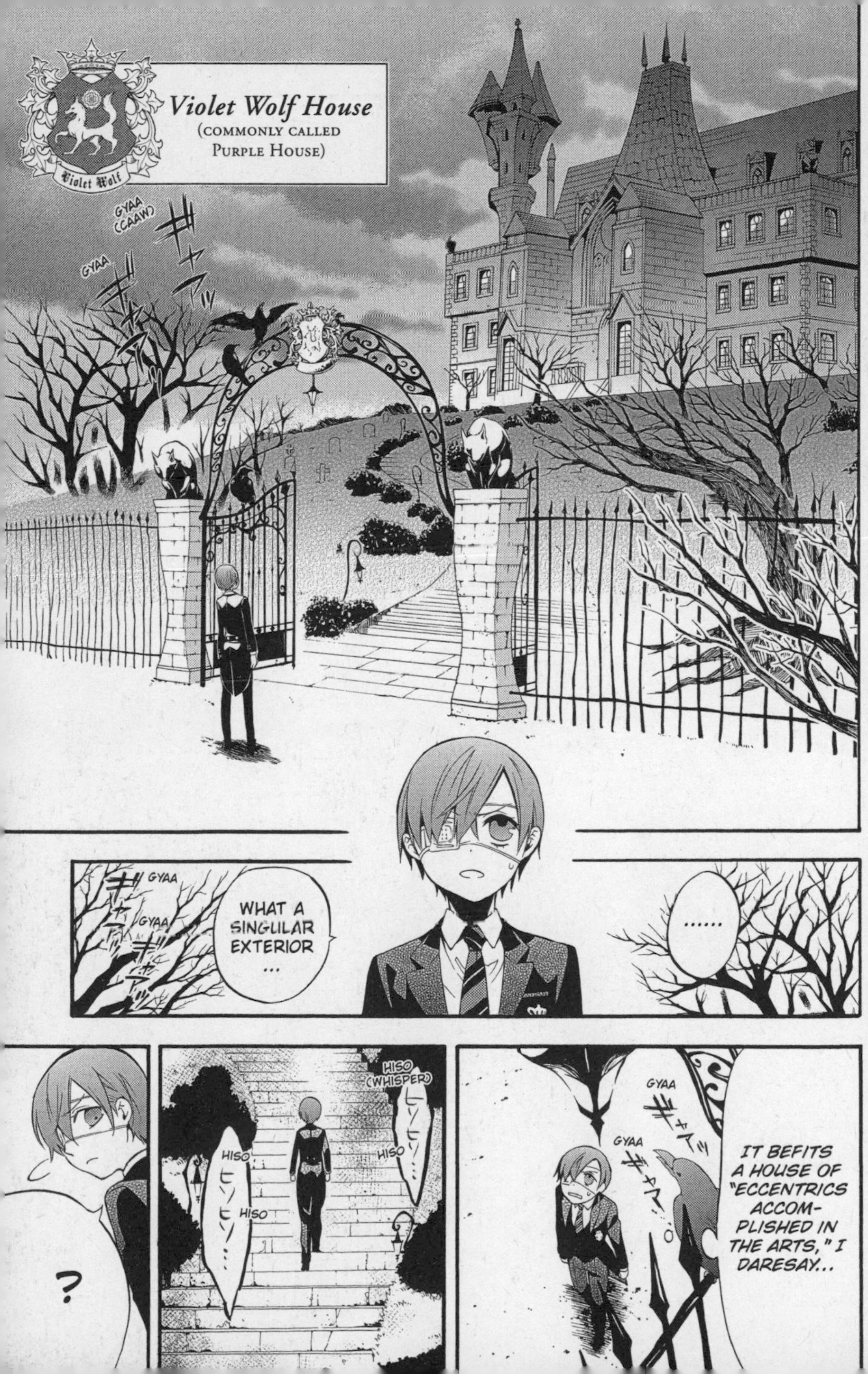
Violet Wolf
Violet Wolf House
(COMMONLY CALLED
PURPLE HOUSE)
GYAA
(CAAW)
GYAA
......
WHAT A SINGULAR EXTERIOR ...
GYAA
GYAA
GYAA
GYAA
IT BEFITS A HOUSE OF "ECCENTRICS ACCOMPLISHED IN THE ARTS," I DARESAY...
HISO
(WHISPER)
HISO
HISO
HISO
?

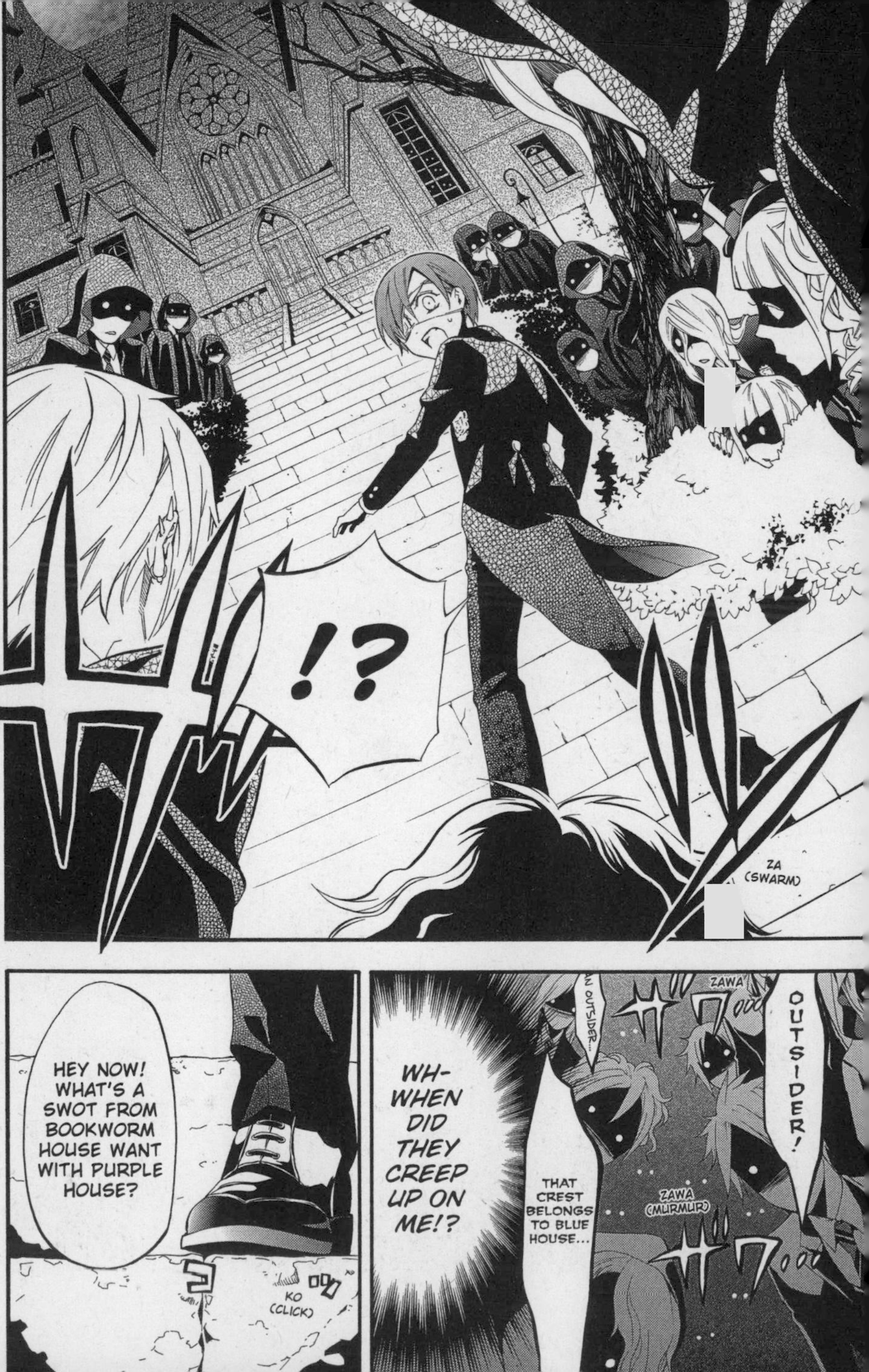
!?
ZA (SWARM)
OUTSIDER!
ZAWA
AN OUTSIDER...
WH-WHEN DID THEY CREEP UP ON ME!?
THAT CREST BELONGS TO BLUE HOUSE...
ZAWA (MURMUR)
HEY NOW! WHAT'S A SWOT FROM BOOKWORM HOUSE WANT WITH PURPLE HOUSE?
KO (CLICK)

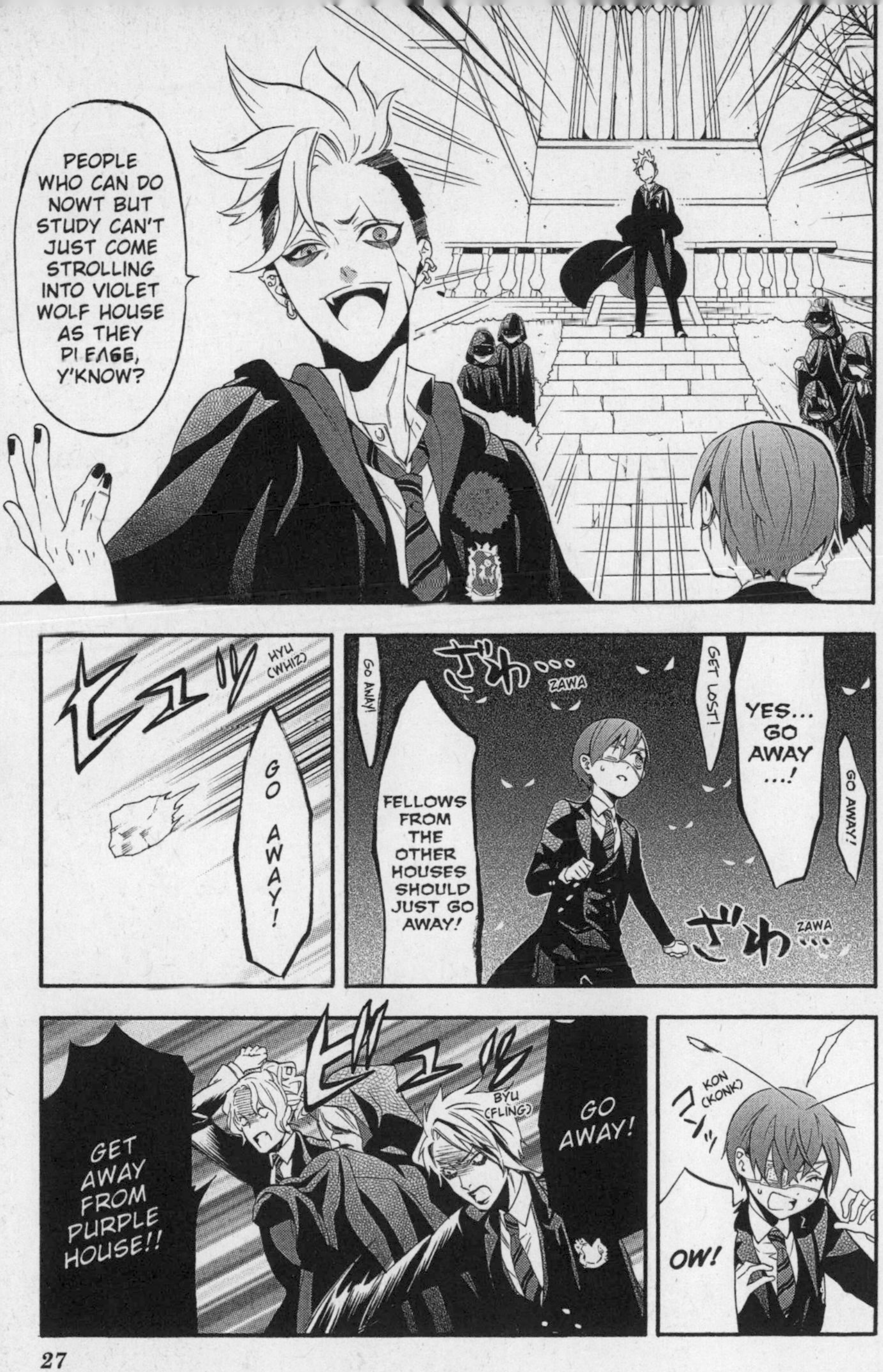
PEOPLE WHO CAN DO NOWT BUT STUDY CAN'T JUST COME STROLLING INTO VIOLET WOLF HOUSE AS THEY PLEASE, Y'KNOW?
YES... GO AWAY ...!
GO AWAY!
GET LOST!
ZAWA
FELLOWS FROM THE OTHER HOUSES SHOULD JUST GO AWAY!
GO AWAY!
ZAWA
HYU (WHIZ)
GO AWAY!
KON (KONK)
OW!
GO AWAY!
BYU (FLING)
GET AWAY FROM PURPLE HOUSE!!

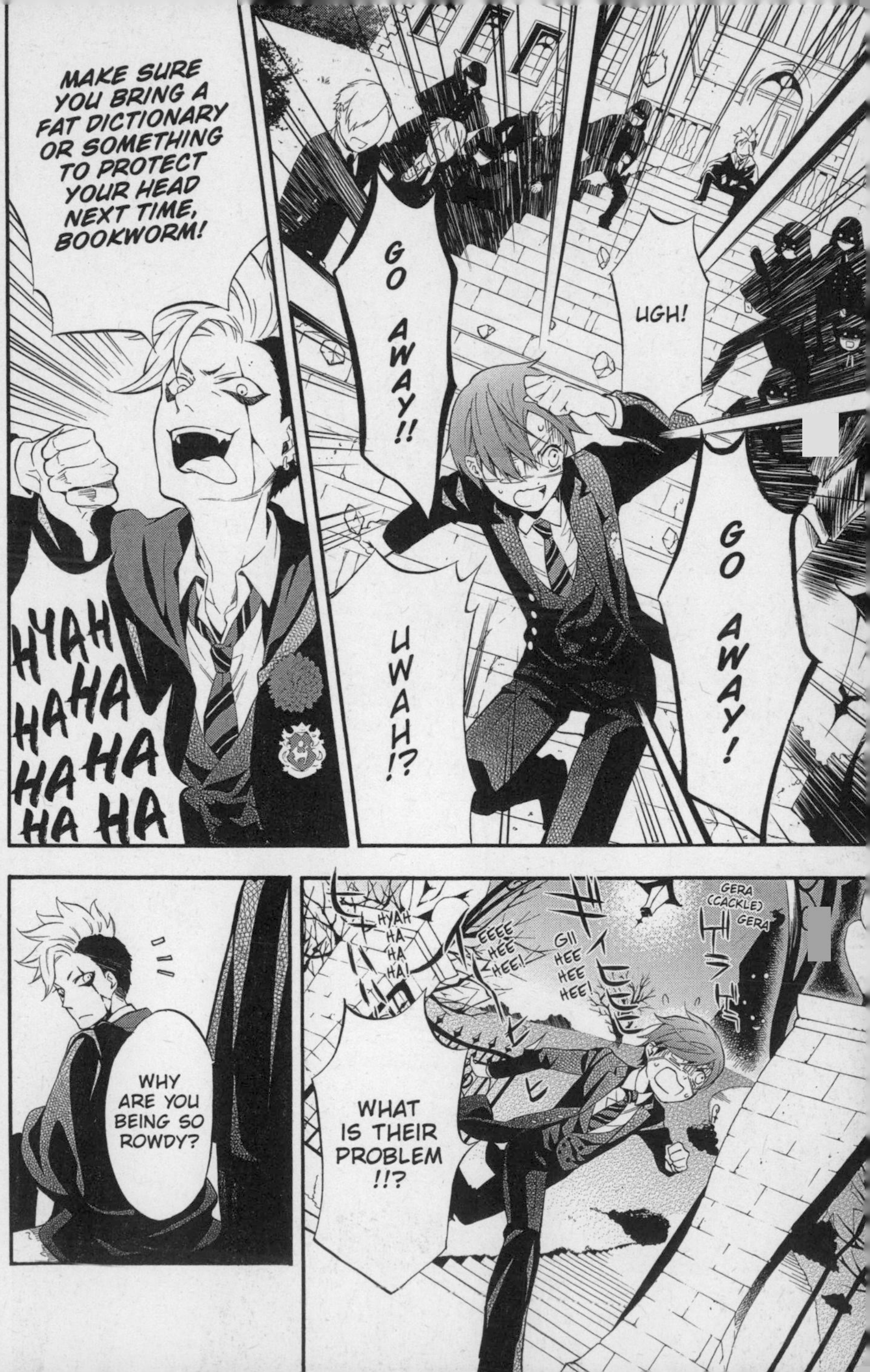
UGH!
GO AWAY!!
GO AWAY!
UWAH!?
MAKE SURE YOU BRING A FAT DICTIONARY OR SOMETHING TO PROTECT YOUR HEAD NEXT TIME, BOOKWORM!
HYAH HA HA HA HA HA HA HA
GERA (CACKLE) GERA
GII HEE HEE HEE!
EEEE HEE HEE!
HYAH HA HA HA!
WHAT IS THEIR PROBLEM!!?
WHY ARE YOU BEING SO ROWDY?

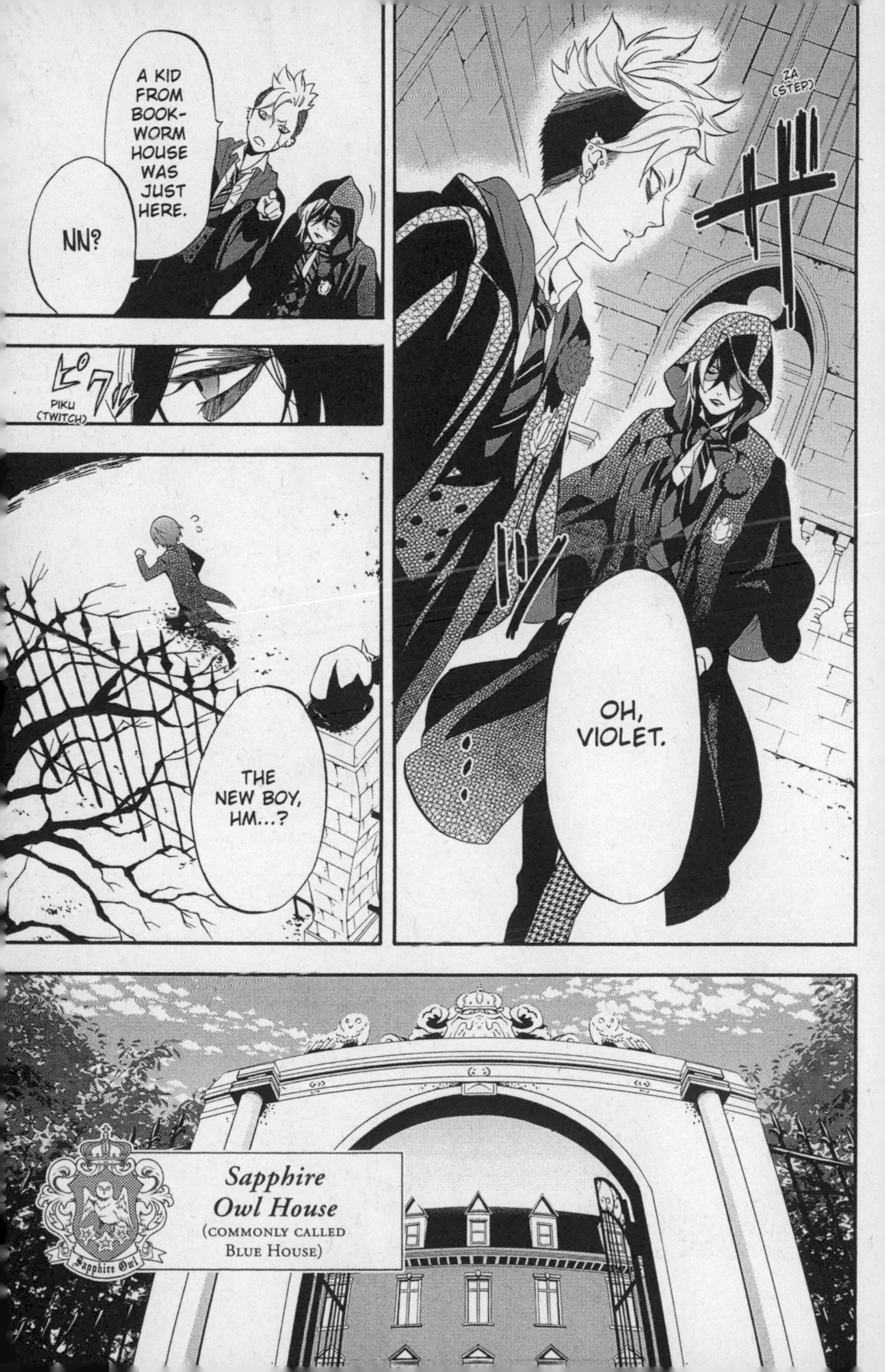
ZA (STEP)
OH, VIOLET.
A KID FROM BOOK-WORM HOUSE WAS JUST HERE.
NN?
PIKU (TWITCH)
THE NEW BOY, HM...?
Sapphire Owl House (COMMONLY CALLED BLUE HOUSE)
Sapphire Owl

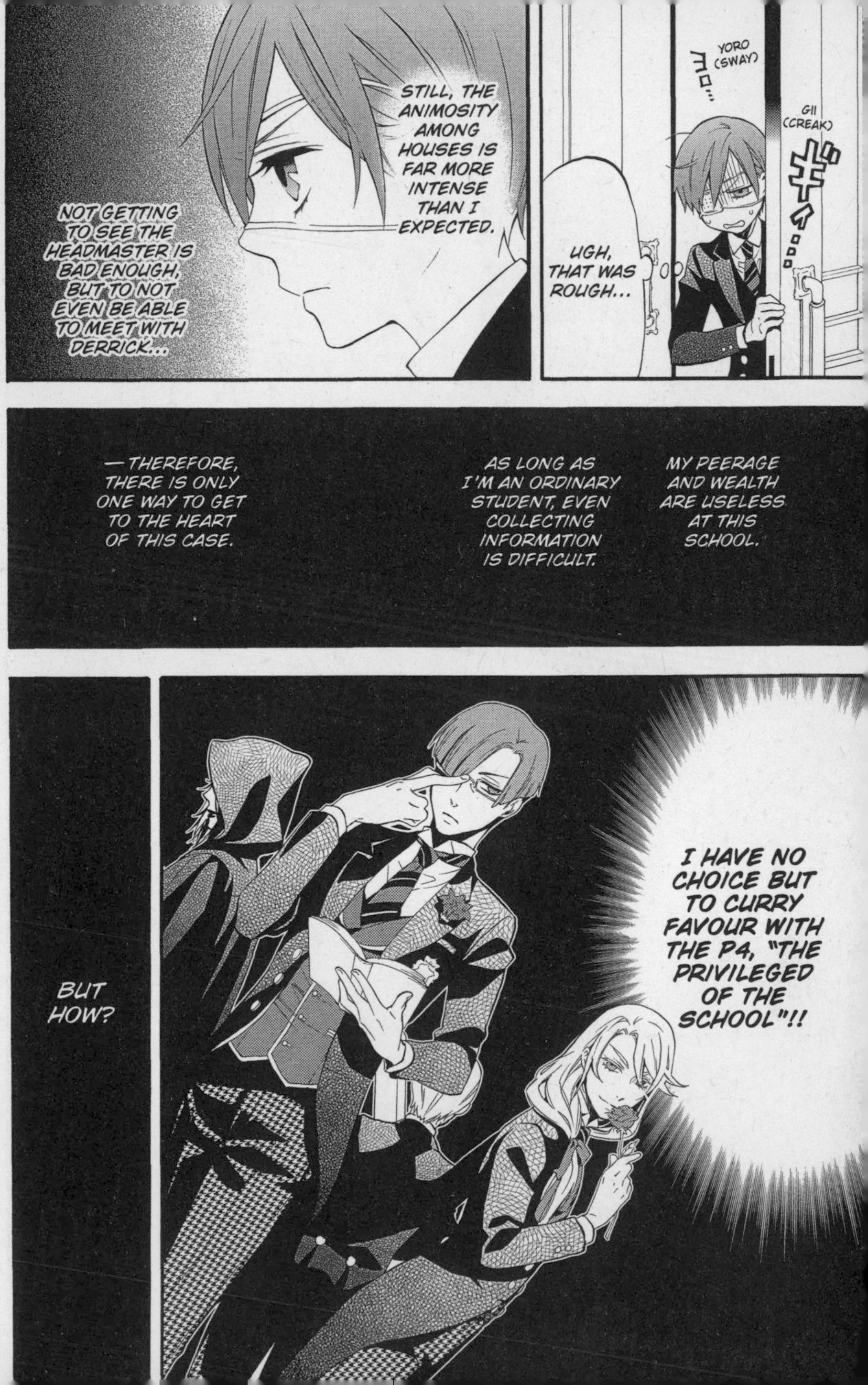
ヨロ…
YORO (SWAY)
ギィ…
GII (CREAK)
UGH, THAT WAS ROUGH...
STILL, THE ANIMOSITY AMONG HOUSES IS FAR MORE INTENSE THAN I EXPECTED.
NOT GETTING TO SEE THE HEADMASTER IS BAD ENOUGH, BUT TO NOT EVEN BE ABLE TO MEET WITH DERRICK...
MY PEERAGE AND WEALTH ARE USELESS AT THIS SCHOOL.
AS LONG AS I'M AN ORDINARY STUDENT, EVEN COLLECTING INFORMATION IS DIFFICULT.
—THEREFORE, THERE IS ONLY ONE WAY TO GET TO THE HEART OF THIS CASE.
I HAVE NO CHOICE BUT TO CURRY FAVOUR WITH THE P4, "THE PRIVILEGED OF THE SCHOOL"!!
BUT HOW?

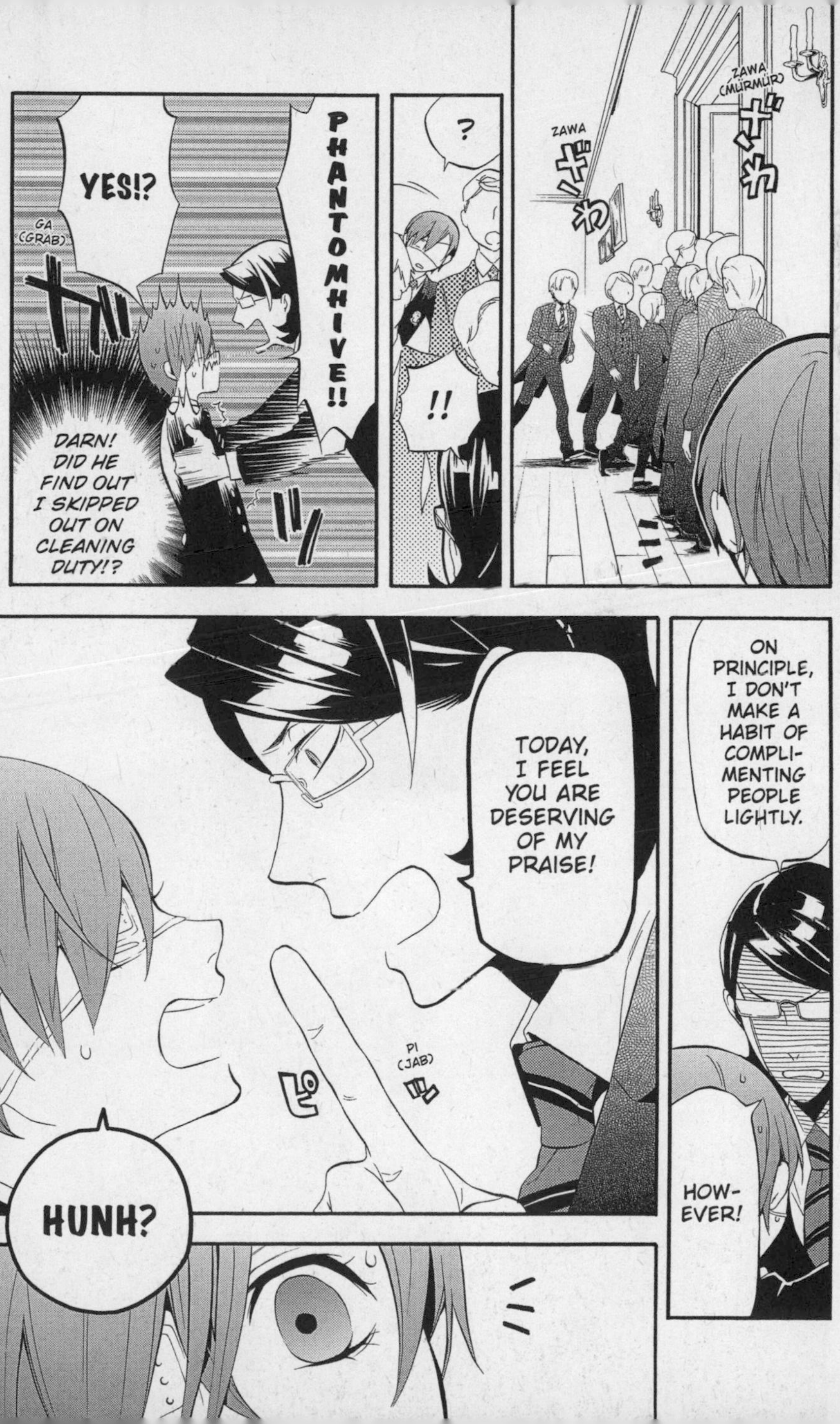
ZAWA (MÜRMÜR)
ZAWA
?
!!
PHANTOMHIVE!!
YES!?
GA (GRAB)
DARN! DID HE FIND OUT I SKIPPED OUT ON CLEANING DUTY!?
ON PRINCIPLE, I DON'T MAKE A HABIT OF COMPLI-MENTING PEOPLE LIGHTLY.
HOW-EVER!
TODAY, I FEEL YOU ARE DESERVING OF MY PRAISE!
PI (JAB)
HUNH?

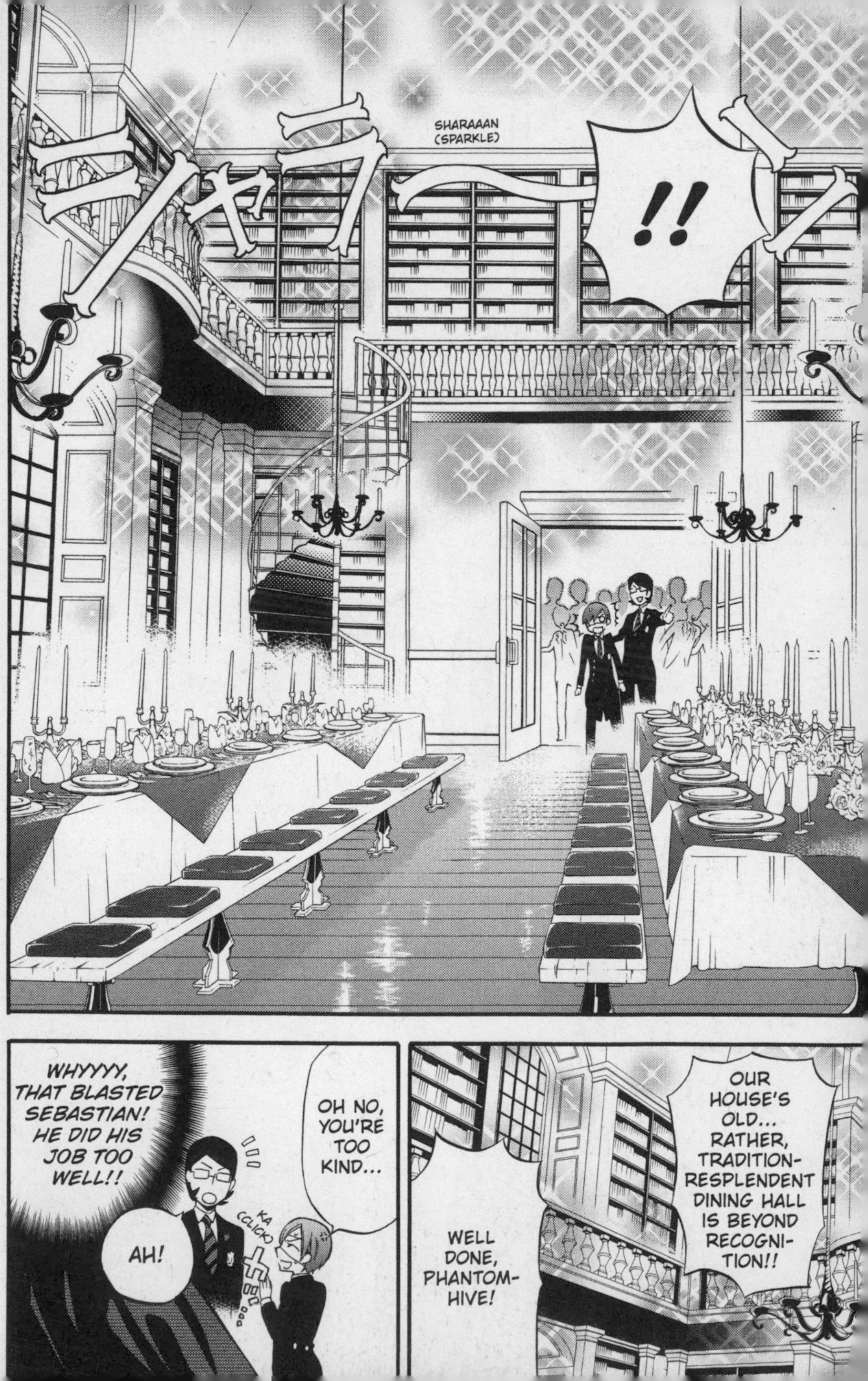
シャラーン
SHARAAAN (SPARKLE)
!!
OUR HOUSE'S OLD... RATHER, TRADITION-RESPLENDENT DINING HALL IS BEYOND RECOGNITION!!
WELL DONE, PHANTOM-HIVE!
OH NO, YOU'RE TOO KIND...
WHYYYY, THAT BLASTED SEBASTIAN! HE DID HIS JOB TOO WELL!!
KA (CLICK)
AH!

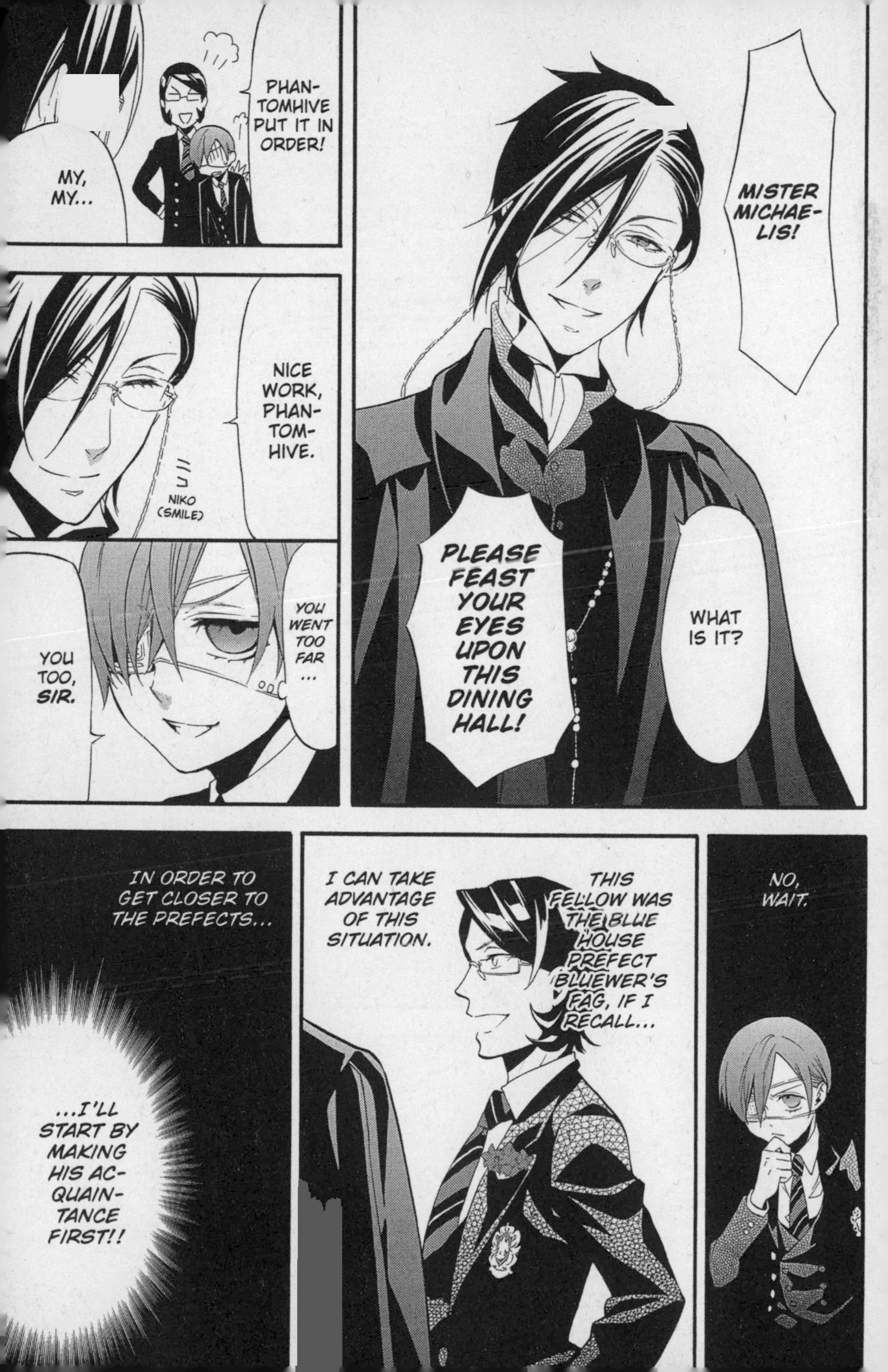

MISTER MICHAELIS!
WHAT IS IT?
PLEASE FEAST YOUR EYES UPON THIS DINING HALL!
PHANTOMHIVE PUT IT IN ORDER!
MY, MY...
NICE WORK, PHANTOMHIVE.
NIKO (SMILE)
YOU WENT TOO FAR...
YOU TOO, SIR.
NO, WAIT.
THIS FELLOW WAS THE BLUE HOUSE PREFECT BLUEWER'S FAG, IF I RECALL...
I CAN TAKE ADVANTAGE OF THIS SITUATION.
IN ORDER TO GET CLOSER TO THE PREFECTS...
...I'LL START BY MAKING HIS ACQUAINTANCE FIRST!!

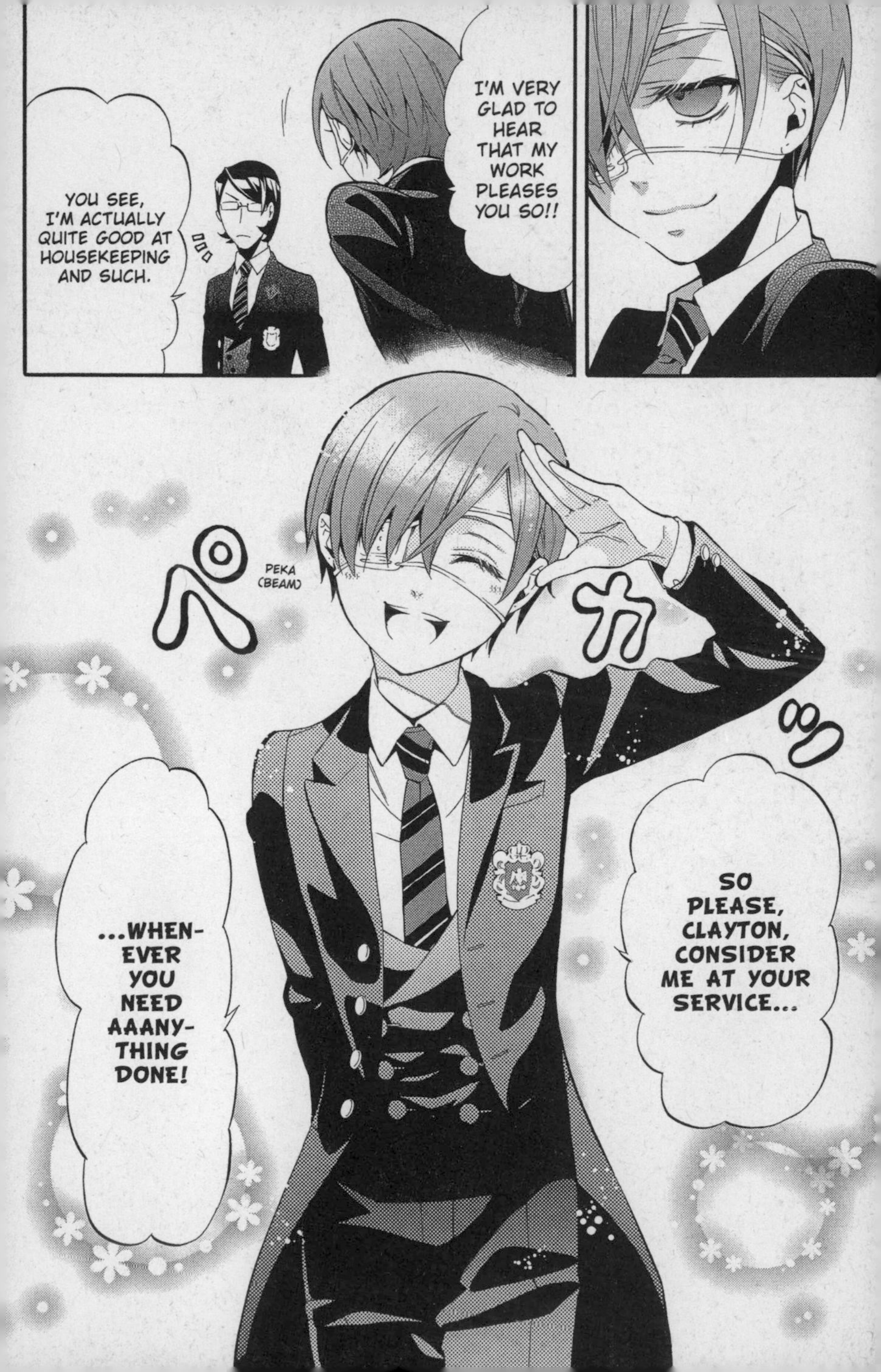
I'M VERY GLAD TO HEAR THAT MY WORK PLEASES YOU SO!!
YOU SEE, I'M ACTUALLY QUITE GOOD AT HOUSEKEEPING AND SUCH.
ペカッ
PEKA (BEAM)
SO PLEASE, CLAYTON, CONSIDER ME AT YOUR SERVICE...
...WHEN-EVER YOU NEED AAANY-THING DONE!

Black Butler

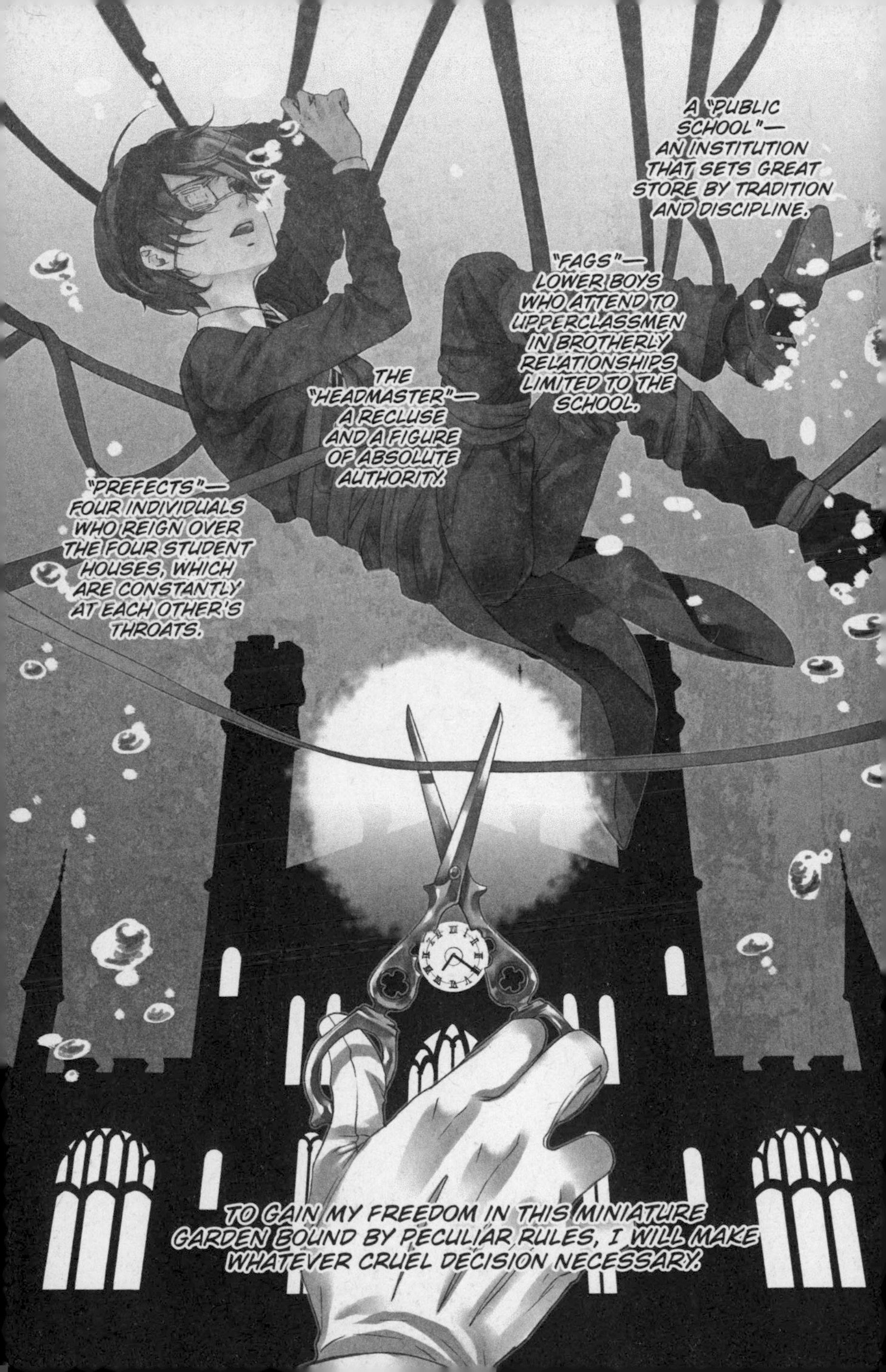
A "PUBLIC SCHOOL"—AN INSTITUTION THAT SETS GREAT STORE BY TRADITION AND DISCIPLINE.
"FAGS"—LOWER BOYS WHO ATTEND TO UPPERCLASSMEN IN BROTHERLY RELATIONSHIPS LIMITED TO THE SCHOOL.
THE "HEADMASTER"—A RECLUSE AND A FIGURE OF ABSOLUTE AUTHORITY.
"PREFECTS"—FOUR INDIVIDUALS WHO REIGN OVER THE FOUR STUDENT HOUSES, WHICH ARE CONSTANTLY AT EACH OTHER'S THROATS.
TO GAIN MY FREEDOM IN THIS MINIATURE GARDEN BOUND BY PECULIAR RULES, I WILL MAKE WHATEVER CRUEL DECISION NECESSARY.

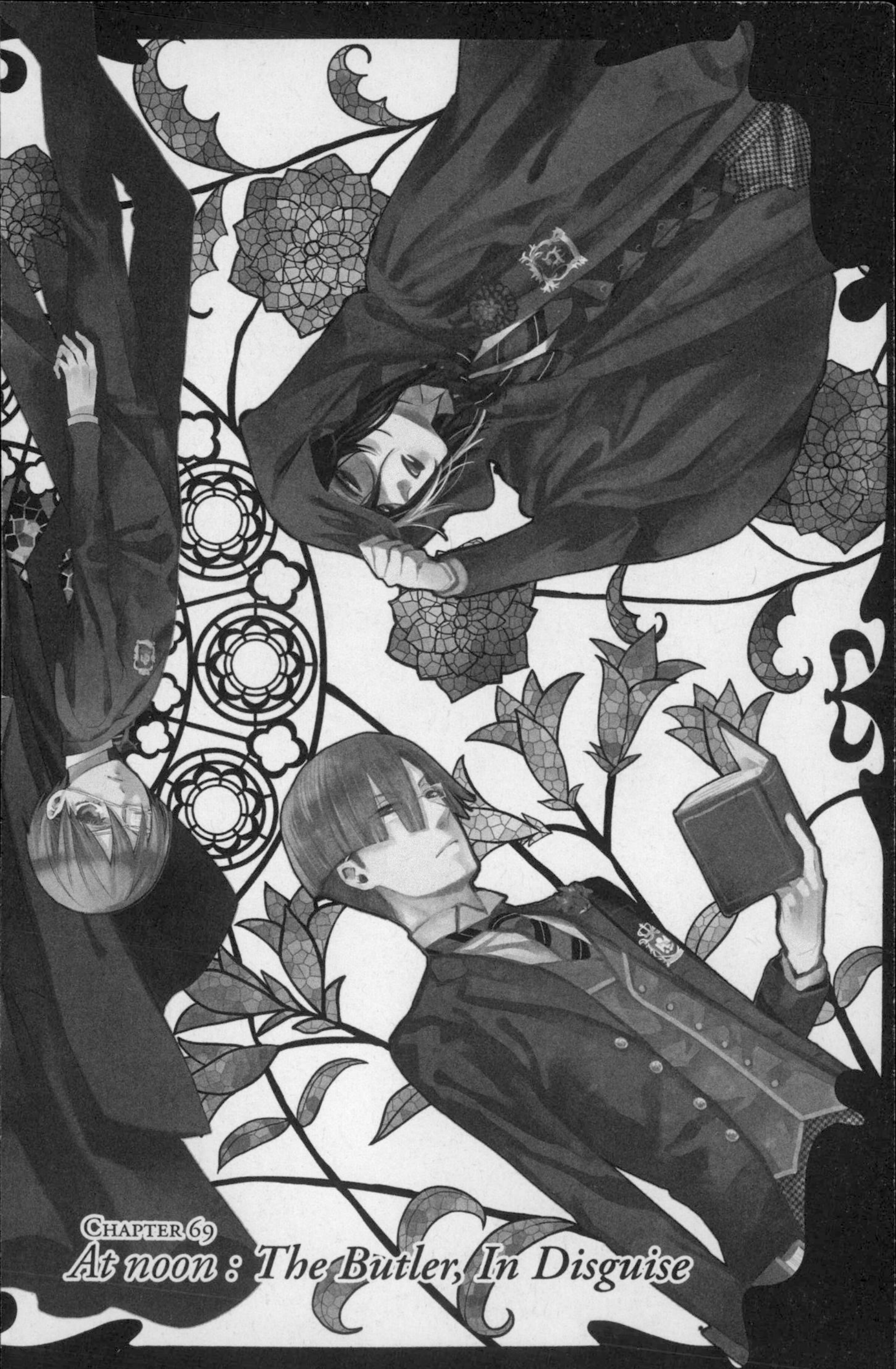
CHAPTER 69
At noon : The Butler, In Disguise

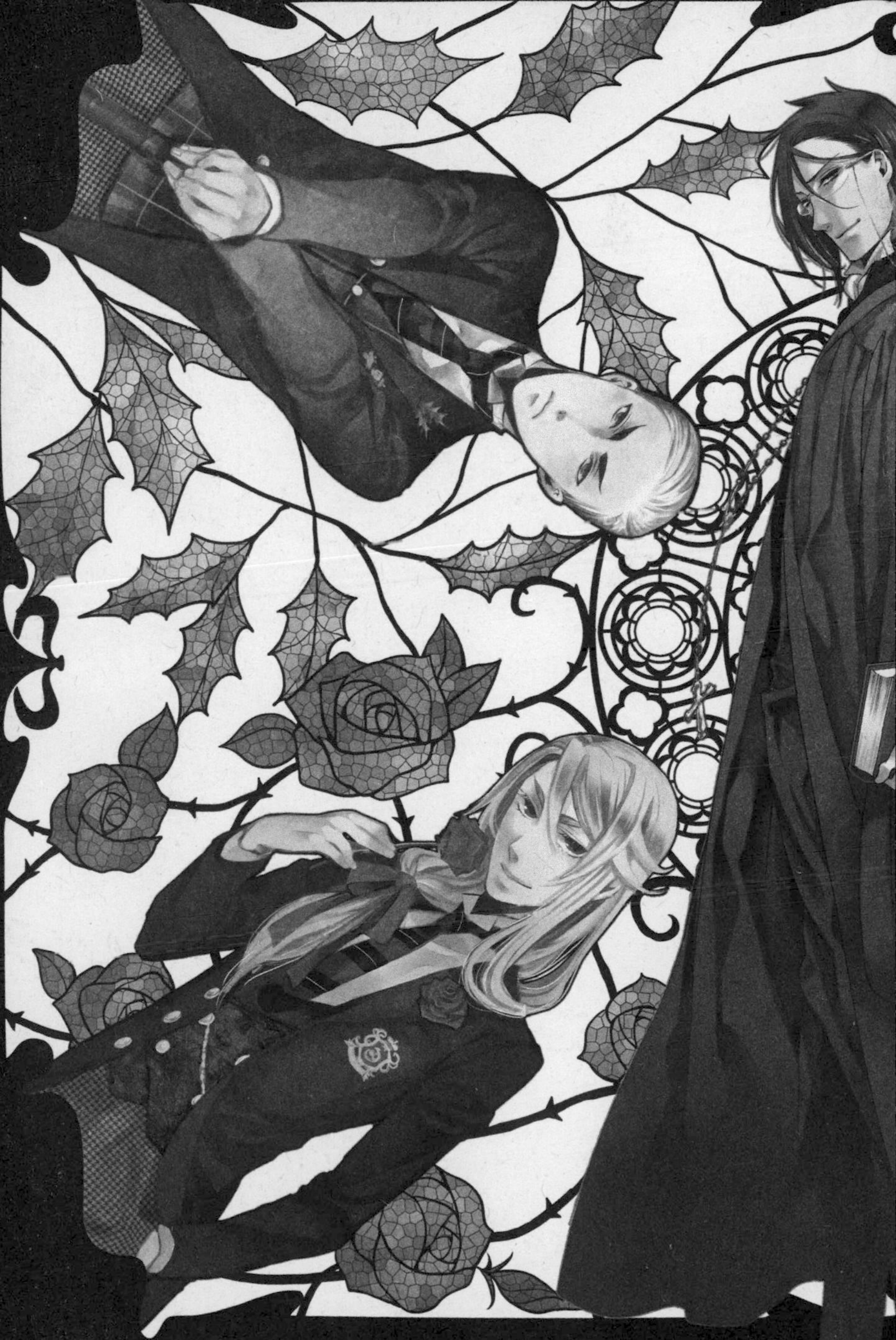

Black Butler

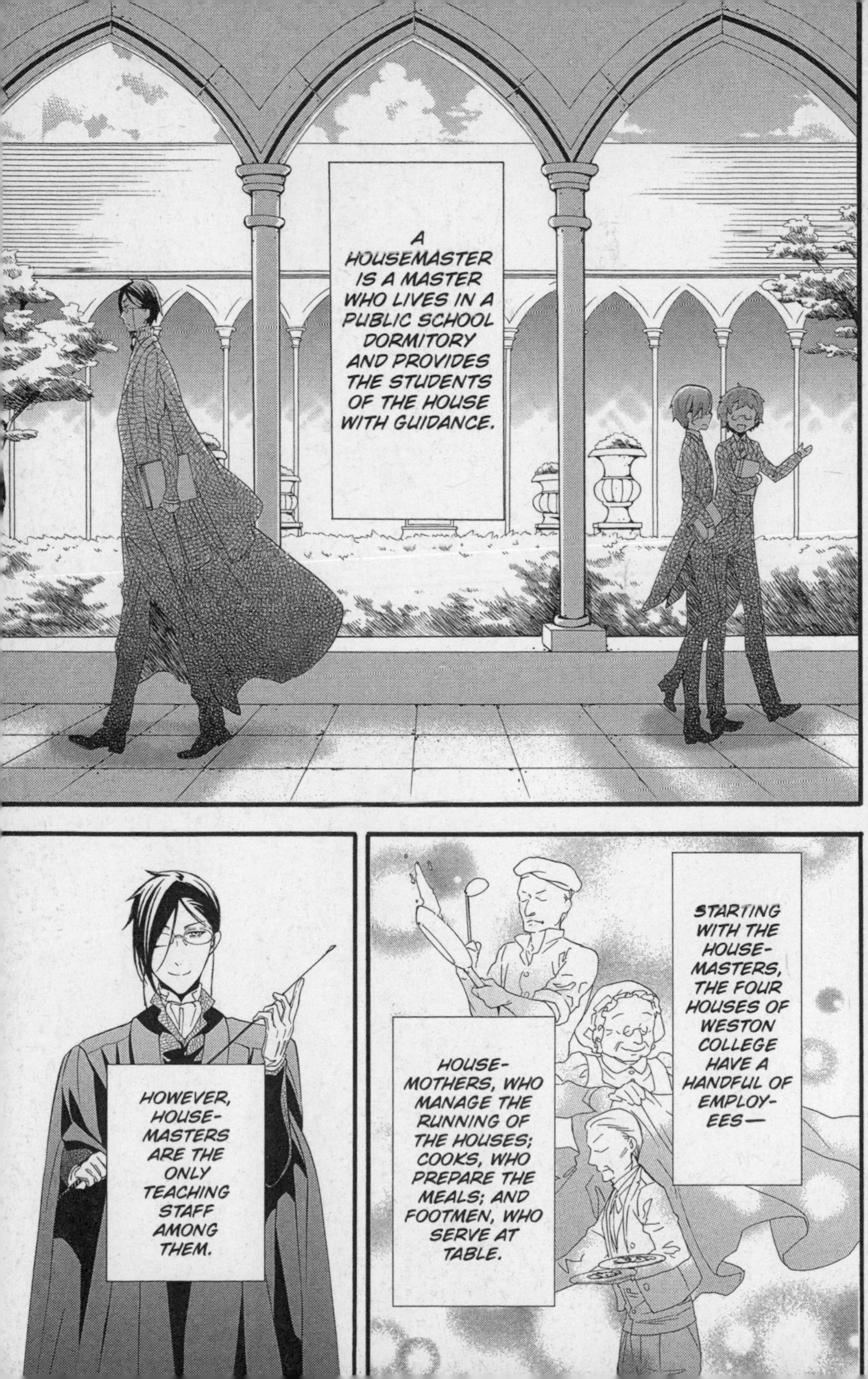
A HOUSEMASTER IS A MASTER WHO LIVES IN A PUBLIC SCHOOL DORMITORY AND PROVIDES THE STUDENTS OF THE HOUSE WITH GUIDANCE.
STARTING WITH THE HOUSE-MASTERS, THE FOUR HOUSES OF WESTON COLLEGE HAVE A HANDFUL OF EMPLOY-EES—
HOUSE-MOTHERS, WHO MANAGE THE RUNNING OF THE HOUSES; COOKS, WHO PREPARE THE MEALS; AND FOOTMEN, WHO SERVE AT TABLE.
HOWEVER, HOUSE-MASTERS ARE THE ONLY TEACHING STAFF AMONG THEM.

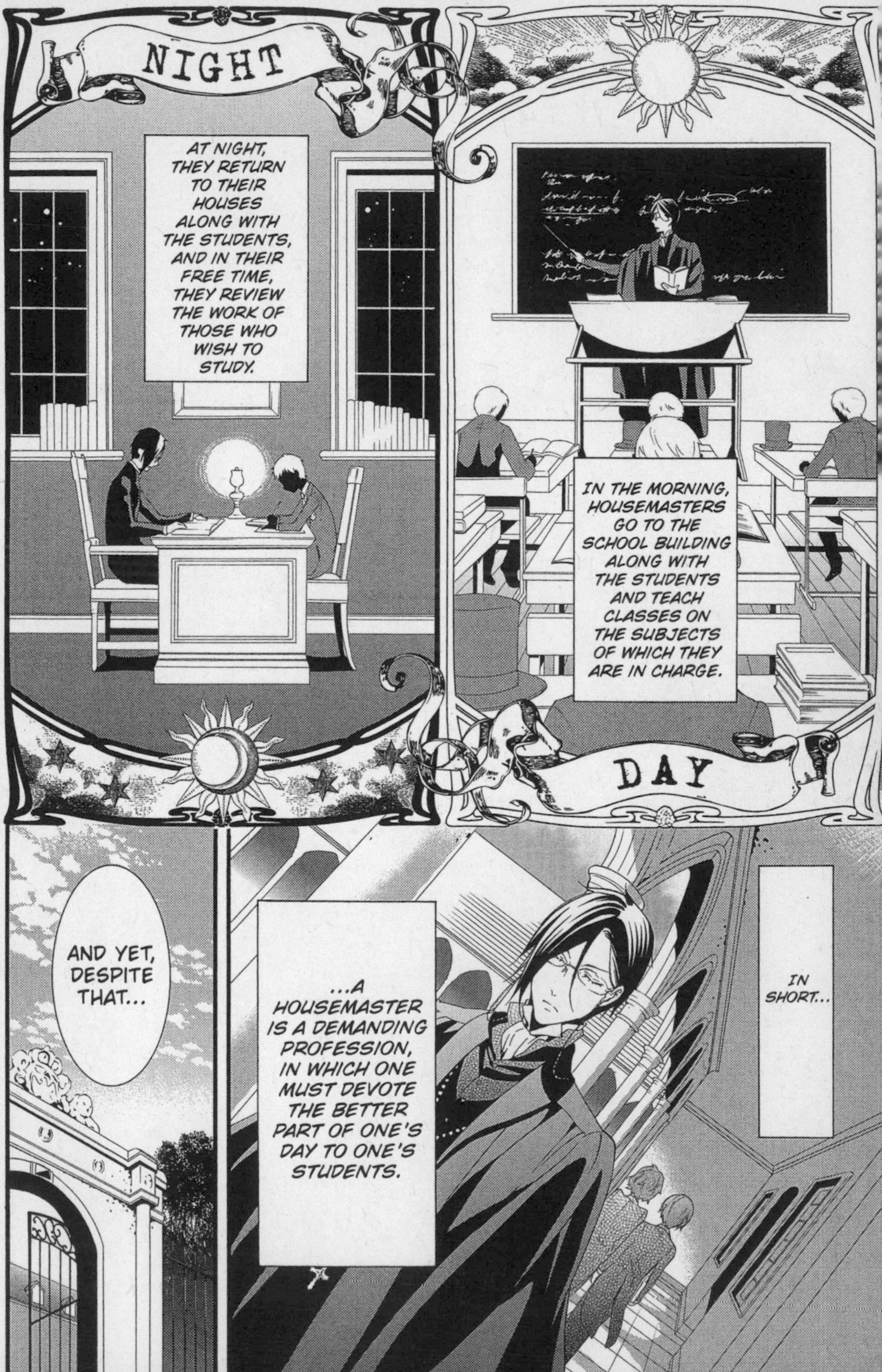
DAY
IN THE MORNING, HOUSEMASTERS GO TO THE SCHOOL BUILDING ALONG WITH THE STUDENTS AND TEACH CLASSES ON THE SUBJECTS OF WHICH THEY ARE IN CHARGE.
NIGHT
AT NIGHT, THEY RETURN TO THEIR HOUSES ALONG WITH THE STUDENTS, AND IN THEIR FREE TIME, THEY REVIEW THE WORK OF THOSE WHO WISH TO STUDY.
IN SHORT...
...A HOUSEMASTER IS A DEMANDING PROFESSION, IN WHICH ONE MUST DEVOTE THE BETTER PART OF ONE'S DAY TO ONE'S STUDENTS.
AND YET, DESPITE THAT...

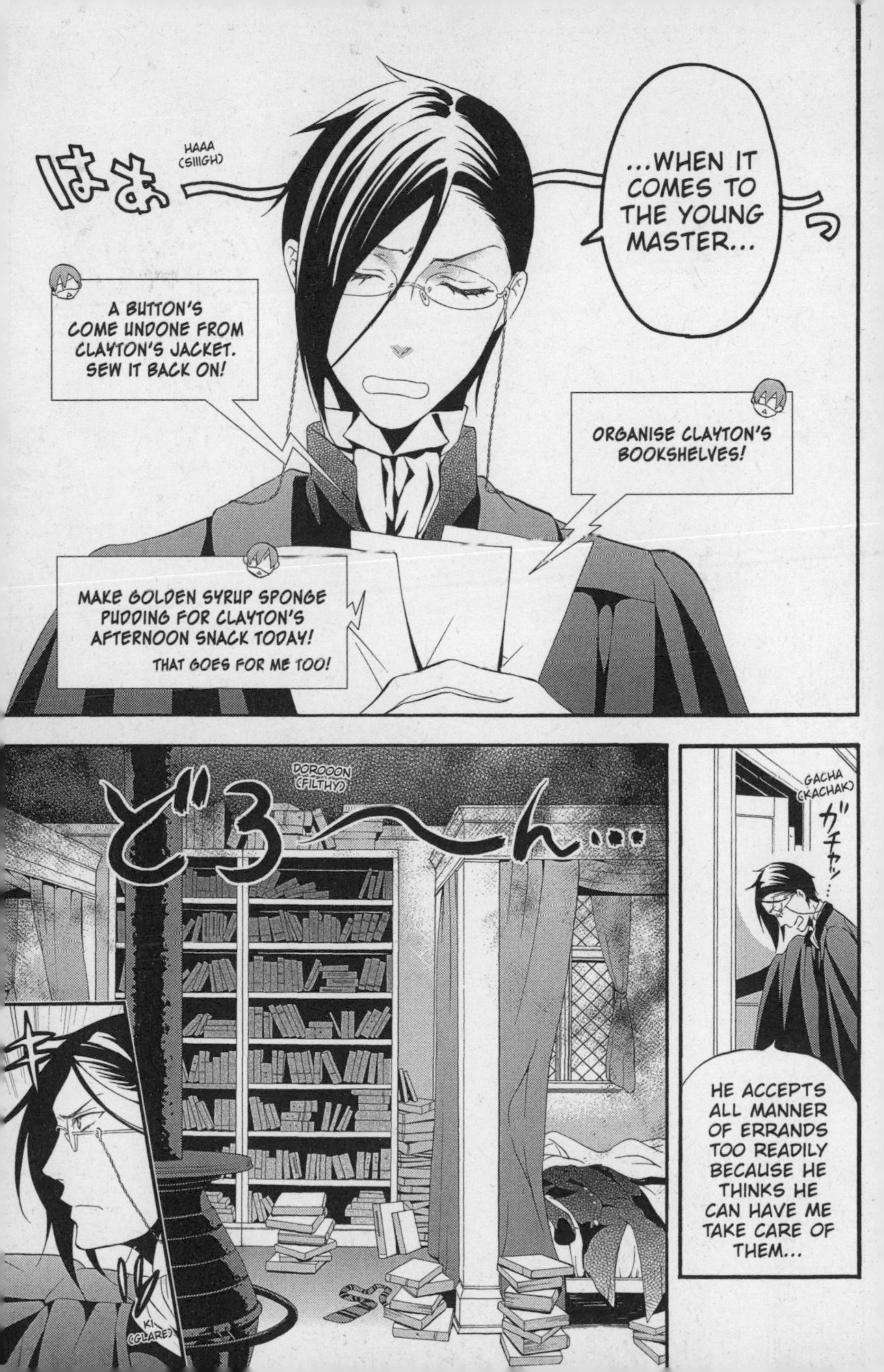
...WHEN IT COMES TO THE YOUNG MASTER...
はぁ
HAAA (SIIIGH)
ORGANISE CLAYTON'S BOOKSHELVES!
A BUTTON'S COME UNDONE FROM CLAYTON'S JACKET. SEW IT BACK ON!
MAKE GOLDEN SYRUP SPONGE PUDDING FOR CLAYTON'S AFTERNOON SNACK TODAY!
THAT GOES FOR ME TOO!
GACHA (KACHAK)
ガチャッ
HE ACCEPTS ALL MANNER OF ERRANDS TOO READILY BECAUSE HE THINKS HE CAN HAVE ME TAKE CARE OF THEM...
DOROOON (FILTHY)
どろ〜ん…
KI (GLARE)

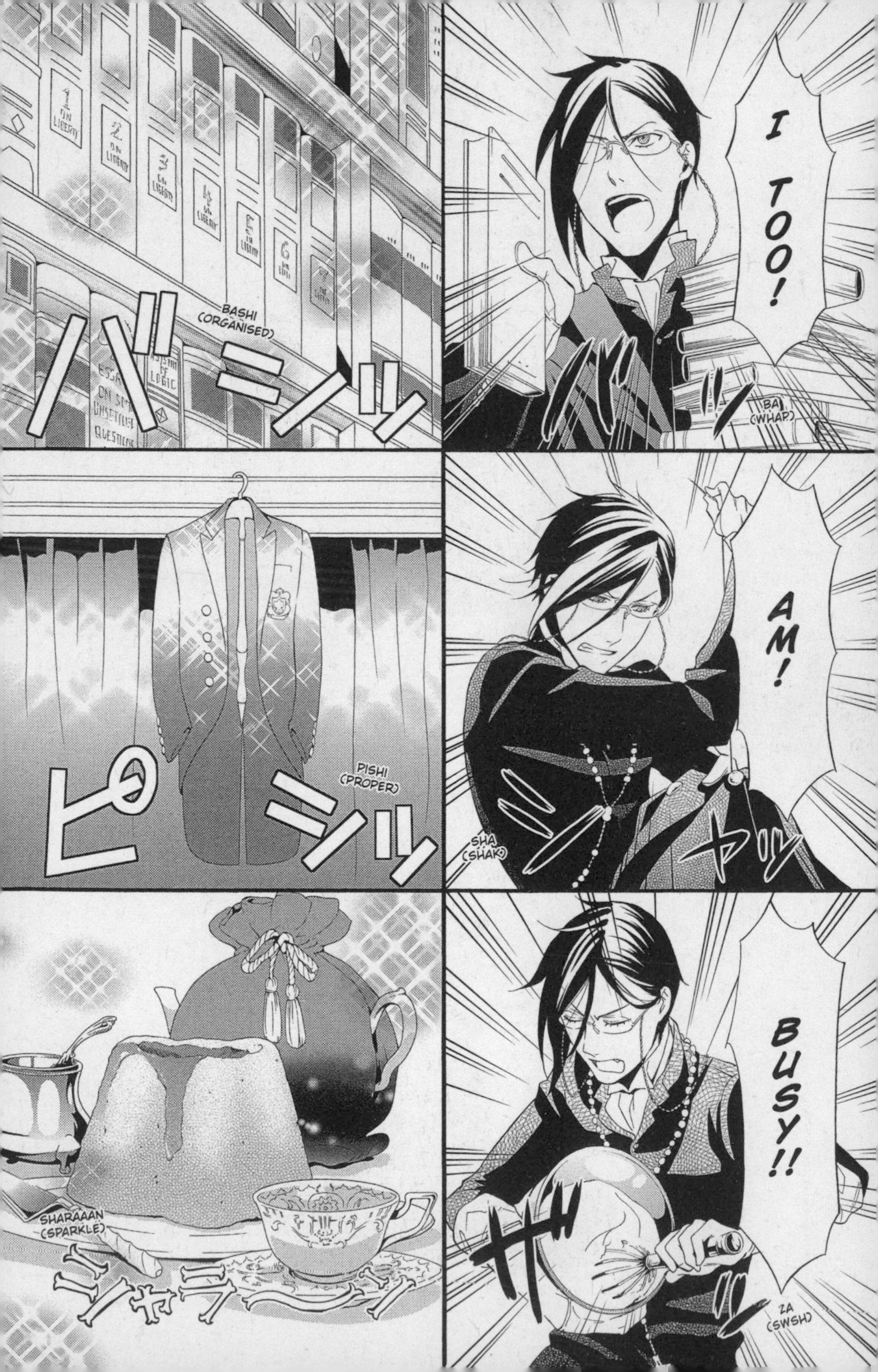
I TOO!
BA (WHAP)
BASHI (ORGANISED)
ON LIBERTY
A SYSTEM OF LOGIC
AM!
SHA (SHAK)
PISHI (PROPER)
BUSY!!
ZA (SWSH)
SHARAAAN (SPARKLE)

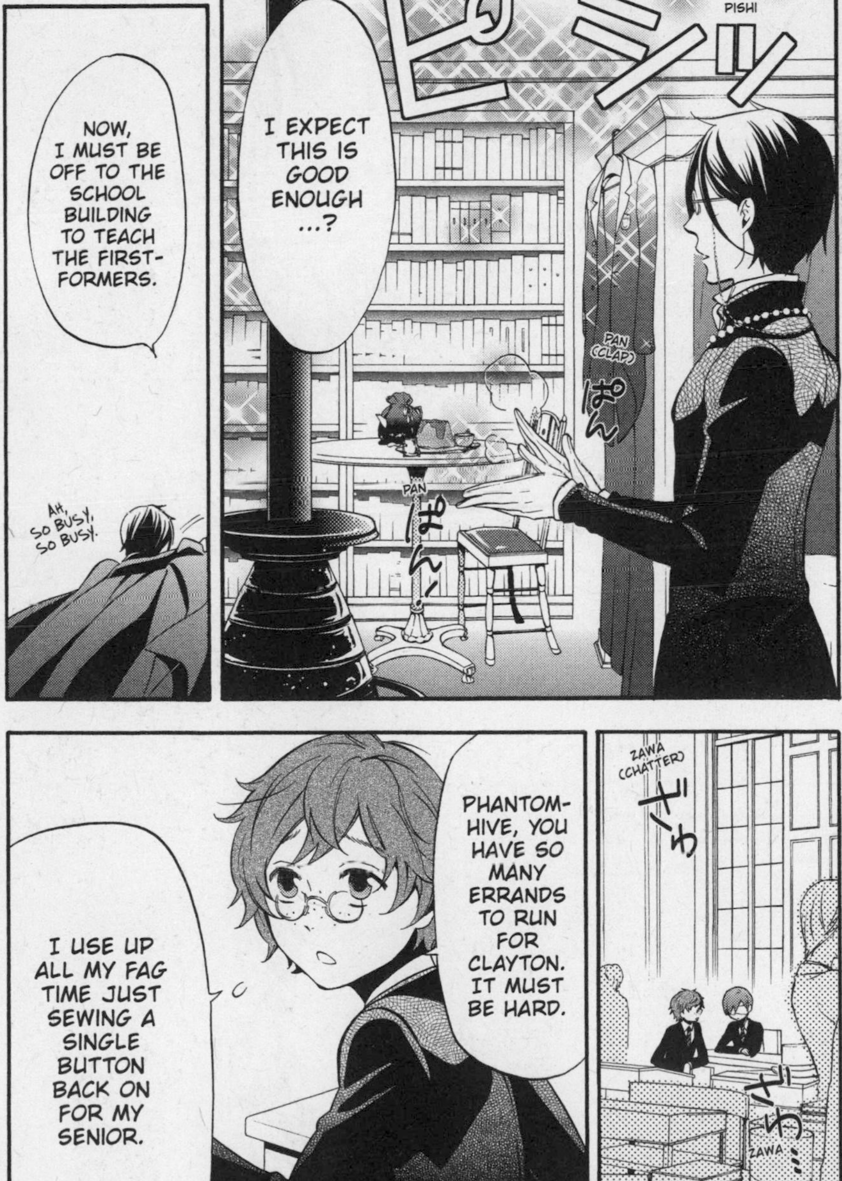
PISHI
I EXPECT THIS IS GOOD ENOUGH ...?
PAN (CLAP)
PAN
NOW, I MUST BE OFF TO THE SCHOOL BUILDING TO TEACH THE FIRST-FORMERS.
AH, SO BUSY, SO BUSY.
ZAWA (CHATTER)
ZAWA
PHANTOM-HIVE, YOU HAVE SO MANY ERRANDS TO RUN FOR CLAYTON. IT MUST BE HARD.
I USE UP ALL MY FAG TIME JUST SEWING A SINGLE BUTTON BACK ON FOR MY SENIOR.

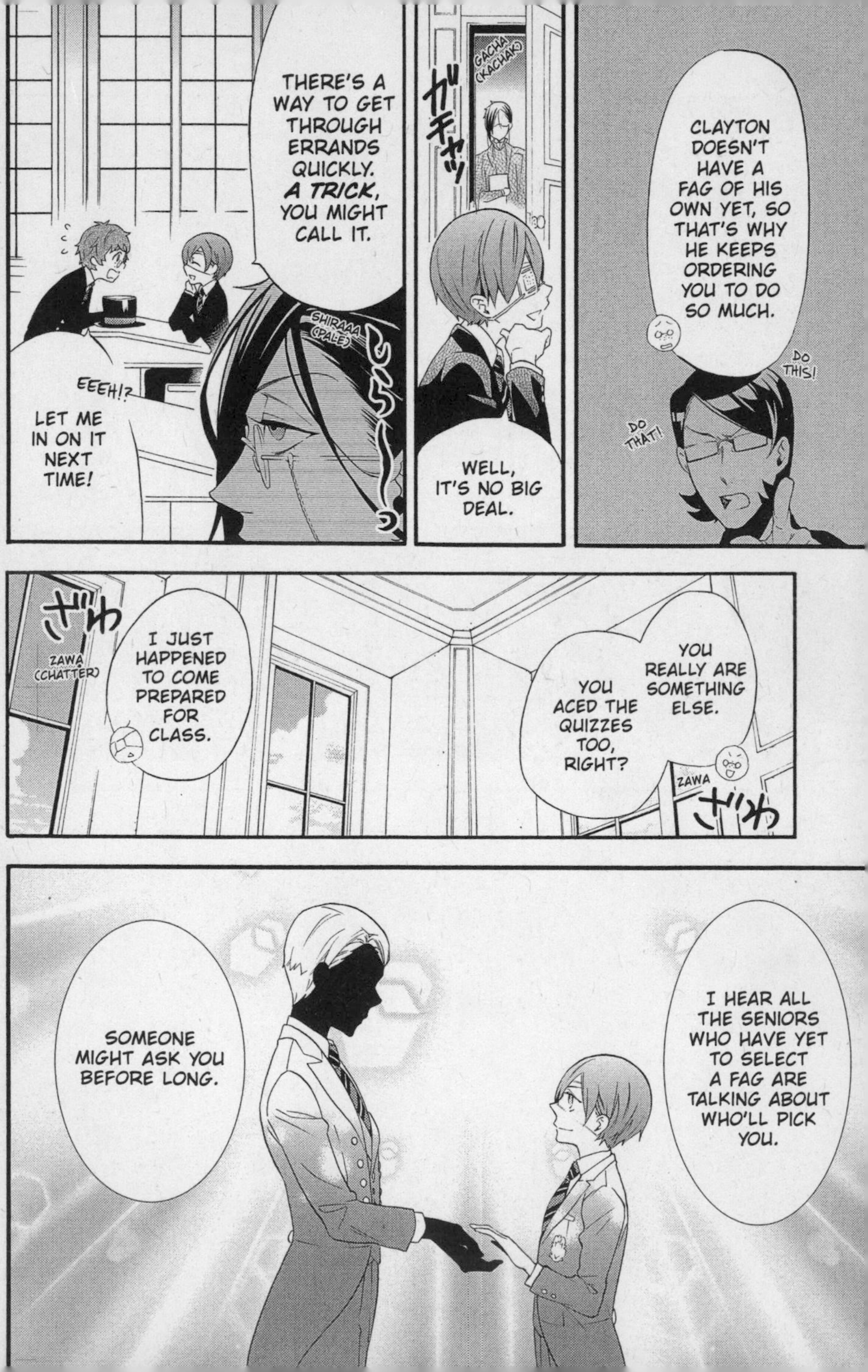
CLAYTON DOESN'T HAVE A FAG OF HIS OWN YET, SO THAT'S WHY HE KEEPS ORDERING YOU TO DO SO MUCH.
DO THIS!
DO THAT!
GACHA (KACHAK)
WELL, IT'S NO BIG DEAL.
THERE'S A WAY TO GET THROUGH ERRANDS QUICKLY. ***A TRICK***, YOU MIGHT CALL IT.
SHIRAAA (PALE)
EEEH!?
LET ME IN ON IT NEXT TIME!
YOU REALLY ARE SOMETHING ELSE.
YOU ACED THE QUIZZES TOO, RIGHT?
ZAWA
I JUST HAPPENED TO COME PREPARED FOR CLASS.
ZAWA (CHATTER)
I HEAR ALL THE SENIORS WHO HAVE YET TO SELECT A FAG ARE TALKING ABOUT WHO'LL PICK YOU.
SOMEONE MIGHT ASK YOU BEFORE LONG.

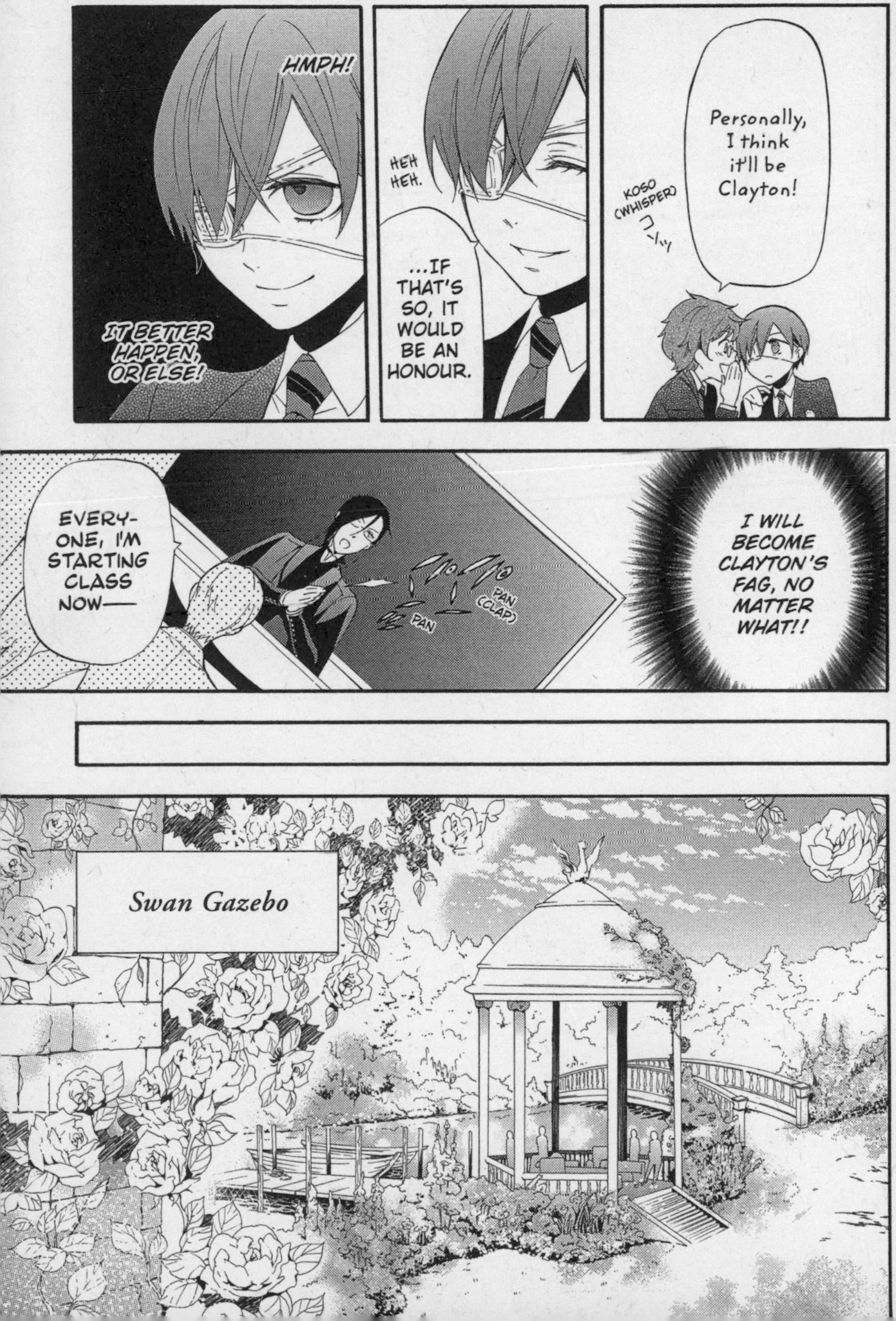

Personally, I think it'll be Clayton!
KOSO (WHISPER)
HEH HEH.
...IF THAT'S SO, IT WOULD BE AN HONOUR.
HMPH!
IT BETTER HAPPEN, OR ELSE!
I WILL BECOME CLAYTON'S FAG, NO MATTER WHAT!!
PAN (CLAP)
PAN
EVERY-ONE, I'M STARTING CLASS NOW—
Swan Gazebo

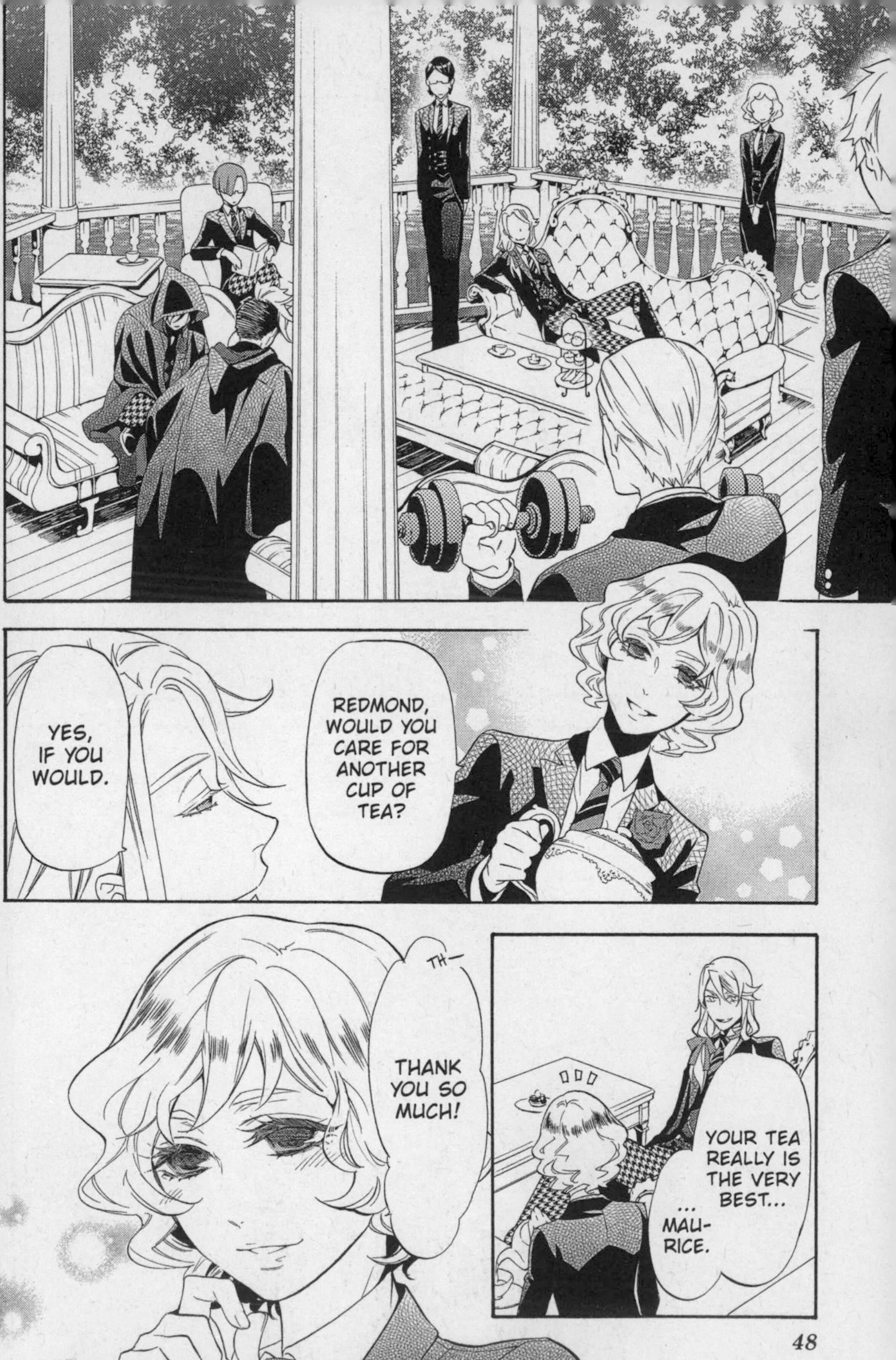
REDMOND, WOULD YOU CARE FOR ANOTHER CUP OF TEA?
YES, IF YOU WOULD.
YOUR TEA REALLY IS THE VERY BEST... ...MAU-RICE.
TH—
THANK YOU SO MUCH!

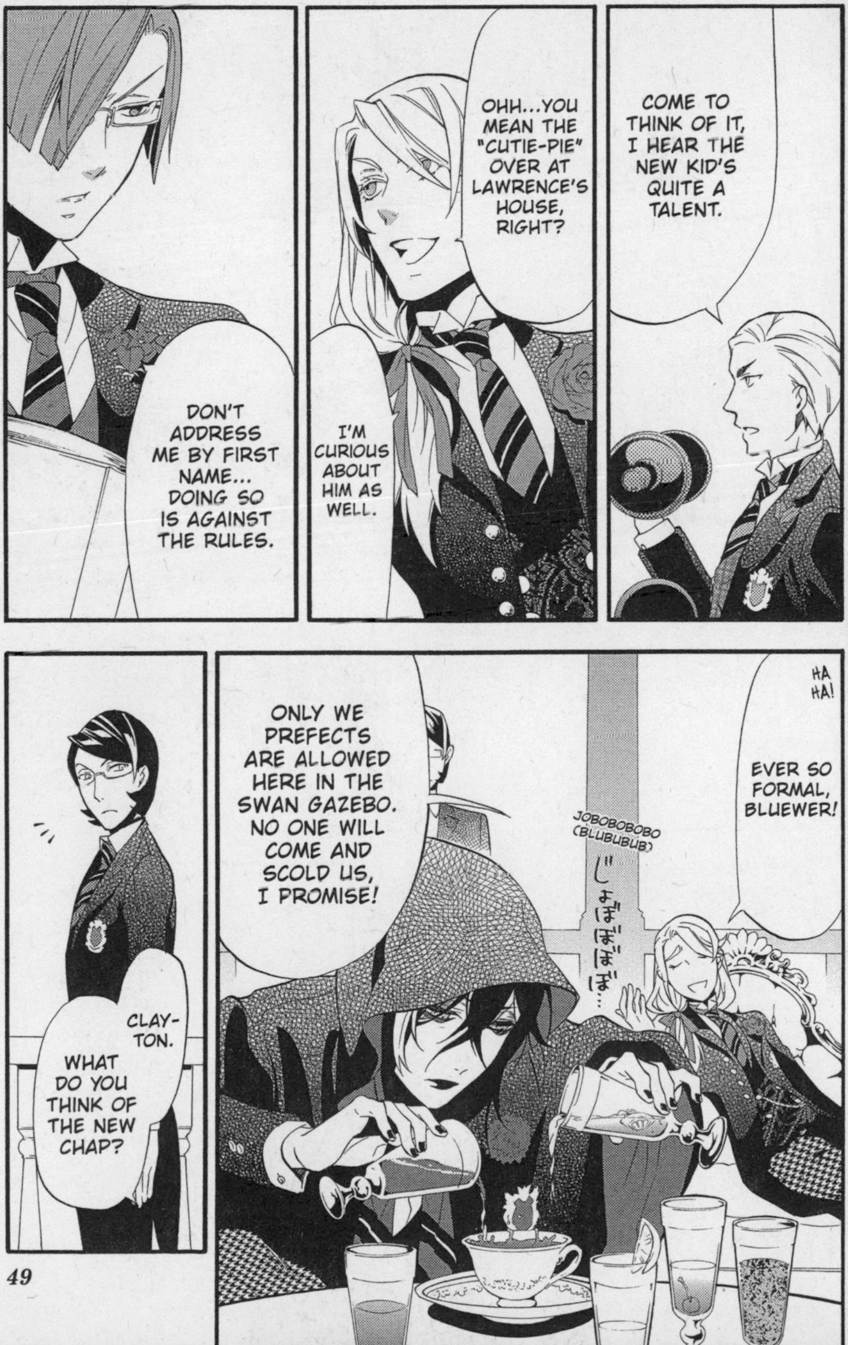
COME TO THINK OF IT, I HEAR THE NEW KID'S QUITE A TALENT.
OHH...YOU MEAN THE "CUTIE-PIE" OVER AT LAWRENCE'S HOUSE, RIGHT?
I'M CURIOUS ABOUT HIM AS WELL.
DON'T ADDRESS ME BY FIRST NAME... DOING SO IS AGAINST THE RULES.
HA HA!
EVER SO FORMAL, BLUEWER!
JOBOBOBOBO (BLUBUBUB)
じょぼぼぼぼ…
ONLY WE PREFECTS ARE ALLOWED HERE IN THE SWAN GAZEBO. NO ONE WILL COME AND SCOLD US, I PROMISE!
CLAY-TON.
WHAT DO YOU THINK OF THE NEW CHAP?

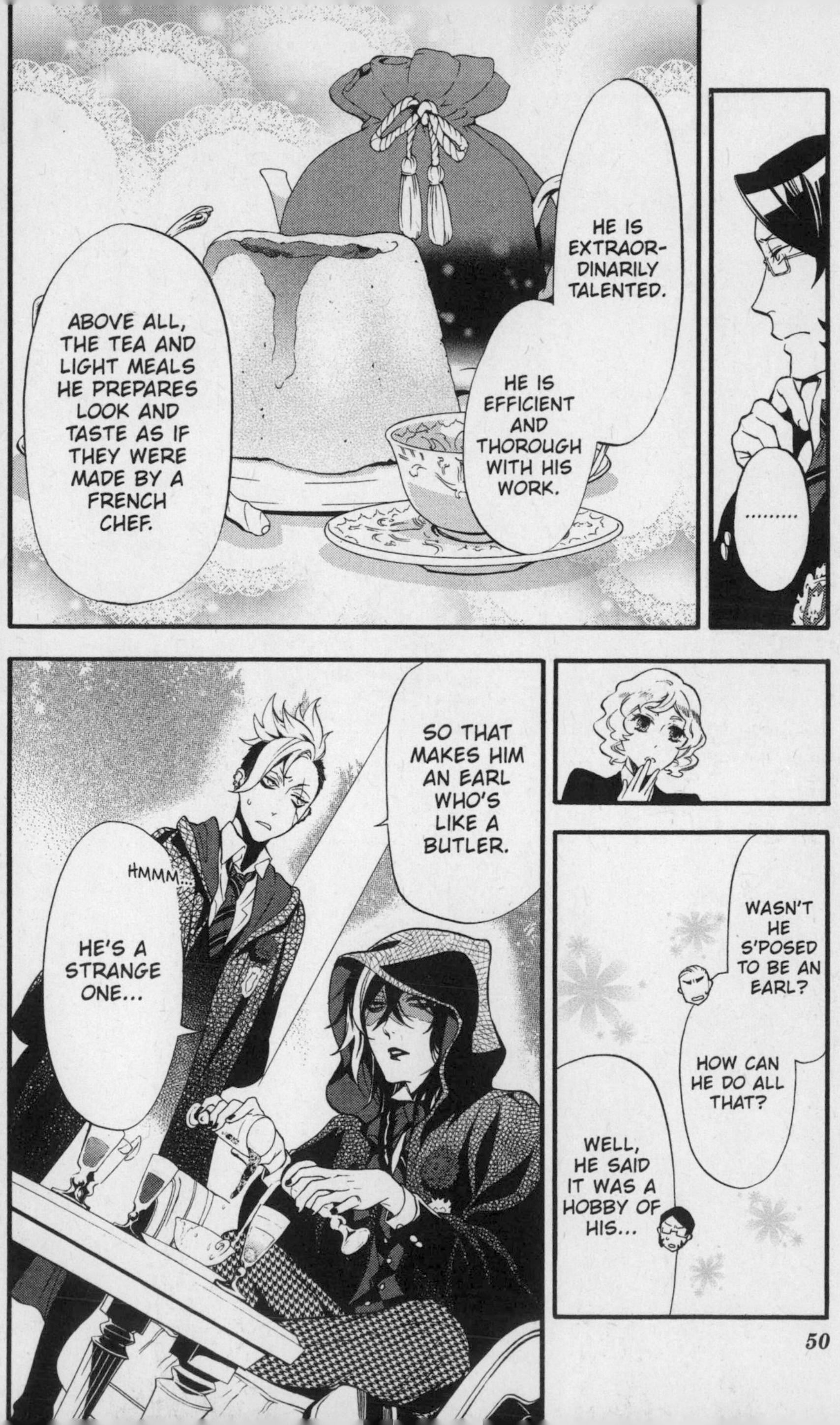
....
HE IS EXTRAOR-DINARILY TALENTED.
HE IS EFFICIENT AND THOROUGH WITH HIS WORK.
ABOVE ALL, THE TEA AND LIGHT MEALS HE PREPARES LOOK AND TASTE AS IF THEY WERE MADE BY A FRENCH CHEF.
WASN'T HE S'POSED TO BE AN EARL?
HOW CAN HE DO ALL THAT?
WELL, HE SAID IT WAS A HOBBY OF HIS...
SO THAT MAKES HIM AN EARL WHO'S LIKE A BUTLER.
HMMM...
HE'S A STRANGE ONE...

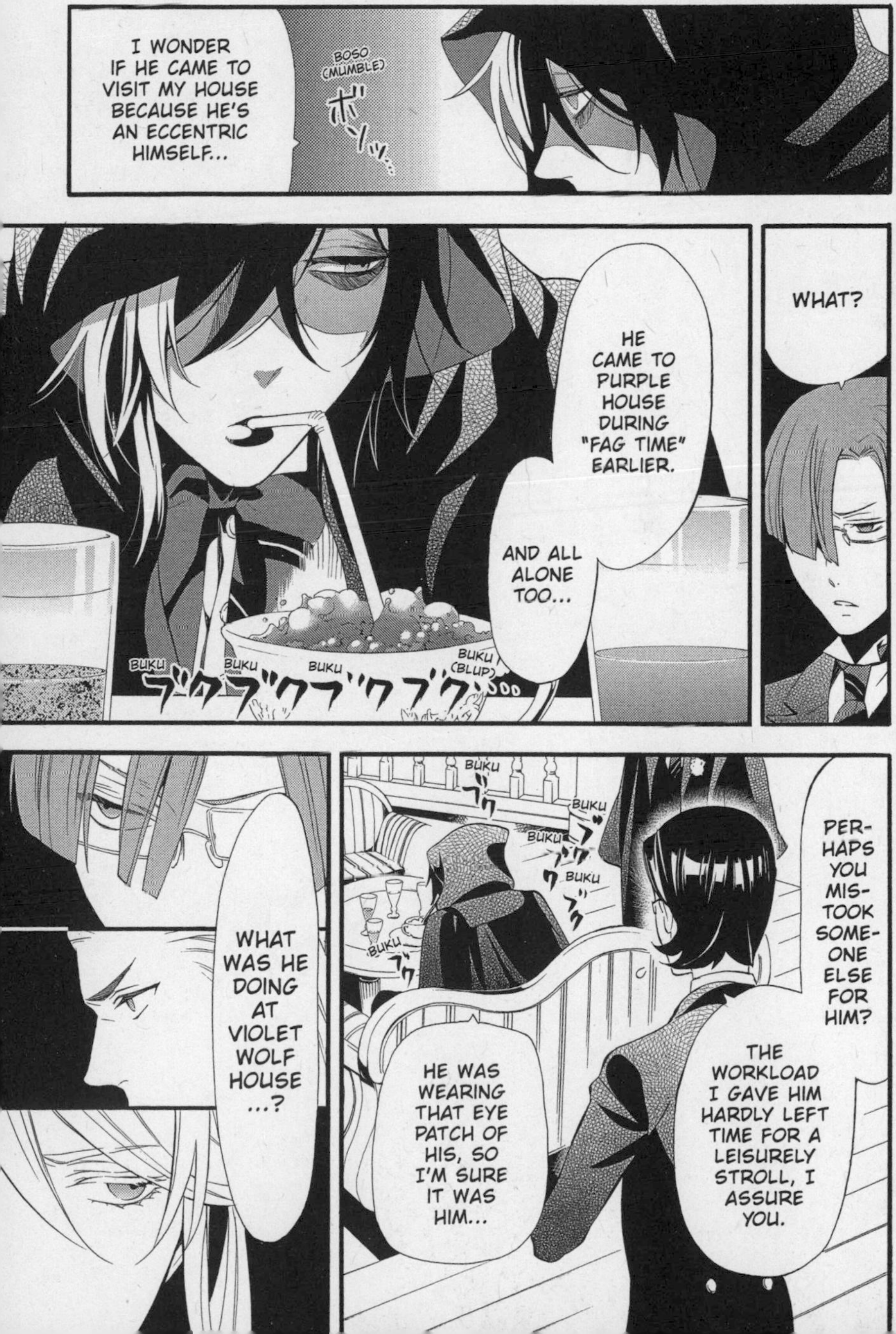
BOSO (MUMBLE)
ボソッ…
I WONDER IF HE CAME TO VISIT MY HOUSE BECAUSE HE'S AN ECCENTRIC HIMSELF…
WHAT?
HE CAME TO PURPLE HOUSE DURING "FAG TIME" EARLIER.
AND ALL ALONE TOO…
BUKU (BLUP)
BUKU
BUKU
BUKU
ブクブクブクブク
PERHAPS YOU MISTOOK SOMEONE ELSE FOR HIM?
THE WORKLOAD I GAVE HIM HARDLY LEFT TIME FOR A LEISURELY STROLL, I ASSURE YOU.
BUKU
BUKU
BUKU
BUKU
BUKU
HE WAS WEARING THAT EYE PATCH OF HIS, SO I'M SURE IT WAS HIM…
WHAT WAS HE DOING AT VIOLET WOLF HOUSE …?

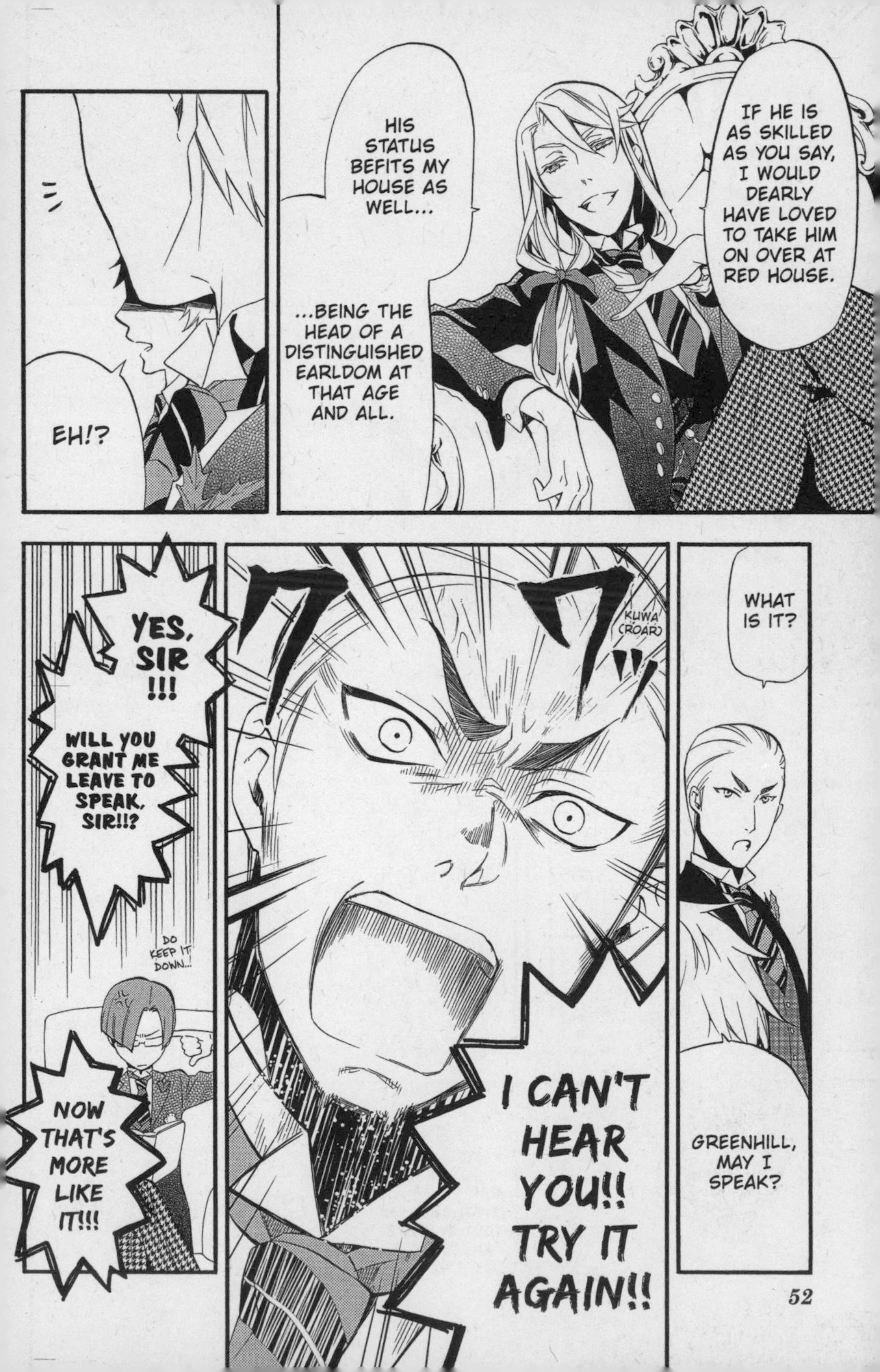
IF HE IS AS SKILLED AS YOU SAY, I WOULD DEARLY HAVE LOVED TO TAKE HIM ON OVER AT RED HOUSE.
HIS STATUS BEFITS MY HOUSE AS WELL...
...BEING THE HEAD OF A DISTINGUISHED EARLDOM AT THAT AGE AND ALL.
EH!?
WHAT IS IT?
GREENHILL, MAY I SPEAK?
KUWA (ROAR)
I CAN'T HEAR YOU!! TRY IT AGAIN!!
YES, SIR!!!
WILL YOU GRANT ME LEAVE TO SPEAK, SIR!!?
DO KEEP IT DOWN...
NOW THAT'S MORE LIKE IT!!!

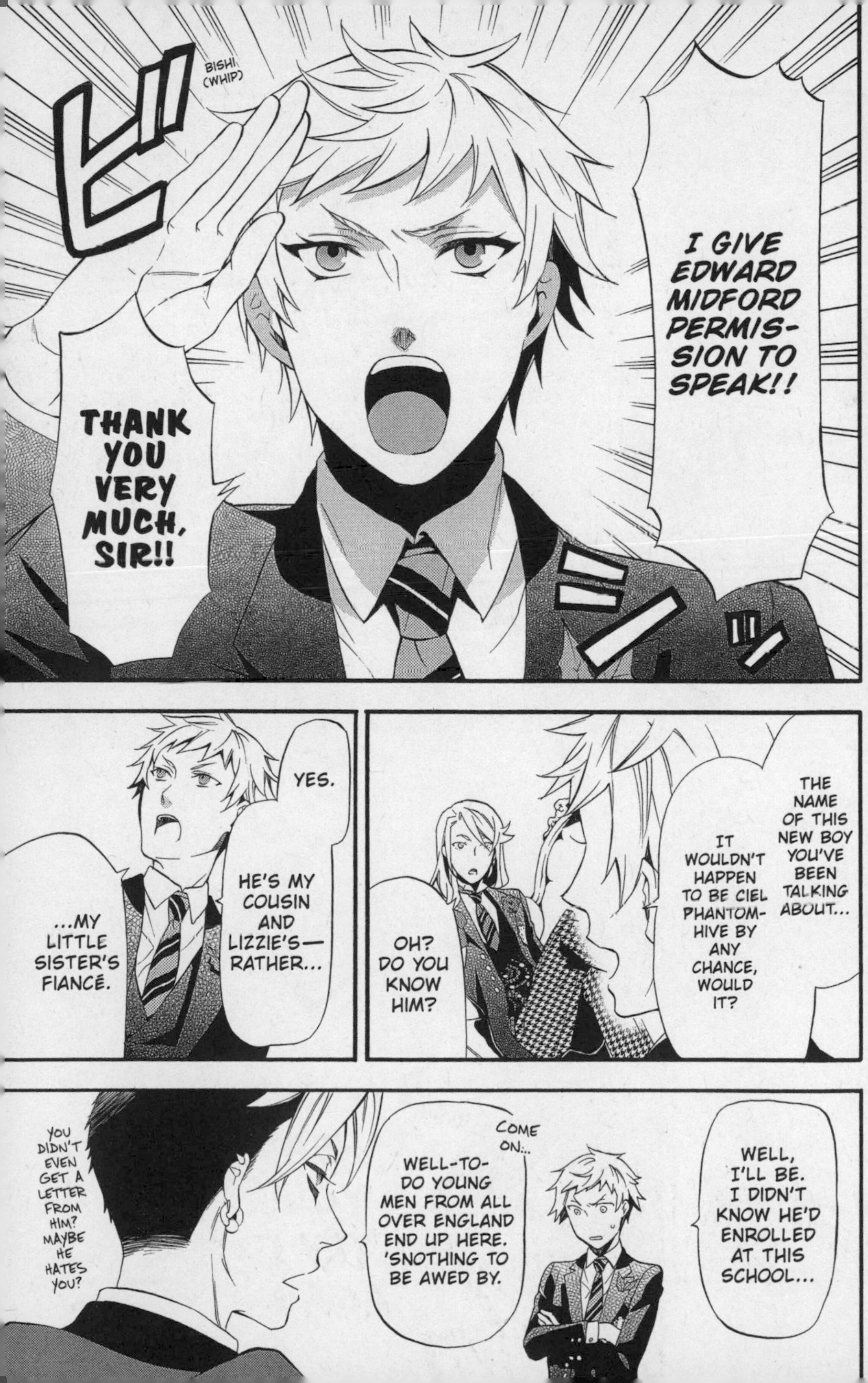
I GIVE EDWARD MIDFORD PERMISSION TO SPEAK!!
BISHI (WHIP)
THANK YOU VERY MUCH, SIR!!
THE NAME OF THIS NEW BOY YOU'VE BEEN TALKING ABOUT...
IT WOULDN'T HAPPEN TO BE CIEL PHANTOMHIVE BY ANY CHANCE, WOULD IT?
OH? DO YOU KNOW HIM?
YES.
HE'S MY COUSIN AND LIZZIE'S—RATHER...
...MY LITTLE SISTER'S FIANCÉ.
WELL, I'LL BE. I DIDN'T KNOW HE'D ENROLLED AT THIS SCHOOL...
COME ON...
WELL-TO-DO YOUNG MEN FROM ALL OVER ENGLAND END UP HERE. 'SNOTHING TO BE AWED BY.
YOU DIDN'T EVEN GET A LETTER FROM HIM? MAYBE HE HATES YOU?

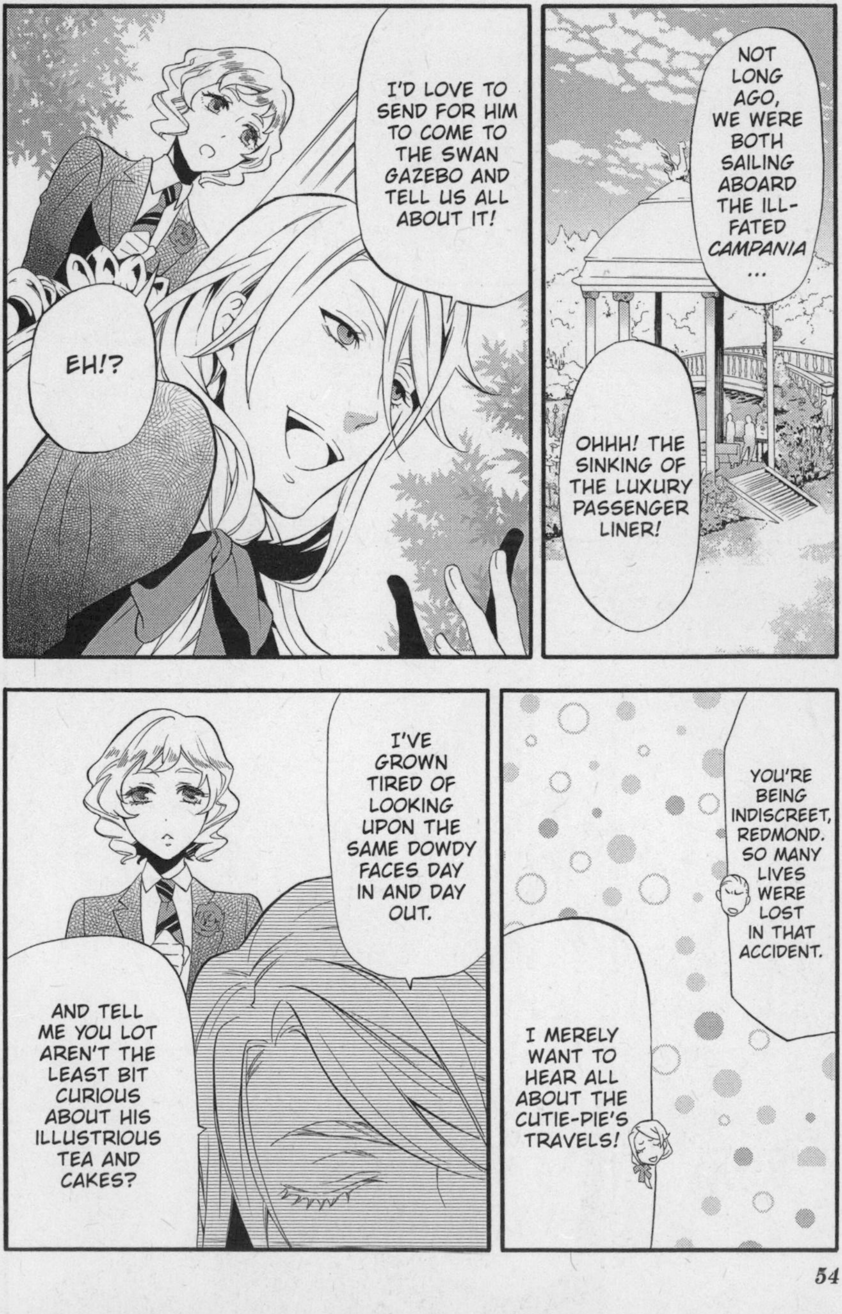
NOT LONG AGO, WE WERE BOTH SAILING ABOARD THE ILL-FATED *CAMPANIA* ...
OHHH! THE SINKING OF THE LUXURY PASSENGER LINER!
I'D LOVE TO SEND FOR HIM TO COME TO THE SWAN GAZEBO AND TELL US ALL ABOUT IT!
EH!?
YOU'RE BEING INDISCREET, REDMOND. SO MANY LIVES WERE LOST IN THAT ACCIDENT.
I MERELY WANT TO HEAR ALL ABOUT THE CUTIE-PIE'S TRAVELS!
I'VE GROWN TIRED OF LOOKING UPON THE SAME DOWDY FACES DAY IN AND DAY OUT.
AND TELL ME YOU LOT AREN'T THE LEAST BIT CURIOUS ABOUT HIS ILLUSTRIOUS TEA AND CAKES?

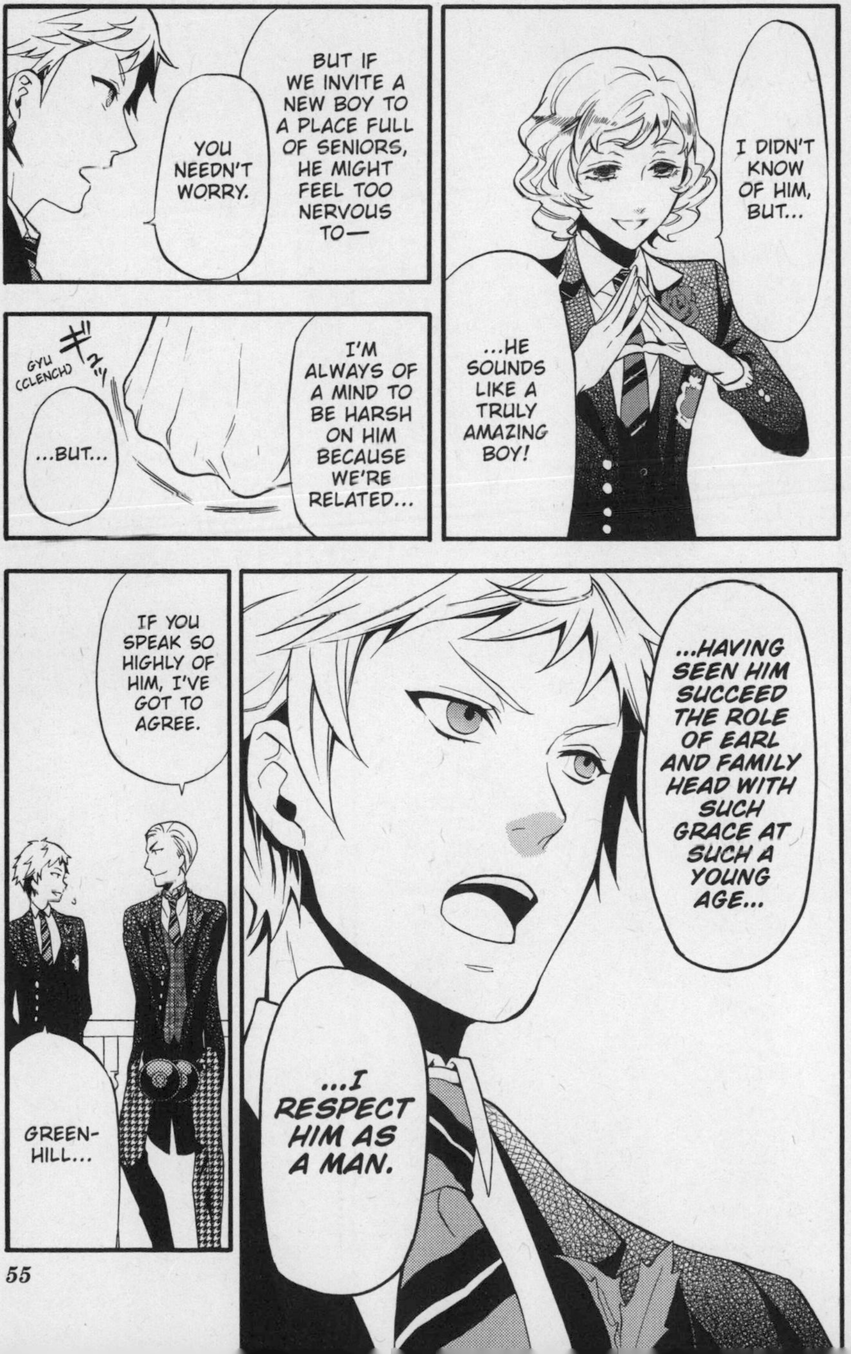
I DIDN'T KNOW OF HIM, BUT...
...HE SOUNDS LIKE A TRULY AMAZING BOY!
BUT IF WE INVITE A NEW BOY TO A PLACE FULL OF SENIORS, HE MIGHT FEEL TOO NERVOUS TO—
YOU NEEDN'T WORRY.
I'M ALWAYS OF A MIND TO BE HARSH ON HIM BECAUSE WE'RE RELATED...
GYU (CLENCH)
...BUT...
...HAVING SEEN HIM SUCCEED THE ROLE OF EARL AND FAMILY HEAD WITH SUCH GRACE AT SUCH A YOUNG AGE...
...I RESPECT HIM AS A MAN.
IF YOU SPEAK SO HIGHLY OF HIM, I'VE GOT TO AGREE.
GREEN-HILL...

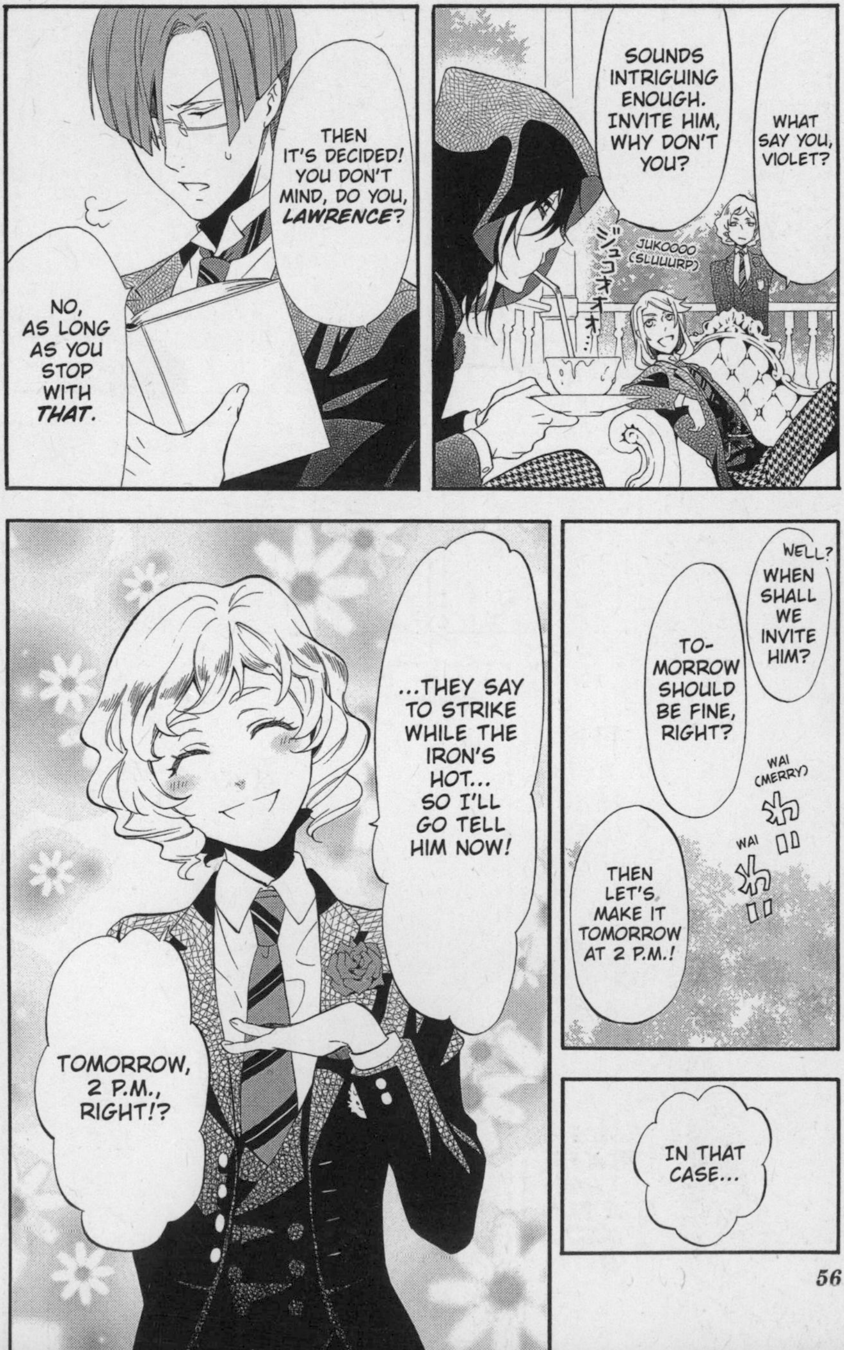
WHAT SAY YOU, VIOLET?
SOUNDS INTRIGUING ENOUGH. INVITE HIM, WHY DON'T YOU?
ジュコオオ…
JUKOOOO (SLUUURP)
THEN IT'S DECIDED! YOU DON'T MIND, DO YOU, *LAWRENCE*?
NO, AS LONG AS YOU STOP WITH *THAT*.
WELL? WHEN SHALL WE INVITE HIM?
TO-MORROW SHOULD BE FINE, RIGHT?
WAI (MERRY)
わい
WAI
わい
THEN LET'S MAKE IT TOMORROW AT 2 P.M.!
IN THAT CASE...
...THEY SAY TO STRIKE WHILE THE IRON'S HOT... SO I'LL GO TELL HIM NOW!
TOMORROW, 2 P.M., RIGHT!?

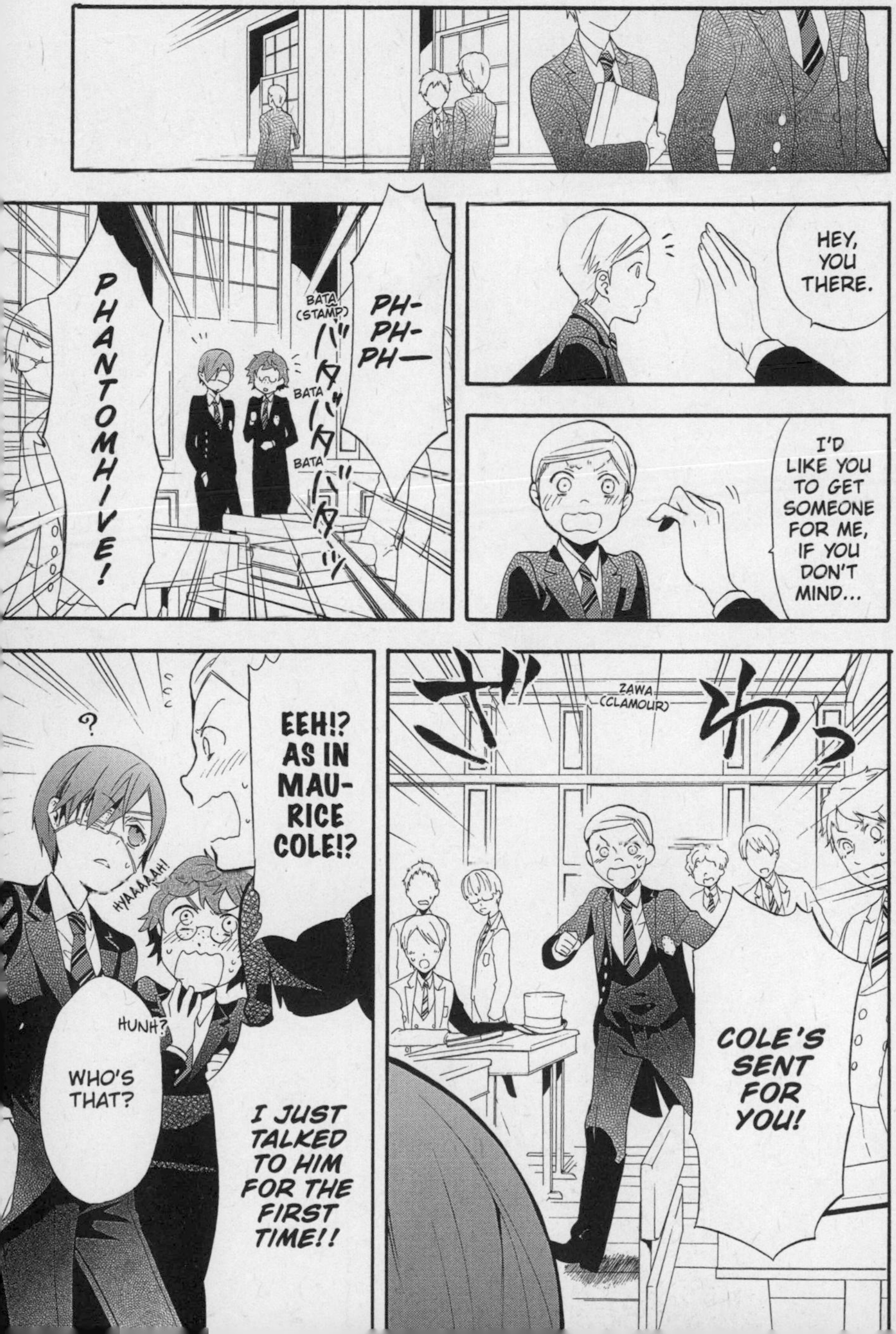
HEY, YOU THERE.
I'D LIKE YOU TO GET SOMEONE FOR ME, IF YOU DON'T MIND...
PH- PH- PH—
BATA (STAMP)
BATA
BATA
PHANTOMHIVE!
ZAWA (CLAMOUR)
COLE'S SENT FOR YOU!
EEH!? AS IN MAURICE COLE!?
HYAAAAAH!
?
HUNH?
WHO'S THAT?
I JUST TALKED TO HIM FOR THE FIRST TIME!!

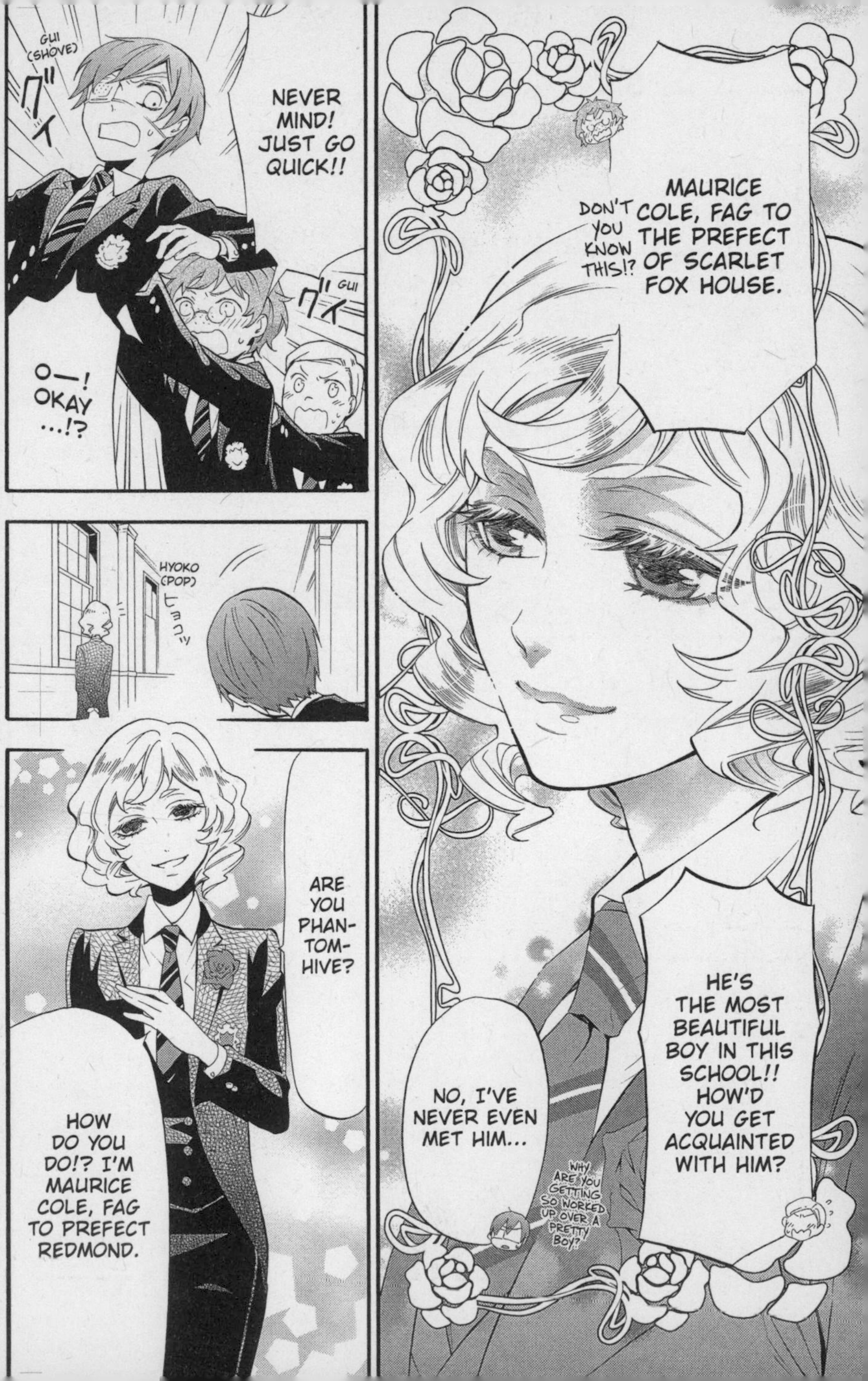
MAURICE COLE, FAG TO THE PREFECT OF SCARLET FOX HOUSE.
DON'T YOU KNOW THIS!?
HE'S THE MOST BEAUTIFUL BOY IN THIS SCHOOL!! HOW'D YOU GET ACQUAINTED WITH HIM?
NO, I'VE NEVER EVEN MET HIM...
WHY ARE YOU GETTING SO WORKED UP OVER A PRETTY BOY?
NEVER MIND! JUST GO QUICK!!
GUI (SHOVE)
グイ
GUI
グイ
O—! OKAY ...!?
HYOKO (POP)
ヒョコッ
ARE YOU PHANTOM-HIVE?
HOW DO YOU DO!? I'M MAURICE COLE, FAG TO PREFECT REDMOND.

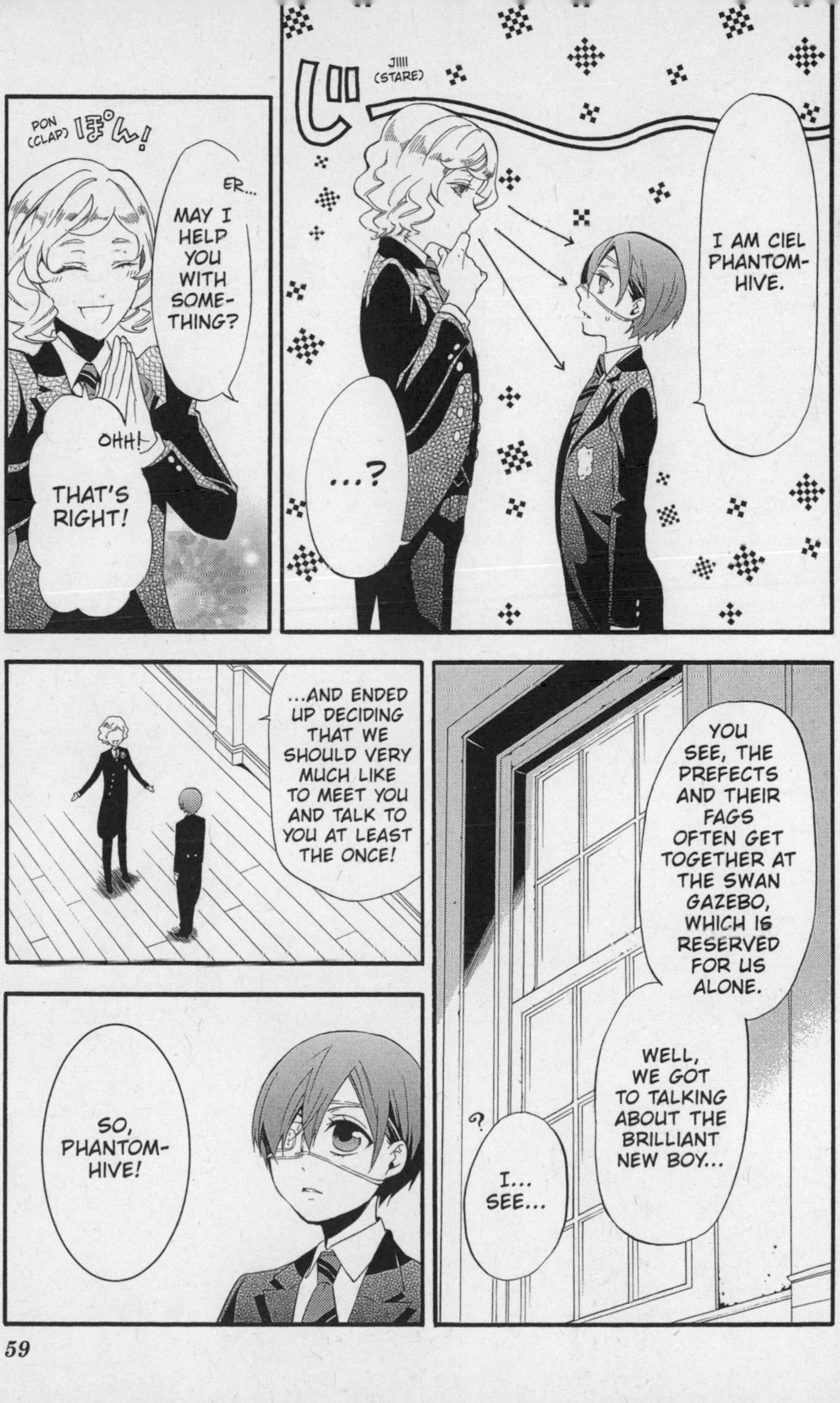
JIIII (STARE)
I AM CIEL PHANTOMHIVE.
...?
ER... MAY I HELP YOU WITH SOMETHING?
PON (CLAP)
OHH! THAT'S RIGHT!
YOU SEE, THE PREFECTS AND THEIR FAGS OFTEN GET TOGETHER AT THE SWAN GAZEBO, WHICH IS RESERVED FOR US ALONE.
WELL, WE GOT TO TALKING ABOUT THE BRILLIANT NEW BOY...
?
I... SEE...
...AND ENDED UP DECIDING THAT WE SHOULD VERY MUCH LIKE TO MEET YOU AND TALK TO YOU AT LEAST THE ONCE!
SO, PHANTOMHIVE!

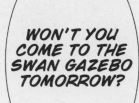

WON'T YOU COME TO THE SWAN GAZEBO TOMORROW?

THIS IS...

...MY CHANCE TO GET CLOSE TO THE P4 IN ONE GO!!

OF COURSE I ACCEPT!

!!

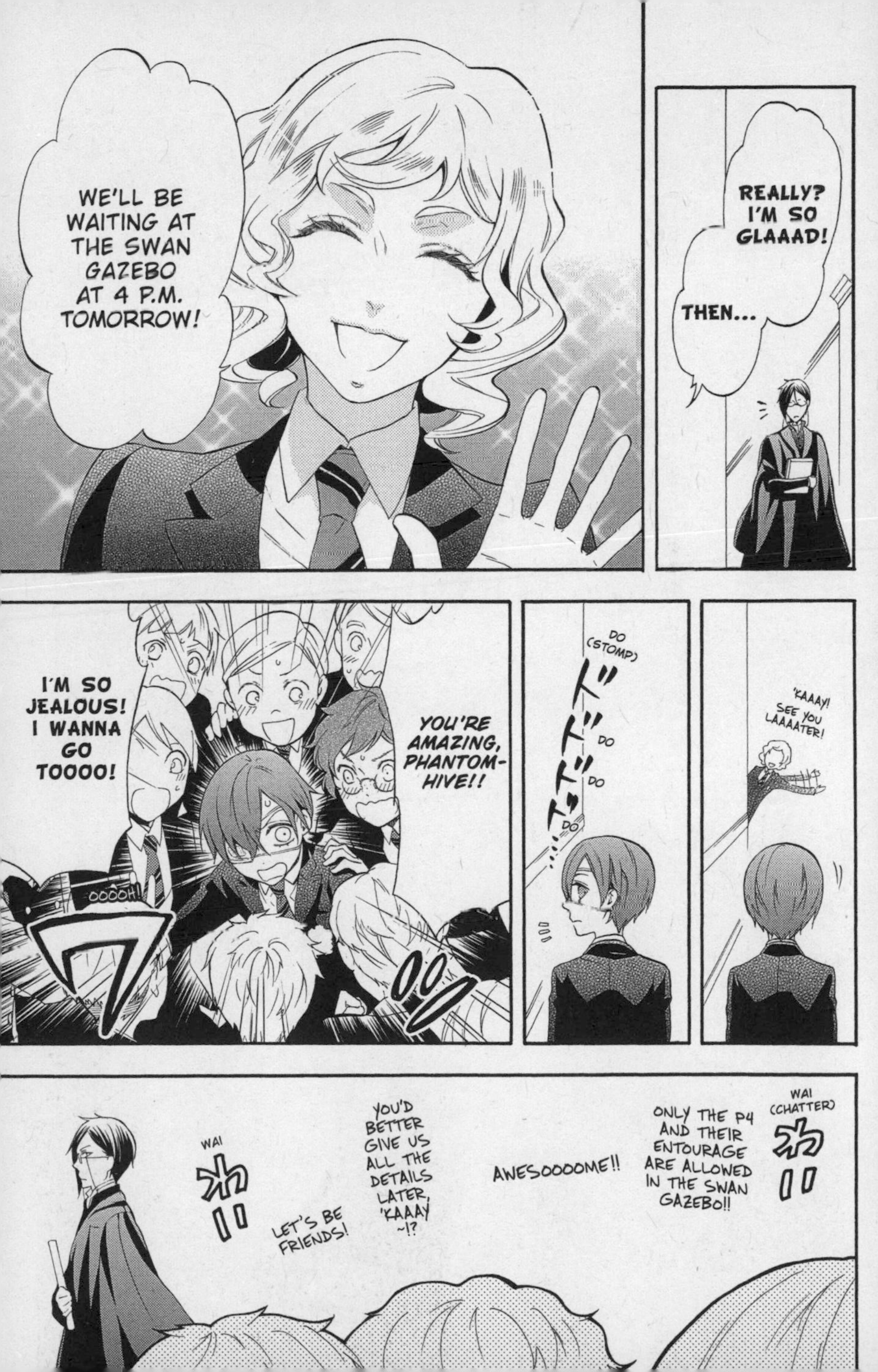
REALLY? I'M SO GLAAAD!
THEN...
WE'LL BE WAITING AT THE SWAN GAZEBO AT 4 P.M. TOMORROW!
'KAAAY! SEE YOU LAAAATER!
DO (STOMP)
DO
DO
DO
YOU'RE AMAZING, PHANTOM-HIVE!!
I'M SO JEALOUS! I WANNA GO TOOOO!
OOOOH!
WAI (CHATTER)
ONLY THE P4 AND THEIR ENTOURAGE ARE ALLOWED IN THE SWAN GAZEBO!!
AWESOOOOME!!
YOU'D BETTER GIVE US ALL THE DETAILS LATER, 'KAAAY~!?
LET'S BE FRIENDS!
WAI

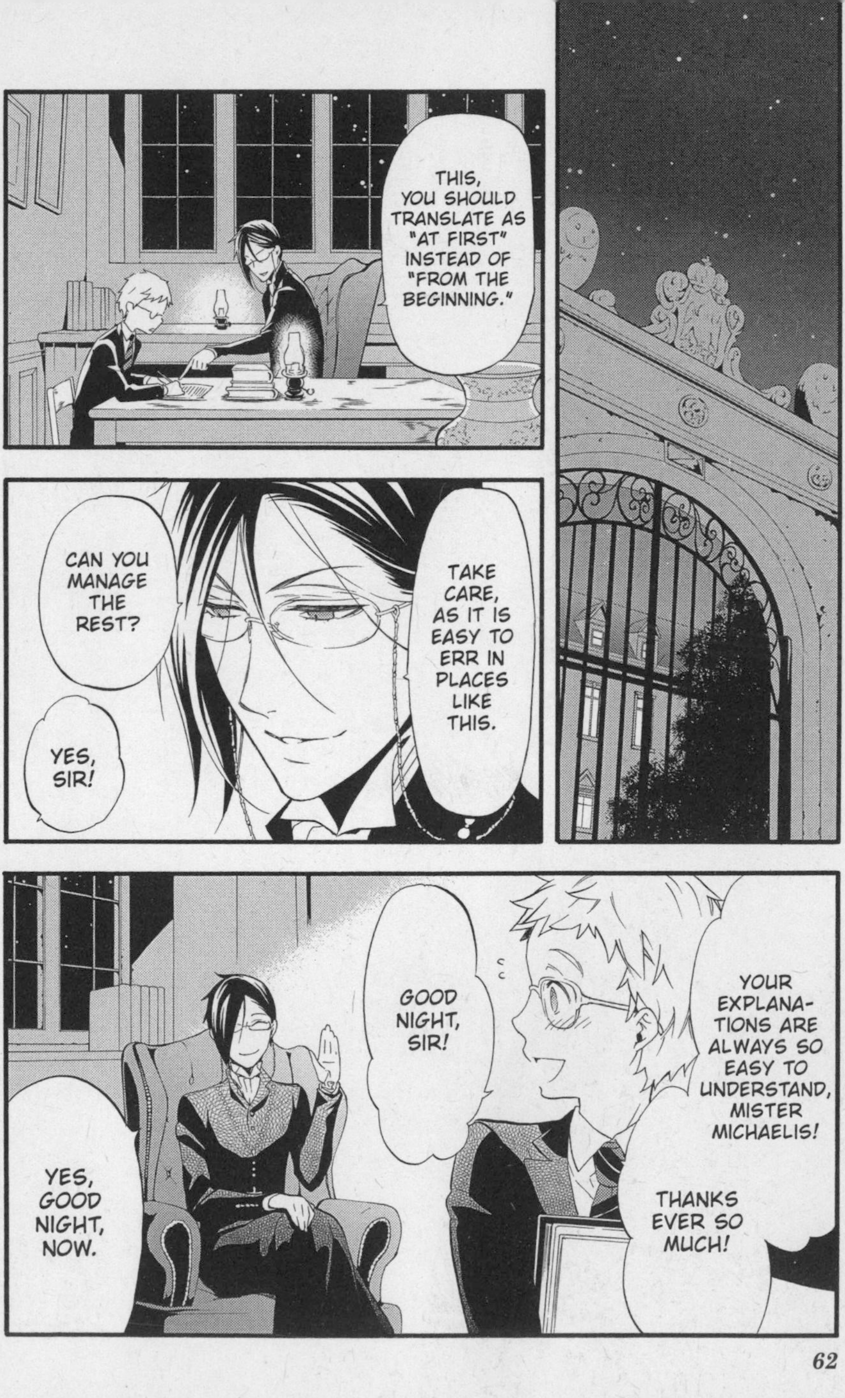
THIS, YOU SHOULD TRANSLATE AS "AT FIRST" INSTEAD OF "FROM THE BEGINNING."
TAKE CARE, AS IT IS EASY TO ERR IN PLACES LIKE THIS.
CAN YOU MANAGE THE REST?
YES, SIR!
YOUR EXPLANATIONS ARE ALWAYS SO EASY TO UNDERSTAND, MISTER MICHAELIS!
THANKS EVER SO MUCH!
GOOD NIGHT, SIR!
YES, GOOD NIGHT, NOW.

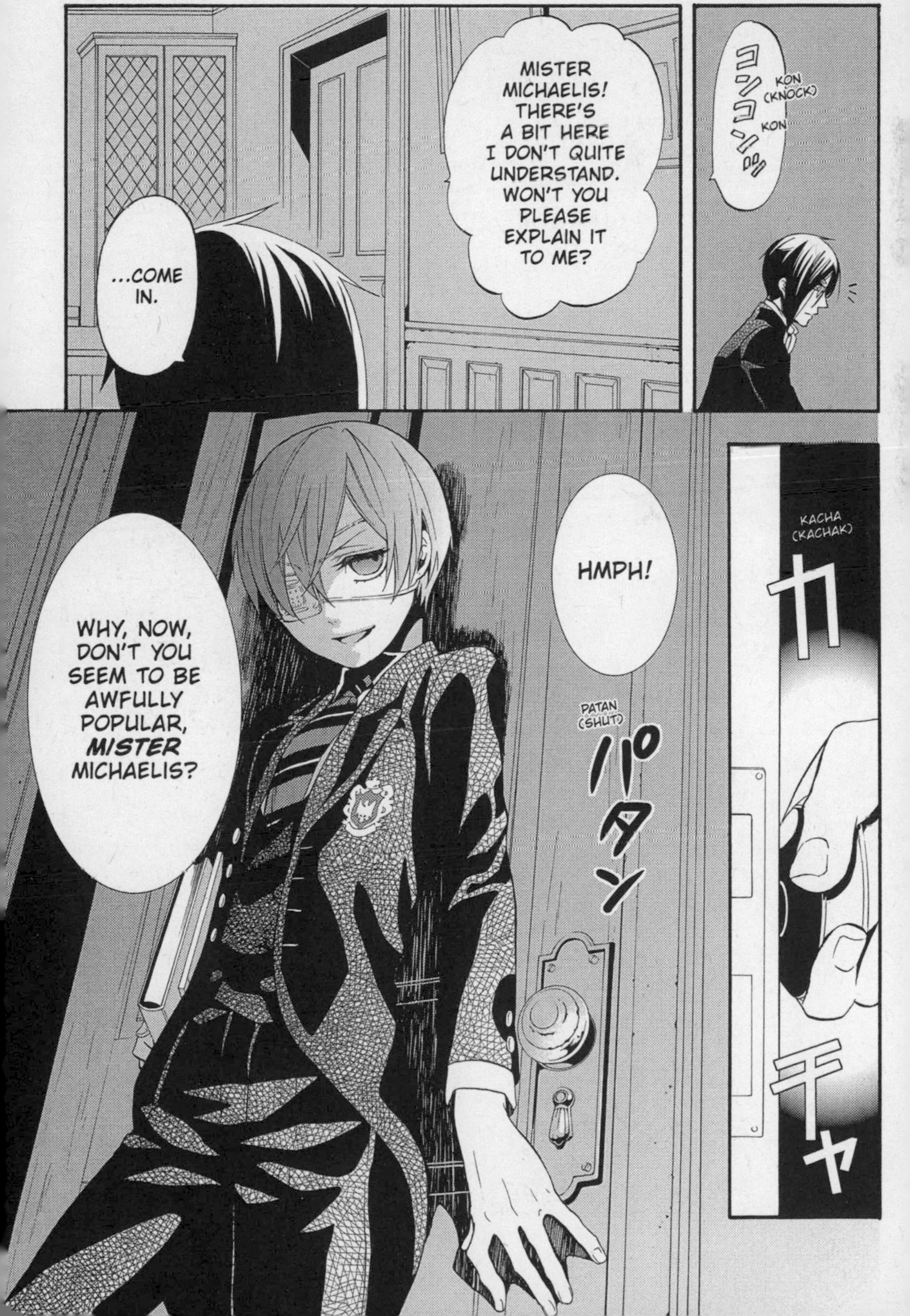
コンコン
KON (KNOCK) KON
MISTER MICHAELIS! THERE'S A BIT HERE I DON'T QUITE UNDERSTAND. WON'T YOU PLEASE EXPLAIN IT TO ME?
...COME IN.
KACHA (KACHAK)
カチャ
HMPH!
PATAN (SHUT)
パタン
WHY, NOW, DON'T YOU SEEM TO BE AWFULLY POPULAR, ***MISTER*** MICHAELIS?

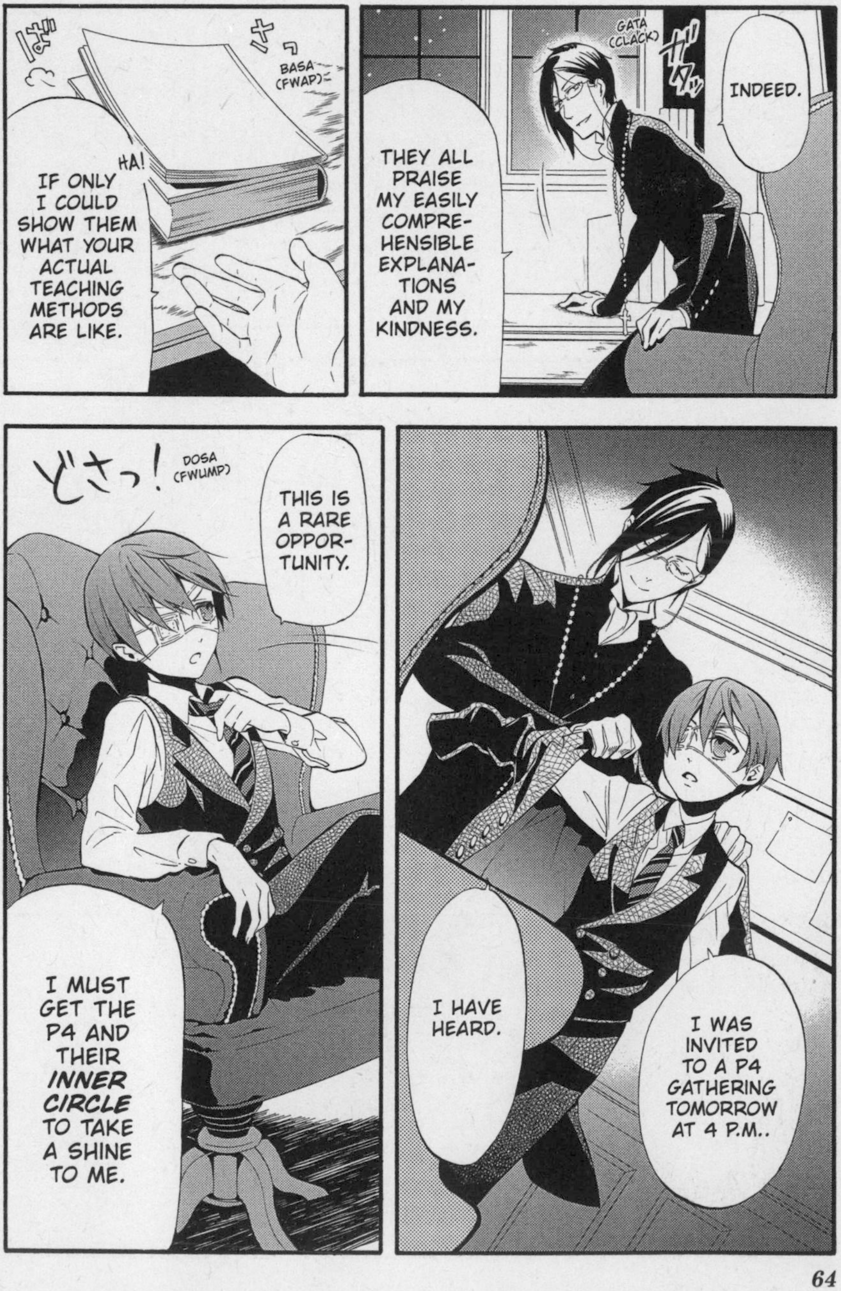
GATA (CLACK)
INDEED.
THEY ALL PRAISE MY EASILY COMPREHENSIBLE EXPLANATIONS AND MY KINDNESS.
BASA (FWAP)
HA!
IF ONLY I COULD SHOW THEM WHAT YOUR ACTUAL TEACHING METHODS ARE LIKE.
I WAS INVITED TO A P4 GATHERING TOMORROW AT 4 P.M..
I HAVE HEARD.
どさっ!
DOSA (FWUMP)
THIS IS A RARE OPPORTUNITY.
I MUST GET THE P4 AND THEIR *INNER CIRCLE* TO TAKE A SHINE TO ME.

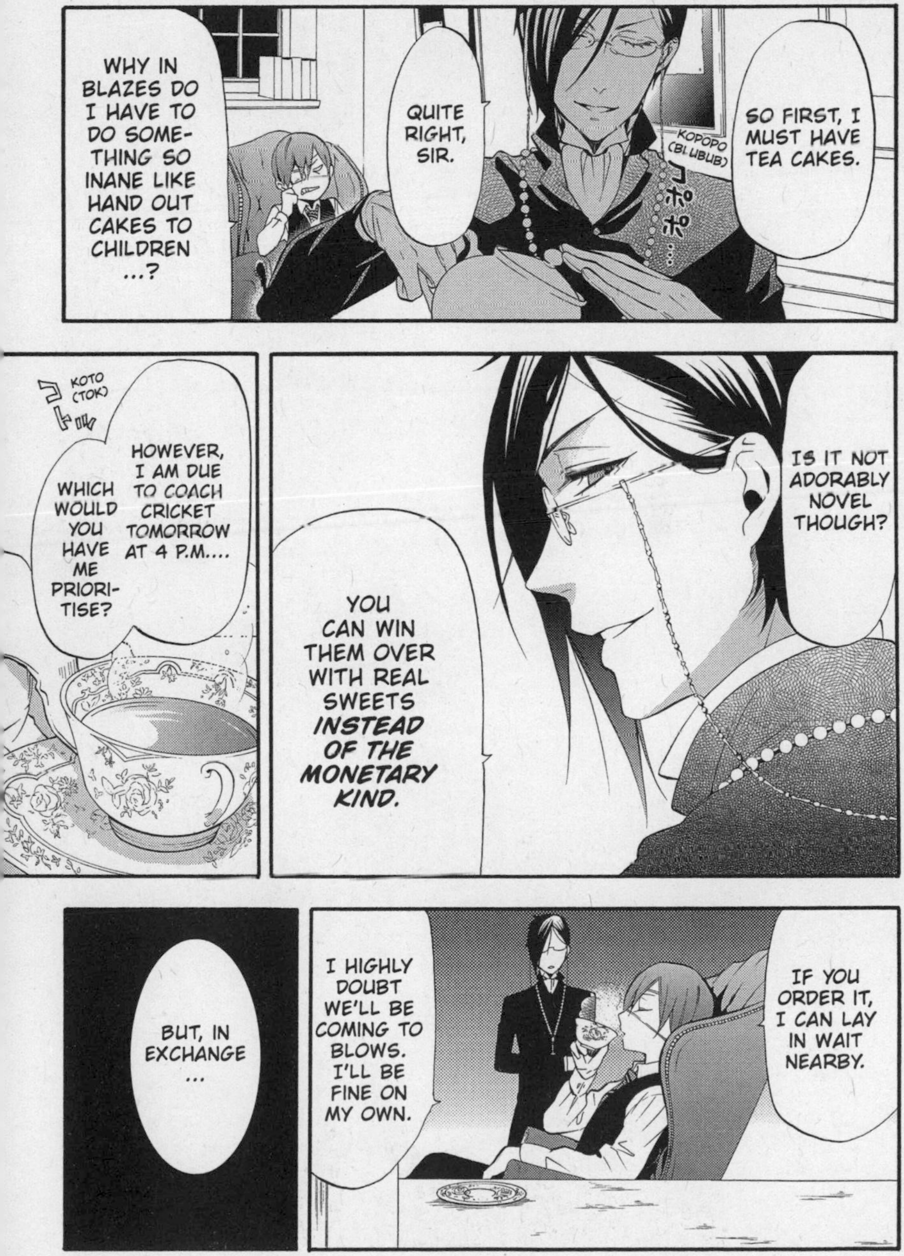
SO FIRST, I MUST HAVE TEA CAKES.
KOPOPO (BLUBUB)
QUITE RIGHT, SIR.
WHY IN BLAZES DO I HAVE TO DO SOMETHING SO INANE LIKE HAND OUT CAKES TO CHILDREN ...?
IS IT NOT ADORABLY NOVEL THOUGH?
YOU CAN WIN THEM OVER WITH REAL SWEETS *INSTEAD OF THE MONETARY KIND.*
KOTO (TOK)
HOWEVER, I AM DUE TO COACH CRICKET TOMORROW AT 4 P.M....
WHICH WOULD YOU HAVE ME PRIORITISE?
IF YOU ORDER IT, I CAN LAY IN WAIT NEARBY.
I HIGHLY DOUBT WE'LL BE COMING TO BLOWS. I'LL BE FINE ON MY OWN.
BUT, IN EXCHANGE ...

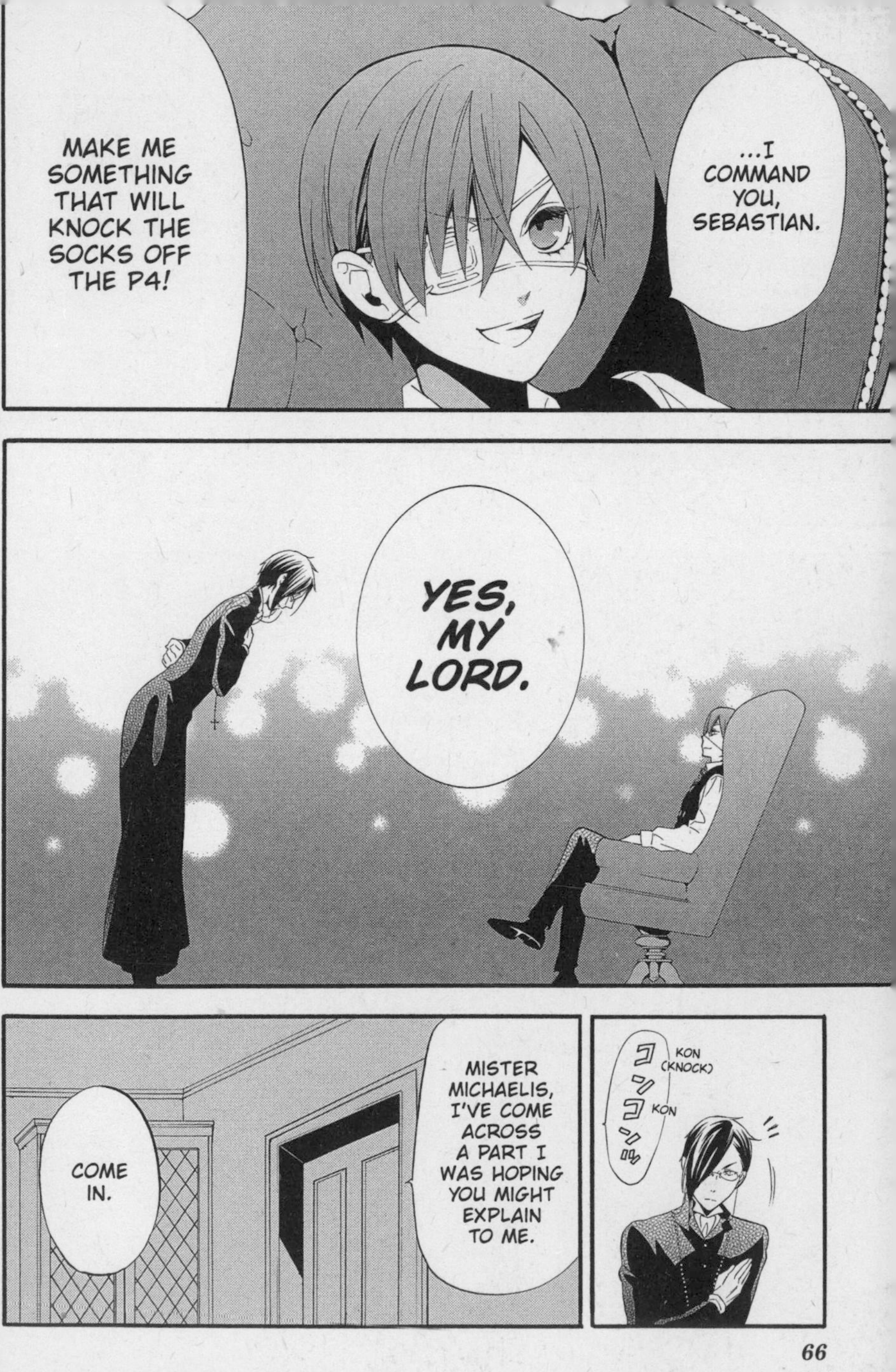
...I COMMAND YOU, SEBASTIAN.
MAKE ME SOMETHING THAT WILL KNOCK THE SOCKS OFF THE P4!
YES, MY LORD.
KON (KNOCK)
KON
MISTER MICHAELIS, I'VE COME ACROSS A PART I WAS HOPING YOU MIGHT EXPLAIN TO ME.
COME IN.

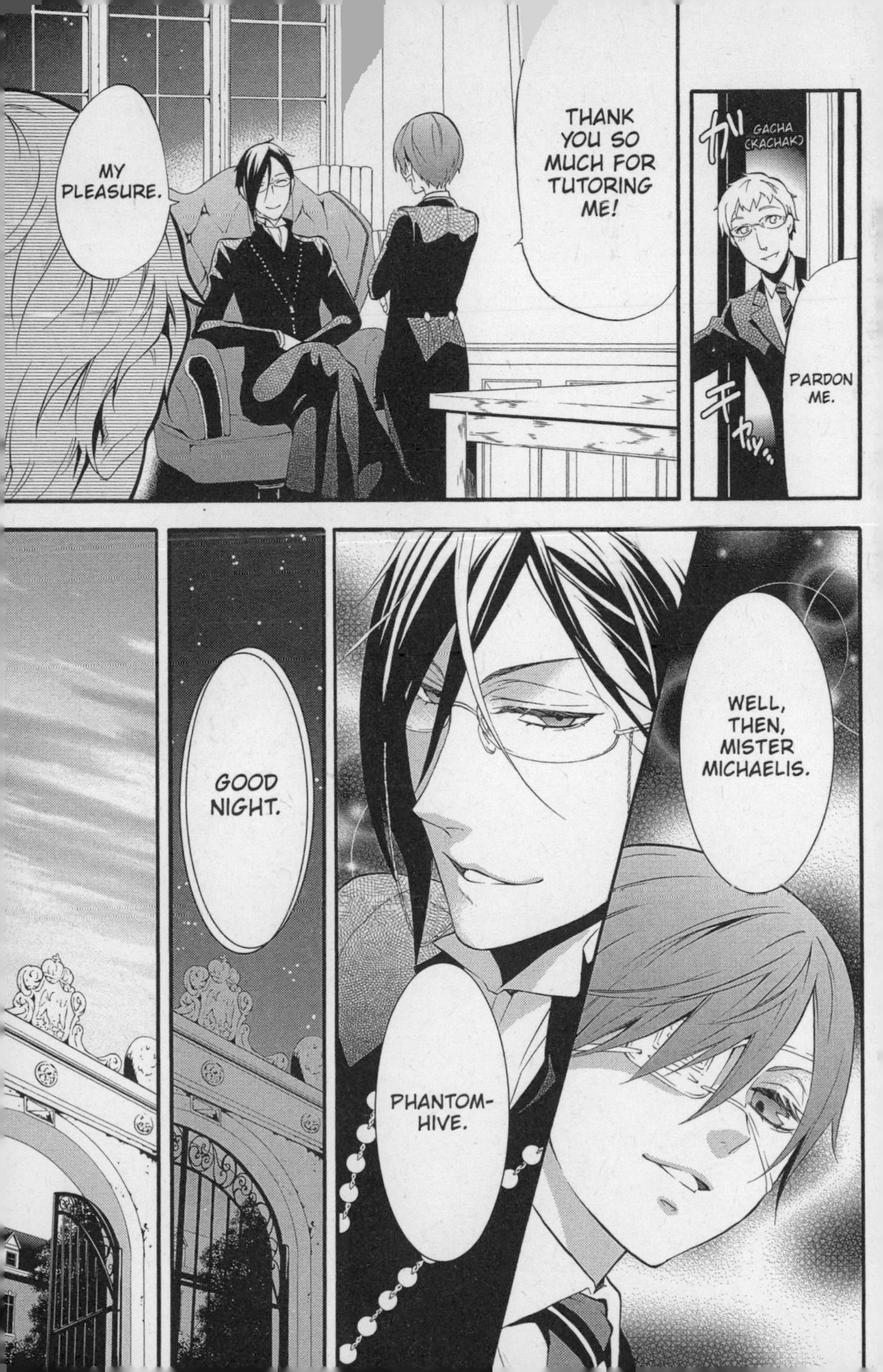
GACHA (KACHAK)
PARDON ME.
THANK YOU SO MUCH FOR TUTORING ME!
MY PLEASURE.
WELL, THEN, MISTER MICHAELIS.
PHANTOM-HIVE.
GOOD NIGHT.

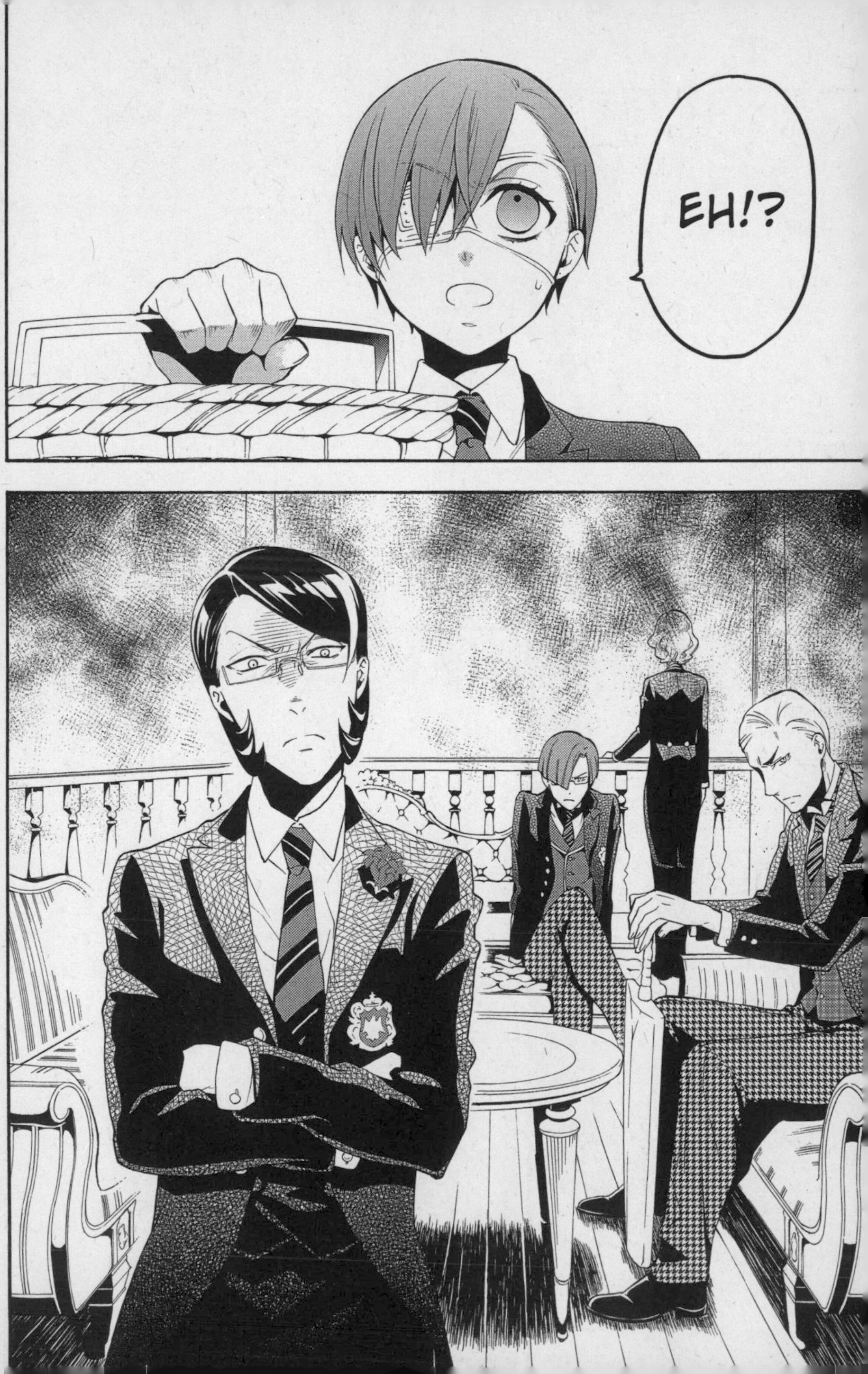
EH!?

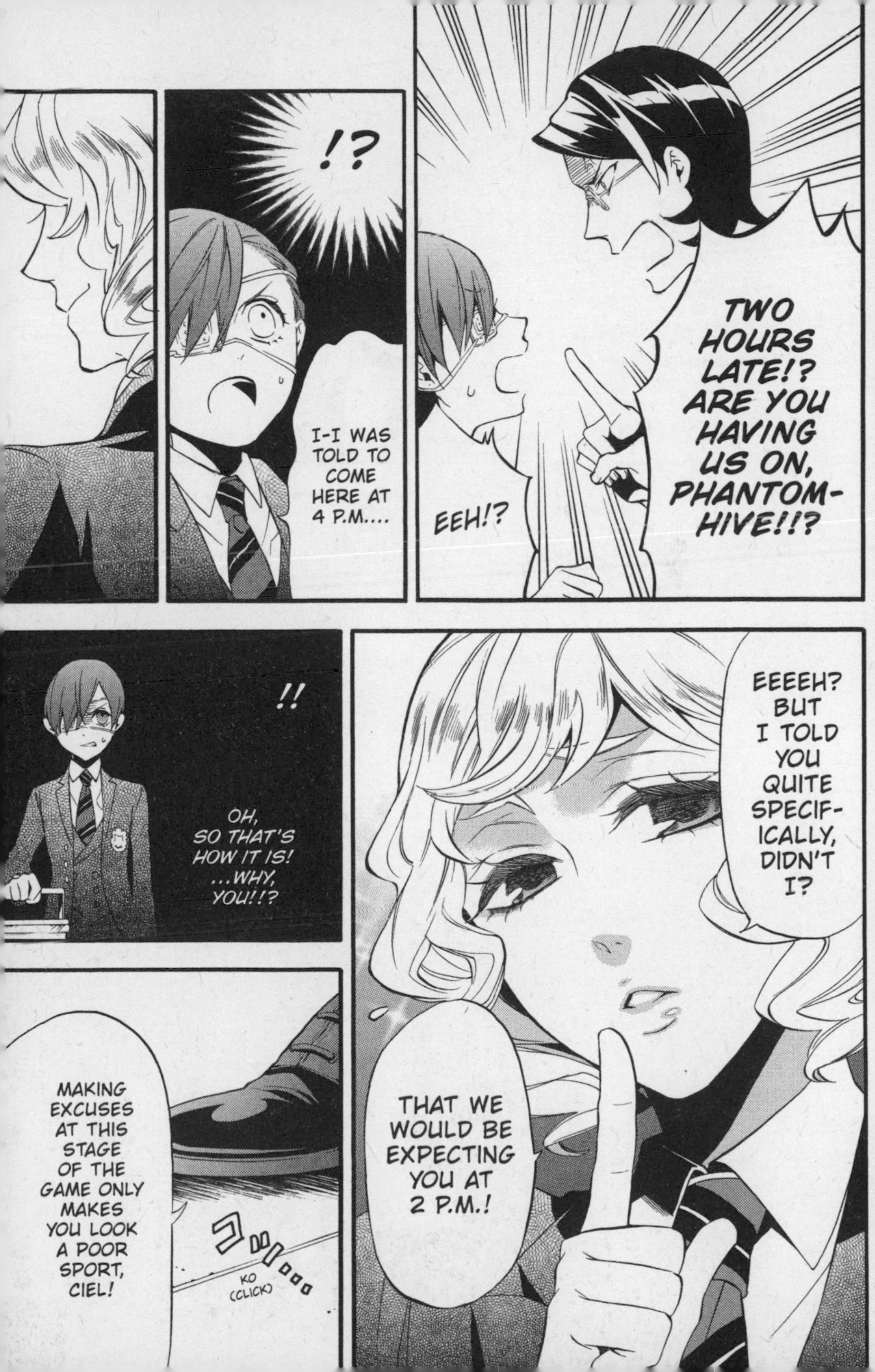
TWO HOURS LATE!? ARE YOU HAVING US ON, PHANTOM-HIVE!!?
EEH!?
!?
I-I WAS TOLD TO COME HERE AT 4 P.M....
EEEEH? BUT I TOLD YOU QUITE SPECIF-ICALLY, DIDN'T I?
THAT WE WOULD BE EXPECTING YOU AT 2 P.M.!
!!
OH, SO THAT'S HOW IT IS! ...WHY, YOU!!?
MAKING EXCUSES AT THIS STAGE OF THE GAME ONLY MAKES YOU LOOK A POOR SPORT, CIEL!
KO (CLICK)

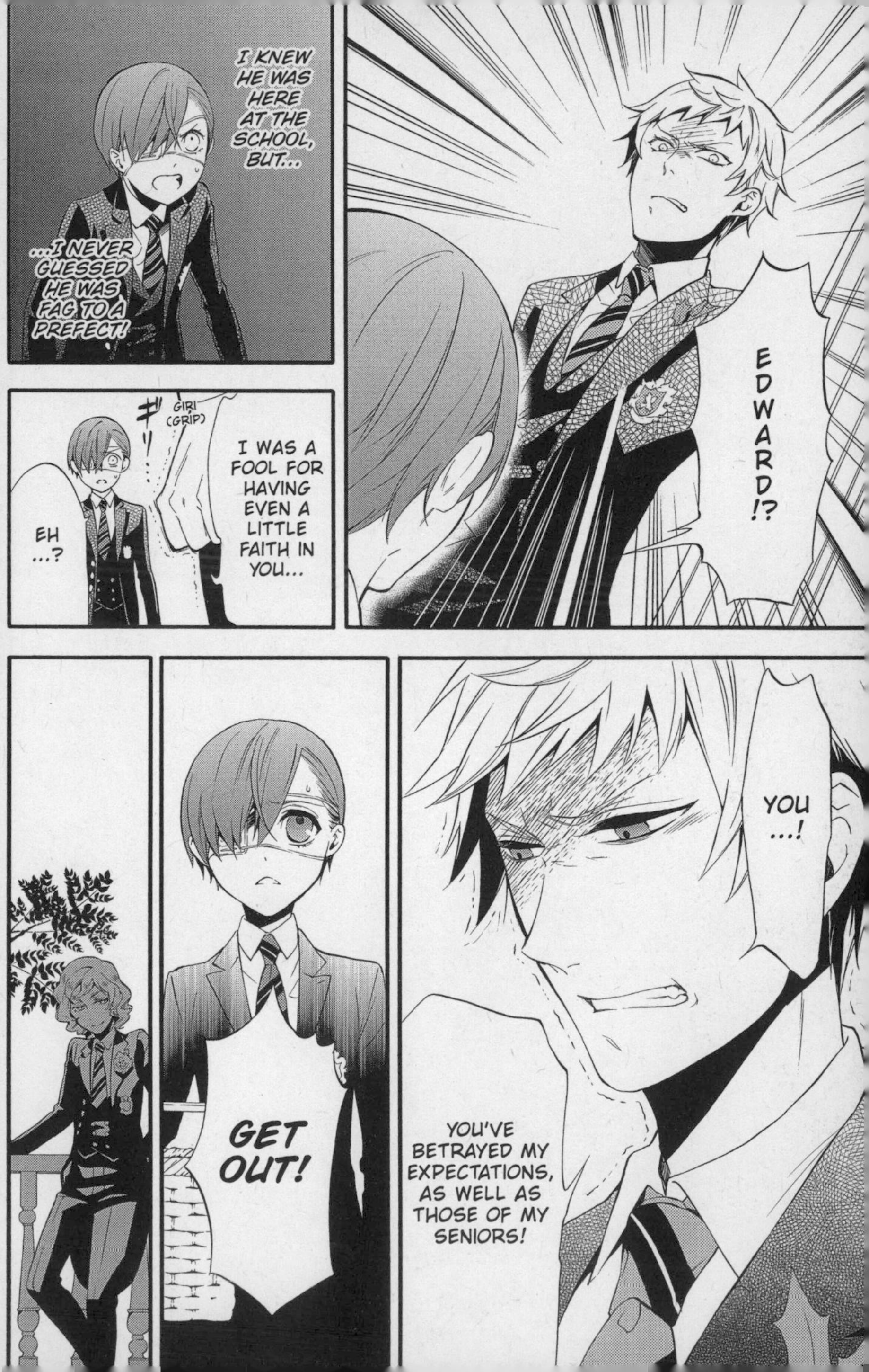
EDWARD!?
I KNEW HE WAS HERE AT THE SCHOOL, BUT...
...I NEVER GUESSED HE WAS FAG TO A PREFECT!
I WAS A FOOL FOR HAVING EVEN A LITTLE FAITH IN YOU...
GIRI (GRIP)
EH ...?
YOU ...!
YOU'VE BETRAYED MY EXPECTATIONS, AS WELL AS THOSE OF MY SENIORS!
GET OUT!

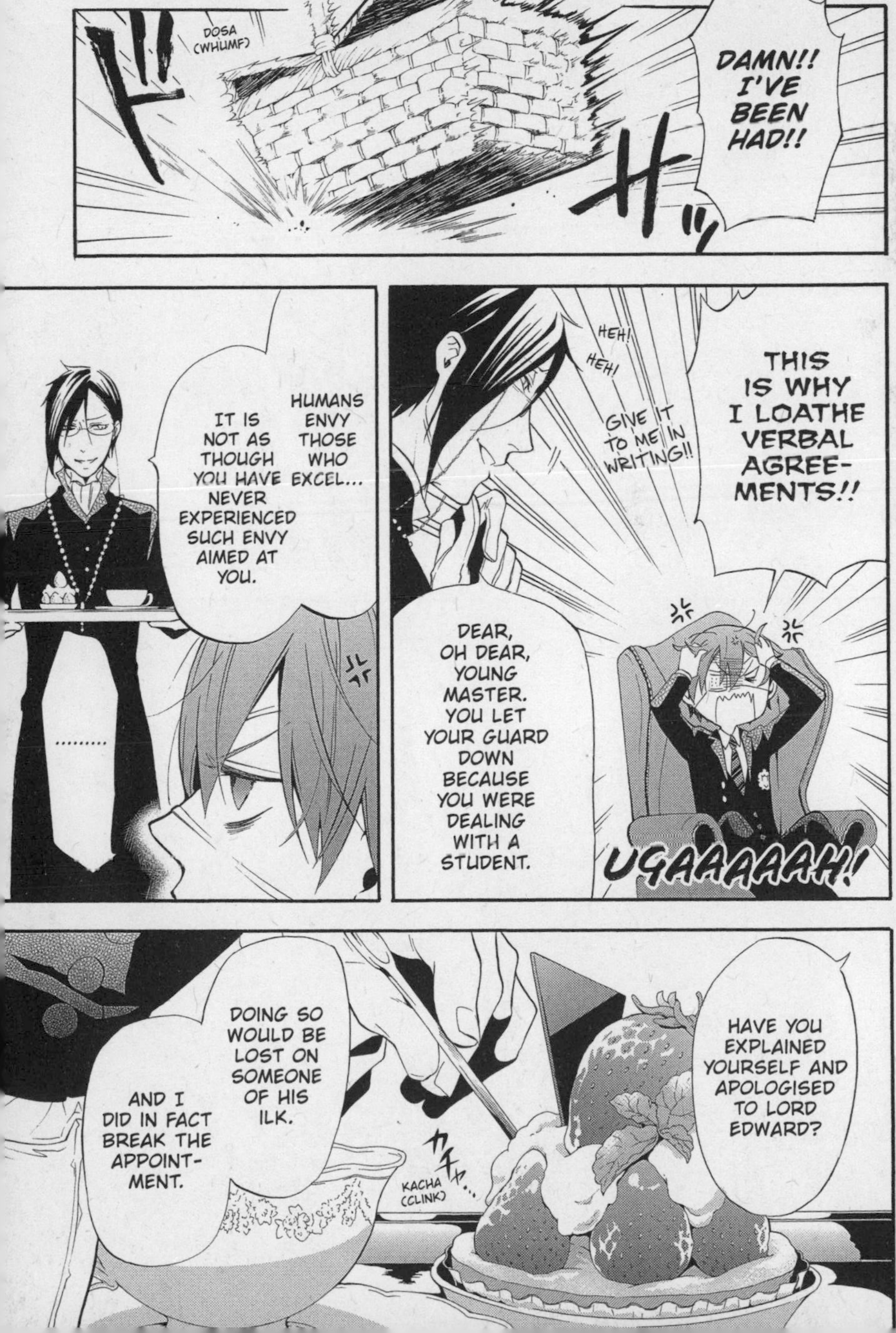
DAMN!! I'VE BEEN HAD!!
DOSA (WHUMF)
THIS IS WHY I LOATHE VERBAL AGREE-MENTS!!
HEH! HEH!
GIVE IT TO ME IN WRITING!!
UGAAAAAAH!
DEAR, OH DEAR, YOUNG MASTER. YOU LET YOUR GUARD DOWN BECAUSE YOU WERE DEALING WITH A STUDENT.
HUMANS ENVY THOSE WHO EXCEL...
IT IS NOT AS THOUGH YOU HAVE NEVER EXPERIENCED SUCH ENVY AIMED AT YOU.
....
HAVE YOU EXPLAINED YOURSELF AND APOLOGISED TO LORD EDWARD?
KACHA (CLINK)
DOING SO WOULD BE LOST ON SOMEONE OF HIS ILK.
AND I DID IN FACT BREAK THE APPOINT-MENT.

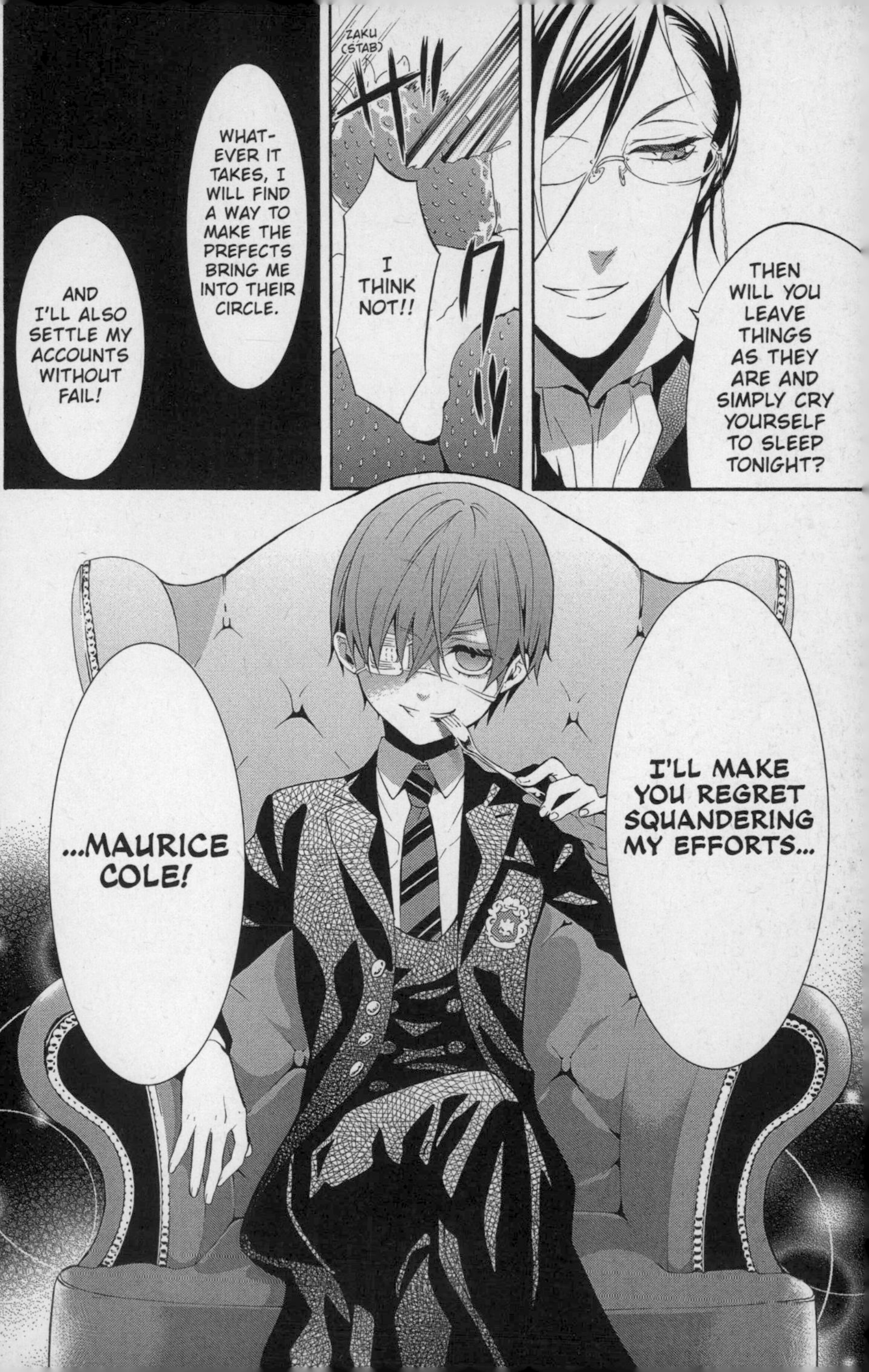
THEN WILL YOU LEAVE THINGS AS THEY ARE AND SIMPLY CRY YOURSELF TO SLEEP TONIGHT?
ZAKU (STAB)
I THINK NOT!!
WHAT-EVER IT TAKES, I WILL FIND A WAY TO MAKE THE PREFECTS BRING ME INTO THEIR CIRCLE.
AND I'LL ALSO SETTLE MY ACCOUNTS WITHOUT FAIL!
I'LL MAKE YOU REGRET SQUANDERING MY EFFORTS...
...MAURICE COLE!

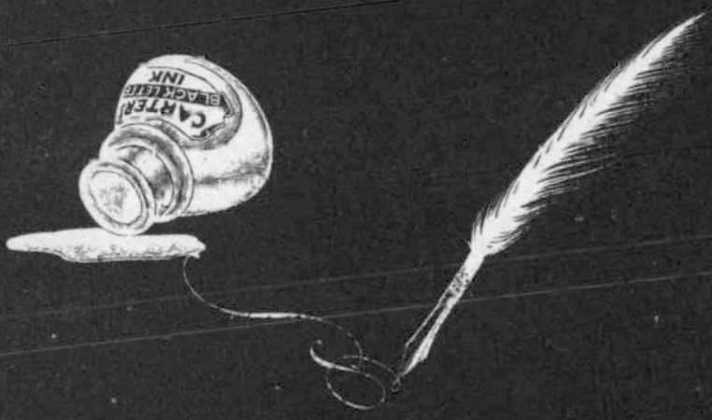
CARTER'S
BLACK
INK

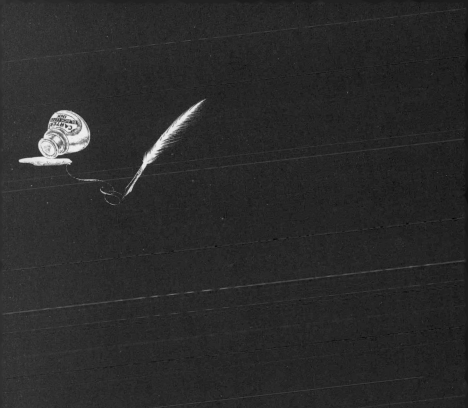

Black Butler

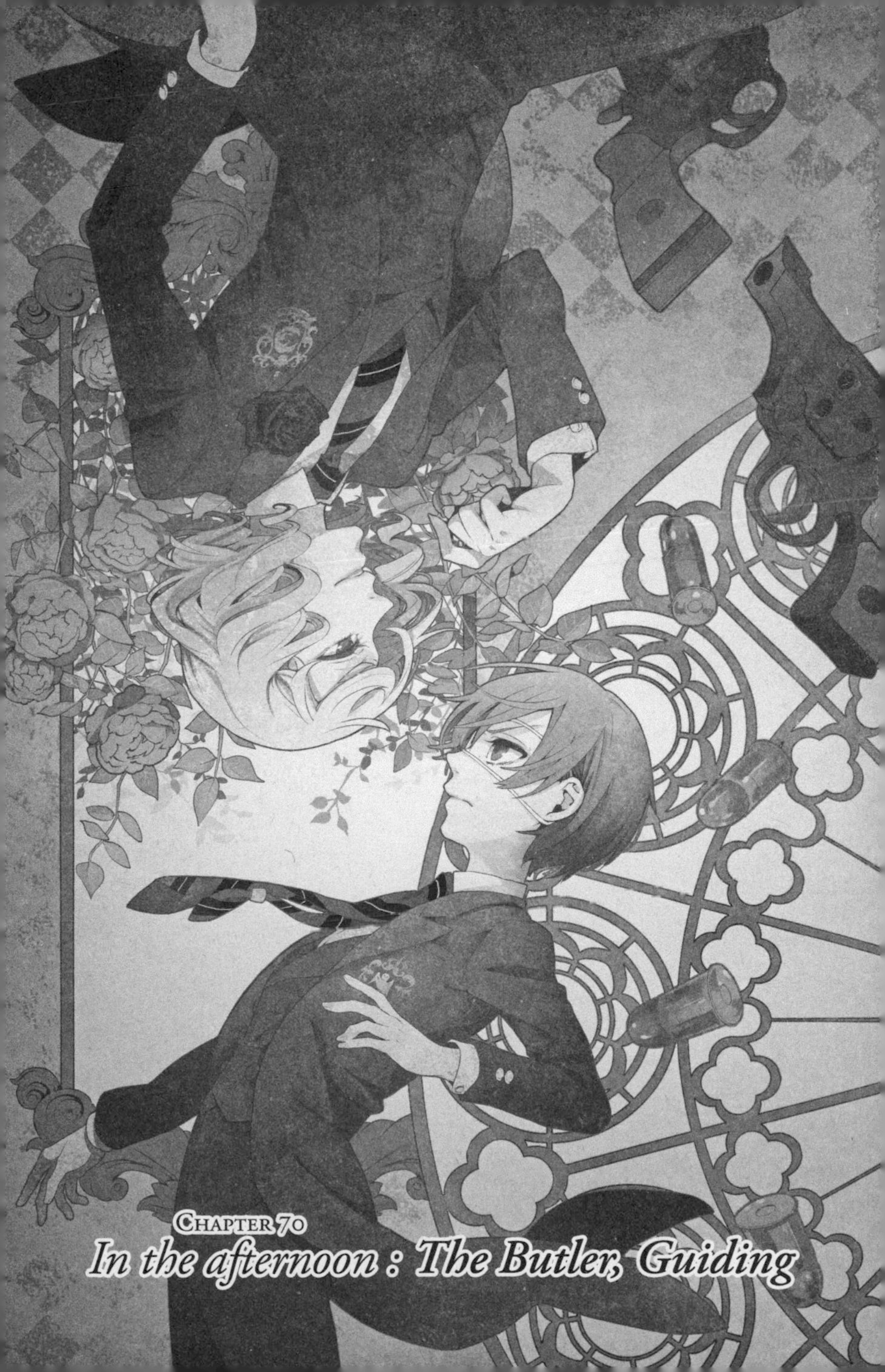

Chapter 70
In the afternoon : The Butler, Guiding

Black Butler

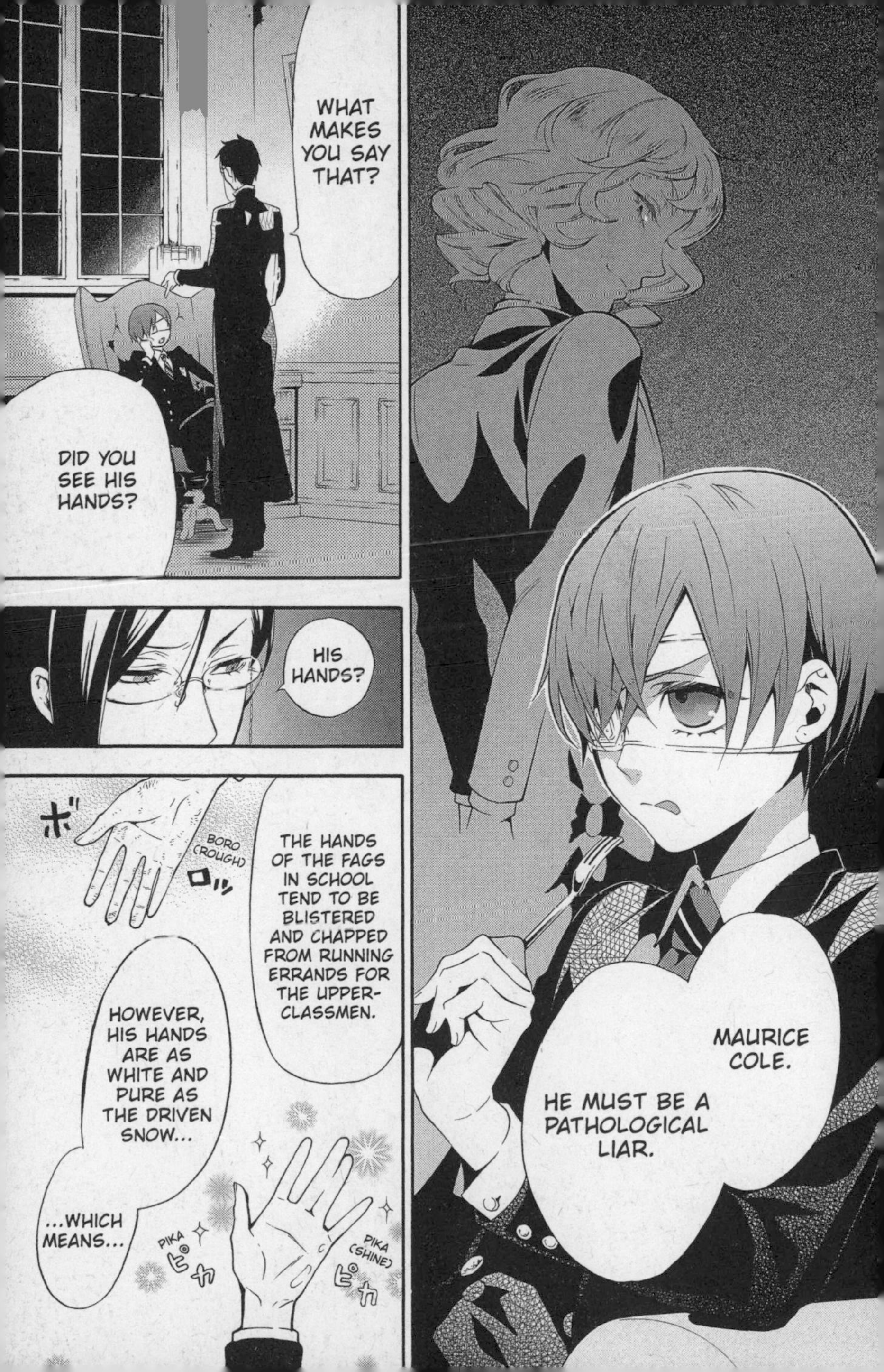
MAURICE COLE.
HE MUST BE A PATHOLOGICAL LIAR.
WHAT MAKES YOU SAY THAT?
DID YOU SEE HIS HANDS?
HIS HANDS?
ボロッ
BORO (ROUGH)
THE HANDS OF THE FAGS IN SCHOOL TEND TO BE BLISTERED AND CHAPPED FROM RUNNING ERRANDS FOR THE UPPER-CLASSMEN.
HOWEVER, HIS HANDS ARE AS WHITE AND PURE AS THE DRIVEN SNOW...
...WHICH MEANS...
ピカ
PIKA
ピカ
PIKA (SHINE)

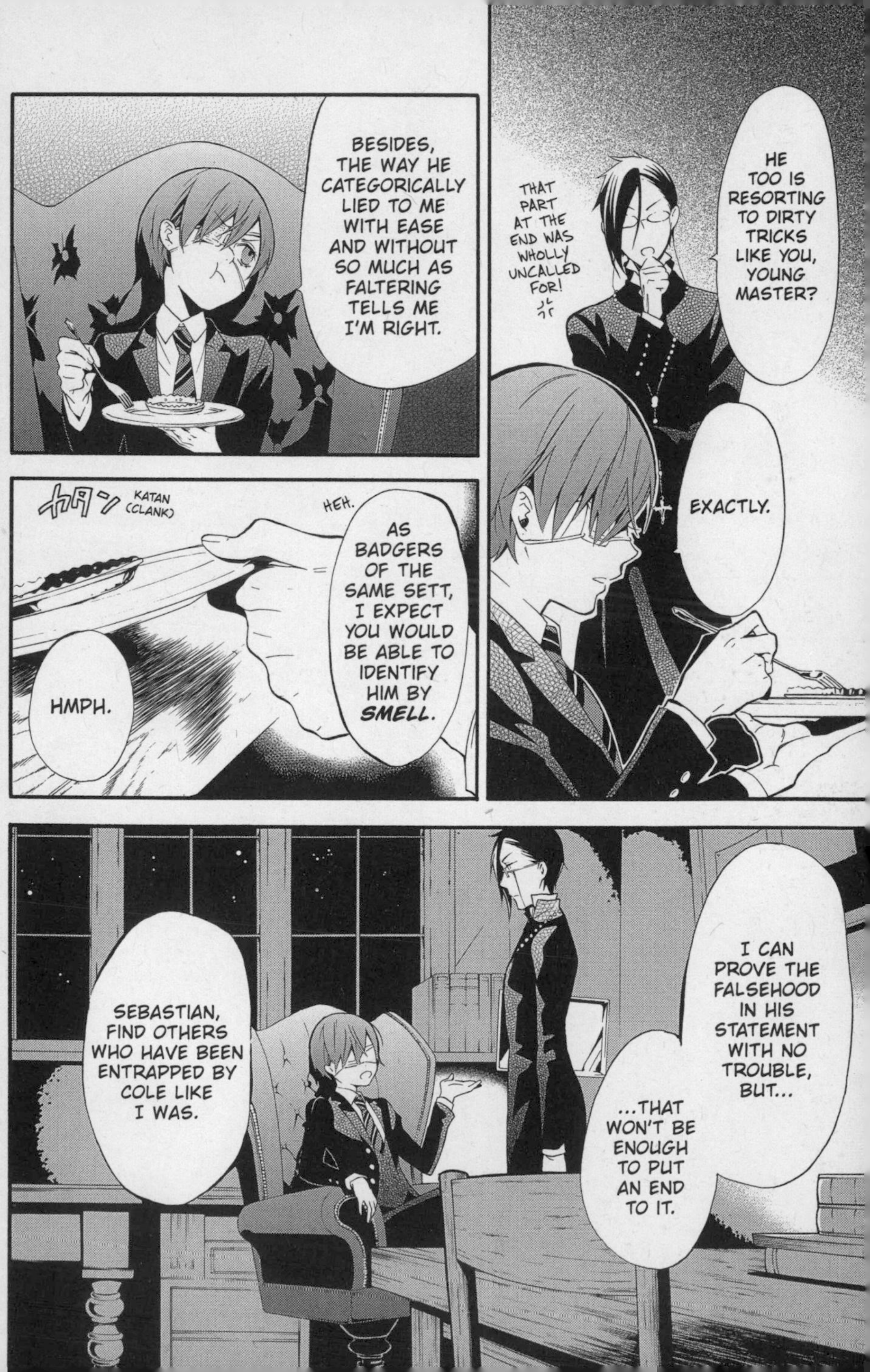
HE TOO IS RESORTING TO DIRTY TRICKS LIKE YOU, YOUNG MASTER?
THAT PART AT THE END WAS WHOLLY UNCALLED FOR!
EXACTLY.
BESIDES, THE WAY HE CATEGORICALLY LIED TO ME WITH EASE AND WITHOUT SO MUCH AS FALTERING TELLS ME I'M RIGHT.
カタン KATAN (CLANK)
HEH.
AS BADGERS OF THE SAME SETT, I EXPECT YOU WOULD BE ABLE TO IDENTIFY HIM BY SMELL.
HMPH.
I CAN PROVE THE FALSEHOOD IN HIS STATEMENT WITH NO TROUBLE, BUT...
...THAT WON'T BE ENOUGH TO PUT AN END TO IT.
SEBASTIAN, FIND OTHERS WHO HAVE BEEN ENTRAPPED BY COLE LIKE I WAS.

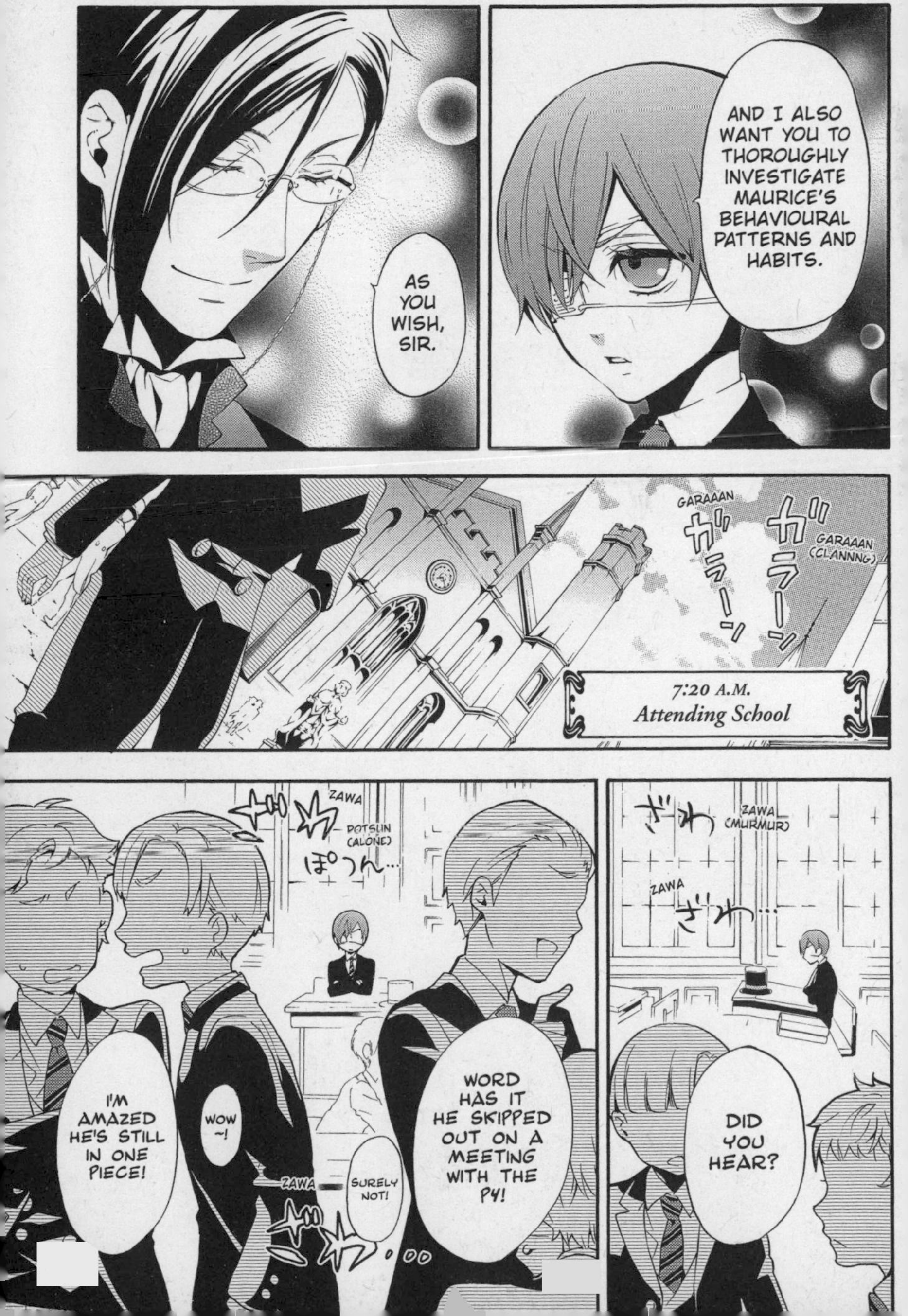

AND I ALSO WANT YOU TO THOROUGHLY INVESTIGATE MAURICE'S BEHAVIOURAL PATTERNS AND HABITS.
AS YOU WISH, SIR.
GARAAAN
ガラーン
GARAAAN (CLANNNG)
ガラーン
7:20 A.M.
Attending School
ZAWA (MURMUR)
ざわ
ZAWA
ざわ…
DID YOU HEAR?
ZAWA
POTSLIN (ALONE)
ぽつん…
WORD HAS IT HE SKIPPED OUT ON A MEETING WITH THE P4!
ZAWA
SURELY NOT!
WOW ~!
I'M AMAZED HE'S STILL IN ONE PIECE!

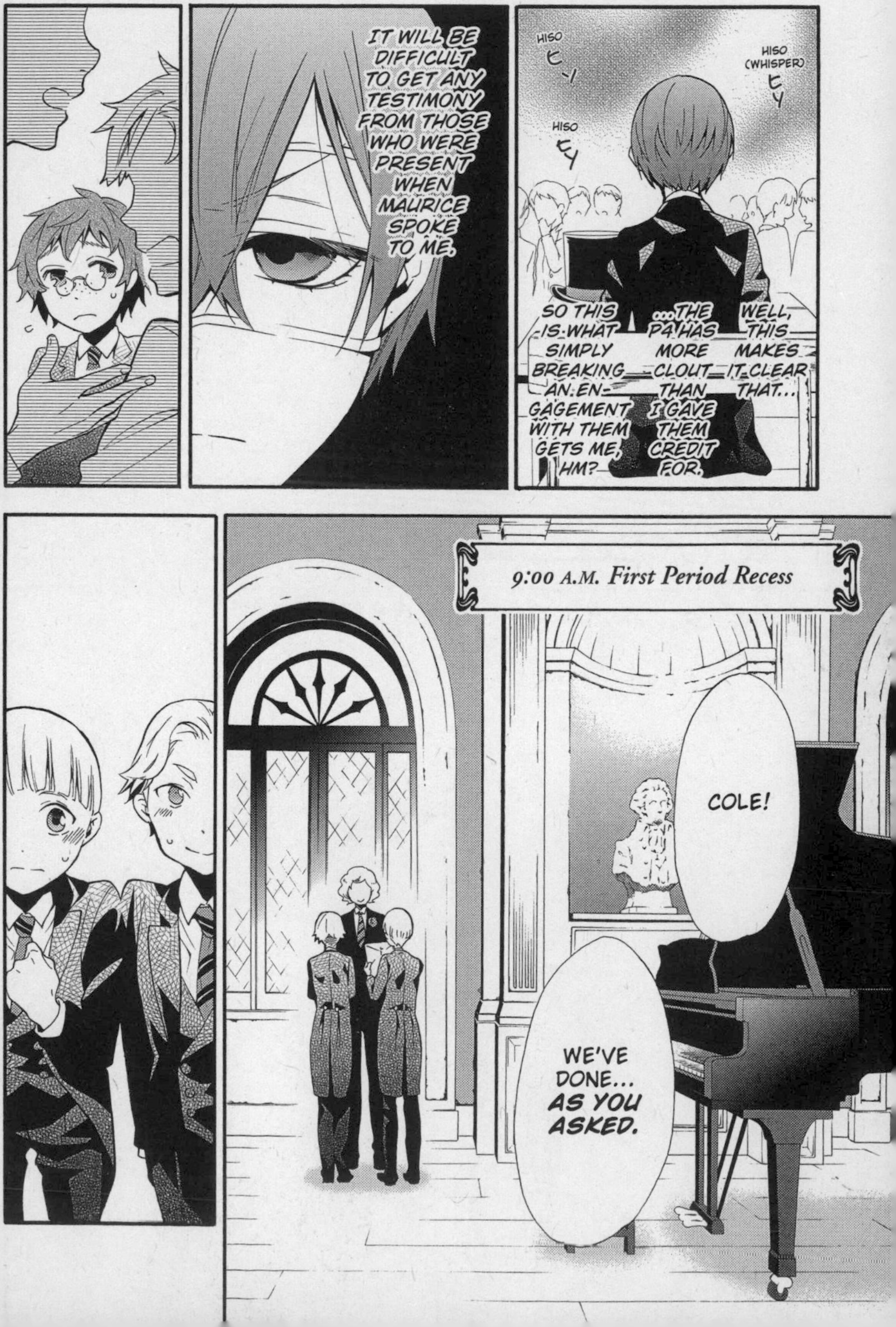
HISO (WHISPER)
ヒソ
HISO
ヒソ
HISO
ヒソ
WELL, THIS MAKES IT CLEAR THAT...
...THE P4 HAS MORE CLOUT THAN I GAVE THEM CREDIT FOR.
SO THIS IS WHAT SIMPLY BREAKING AN EN-GAGEMENT WITH THEM GETS ME, HM?
IT WILL BE DIFFICULT TO GET ANY TESTIMONY FROM THOSE WHO WERE PRESENT WHEN MAURICE SPOKE TO ME.
9:00 A.M. First Period Recess
COLE!
WE'VE DONE... AS YOU ASKED.

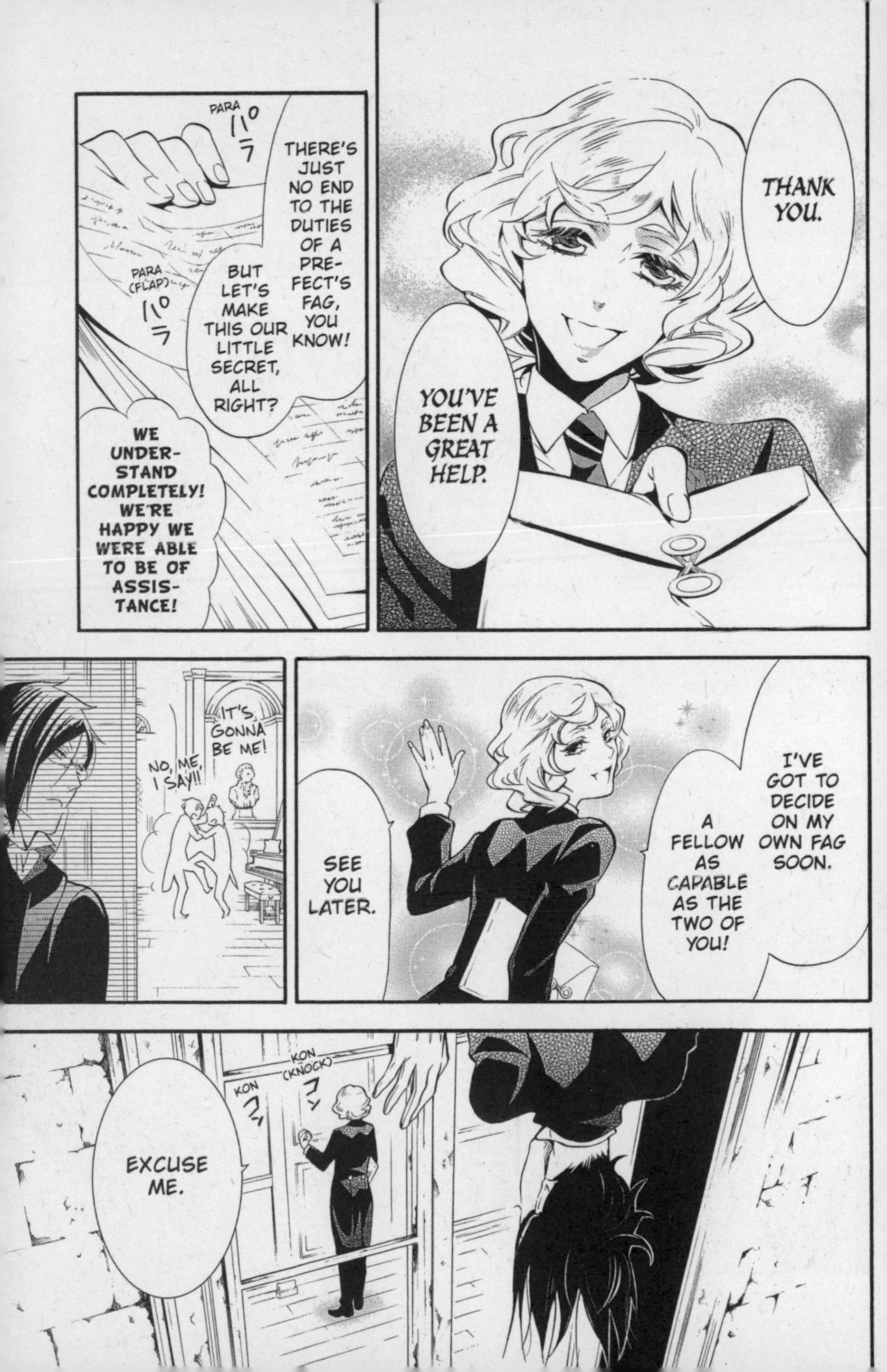
THANK YOU.
YOU'VE BEEN A GREAT HELP.
PARA パラ
THERE'S JUST NO END TO THE DUTIES OF A PRE-FECT'S FAG, YOU KNOW!
PARA (FLAP) パラ
BUT LET'S MAKE THIS OUR LITTLE SECRET, ALL RIGHT?
WE UNDER-STAND COMPLETELY! WE'RE HAPPY WE WERE ABLE TO BE OF ASSIS-TANCE!
I'VE GOT TO DECIDE ON MY OWN FAG SOON.
A FELLOW AS CAPABLE AS THE TWO OF YOU!
SEE YOU LATER.
IT'S GONNA BE ME!
NO, ME, I SAY!!
KON (KNOCK) コン
KON コン
EXCUSE ME.

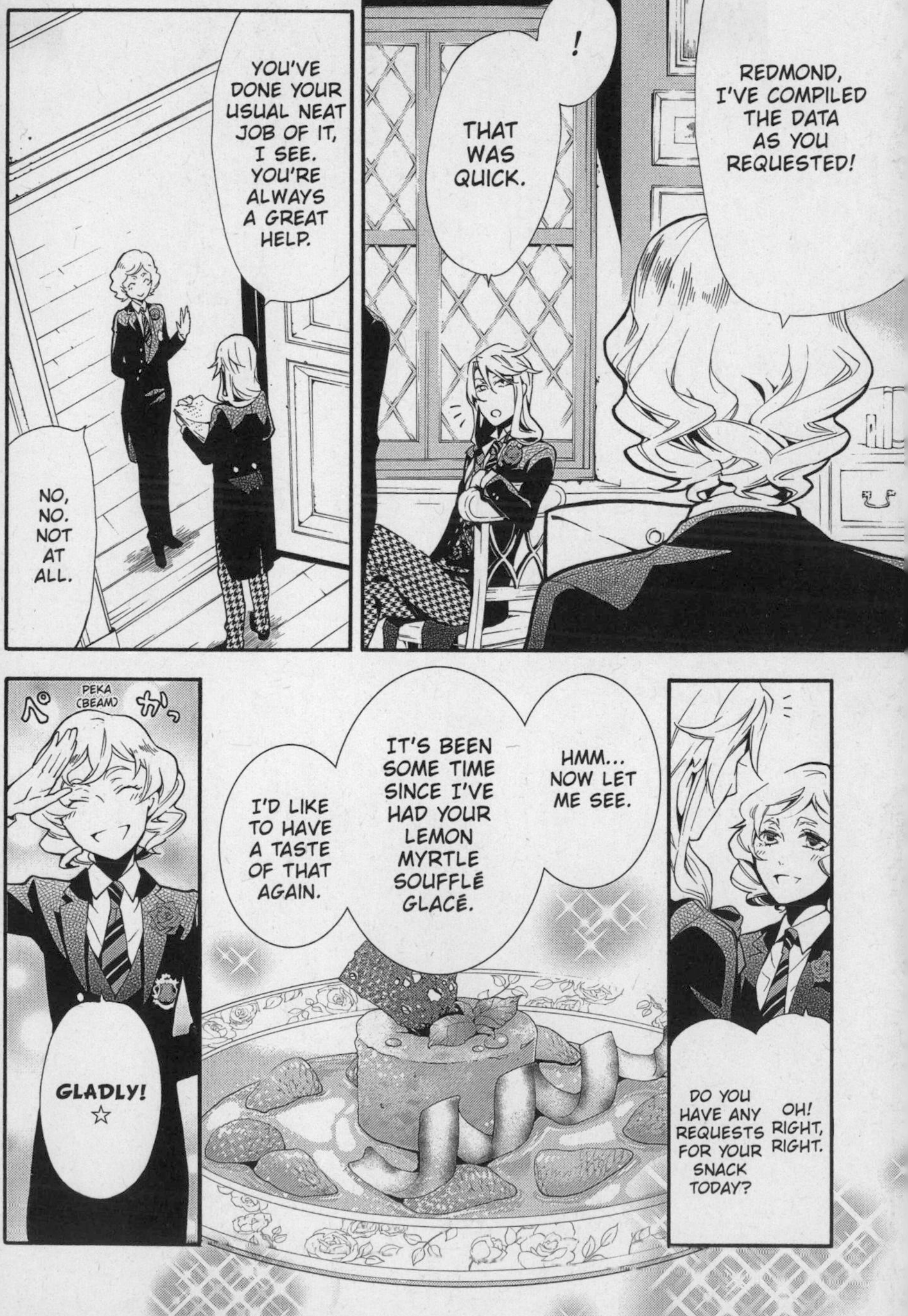
REDMOND, I'VE COMPILED THE DATA AS YOU REQUESTED!
!
THAT WAS QUICK.
YOU'VE DONE YOUR USUAL NEAT JOB OF IT, I SEE. YOU'RE ALWAYS A GREAT HELP.
NO, NO. NOT AT ALL.
OH! RIGHT, RIGHT.
DO YOU HAVE ANY REQUESTS FOR YOUR SNACK TODAY?
HMM... NOW LET ME SEE.
IT'S BEEN SOME TIME SINCE I'VE HAD YOUR LEMON MYRTLE SOUFFLÉ GLACÉ.
I'D LIKE TO HAVE A TASTE OF THAT AGAIN.
PEKA (BEAM)
GLADLY! ☆

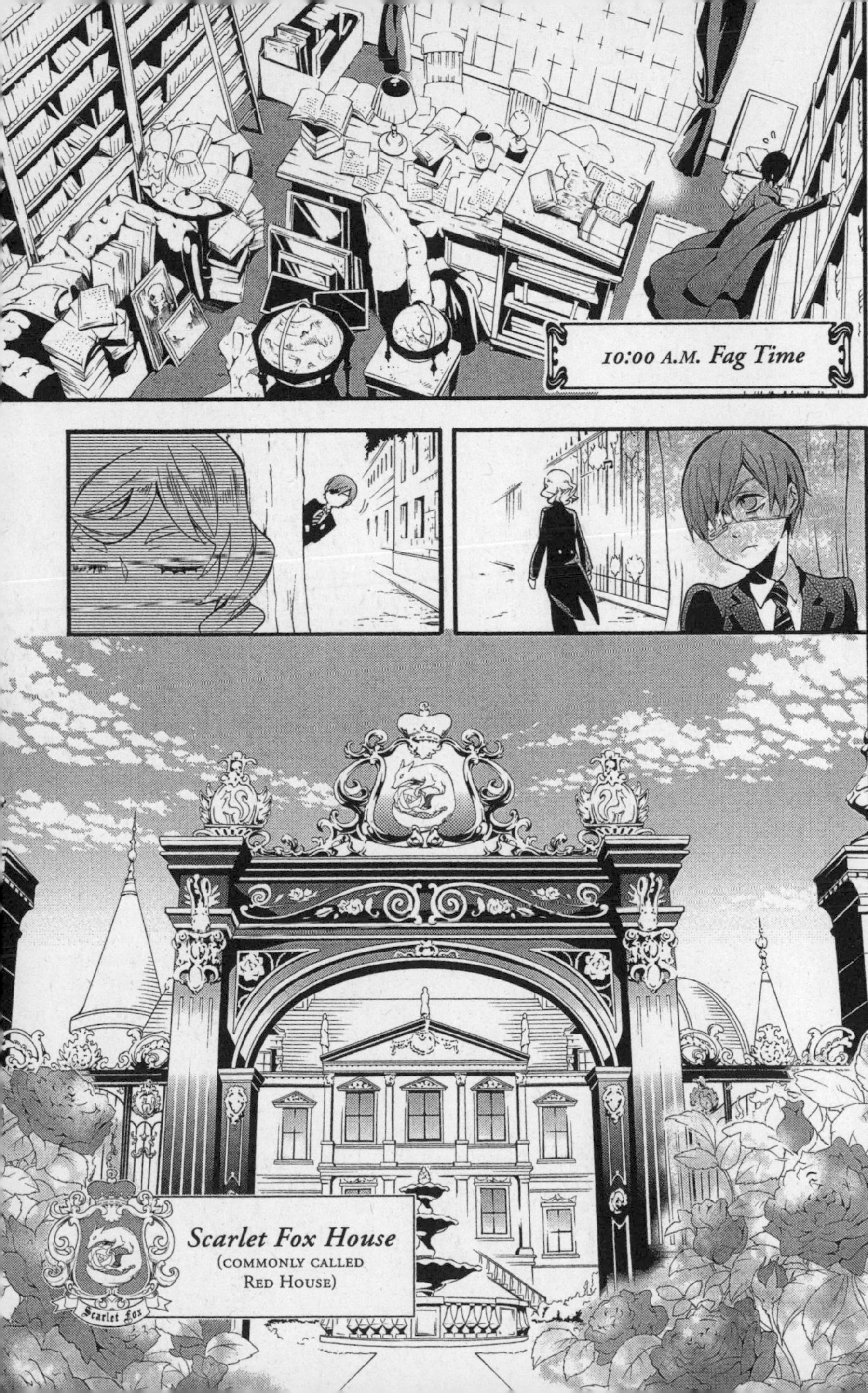
10:00 A.M. Fag Time
Scarlet Fox House
(COMMONLY CALLED
RED HOUSE)
Scarlet Fox

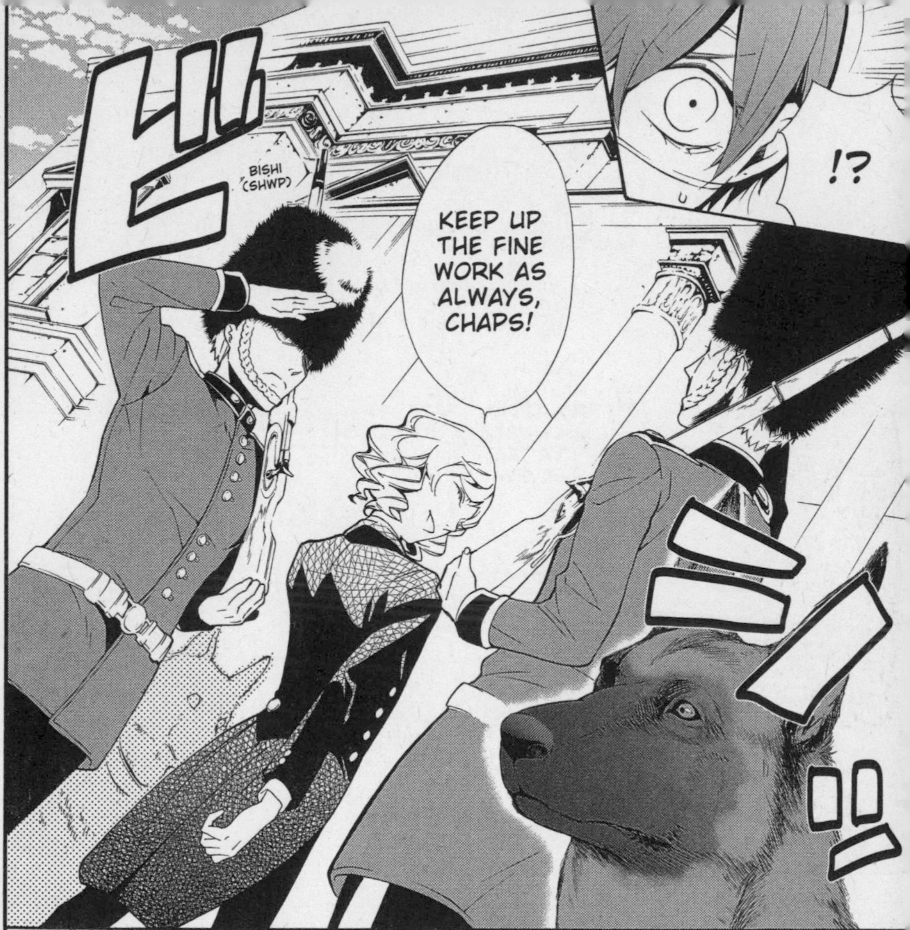
!?
KEEP UP THE FINE WORK AS ALWAYS, CHAPS!
BISHI (SHWP)

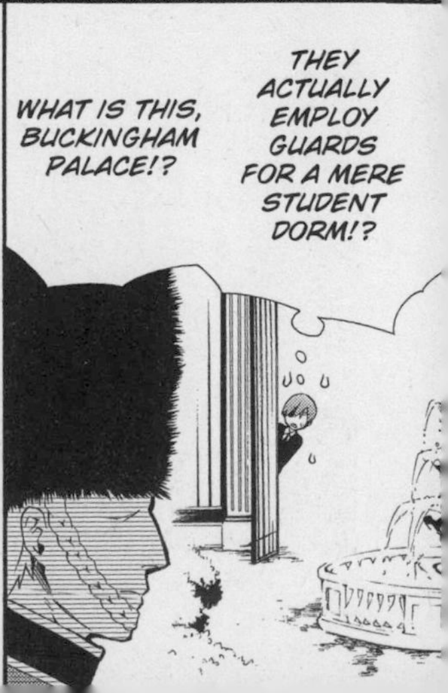
THEY ACTUALLY EMPLOY GUARDS FOR A MERE STUDENT DORM!?
WHAT IS THIS, BUCKINGHAM PALACE!?

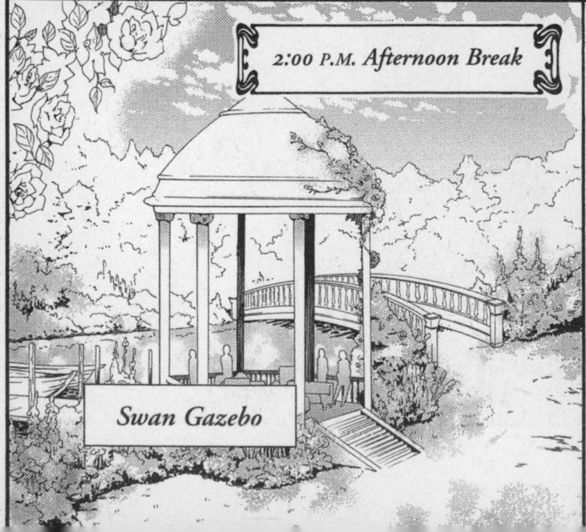
2:00 P.M. Afternoon Break
Swan Gazebo

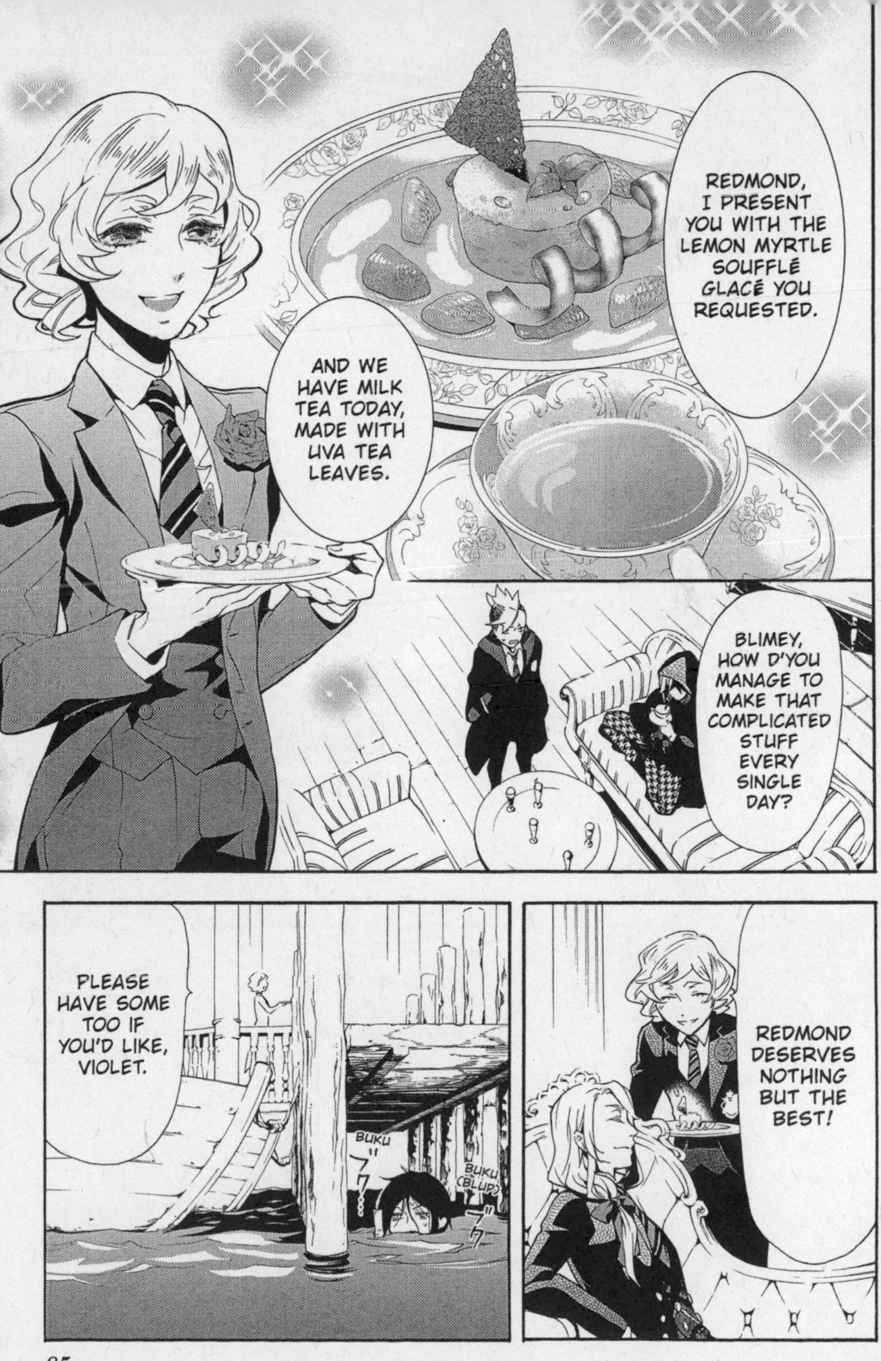
REDMOND, I PRESENT YOU WITH THE LEMON MYRTLE SOUFFLÉ GLACÉ YOU REQUESTED.
AND WE HAVE MILK TEA TODAY, MADE WITH UVA TEA LEAVES.
BLIMEY, HOW D'YOU MANAGE TO MAKE THAT COMPLICATED STUFF EVERY SINGLE DAY?
REDMOND DESERVES NOTHING BUT THE BEST!
PLEASE HAVE SOME TOO IF YOU'D LIKE, VIOLET.
BUKU
BUKU (BLUP)

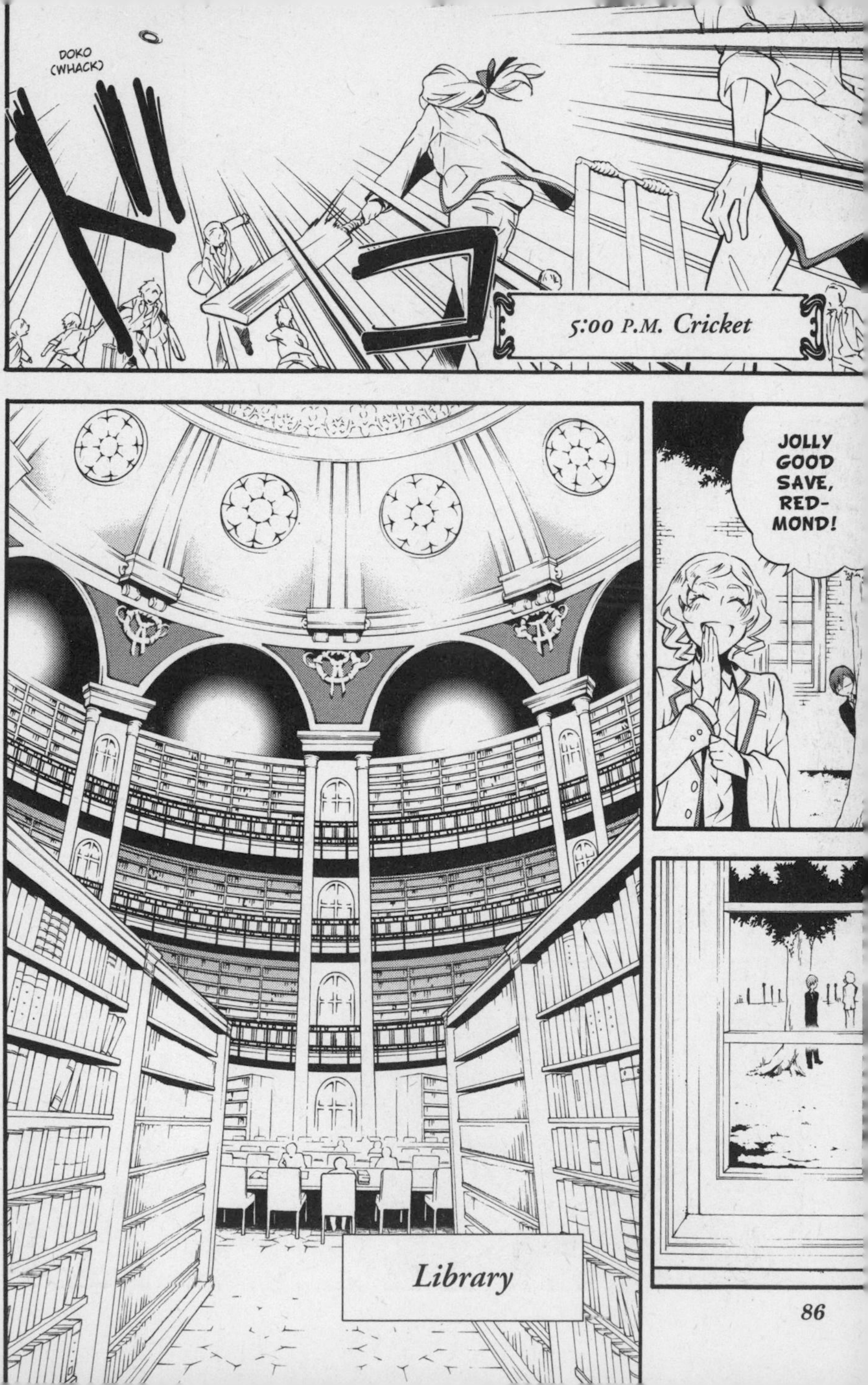
5:00 P.M. Cricket
DOKO (WHACK)
JOLLY GOOD SAVE, RED-MOND!
Library

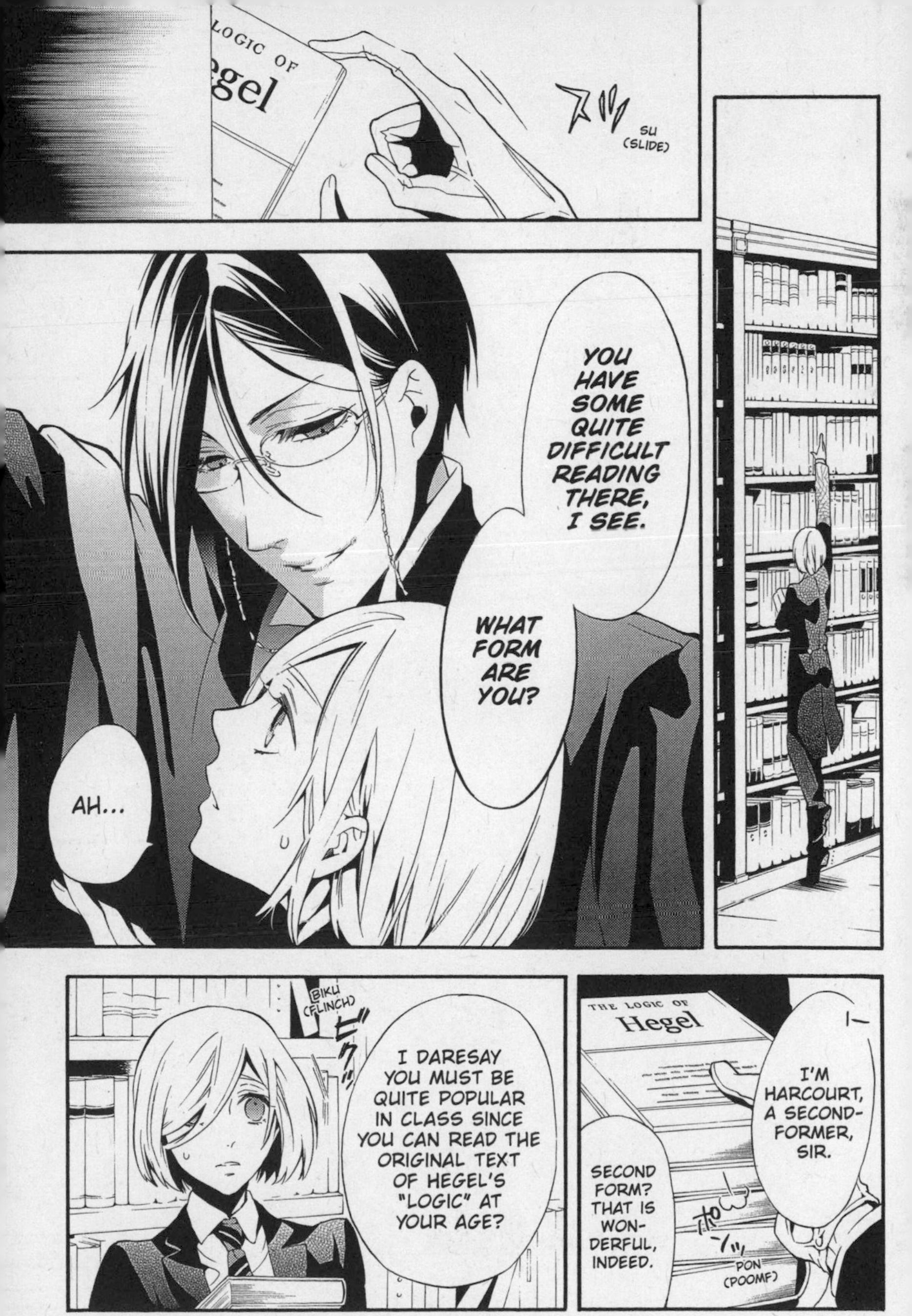
LOGIC OF
Hegel
SU (SLIDE)
YOU HAVE SOME QUITE DIFFICULT READING THERE, I SEE.
WHAT FORM ARE YOU?
AH...
THE LOGIC OF
Hegel
I—
I'M HARCOURT, A SECOND-FORMER, SIR.
SECOND FORM? THAT IS WON-DERFUL, INDEED.
PON (POOMF)
BIKU (FLINCH)
I DARESAY YOU MUST BE QUITE POPULAR IN CLASS SINCE YOU CAN READ THE ORIGINAL TEXT OF HEGEL'S "LOGIC" AT YOUR AGE?

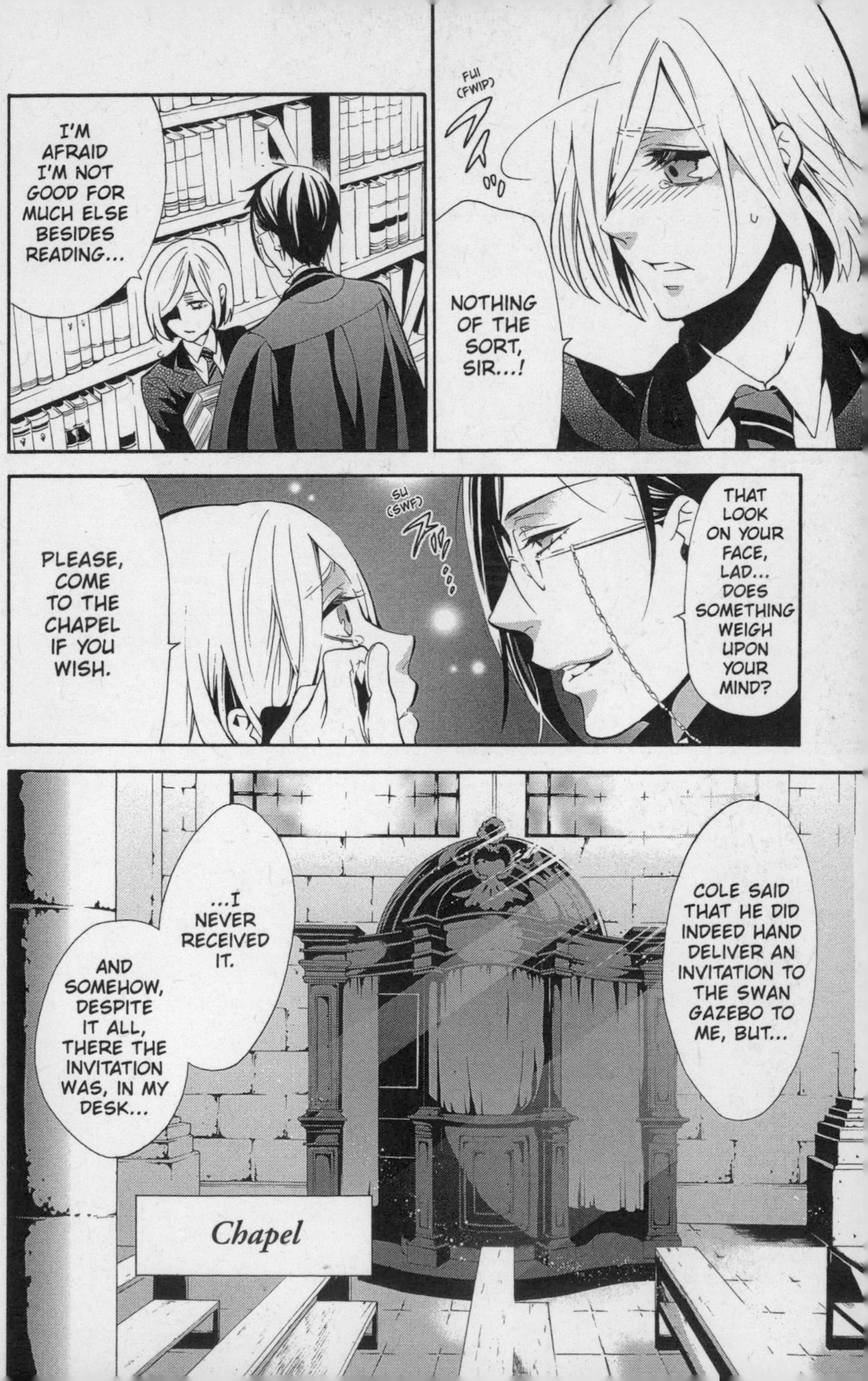
FUI (FWIP)
NOTHING OF THE SORT, SIR...!
I'M AFRAID I'M NOT GOOD FOR MUCH ELSE BESIDES READING...
SU (SWF)
THAT LOOK ON YOUR FACE, LAD... DOES SOMETHING WEIGH UPON YOUR MIND?
PLEASE, COME TO THE CHAPEL IF YOU WISH.
COLE SAID THAT HE DID INDEED HAND DELIVER AN INVITATION TO THE SWAN GAZEBO TO ME, BUT...
...I NEVER RECEIVED IT.
AND SOMEHOW, DESPITE IT ALL, THERE THE INVITATION WAS, IN MY DESK...
Chapel

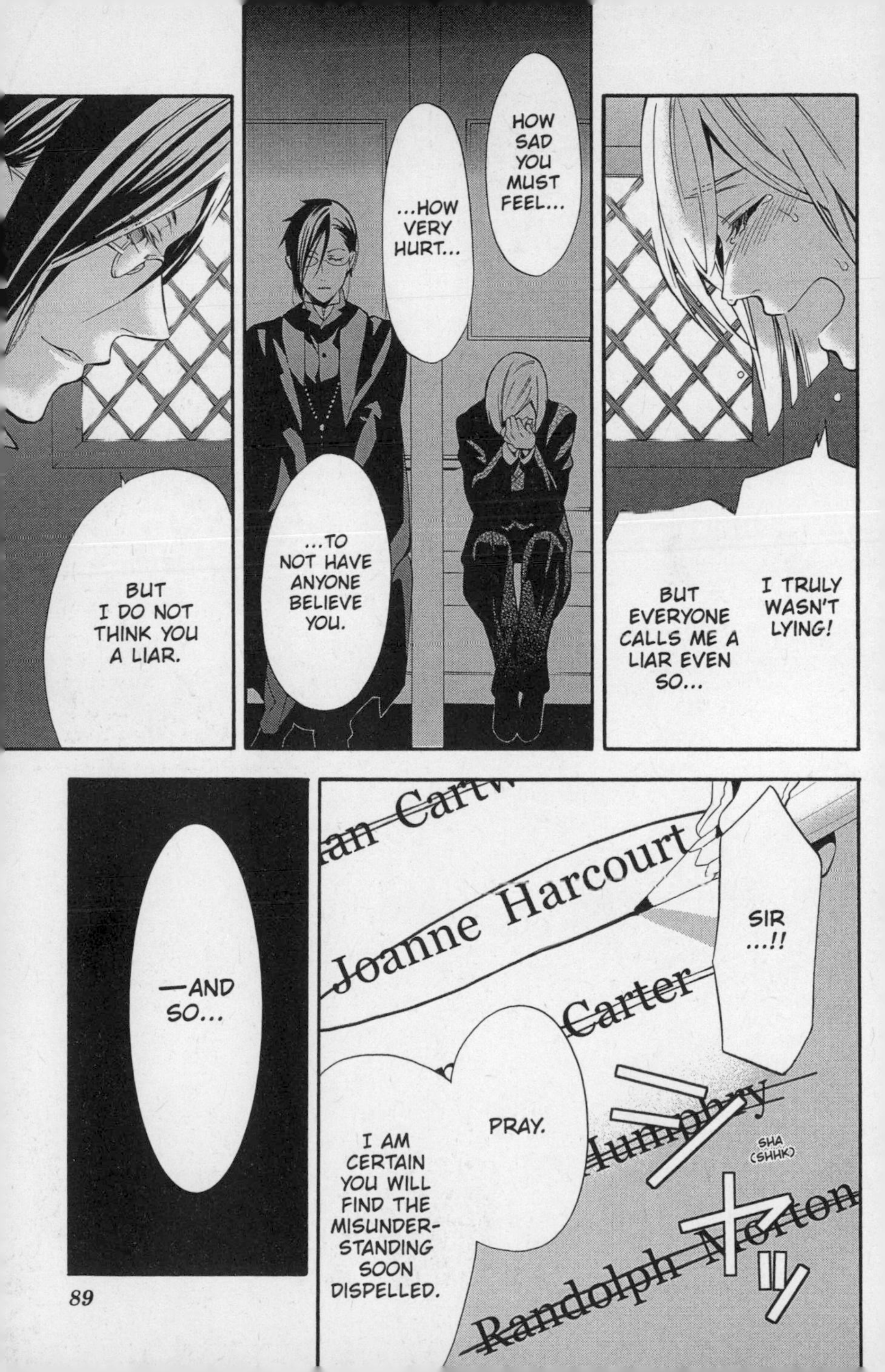
I TRULY WASN'T LYING!
BUT EVERYONE CALLS ME A LIAR EVEN SO...
HOW SAD YOU MUST FEEL...
...HOW VERY HURT...
...TO NOT HAVE ANYONE BELIEVE YOU.
BUT I DO NOT THINK YOU A LIAR.
Joanne Harcourt
Carter
SIR ...!!
PRAY.
I AM CERTAIN YOU WILL FIND THE MISUNDER-STANDING SOON DISPELLED.
Randolph Morton
SHA (SHHK)
—AND SO...

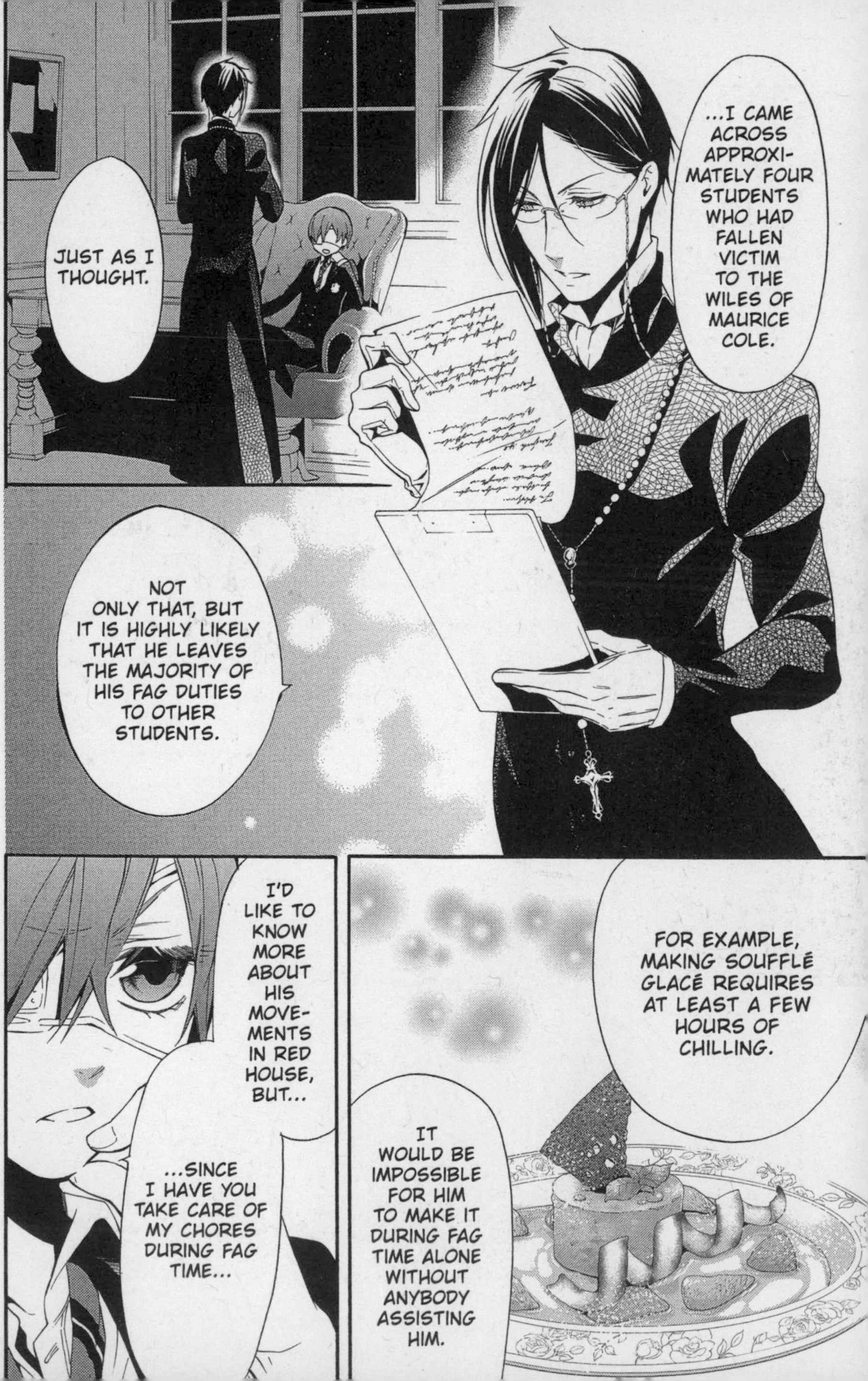
...I CAME ACROSS APPROXI-MATELY FOUR STUDENTS WHO HAD FALLEN VICTIM TO THE WILES OF MAURICE COLE.
JUST AS I THOUGHT.
NOT ONLY THAT, BUT IT IS HIGHLY LIKELY THAT HE LEAVES THE MAJORITY OF HIS FAG DUTIES TO OTHER STUDENTS.
FOR EXAMPLE, MAKING SOUFFLÉ GLACÉ REQUIRES AT LEAST A FEW HOURS OF CHILLING.
IT WOULD BE IMPOSSIBLE FOR HIM TO MAKE IT DURING FAG TIME ALONE WITHOUT ANYBODY ASSISTING HIM.
I'D LIKE TO KNOW MORE ABOUT HIS MOVE-MENTS IN RED HOUSE, BUT...
...SINCE I HAVE YOU TAKE CARE OF MY CHORES DURING FAG TIME...

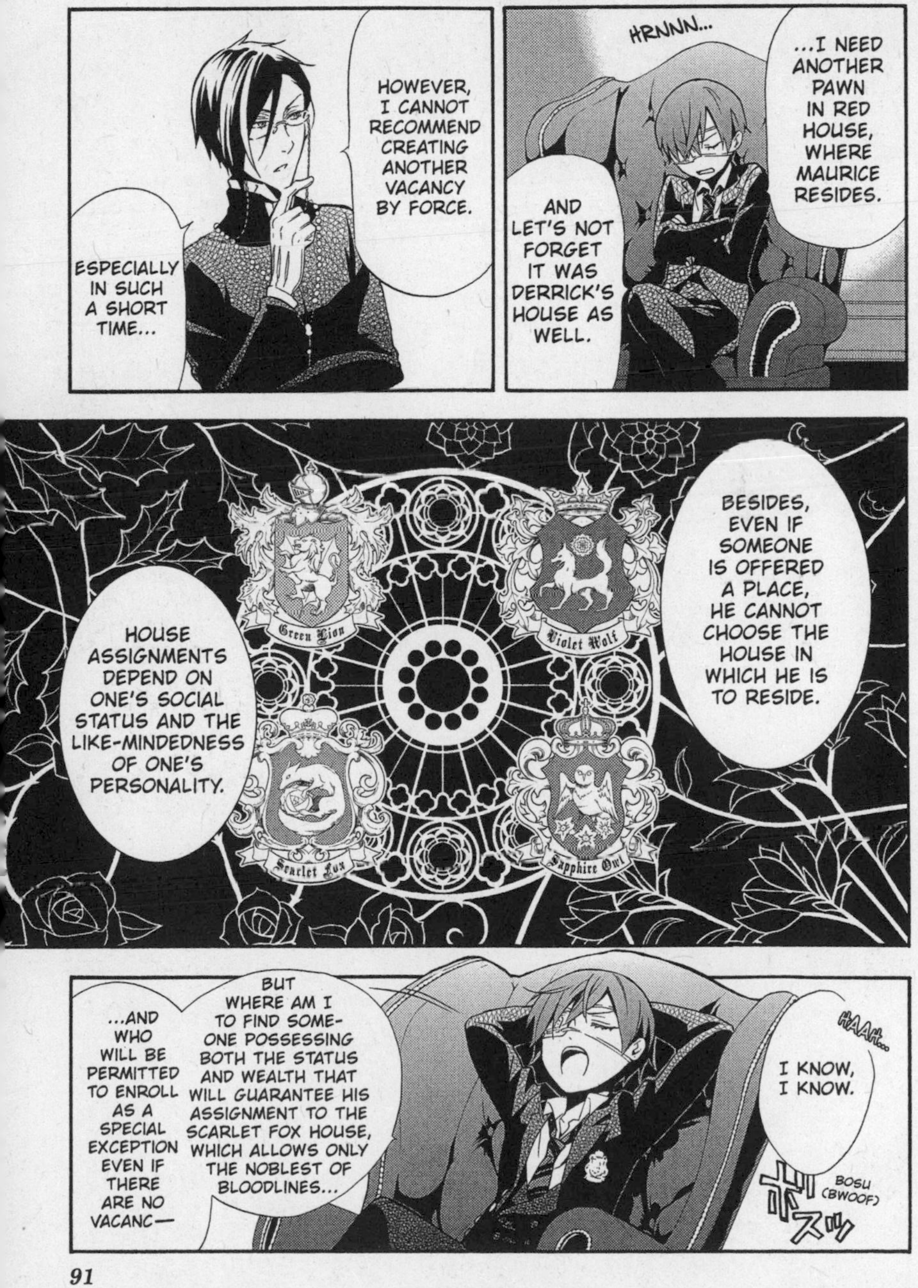
HRNNN...
...I NEED ANOTHER PAWN IN RED HOUSE, WHERE MAURICE RESIDES.
AND LET'S NOT FORGET IT WAS DERRICK'S HOUSE AS WELL.
HOWEVER, I CANNOT RECOMMEND CREATING ANOTHER VACANCY BY FORCE.
ESPECIALLY IN SUCH A SHORT TIME...
BESIDES, EVEN IF SOMEONE IS OFFERED A PLACE, HE CANNOT CHOOSE THE HOUSE IN WHICH HE IS TO RESIDE.
Violet Wolf
Green Lion
Sapphire Owl
Scarlet Fox
HOUSE ASSIGNMENTS DEPEND ON ONE'S SOCIAL STATUS AND THE LIKE-MINDEDNESS OF ONE'S PERSONALITY.
HAAH...
I KNOW, I KNOW.
ボスッ
BOSU (BWOOF)
BUT WHERE AM I TO FIND SOME-ONE POSSESSING BOTH THE STATUS AND WEALTH THAT WILL GUARANTEE HIS ASSIGNMENT TO THE SCARLET FOX HOUSE, WHICH ALLOWS ONLY THE NOBLEST OF BLOODLINES...
...AND WHO WILL BE PERMITTED TO ENROLL AS A SPECIAL EXCEPTION EVEN IF THERE ARE NO VACANC—

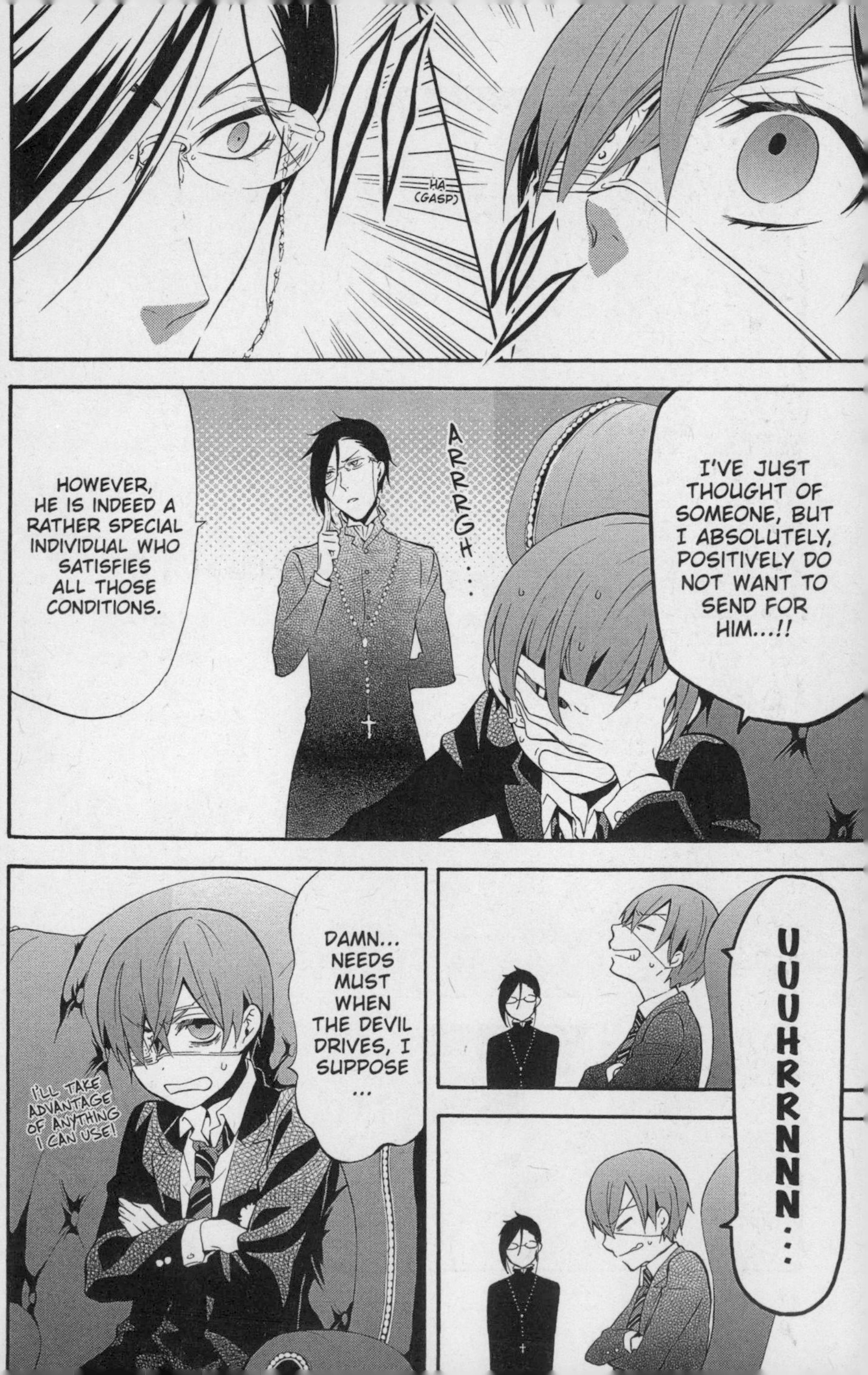
HA (GASP)
I'VE JUST THOUGHT OF SOMEONE, BUT I ABSOLUTELY, POSITIVELY DO NOT WANT TO SEND FOR HIM...!!
ARRRGH...
HOWEVER, HE IS INDEED A RATHER SPECIAL INDIVIDUAL WHO SATISFIES ALL THOSE CONDITIONS.
UUUHRRNNN...
DAMN... NEEDS MUST WHEN THE DEVIL DRIVES, I SUPPOSE...
I'LL TAKE ADVANTAGE OF ANYTHING I CAN USE!

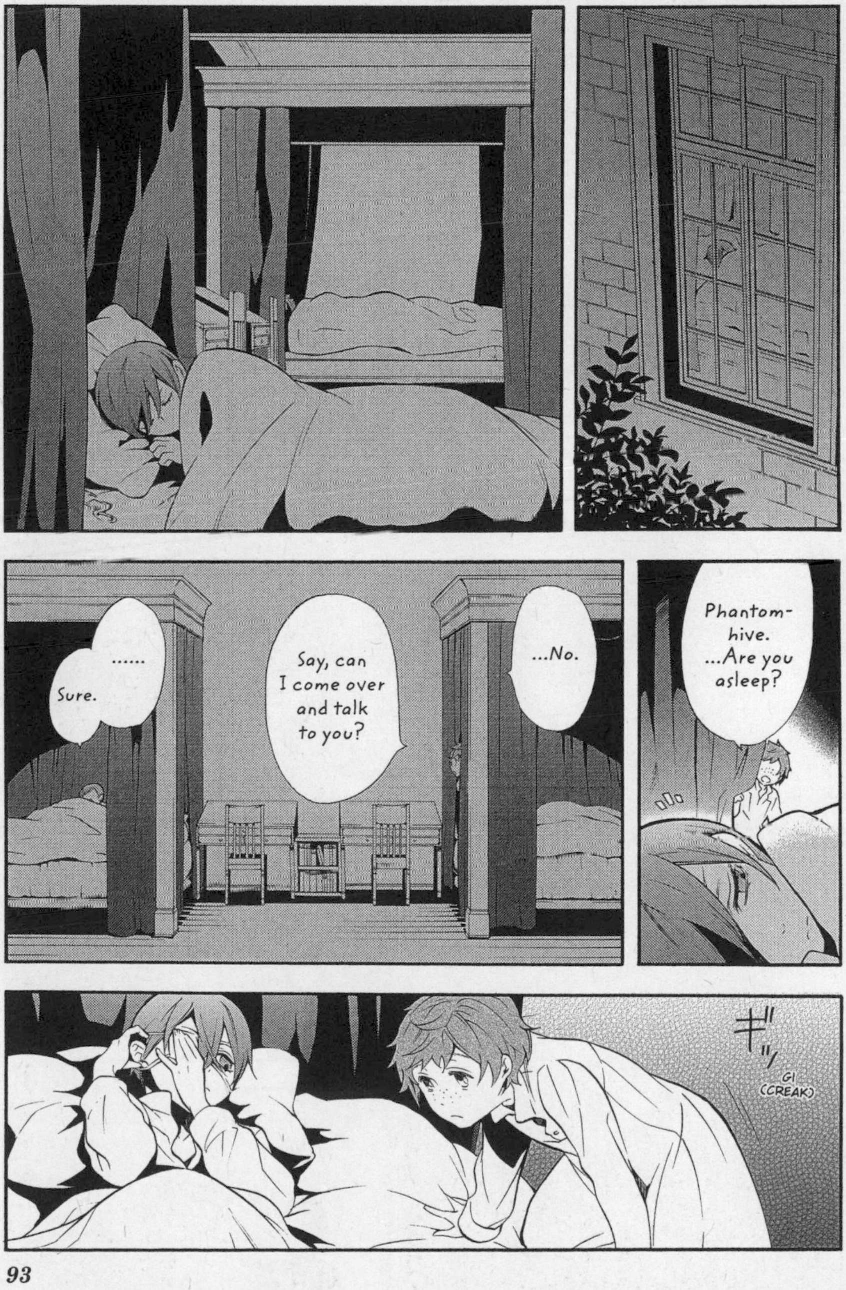
Phantom-hive. ...Are you asleep?
...No.
Say, can I come over and talk to you?
......
Sure.
ギッ
GI (CREAK)

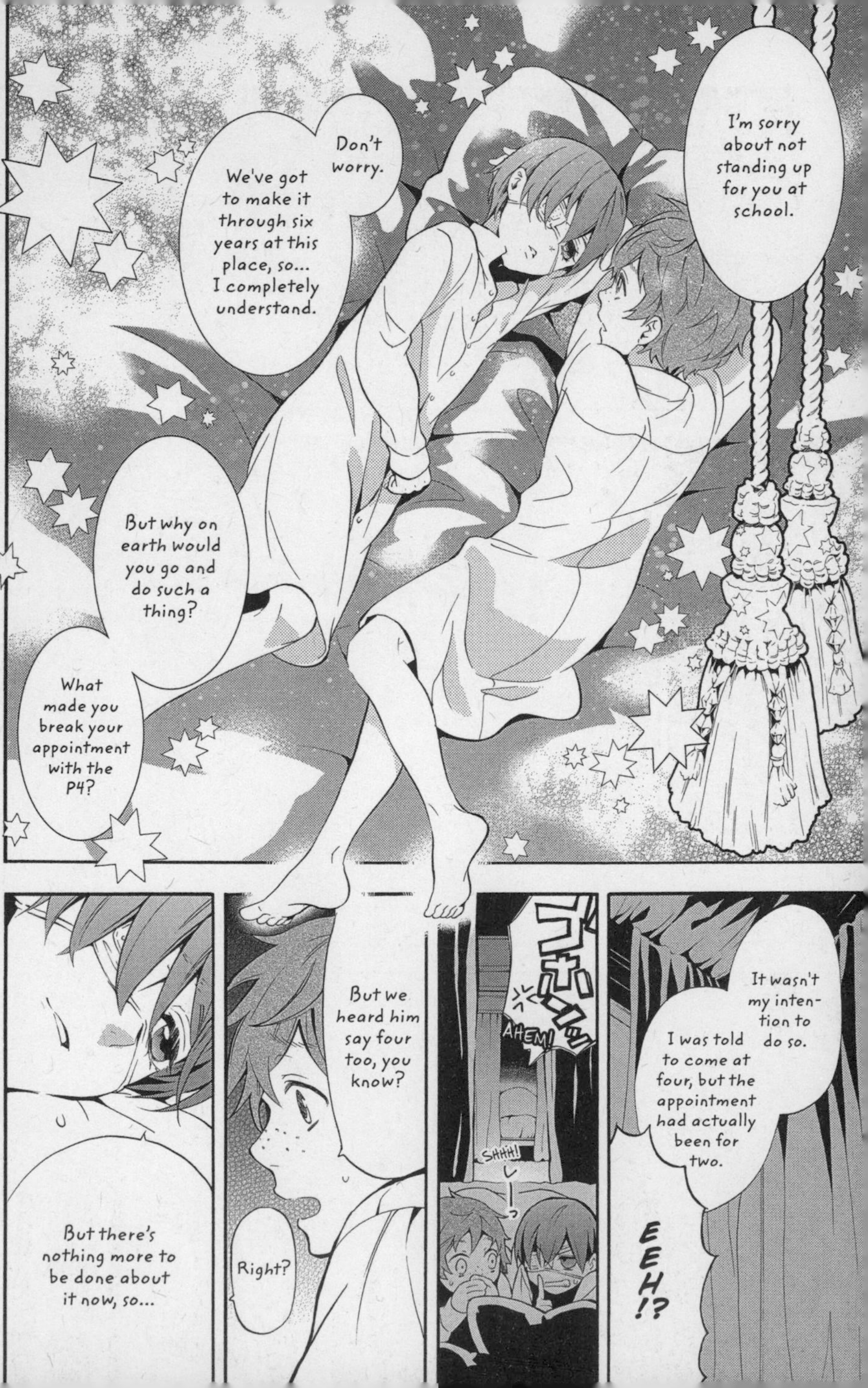
I'm sorry about not standing up for you at school.
Don't worry.
We've got to make it through six years at this place, so... I completely understand.
But why on earth would you go and do such a thing?
What made you break your appointment with the P4?
It wasn't my intention to do so.
I was told to come at four, but the appointment had actually been for two.
EEH!?
AHEM!
SHHH!
But we heard him say four too, you know?
Right?
But there's nothing more to be done about it now, so...

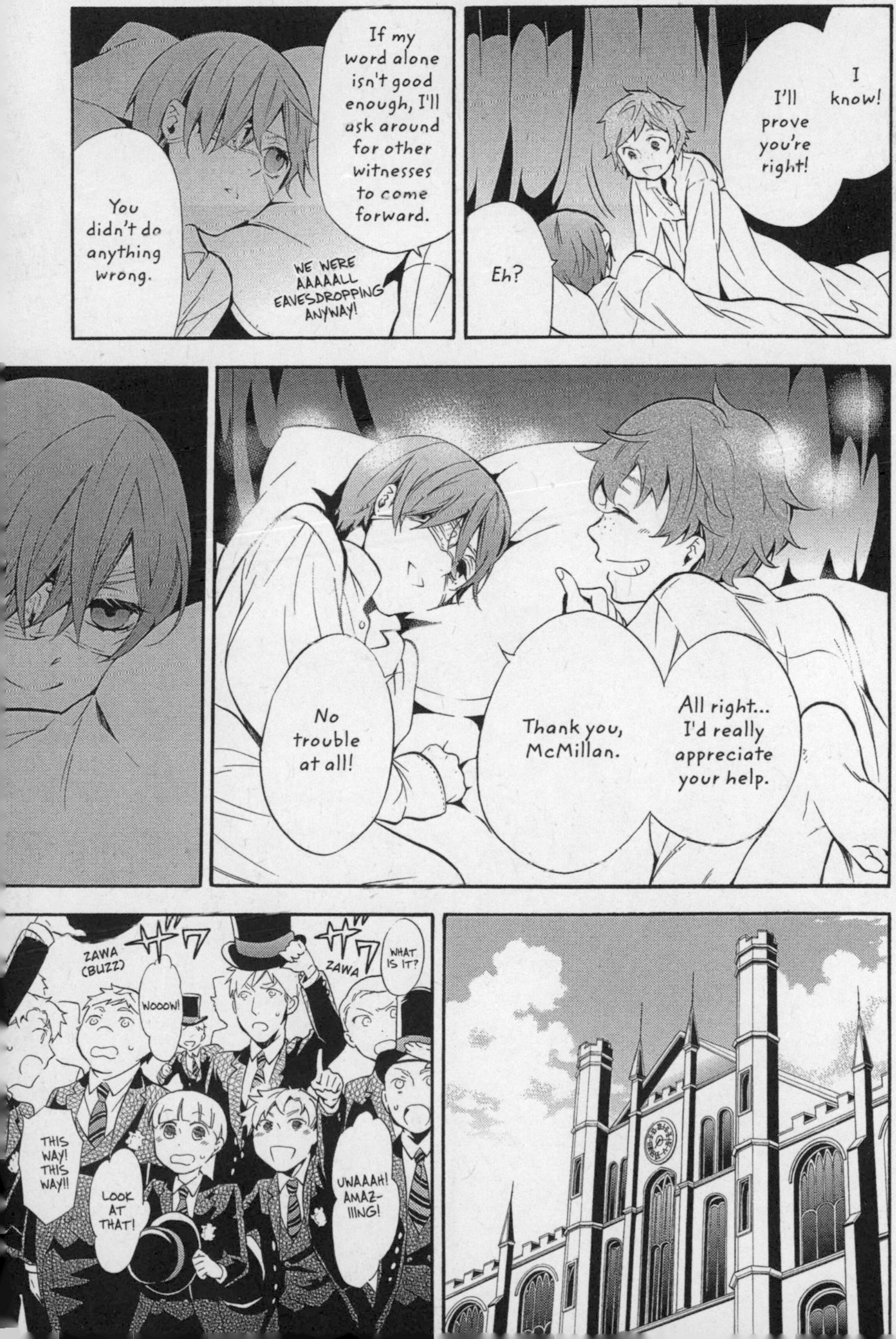
I know!
I'll prove you're right!
Eh?
If my word alone isn't good enough, I'll ask around for other witnesses to come forward.
You didn't do anything wrong.
WE WERE AAAAALL EAVESDROPPING ANYWAY!
All right... I'd really appreciate your help.
Thank you, McMillan.
No trouble at all!
ザワ
WHAT IS IT?
ZAWA
ザワ
ZAWA (BUZZ)
WOOOW!
UWAAAH! AMAZ-IIING!
THIS WAY! THIS WAY!!
LOOK AT THAT!

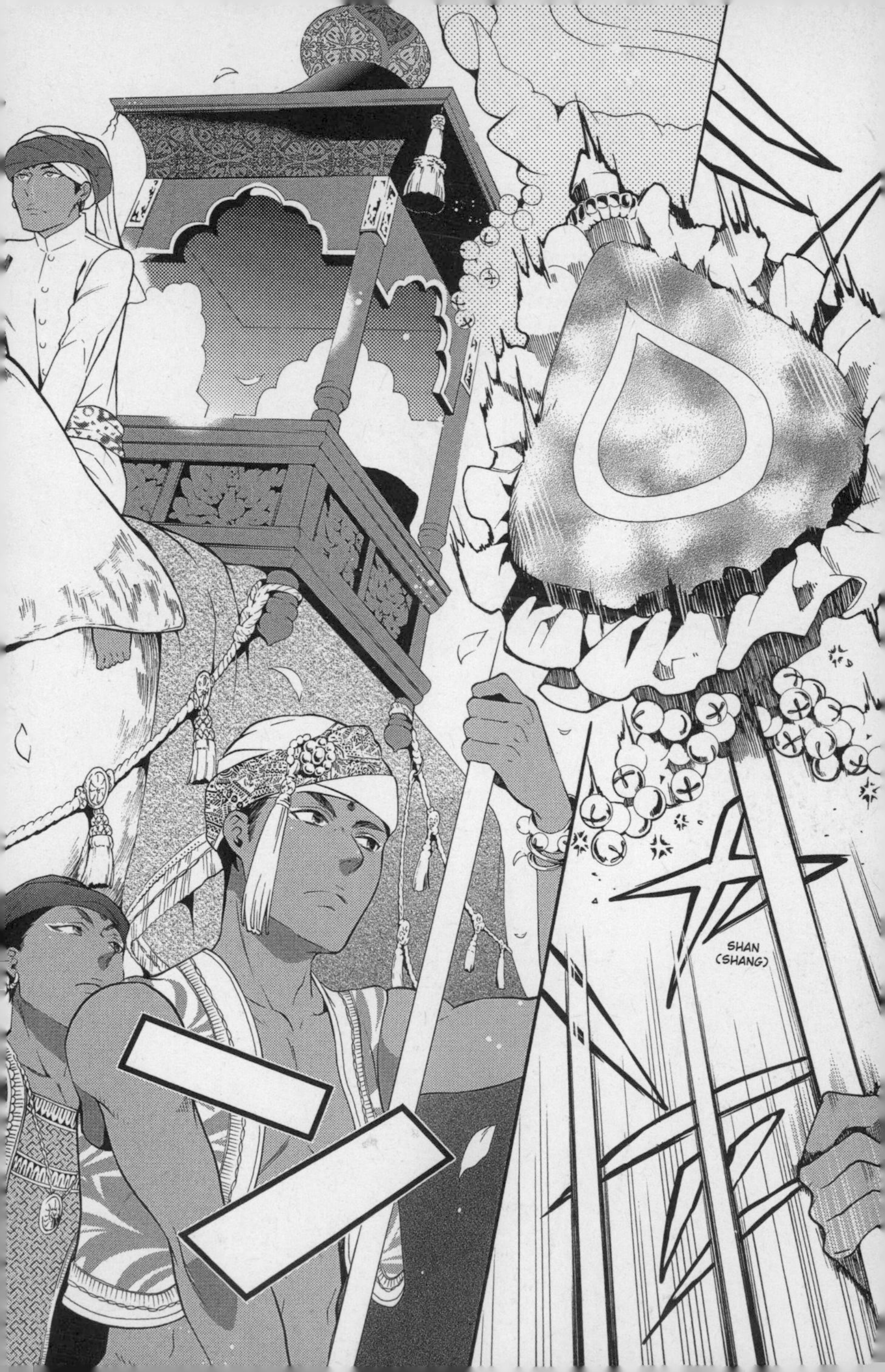
SHAN
(SHANG)

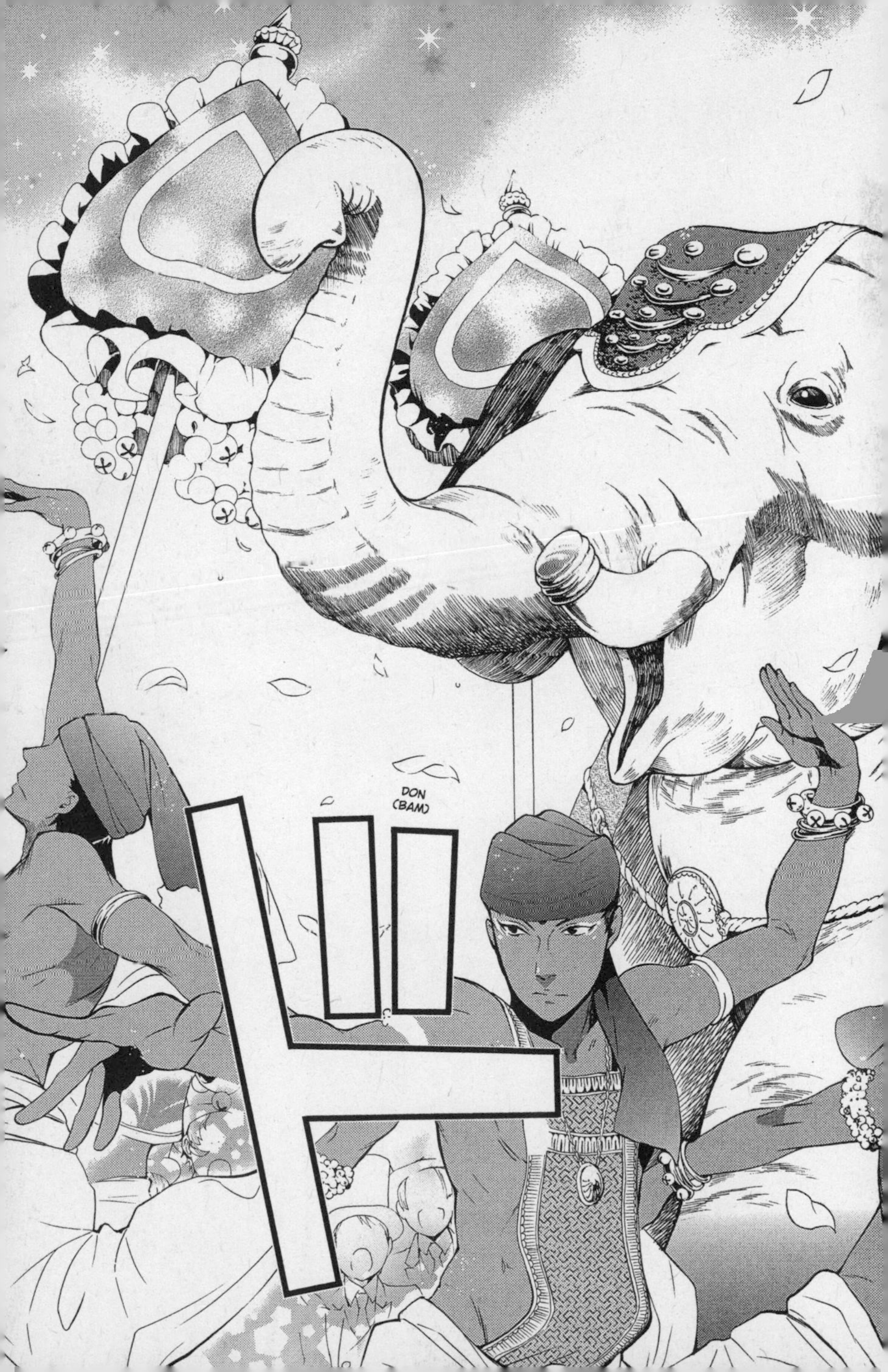
DON
(BAM)

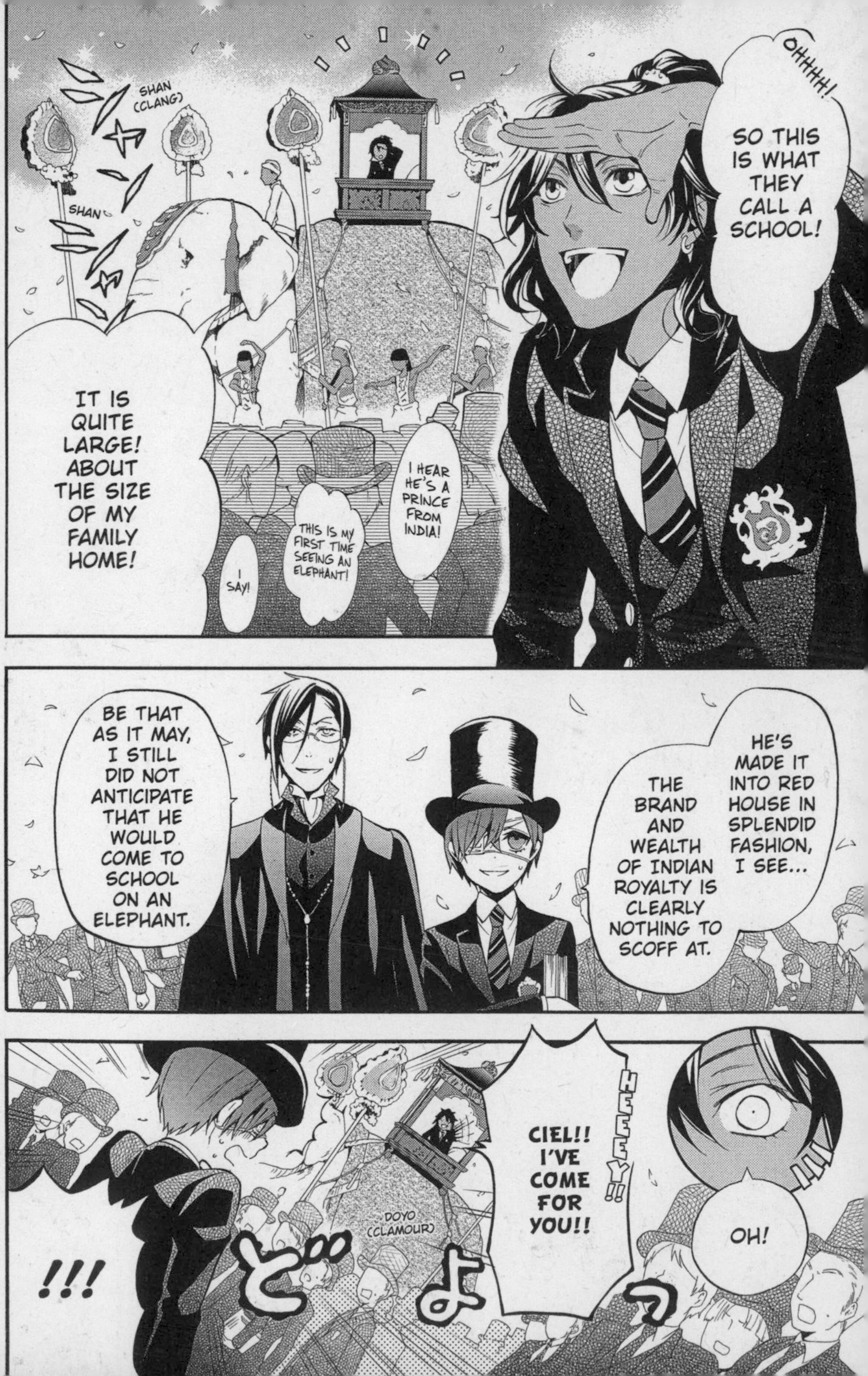
OHHHH!
SO THIS IS WHAT THEY CALL A SCHOOL!
SHAN (CLANG)
SHAN
IT IS QUITE LARGE! ABOUT THE SIZE OF MY FAMILY HOME!
I HEAR HE'S A PRINCE FROM INDIA!
THIS IS MY FIRST TIME SEEING AN ELEPHANT!
I SAY!
HE'S MADE IT INTO RED HOUSE IN SPLENDID FASHION, I SEE...
THE BRAND AND WEALTH OF INDIAN ROYALTY IS CLEARLY NOTHING TO SCOFF AT.
BE THAT AS IT MAY, I STILL DID NOT ANTICIPATE THAT HE WOULD COME TO SCHOOL ON AN ELEPHANT.
OH!
HEEEY!!
CIEL!! I'VE COME FOR YOU!!
DOYO (CLAMOUR)
どよっ
!!!

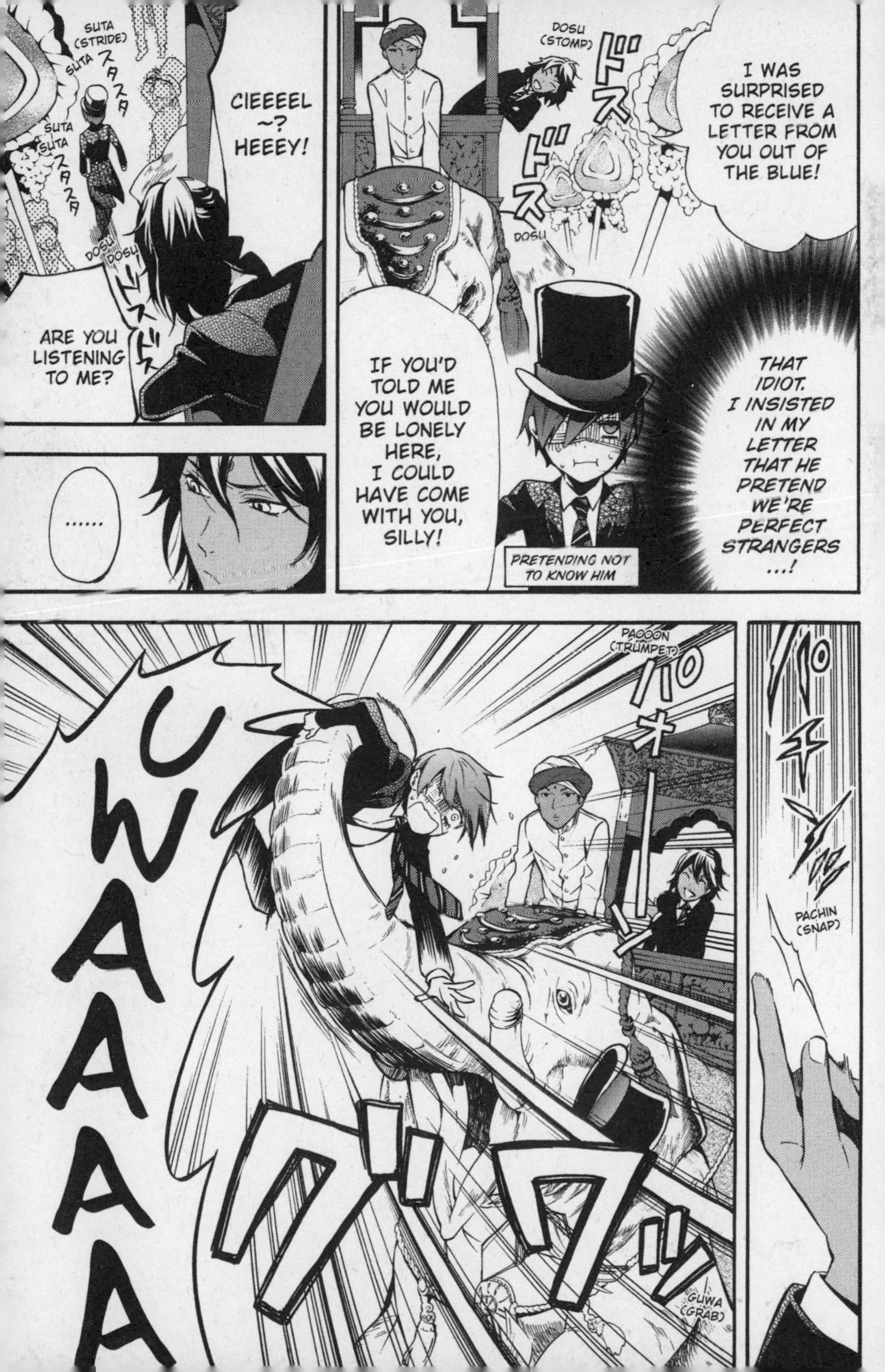
DOSU (STOMP)
I WAS SURPRISED TO RECEIVE A LETTER FROM YOU OUT OF THE BLUE!
DOSU
THAT IDIOT. I INSISTED IN MY LETTER THAT HE PRETEND WE'RE PERFECT STRANGERS ...!
IF YOU'D TOLD ME YOU WOULD BE LONELY HERE, I COULD HAVE COME WITH YOU, SILLY!
PRETENDING NOT TO KNOW HIM
CIEEEEL ~? HEEEY!
SUTA (STRIDE) SUTA
SUTA SUTA
DOSU DOSU
ARE YOU LISTENING TO ME?
......
PACHIN (SNAP)
PAOOON (TRUMPET)
UWAAAAA
GUWA (GRAB)

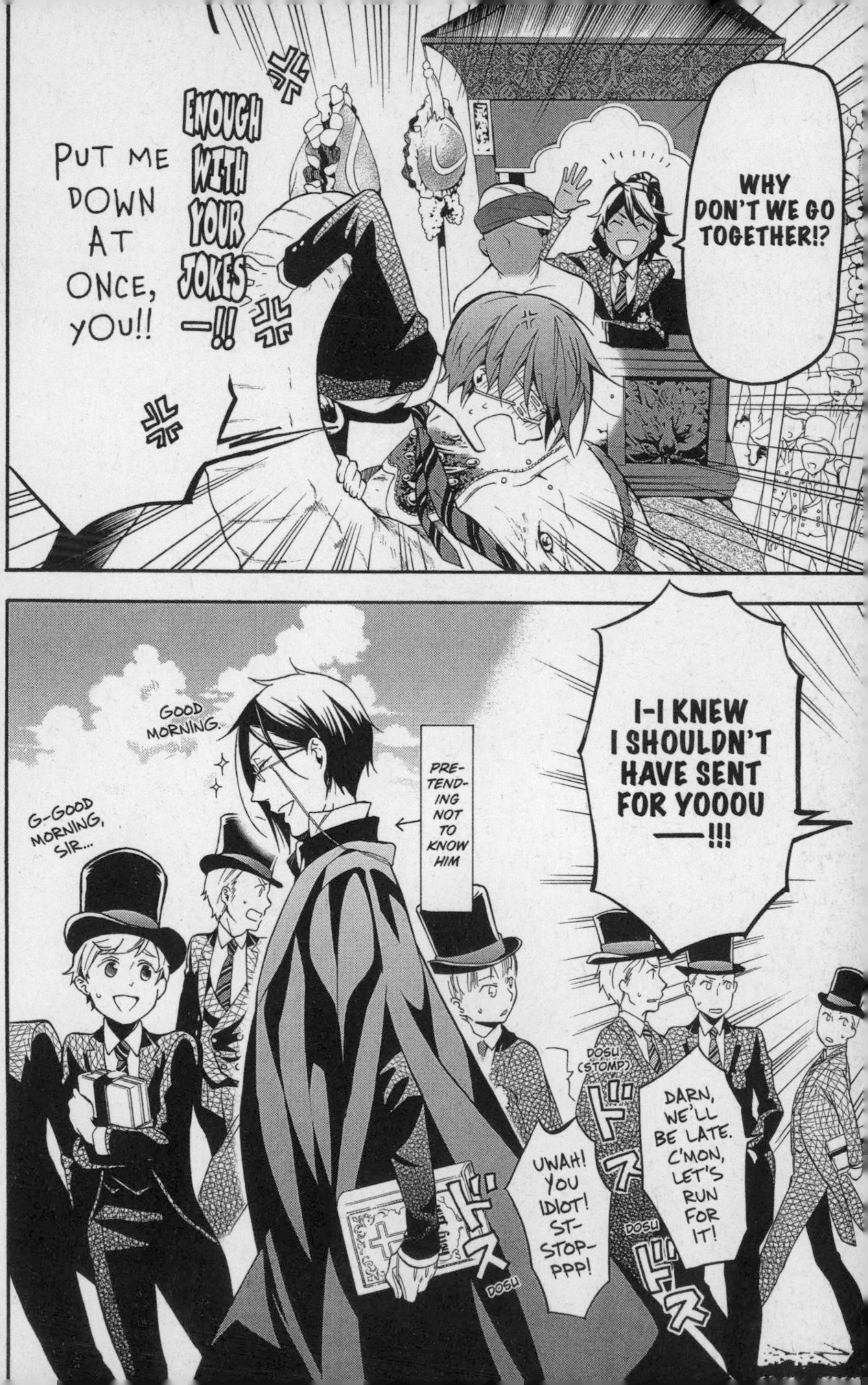
WHY DON'T WE GO TOGETHER!?
ENOUGH WITH YOUR JOKES—!!
PUT ME DOWN AT ONCE, YOU!!
I-I KNEW I SHOULDN'T HAVE SENT FOR YOOOU—!!!
DARN, WE'LL BE LATE. C'MON, LET'S RUN FOR IT!
DOSU (STOMP)
DOSU
UWAH! YOU IDIOT! ST-STOPPPP!
DOSU
PRETENDING NOT TO KNOW HIM
GOOD MORNING.
G-GOOD MORNING, SIR...

Black Butler

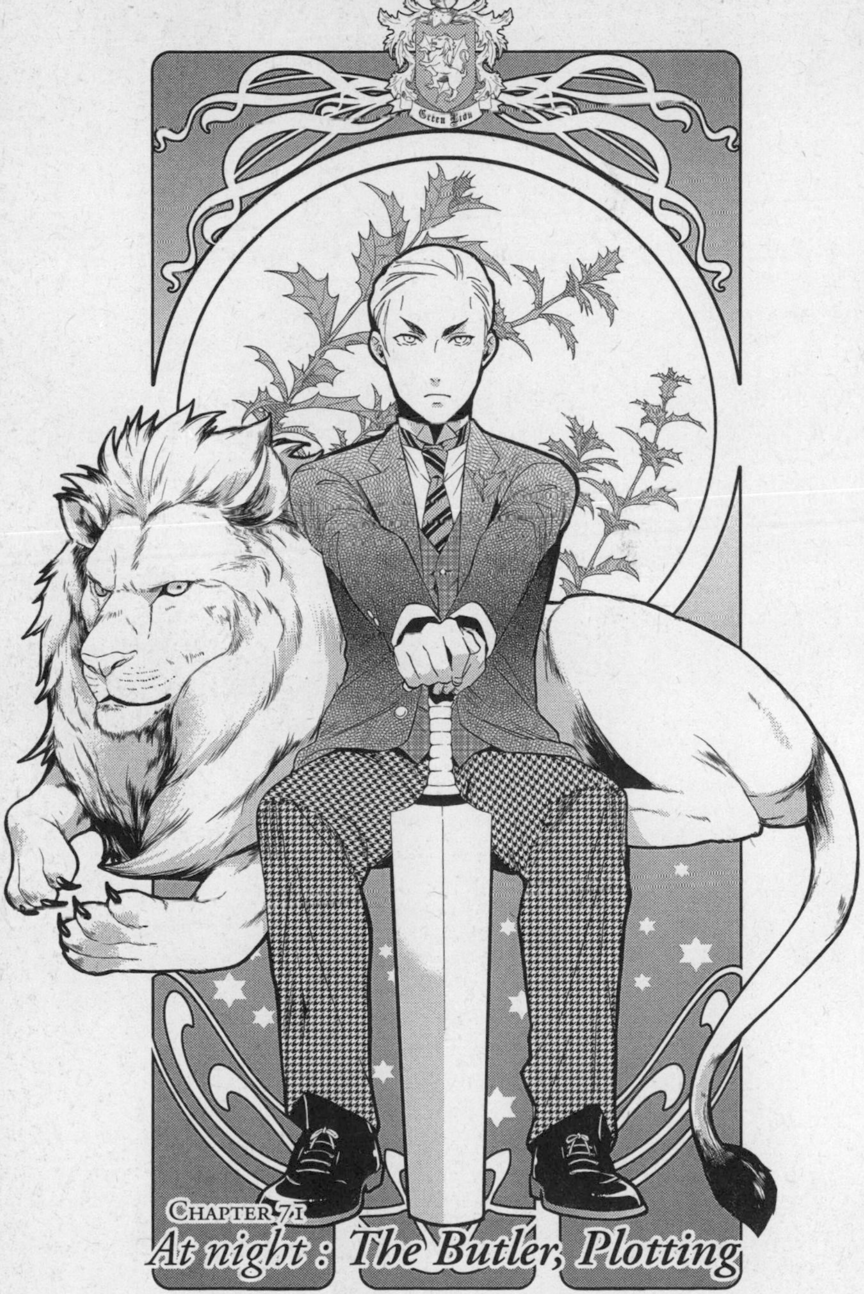

Chapter 71
At night : The Butler, Plotting

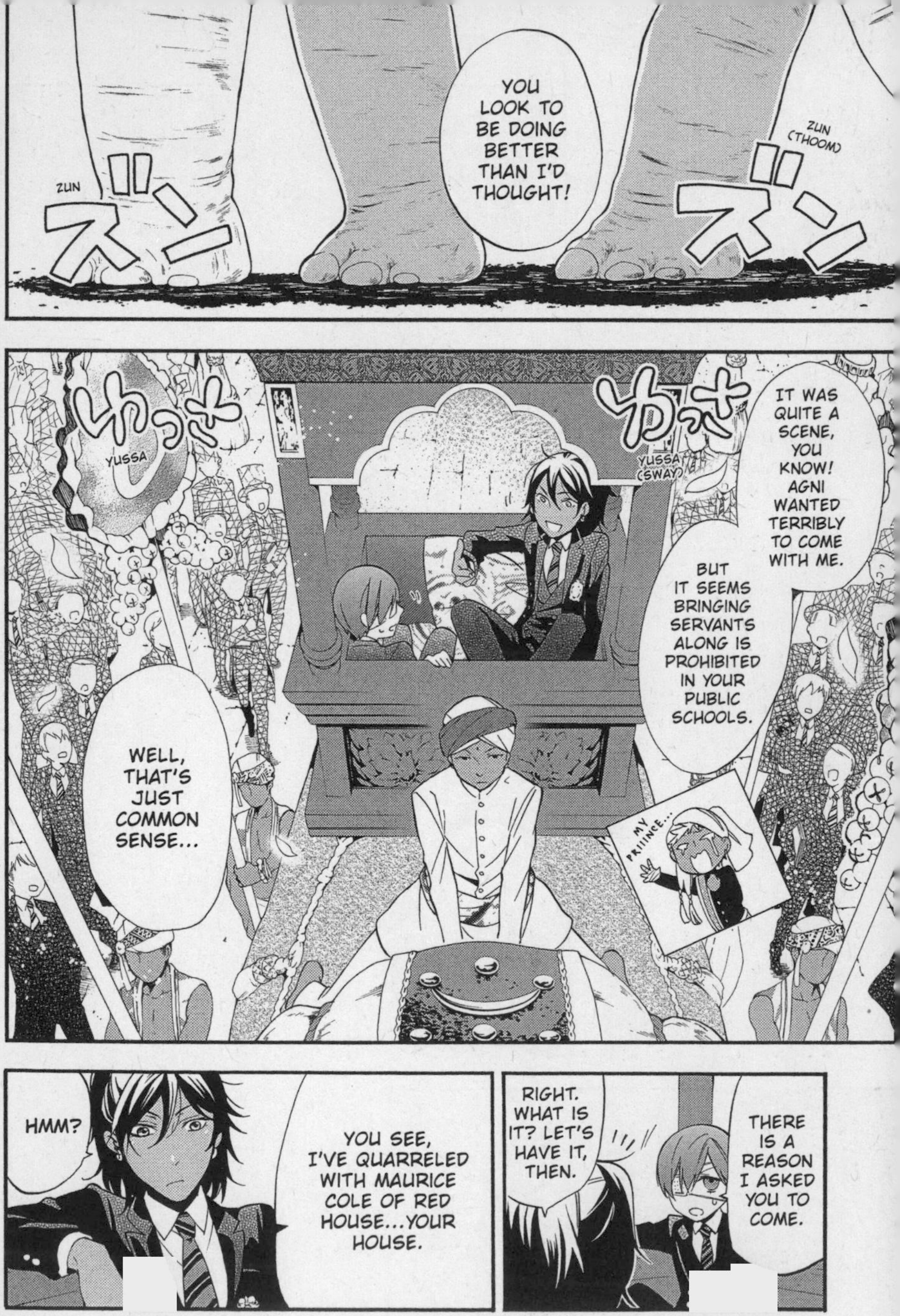
ZUN (THOOM)
ズン
YOU LOOK TO BE DOING BETTER THAN I'D THOUGHT!
ZUN
ズン
YUSSA (SWAY)
ゆっさ
IT WAS QUITE A SCENE, YOU KNOW! AGNI WANTED TERRIBLY TO COME WITH ME.
BUT IT SEEMS BRINGING SERVANTS ALONG IS PROHIBITED IN YOUR PUBLIC SCHOOLS.
MY PRIIINCE...
YUSSA
ゆっさ
WELL, THAT'S JUST COMMON SENSE...
THERE IS A REASON I ASKED YOU TO COME.
RIGHT. WHAT IS IT? LET'S HAVE IT, THEN.
YOU SEE, I'VE QUARRELED WITH MAURICE COLE OF RED HOUSE...YOUR HOUSE.
HMM?

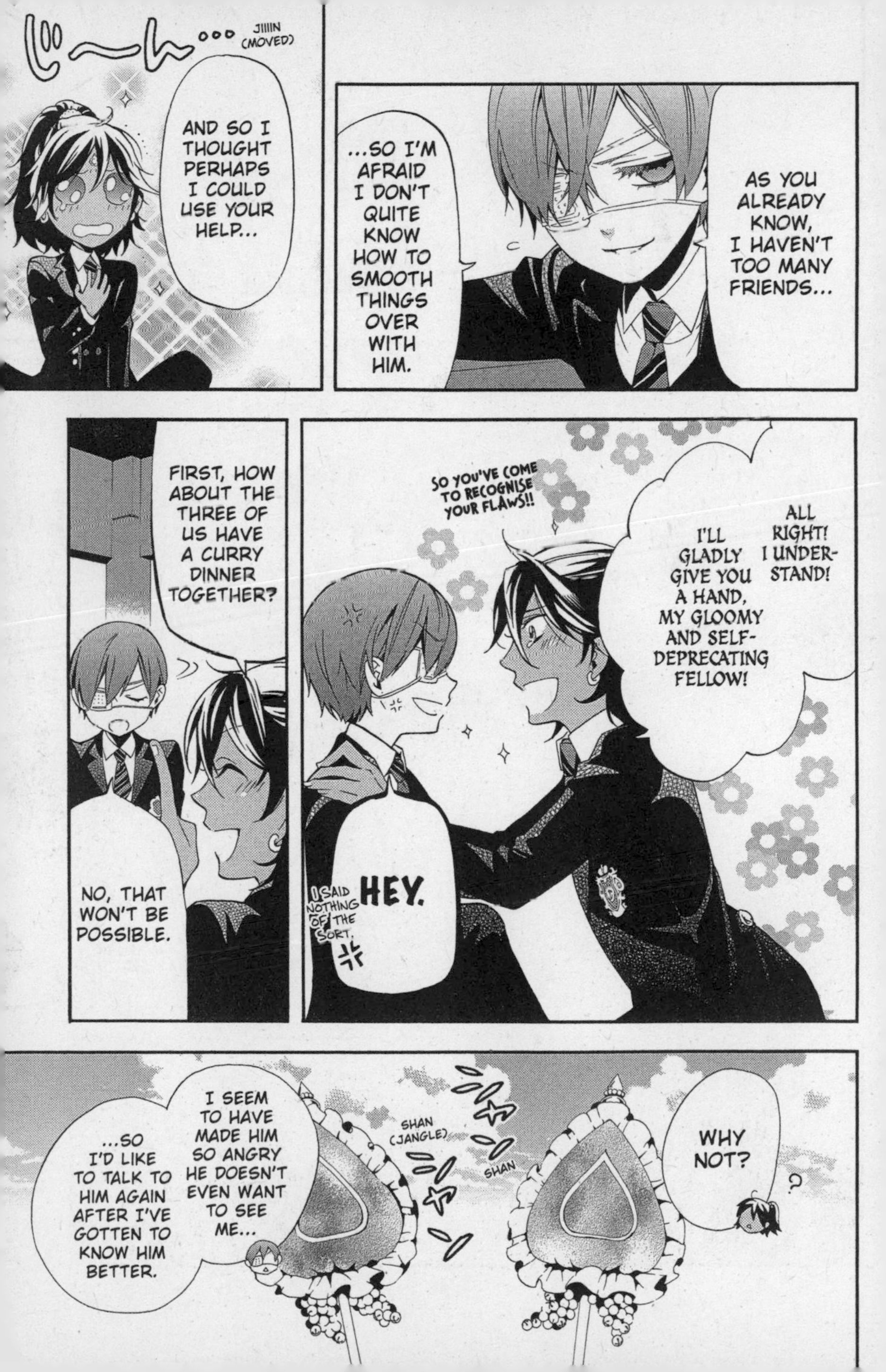
AS YOU ALREADY KNOW, I HAVEN'T TOO MANY FRIENDS...
...SO I'M AFRAID I DON'T QUITE KNOW HOW TO SMOOTH THINGS OVER WITH HIM.
じ〜ん…
JIIIIN (MOVED)
AND SO I THOUGHT PERHAPS I COULD USE YOUR HELP...
ALL RIGHT! I UNDERSTAND!
I'LL GLADLY GIVE YOU A HAND, MY GLOOMY AND SELF-DEPRECATING FELLOW!
SO YOU'VE COME TO RECOGNISE YOUR FLAWS!!
HEY.
I SAID NOTHING OF THE SORT.
FIRST, HOW ABOUT THE THREE OF US HAVE A CURRY DINNER TOGETHER?
NO, THAT WON'T BE POSSIBLE.
WHY NOT?
SHAN
SHAN (JANGLE)
I SEEM TO HAVE MADE HIM SO ANGRY HE DOESN'T EVEN WANT TO SEE ME...
...SO I'D LIKE TO TALK TO HIM AGAIN AFTER I'VE GOTTEN TO KNOW HIM BETTER.

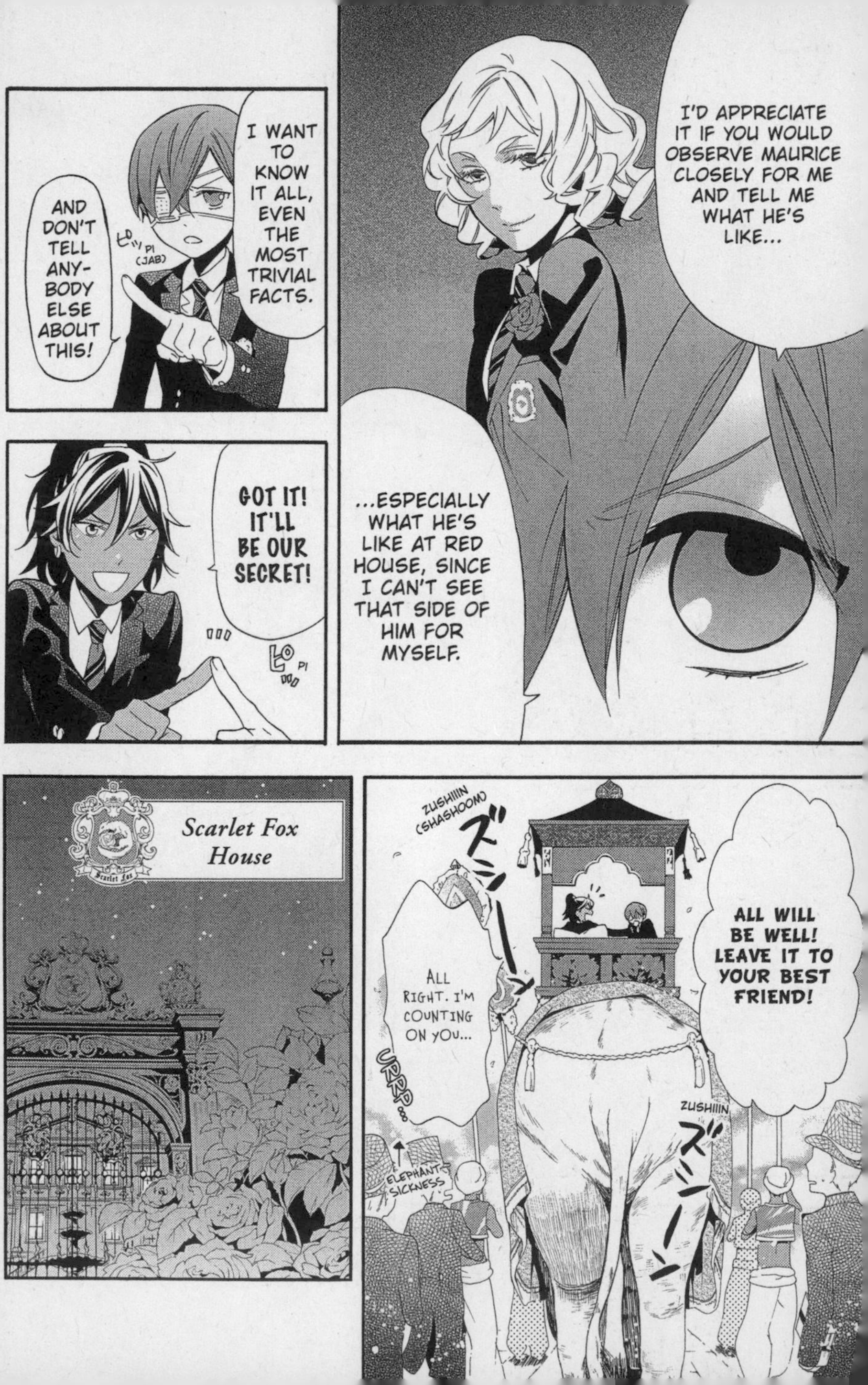
I'D APPRECIATE IT IF YOU WOULD OBSERVE MAURICE CLOSELY FOR ME AND TELL ME WHAT HE'S LIKE...
...ESPECIALLY WHAT HE'S LIKE AT RED HOUSE, SINCE I CAN'T SEE THAT SIDE OF HIM FOR MYSELF.
I WANT TO KNOW IT ALL, EVEN THE MOST TRIVIAL FACTS.
AND DON'T TELL ANYBODY ELSE ABOUT THIS!
PI (JAB)
GOT IT! IT'LL BE OUR SECRET!
PI
ZUSHIIIN (SHASHOOM)
ALL WILL BE WELL! LEAVE IT TO YOUR BEST FRIEND!
ALL RIGHT. I'M COUNTING ON YOU...
URPP...
ELEPHANT SICKNESS
ZUSHIIIN
Scarlet Fox House
Scarlet Fox

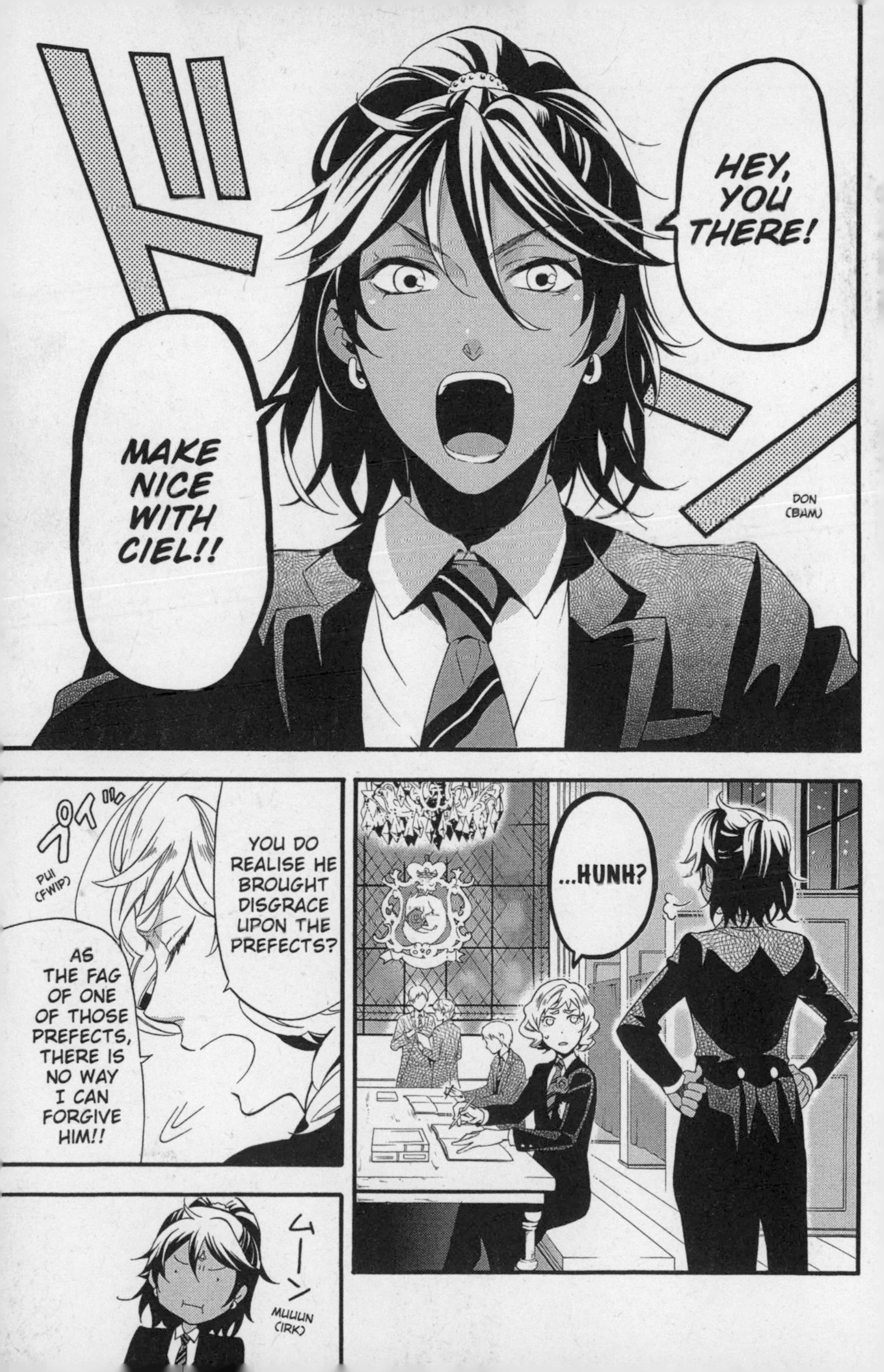
HEY, YOU THERE!
MAKE NICE WITH CIEL!!
DON (BAM)
...HUNH?
YOU DO REALISE HE BROUGHT DISGRACE UPON THE PREFECTS?
AS THE FAG OF ONE OF THOSE PREFECTS, THERE IS NO WAY I CAN FORGIVE HIM!!
PUI (FWIP)
MUUUN (IRK)

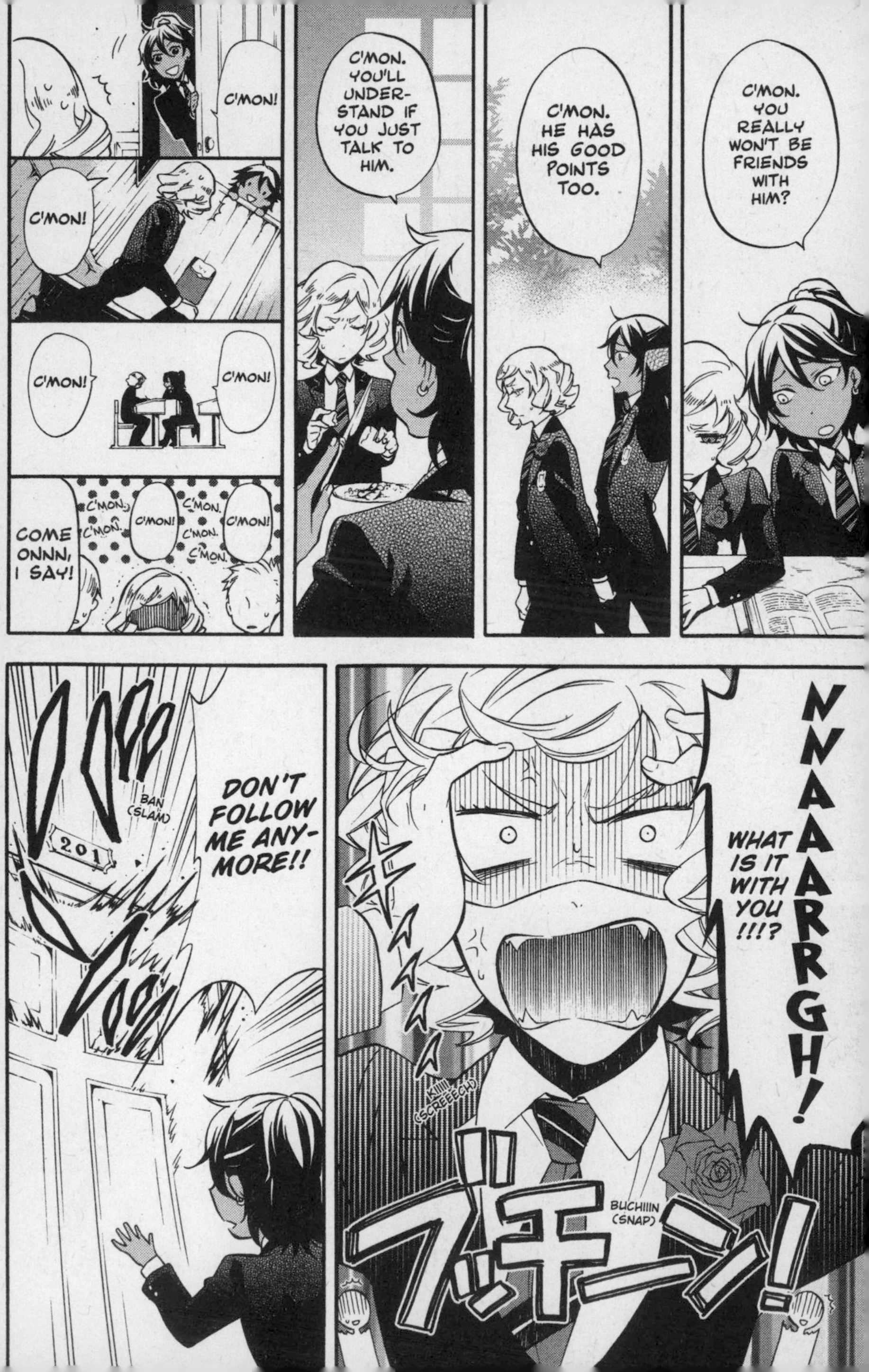
C'MON. YOU REALLY WON'T BE FRIENDS WITH HIM?
C'MON. HE HAS HIS GOOD POINTS TOO.
C'MON. YOU'LL UNDER-STAND IF YOU JUST TALK TO HIM.
C'MON!
C'MON!
C'MON!
C'MON!
C'MON!
C'MON. C'MON. C'MON.
C'MON!
C'MON. C'MON.
COME ONNN, I SAY!
NNAAARRGH!
WHAT IS IT WITH YOU!!!?
KIIIII (SCREEECH)
BUCHIIIN (SNAP)
DON'T FOLLOW ME ANY-MORE!!
BAN (SLAM)
201

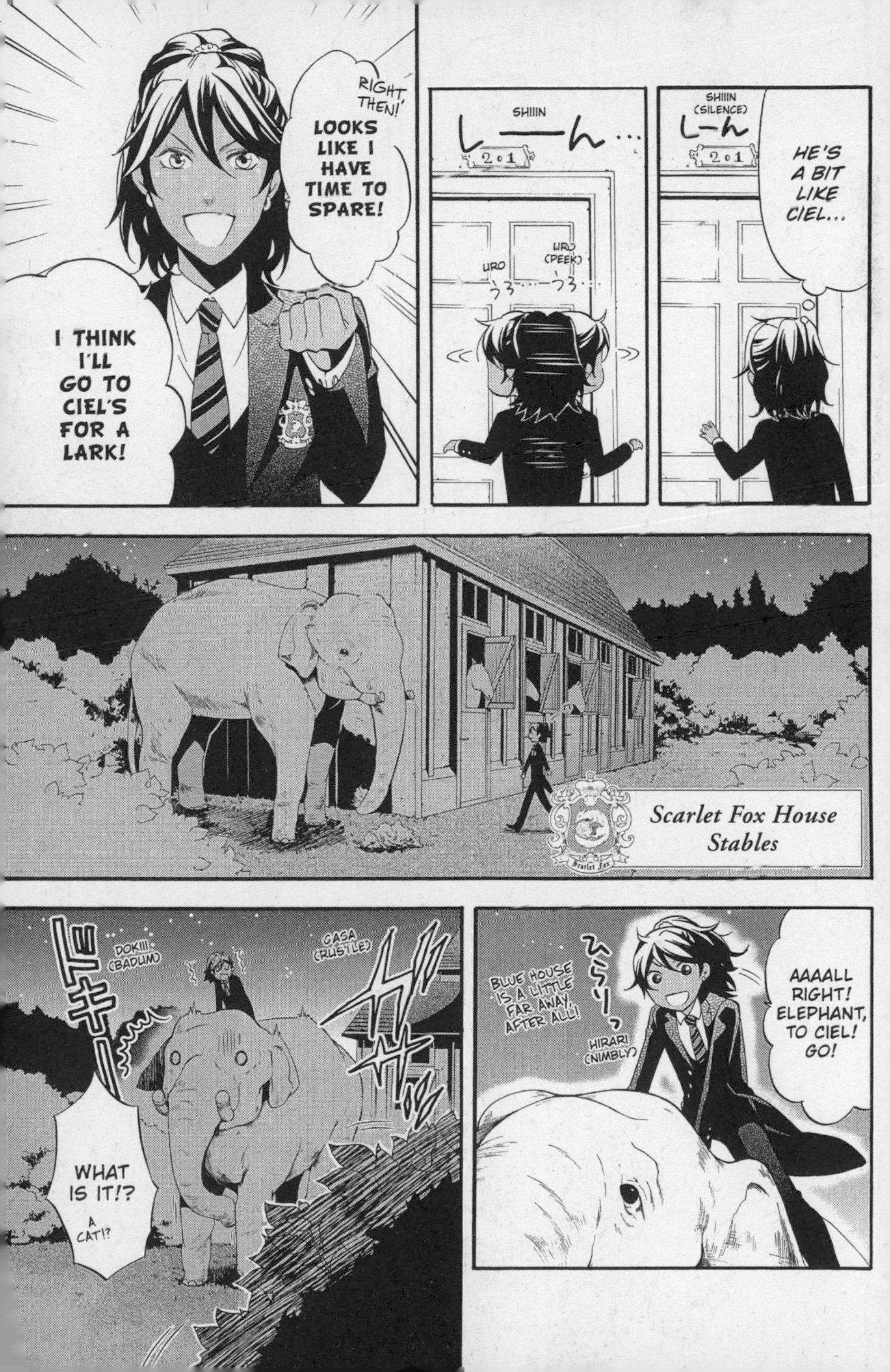

SHIIIN (SILENCE)
しーん
HE'S A BIT LIKE CIEL...
SHIIIN
し――ん…
URO (PEEK)
URO
RIGHT THEN!
LOOKS LIKE I HAVE TIME TO SPARE!
I THINK I'LL GO TO CIEL'S FOR A LARK!
Scarlet Fox House Stables
AAAALL RIGHT! ELEPHANT, TO CIEL! GO!
BLUE HOUSE IS A LITTLE FAR AWAY, AFTER ALL!
HIRARI (NIMBLY)
GASA (RUSTLE)
DOKI!!! (BADUM)
WHAT IS IT!?
A CAT!?

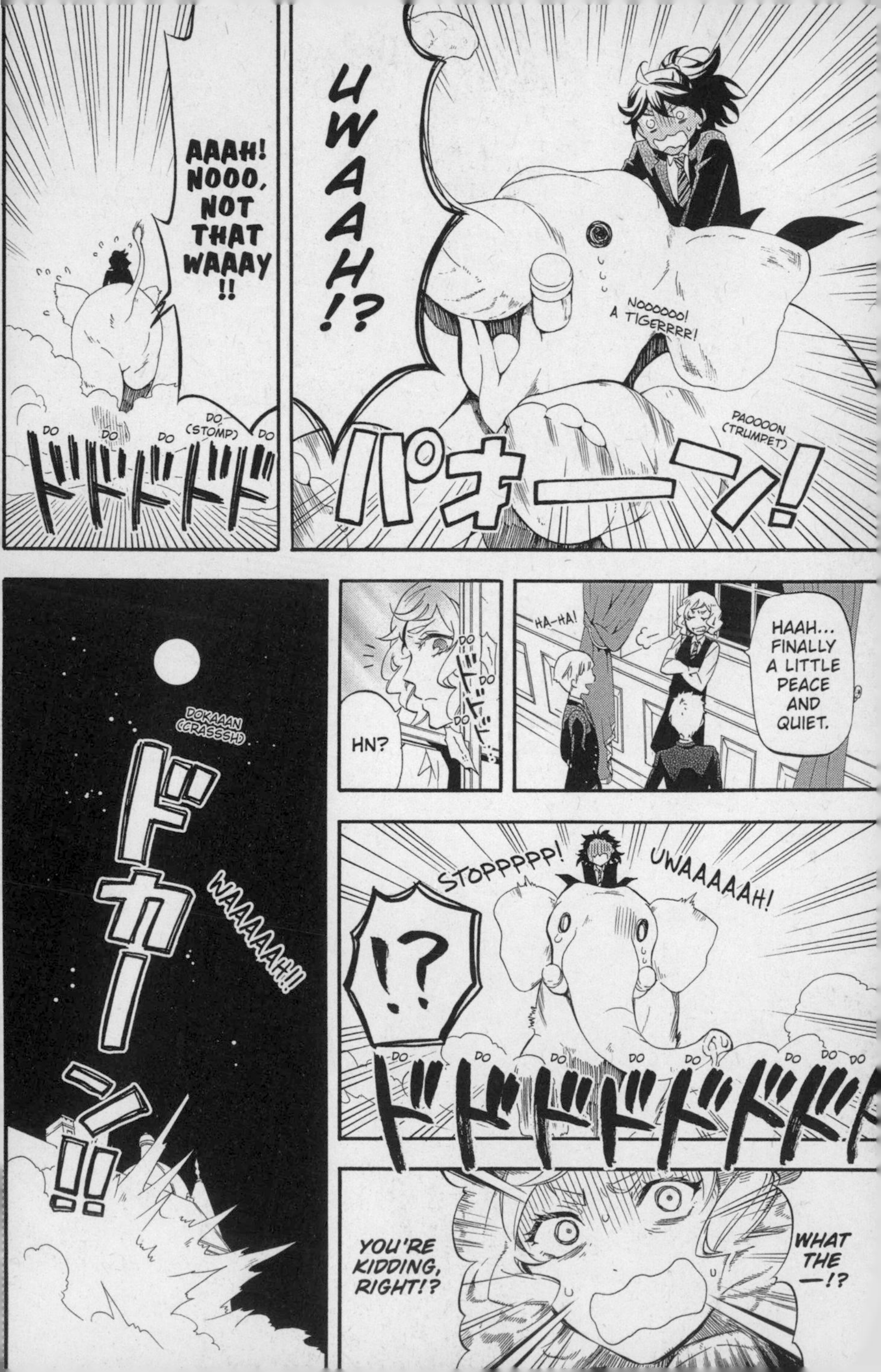
UWAAAH!?
NOOOOOO! A TIGERRRR!
PAOOOON (TRUMPET)
AAAH! NOOO, NOT THAT WAAAY!!
DO DO DO DO (STOMP) DO
HAAH... FINALLY A LITTLE PEACE AND QUIET.
HA-HA!
DO DO DO
HN?
UWAAAAAAH!
STOPPPPP!
!?
DO DO DO DO DO DO DO DO
WHAT THE—!?
YOU'RE KIDDING, RIGHT!?
DOKAAAN (CRASSSH)
WAAAAAH!!

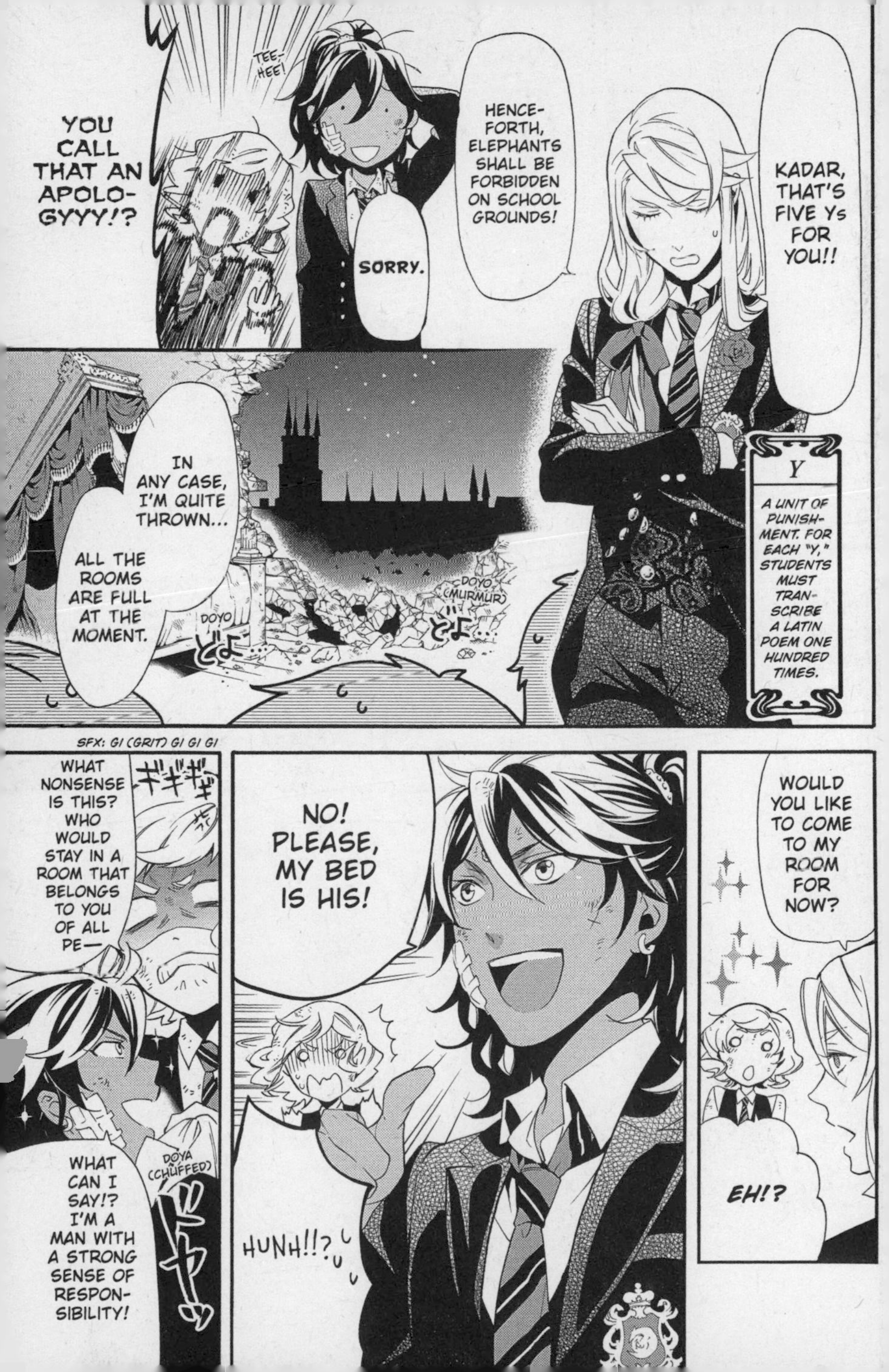

KADAR, THAT'S FIVE Ys FOR YOU!!
Y
A UNIT OF PUNISHMENT. FOR EACH "Y," STUDENTS MUST TRANSCRIBE A LATIN POEM ONE HUNDRED TIMES.
HENCEFORTH, ELEPHANTS SHALL BE FORBIDDEN ON SCHOOL GROUNDS!
SORRY.
TEE-HEE!
YOU CALL THAT AN APOLOGYYY!?
DOYO (MURMUR)
どよ…
IN ANY CASE, I'M QUITE THROWN…
ALL THE ROOMS ARE FULL AT THE MOMENT.
DOYO
どよ…
WOULD YOU LIKE TO COME TO MY ROOM FOR NOW?
EH!?
NO! PLEASE, MY BED IS HIS!
HUNH!!?
SFX: GI (GRIT) GI GI GI
ギギギギ
WHAT NONSENSE IS THIS? WHO WOULD STAY IN A ROOM THAT BELONGS TO YOU OF ALL PE—
DOYA (CHUFFED)
ドヤッ
WHAT CAN I SAY!? I'M A MAN WITH A STRONG SENSE OF RESPONSIBILITY!

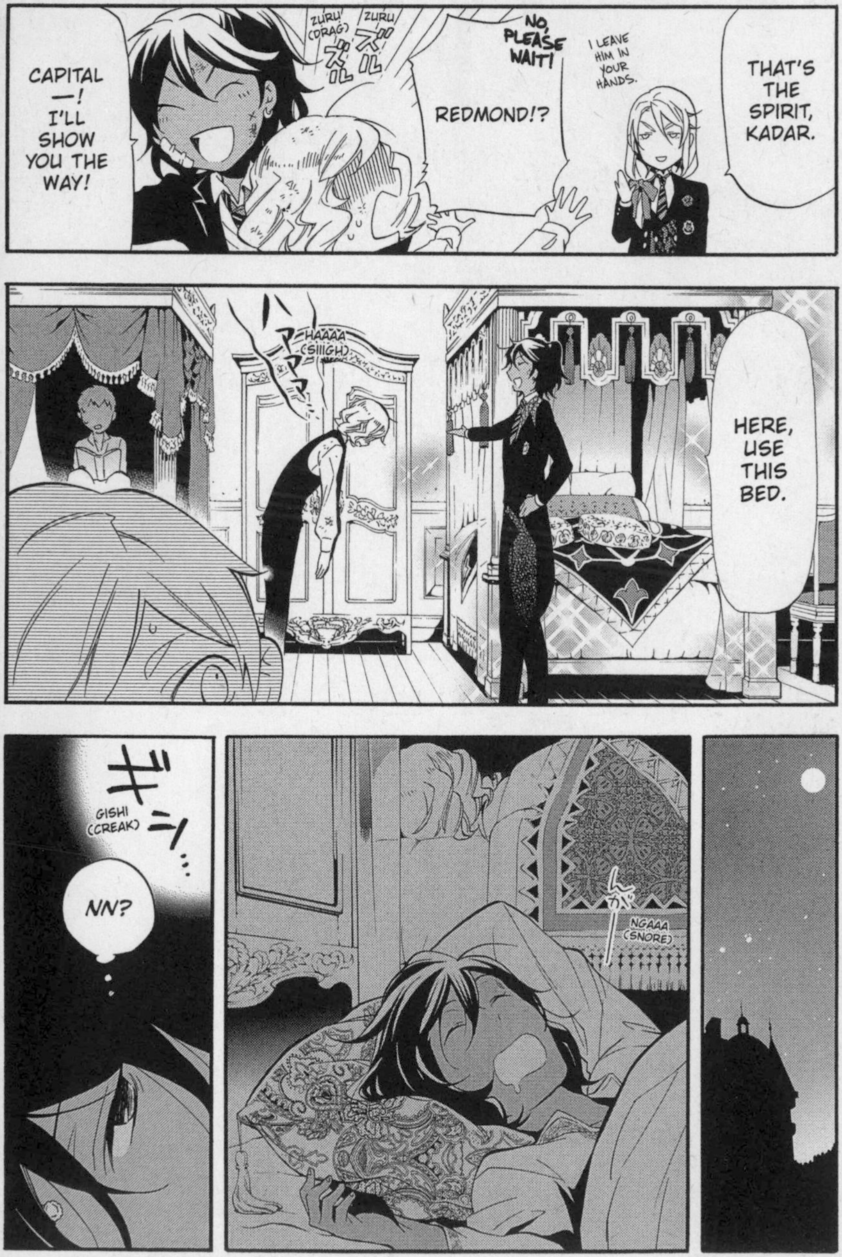
THAT'S THE SPIRIT, KADAR.
I LEAVE HIM IN YOUR HANDS.
NO, PLEASE WAIT!
REDMOND!?
ZURU (DRAG)
ZURU
CAPITAL—! I'LL SHOW YOU THE WAY!
HERE, USE THIS BED.
HAAAA (SIIIGH)
NGAAA (SNORE)
GISHI (CREAK)
NN?

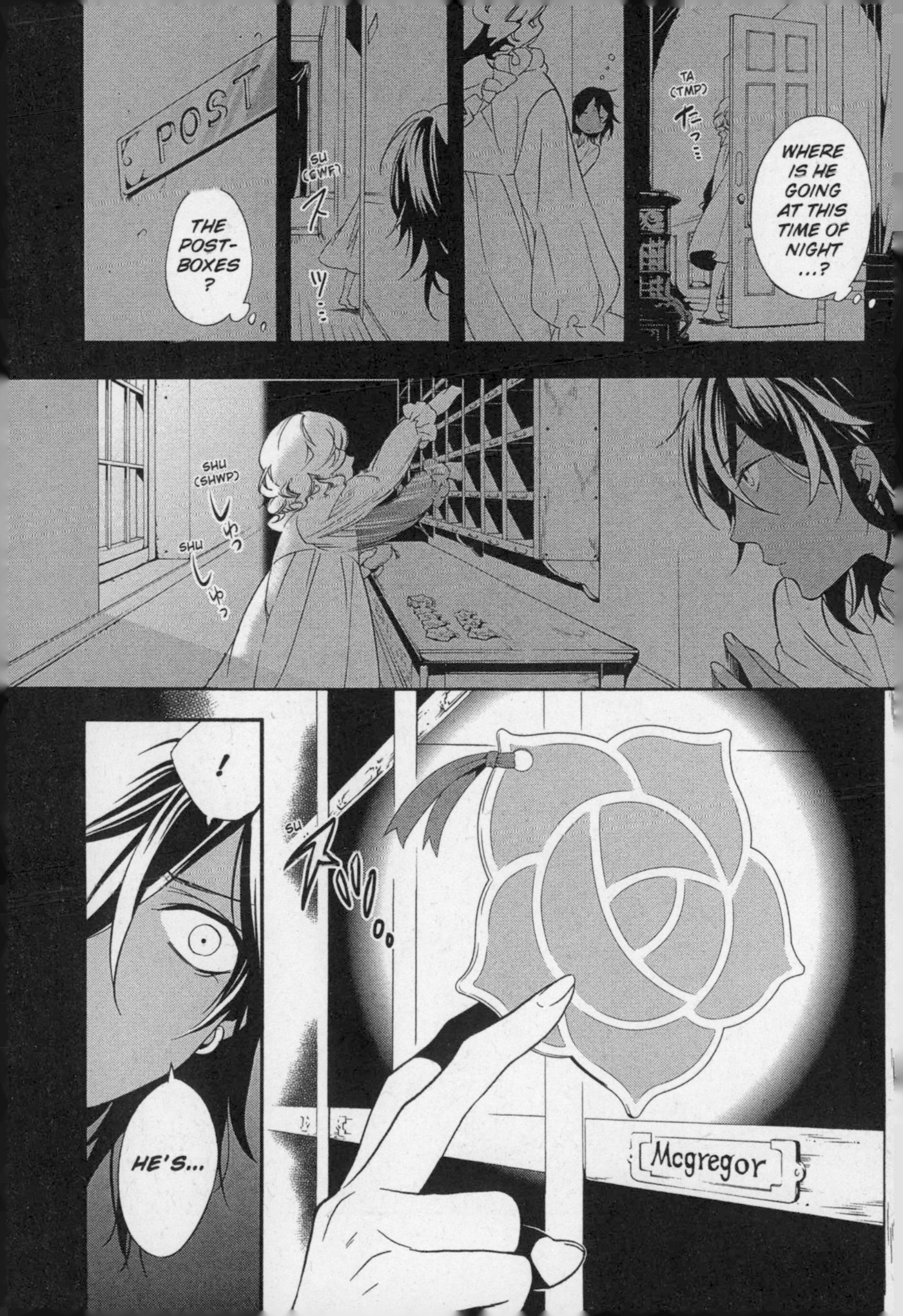
TA (TMP)
WHERE IS HE GOING AT THIS TIME OF NIGHT ...?
SU (SWF)
THE POST-BOXES ?
POST
SHU (SHWP)
SHU
SU
Mcgregor
!
HE'S...

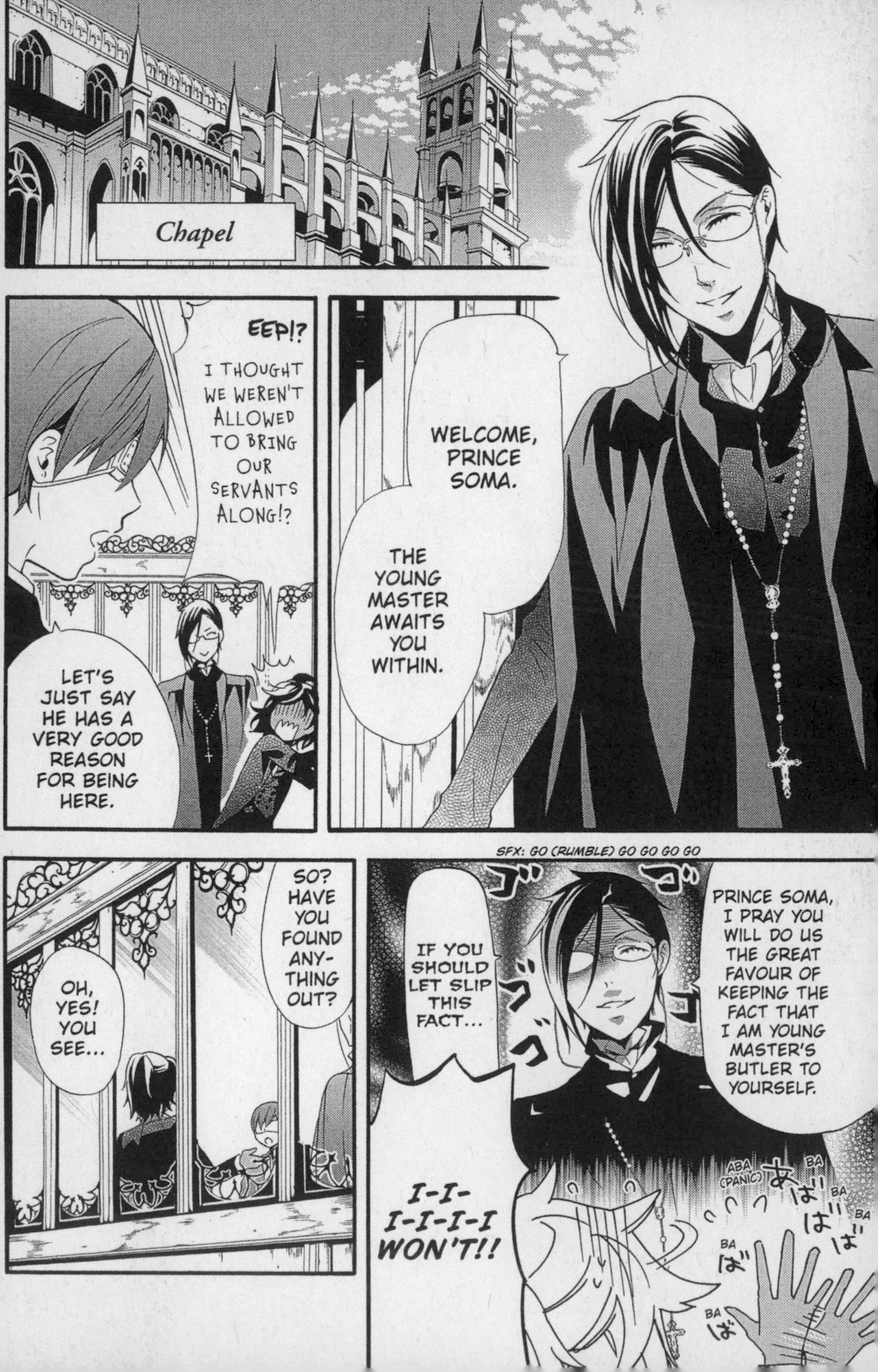
Chapel
WELCOME, PRINCE SOMA.
THE YOUNG MASTER AWAITS YOU WITHIN.
EEP!?
I THOUGHT WE WEREN'T ALLOWED TO BRING OUR SERVANTS ALONG!?
LET'S JUST SAY HE HAS A VERY GOOD REASON FOR BEING HERE.
SFX: GO (RUMBLE) GO GO GO GO
PRINCE SOMA, I PRAY YOU WILL DO US THE GREAT FAVOUR OF KEEPING THE FACT THAT I AM YOUNG MASTER'S BUTLER TO YOURSELF.
IF YOU SHOULD LET SLIP THIS FACT...
ABA (PANIC)
BA
BA
BA
BA
BA
I-I-I-I-I-I WON'T!!
SO? HAVE YOU FOUND ANY-THING OUT?
OH, YES! YOU SEE...

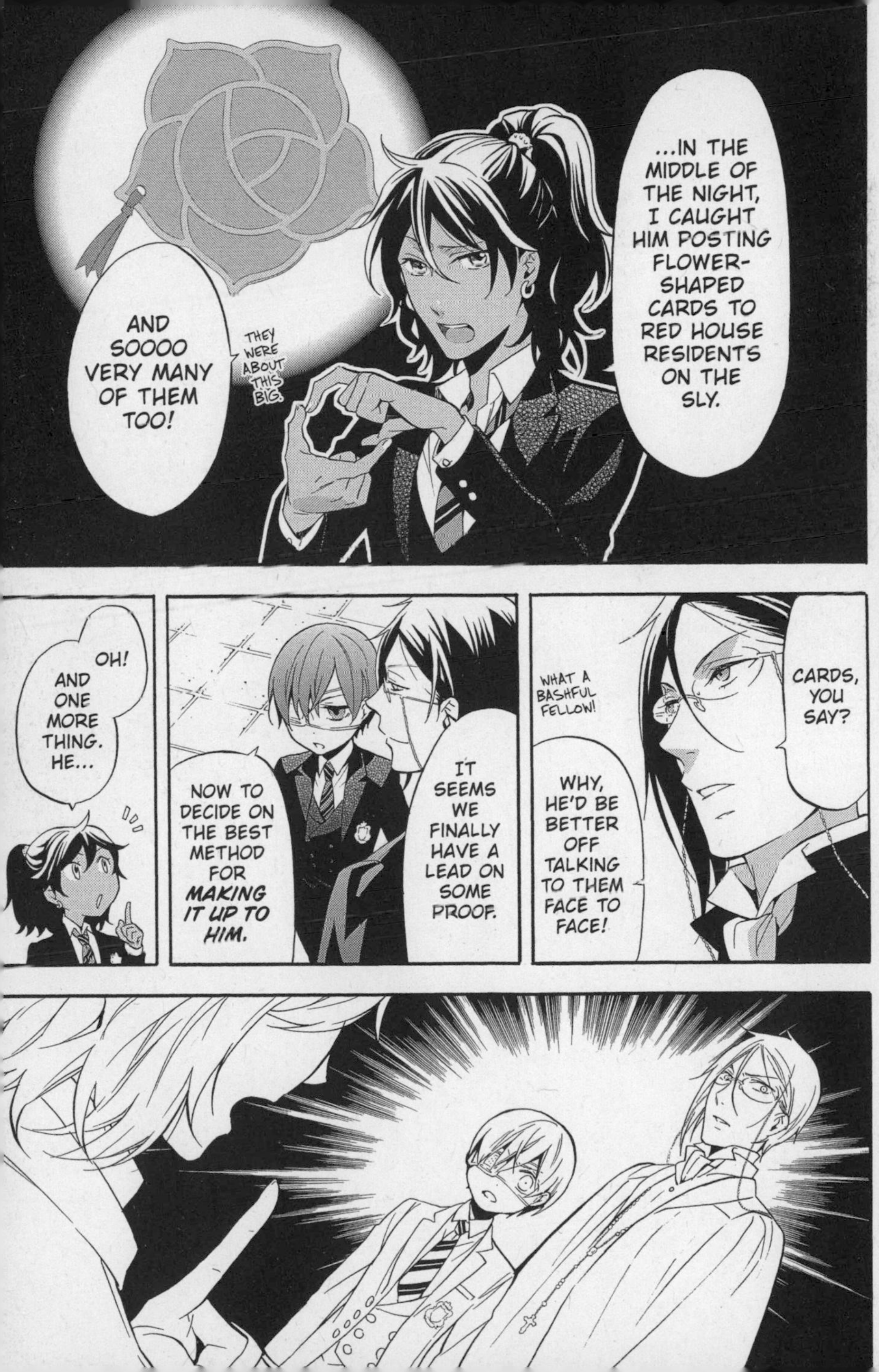
...IN THE MIDDLE OF THE NIGHT, I CAUGHT HIM POSTING FLOWER-SHAPED CARDS TO RED HOUSE RESIDENTS ON THE SLY.
THEY WERE ABOUT THIS BIG.
AND SOOOO VERY MANY OF THEM TOO!
CARDS, YOU SAY?
WHAT A BASHFUL FELLOW!
WHY, HE'D BE BETTER OFF TALKING TO THEM FACE TO FACE!
IT SEEMS WE FINALLY HAVE A LEAD ON SOME PROOF.
NOW TO DECIDE ON THE BEST METHOD FOR *MAKING IT UP TO HIM.*
OH! AND ONE MORE THING. HE...

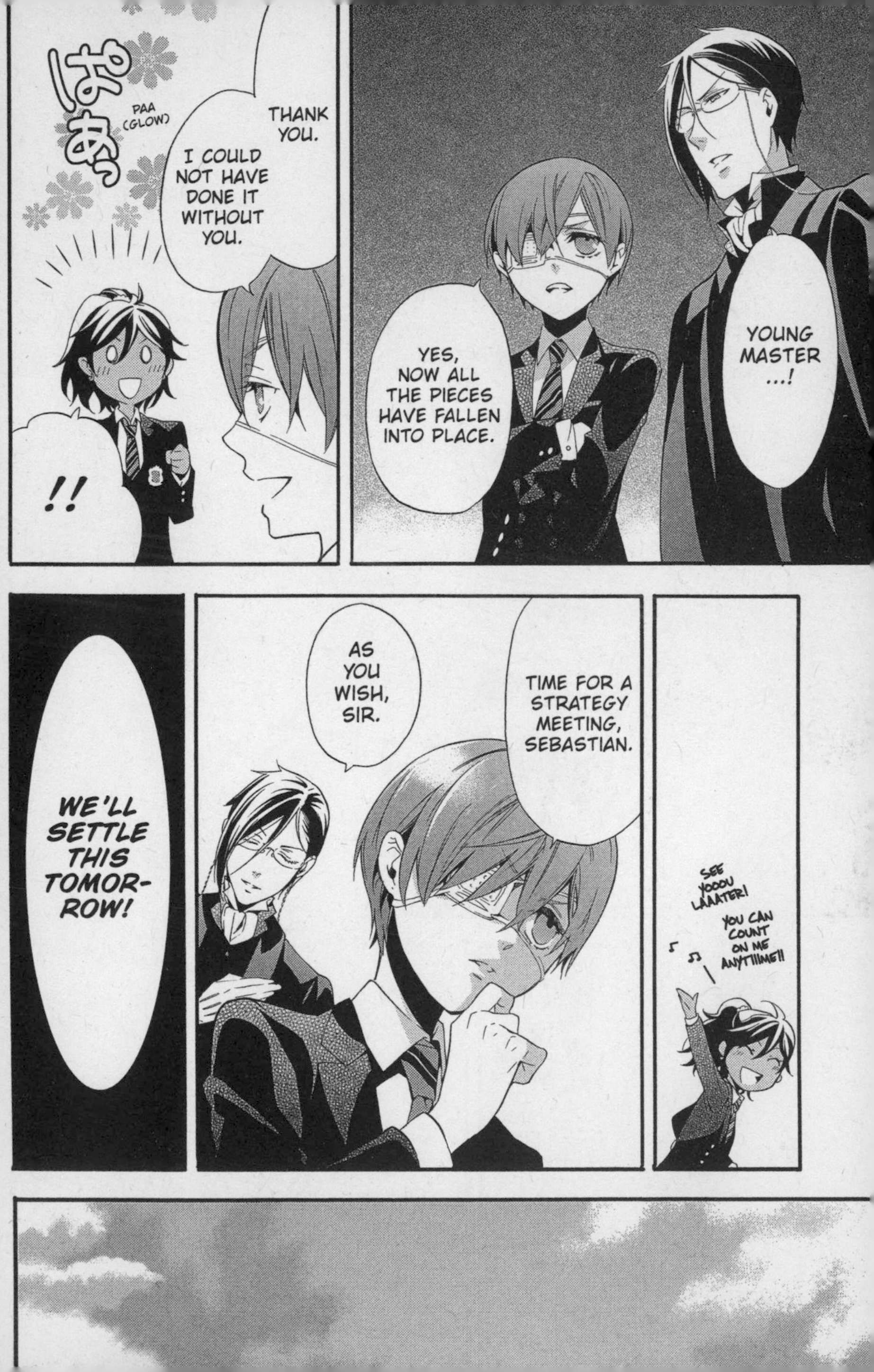
YOUNG MASTER ...!
YES, NOW ALL THE PIECES HAVE FALLEN INTO PLACE.
THANK YOU.
I COULD NOT HAVE DONE IT WITHOUT YOU.
ぱぁっ
PAA (GLOW)
!!
SEE YOOOU LAAATER!
YOU CAN COUNT ON ME ANYTIIIME!!
TIME FOR A STRATEGY MEETING, SEBASTIAN.
AS YOU WISH, SIR.
WE'LL SETTLE THIS TOMOR-ROW!

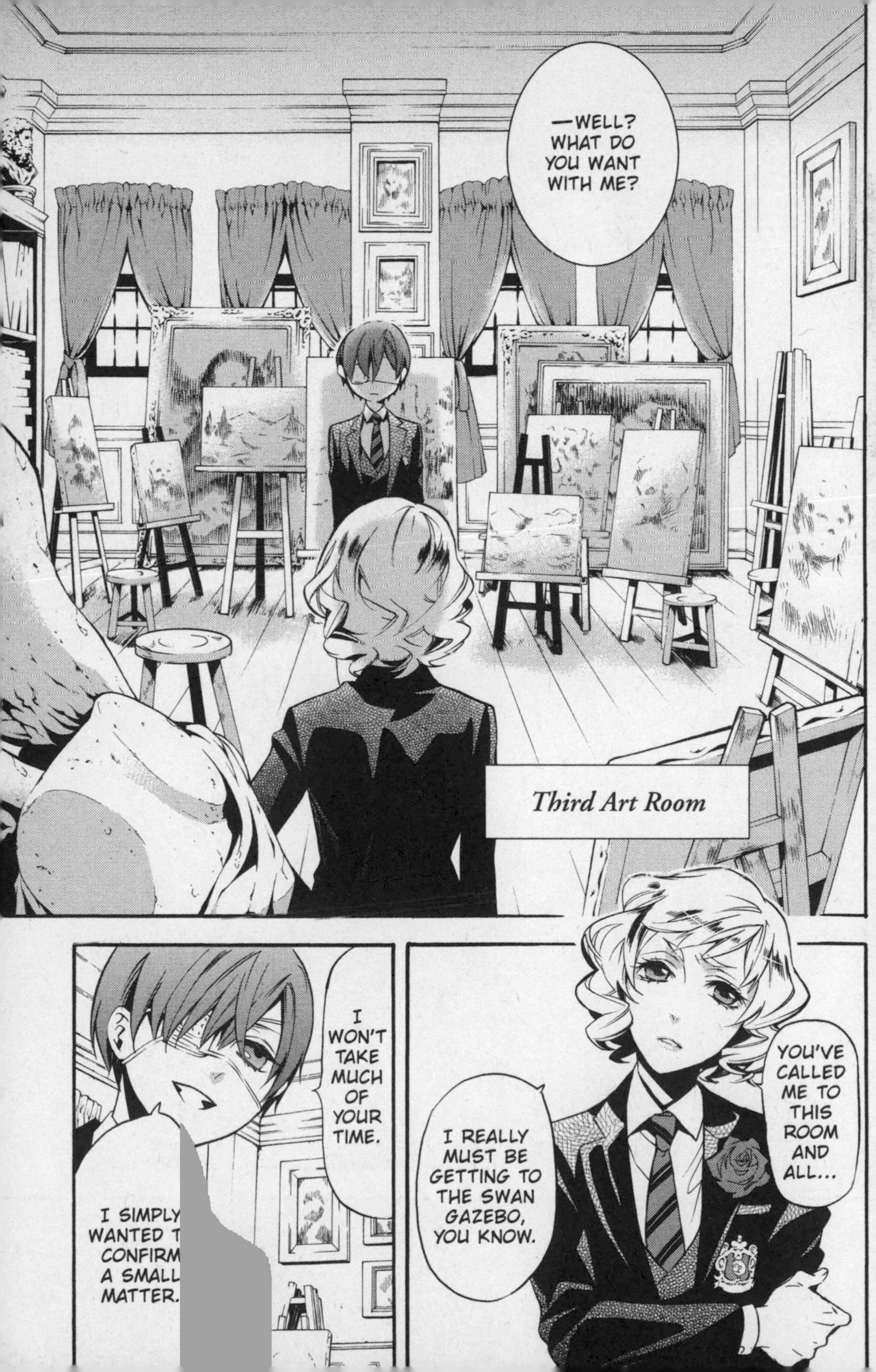
—WELL? WHAT DO YOU WANT WITH ME?
Third Art Room
YOU'VE CALLED ME TO THIS ROOM AND ALL...
I REALLY MUST BE GETTING TO THE SWAN GAZEBO, YOU KNOW.
I WON'T TAKE MUCH OF YOUR TIME.
I SIMPLY WANTED T CONFIRM A SMALL MATTER.

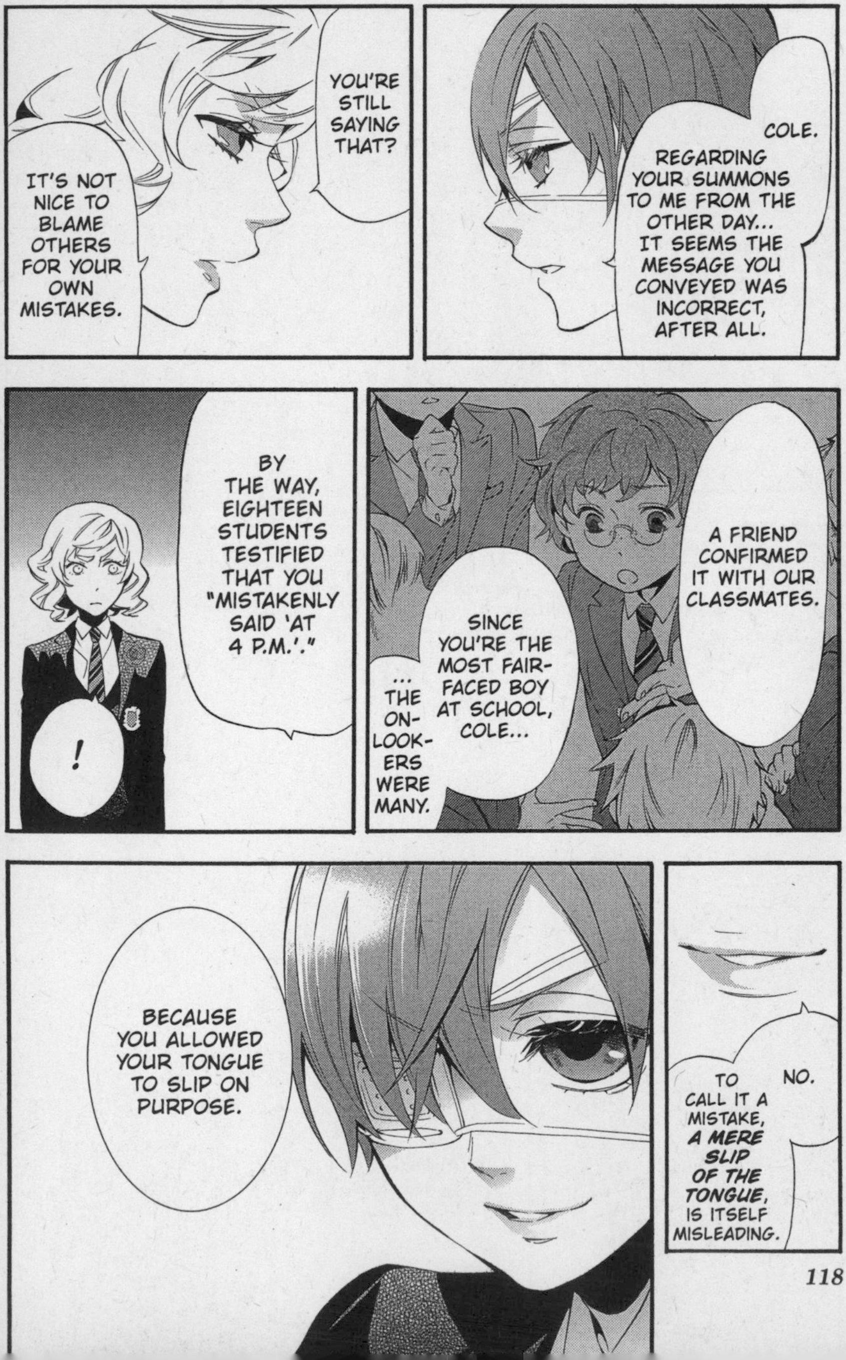
COLE. REGARDING YOUR SUMMONS TO ME FROM THE OTHER DAY... IT SEEMS THE MESSAGE YOU CONVEYED WAS INCORRECT, AFTER ALL.
YOU'RE STILL SAYING THAT?
IT'S NOT NICE TO BLAME OTHERS FOR YOUR OWN MISTAKES.
A FRIEND CONFIRMED IT WITH OUR CLASSMATES.
SINCE YOU'RE THE MOST FAIR-FACED BOY AT SCHOOL, COLE...
...THE ON-LOOKERS WERE MANY.
BY THE WAY, EIGHTEEN STUDENTS TESTIFIED THAT YOU "MISTAKENLY SAID 'AT 4 P.M.'."
!
NO.
TO CALL IT A MISTAKE, ***A MERE SLIP OF THE TONGUE***, IS ITSELF MISLEADING.
BECAUSE YOU ALLOWED YOUR TONGUE TO SLIP ON PURPOSE.

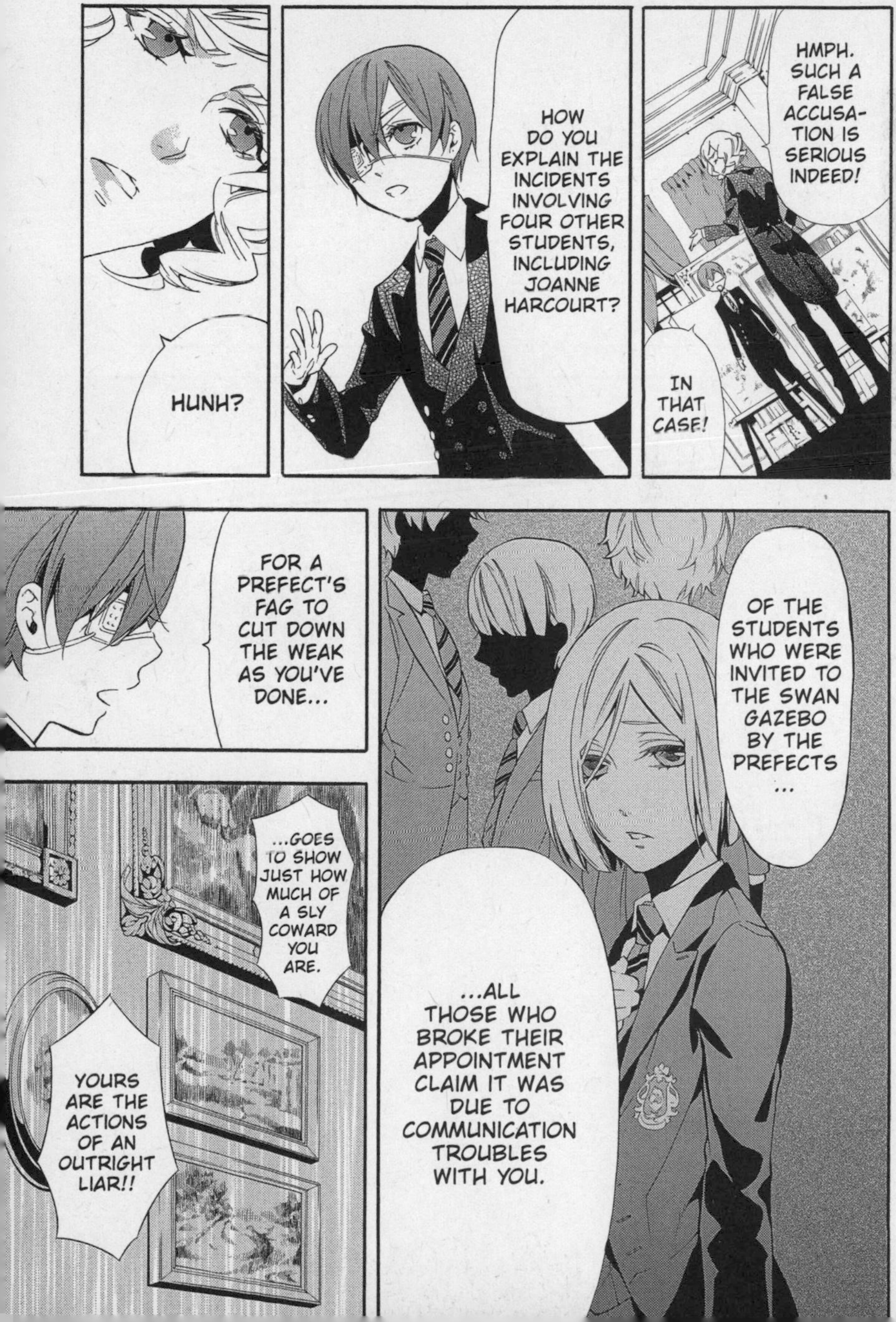
HMPH. SUCH A FALSE ACCUSATION IS SERIOUS INDEED!
IN THAT CASE!
HOW DO YOU EXPLAIN THE INCIDENTS INVOLVING FOUR OTHER STUDENTS, INCLUDING JOANNE HARCOURT?
HUNH?
OF THE STUDENTS WHO WERE INVITED TO THE SWAN GAZEBO BY THE PREFECTS...
...ALL THOSE WHO BROKE THEIR APPOINTMENT CLAIM IT WAS DUE TO COMMUNICATION TROUBLES WITH YOU.
FOR A PREFECT'S FAG TO CUT DOWN THE WEAK AS YOU'VE DONE...
...GOES TO SHOW JUST HOW MUCH OF A SLY COWARD YOU ARE.
YOURS ARE THE ACTIONS OF AN OUTRIGHT LIAR!!

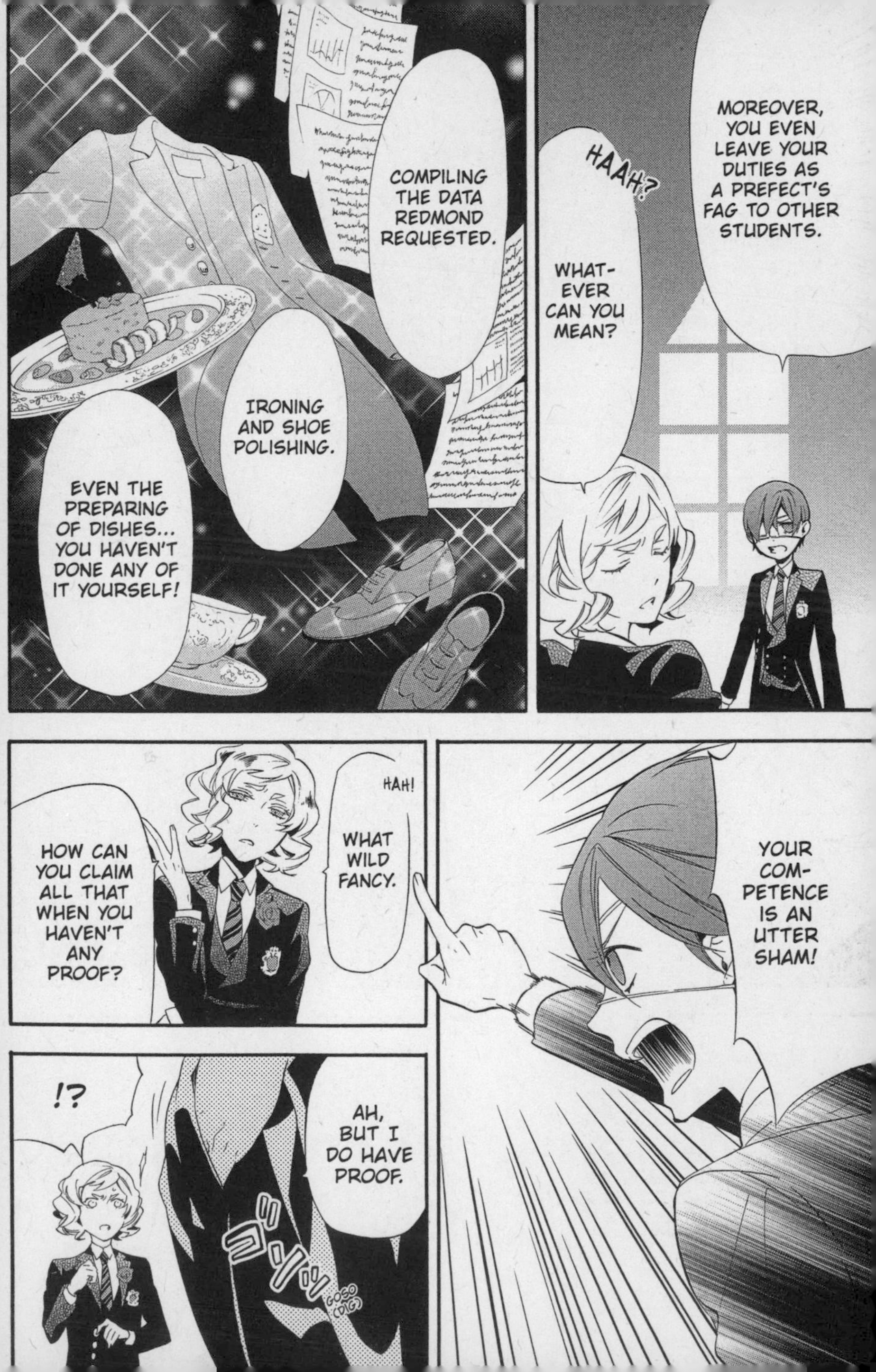
MOREOVER, YOU EVEN LEAVE YOUR DUTIES AS A PREFECT'S FAG TO OTHER STUDENTS.
HAAAH?
WHAT-EVER CAN YOU MEAN?
COMPILING THE DATA REDMOND REQUESTED.
IRONING AND SHOE POLISHING.
EVEN THE PREPARING OF DISHES... YOU HAVEN'T DONE ANY OF IT YOURSELF!
YOUR COM-PETENCE IS AN UTTER SHAM!
HAH!
WHAT WILD FANCY.
HOW CAN YOU CLAIM ALL THAT WHEN YOU HAVEN'T ANY PROOF?
AH, BUT I DO HAVE PROOF.
GOSO (DIG)
!?

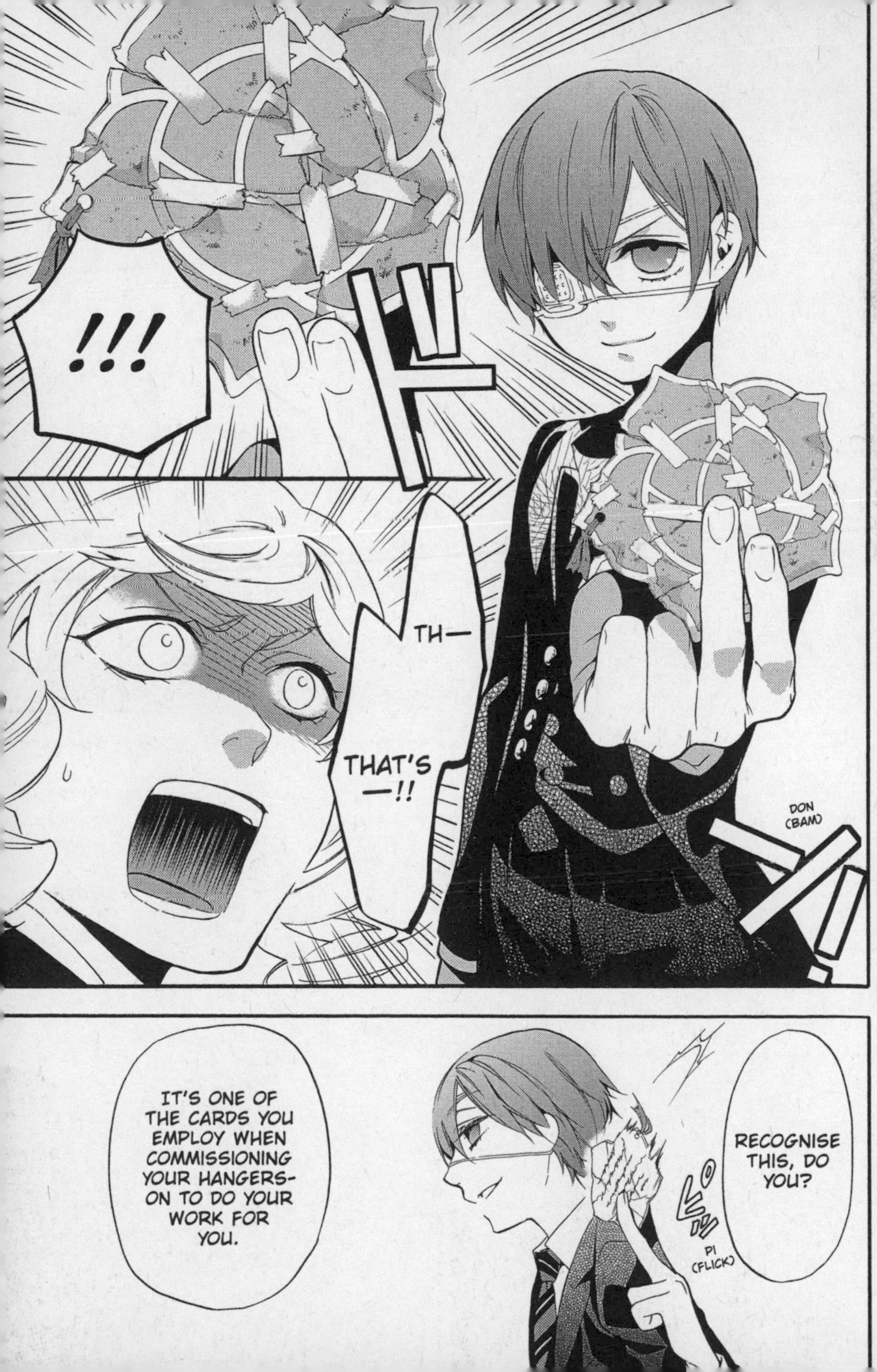
DON (BAM)
!!!
TH—
THAT'S—!!
RECOGNISE THIS, DO YOU?
PI (FLICK)
IT'S ONE OF THE CARDS YOU EMPLOY WHEN COMMISSIONING YOUR HANGERS-ON TO DO YOUR WORK FOR YOU.

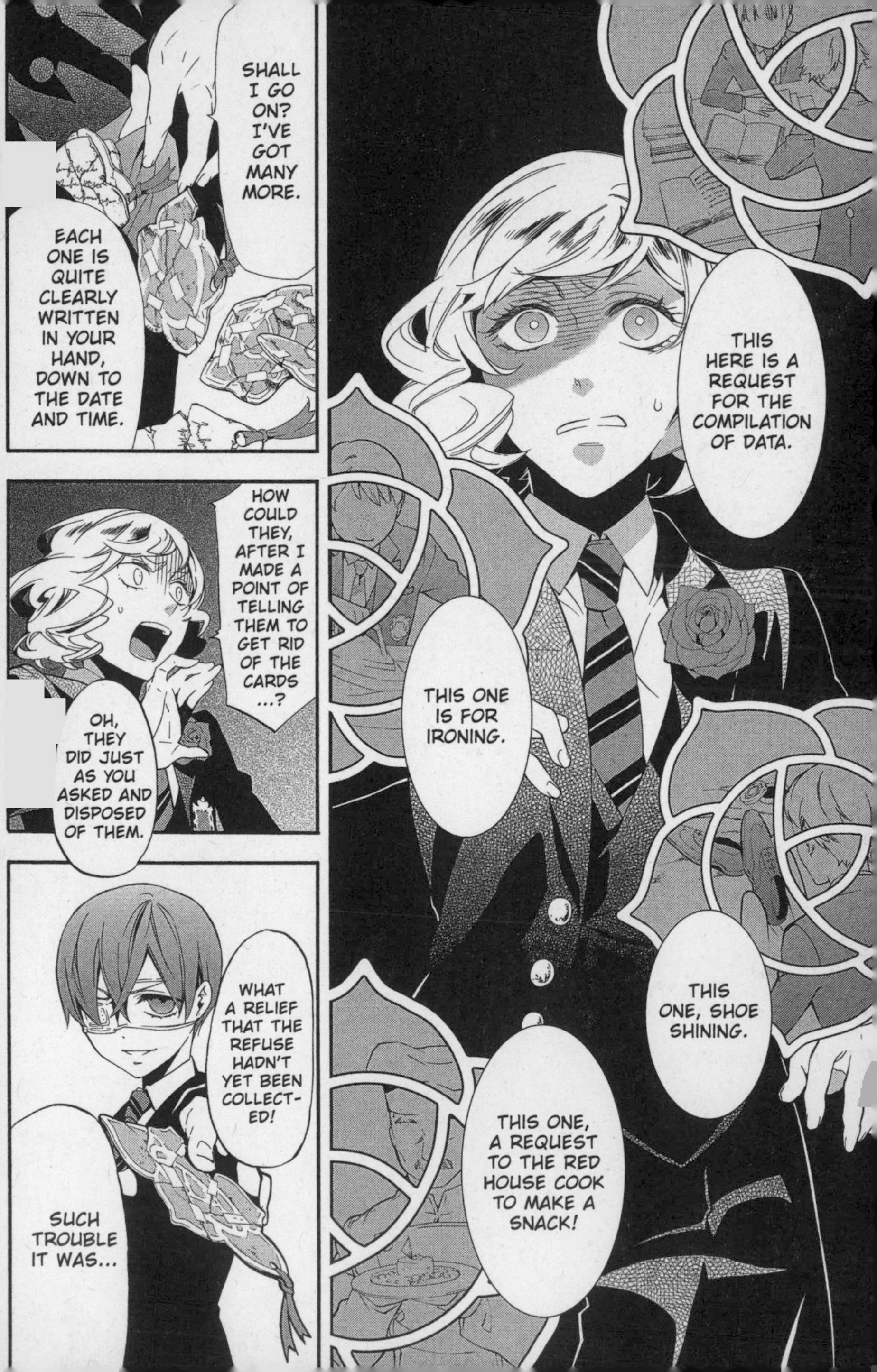
THIS HERE IS A REQUEST FOR THE COMPILATION OF DATA.
THIS ONE IS FOR IRONING.
THIS ONE, SHOE SHINING.
THIS ONE, A REQUEST TO THE RED HOUSE COOK TO MAKE A SNACK!
SHALL I GO ON? I'VE GOT MANY MORE.
EACH ONE IS QUITE CLEARLY WRITTEN IN YOUR HAND, DOWN TO THE DATE AND TIME.
HOW COULD THEY, AFTER I MADE A POINT OF TELLING THEM TO GET RID OF THE CARDS ...?
OH, THEY DID JUST AS YOU ASKED AND DISPOSED OF THEM.
WHAT A RELIEF THAT THE REFUSE HADN'T YET BEEN COLLECT-ED!
SUCH TROUBLE IT WAS...

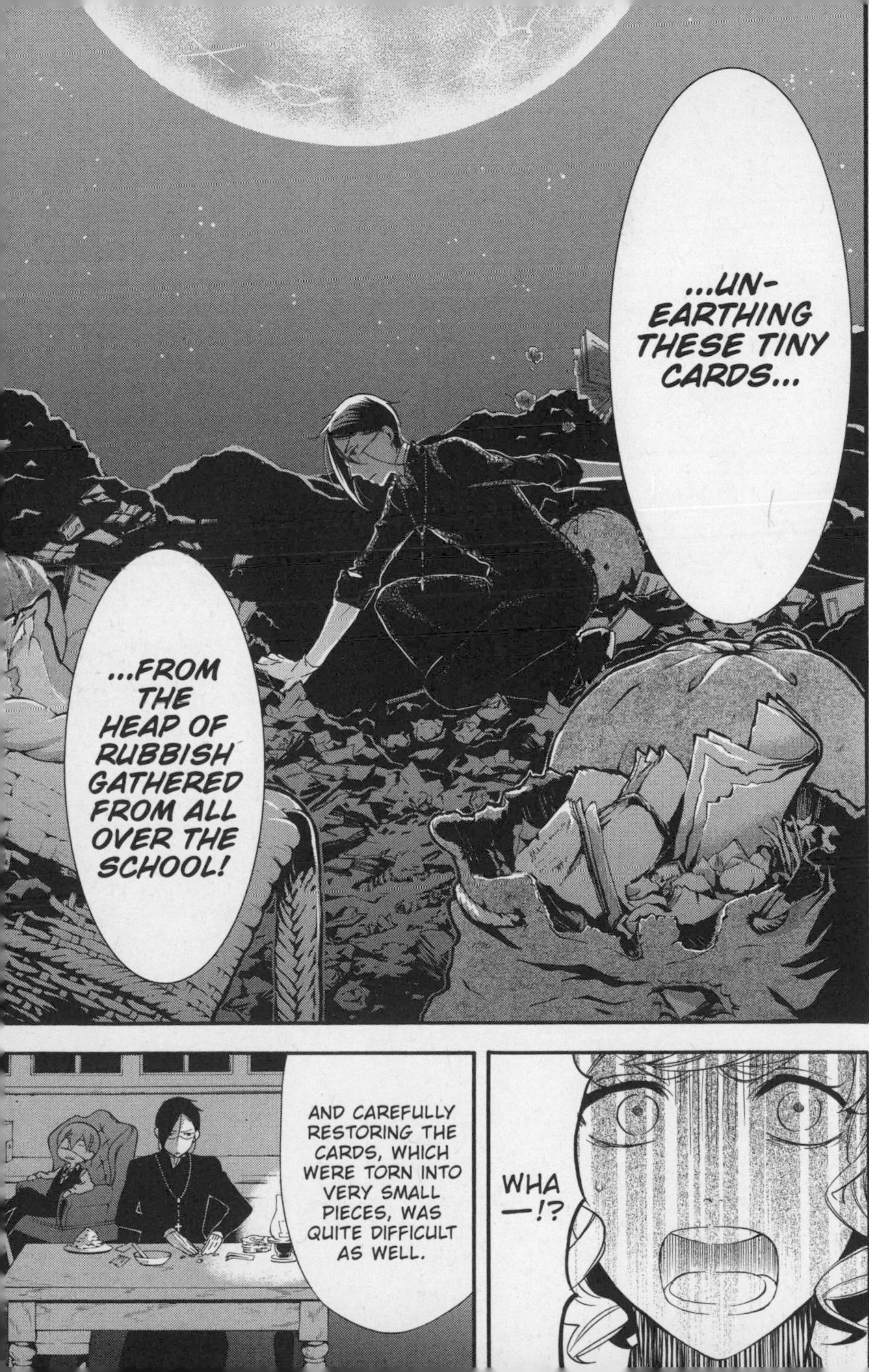
...UN-EARTHING THESE TINY CARDS...
...FROM THE HEAP OF RUBBISH GATHERED FROM ALL OVER THE SCHOOL!
AND CAREFULLY RESTORING THE CARDS, WHICH WERE TORN INTO VERY SMALL PIECES, WAS QUITE DIFFICULT AS WELL.
WHA—!?

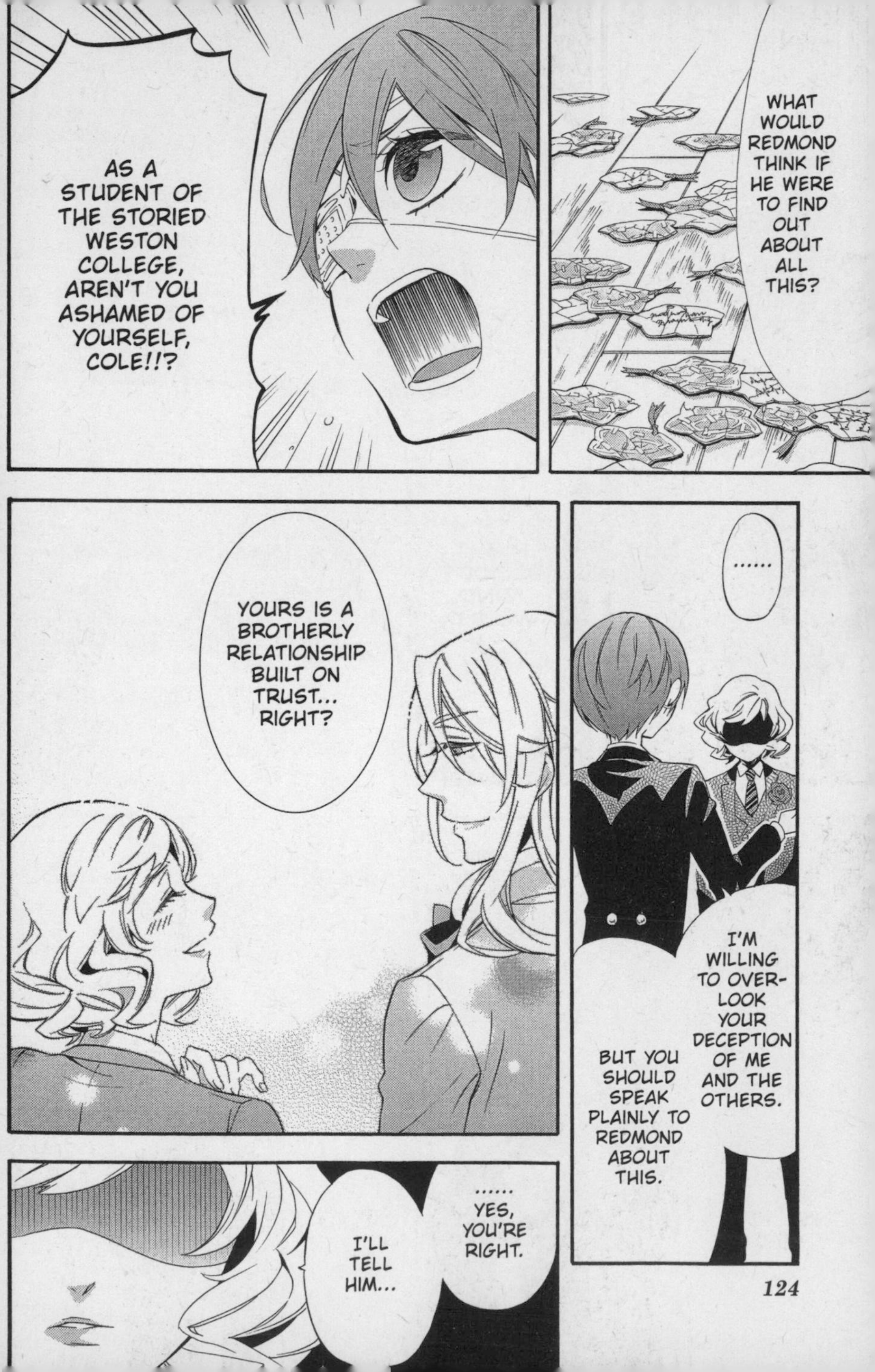
WHAT WOULD REDMOND THINK IF HE WERE TO FIND OUT ABOUT ALL THIS?
AS A STUDENT OF THE STORIED WESTON COLLEGE, AREN'T YOU ASHAMED OF YOURSELF, COLE!!?
......
I'M WILLING TO OVER-LOOK YOUR DECEPTION OF ME AND THE OTHERS.
BUT YOU SHOULD SPEAK PLAINLY TO REDMOND ABOUT THIS.
YOURS IS A BROTHERLY RELATIONSHIP BUILT ON TRUST... RIGHT?
...... YES, YOU'RE RIGHT.
I'LL TELL HIM...

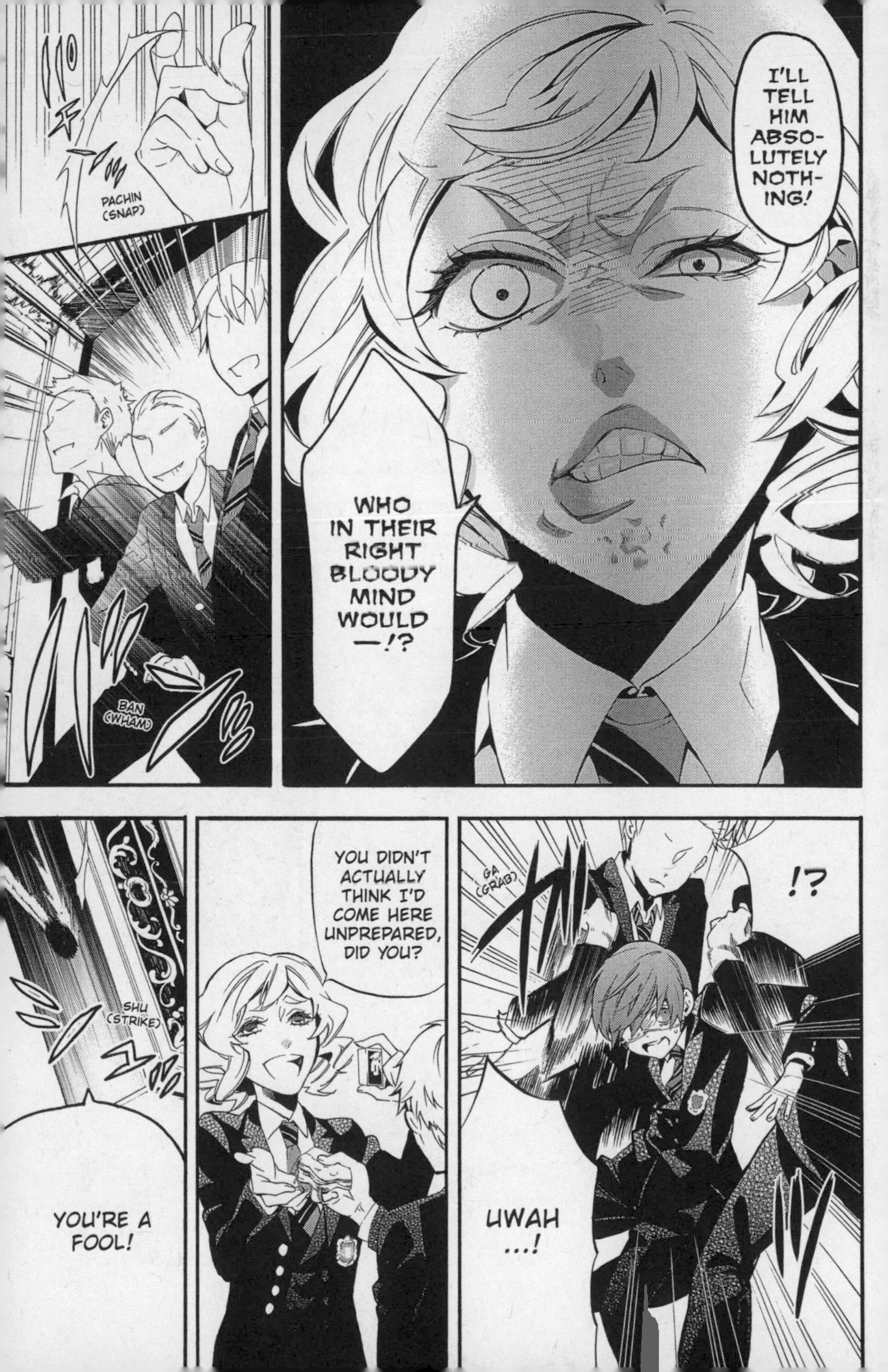
I'LL TELL HIM ABSO-LUTELY NOTH-ING!
WHO IN THEIR RIGHT BLOODY MIND WOULD —!?
PACHIN (SNAP)
BAN (WHAM)
!?
GA (GRAB)
UWAH ...!
YOU DIDN'T ACTUALLY THINK I'D COME HERE UNPREPARED, DID YOU?
SHU (STRIKE)
YOU'RE A FOOL!

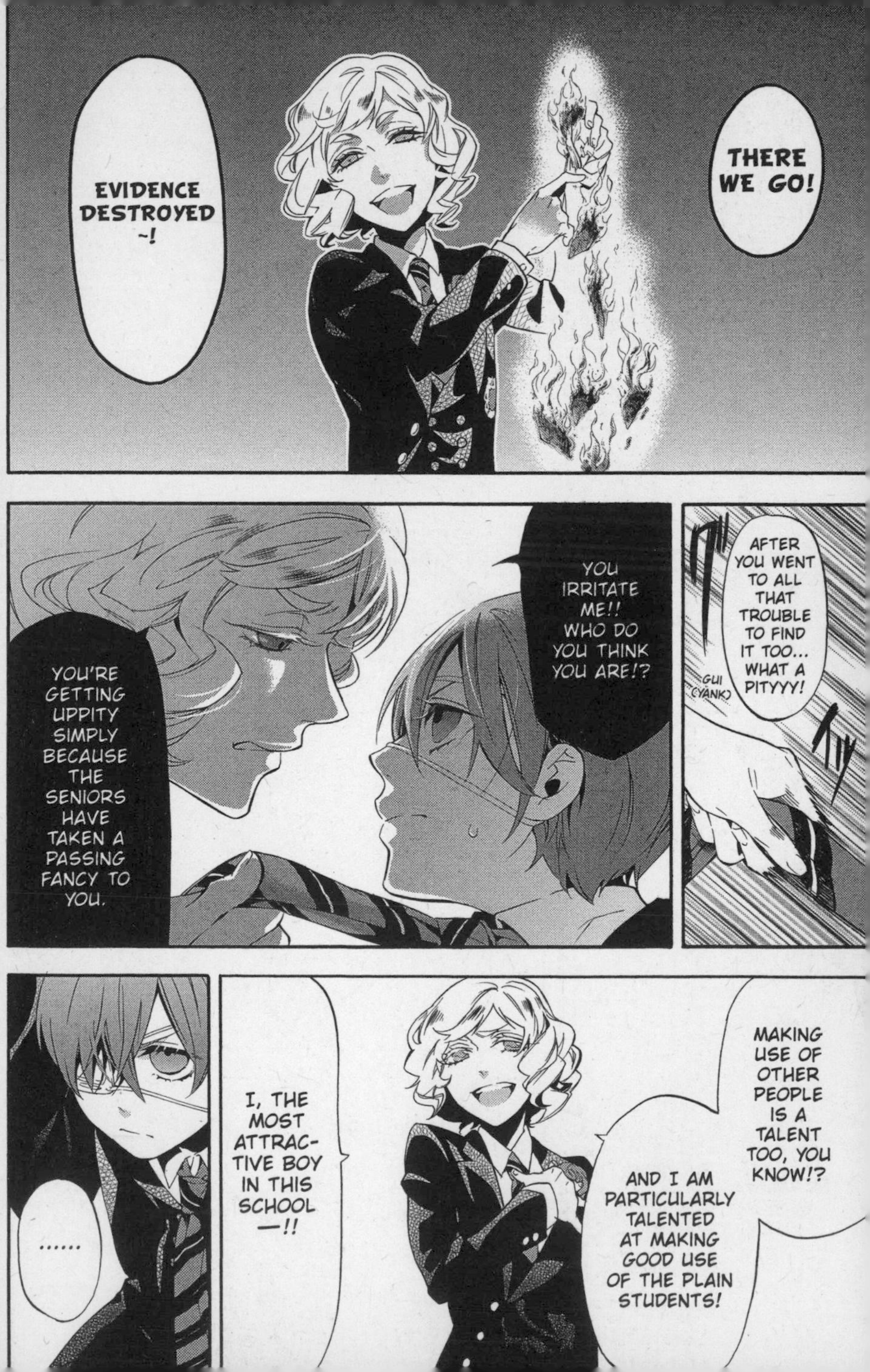
THERE WE GO!
EVIDENCE DESTROYED ~!
GUI (YANK)
AFTER YOU WENT TO ALL THAT TROUBLE TO FIND IT TOO... WHAT A PITYYY!
YOU IRRITATE ME!! WHO DO YOU THINK YOU ARE!?
YOU'RE GETTING UPPITY SIMPLY BECAUSE THE SENIORS HAVE TAKEN A PASSING FANCY TO YOU.
MAKING USE OF OTHER PEOPLE IS A TALENT TOO, YOU KNOW!?
AND I AM PARTICULARLY TALENTED AT MAKING GOOD USE OF THE PLAIN STUDENTS!
I, THE MOST ATTRACTIVE BOY IN THIS SCHOOL —!!
......

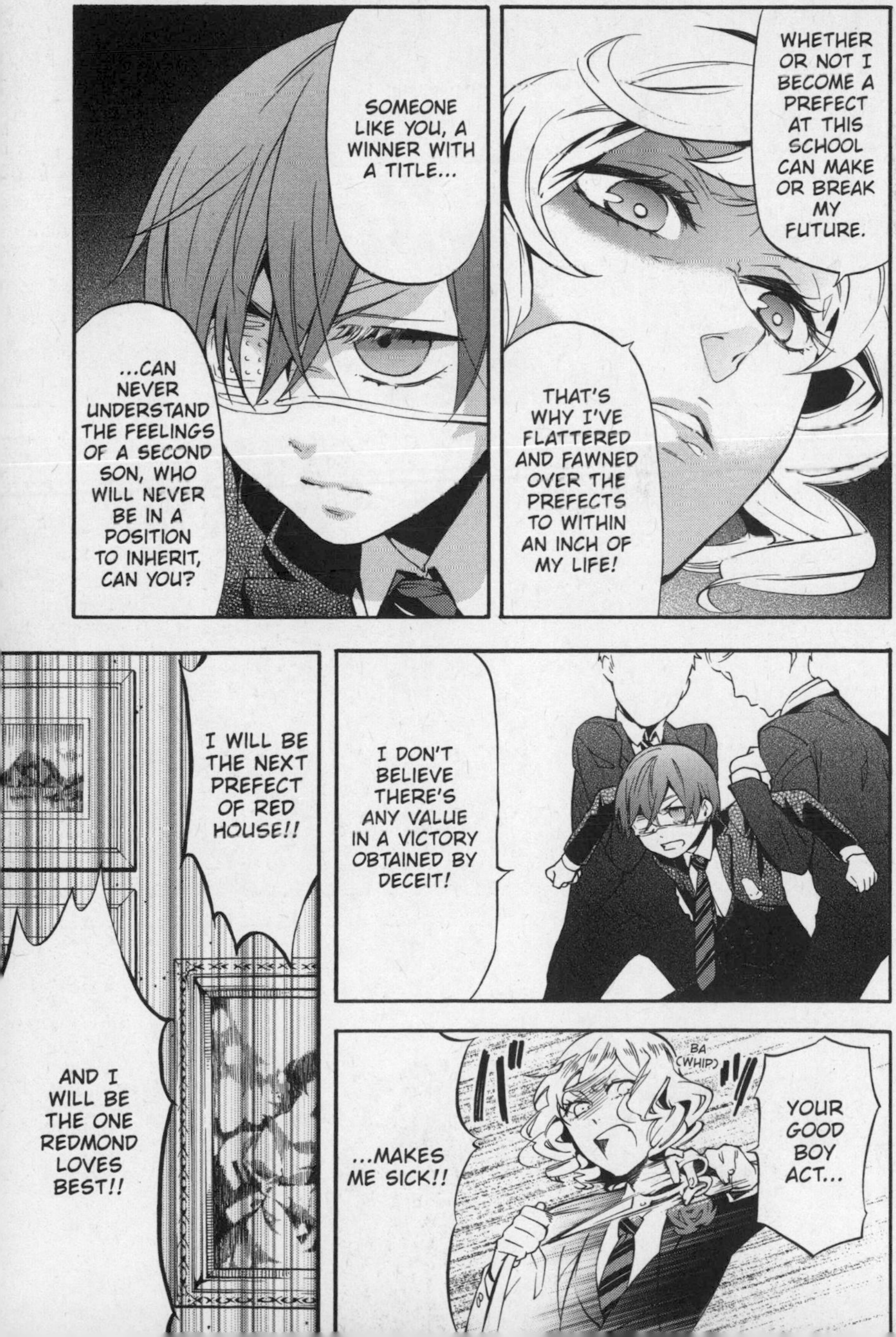
WHETHER OR NOT I BECOME A PREFECT AT THIS SCHOOL CAN MAKE OR BREAK MY FUTURE.
THAT'S WHY I'VE FLATTERED AND FAWNED OVER THE PREFECTS TO WITHIN AN INCH OF MY LIFE!
SOMEONE LIKE YOU, A WINNER WITH A TITLE...
...CAN NEVER UNDERSTAND THE FEELINGS OF A SECOND SON, WHO WILL NEVER BE IN A POSITION TO INHERIT, CAN YOU?
I DON'T BELIEVE THERE'S ANY VALUE IN A VICTORY OBTAINED BY DECEIT!
YOUR GOOD BOY ACT...
BA (WHIP)
...MAKES ME SICK!!
I WILL BE THE NEXT PREFECT OF RED HOUSE!!
AND I WILL BE THE ONE REDMOND LOVES BEST!!

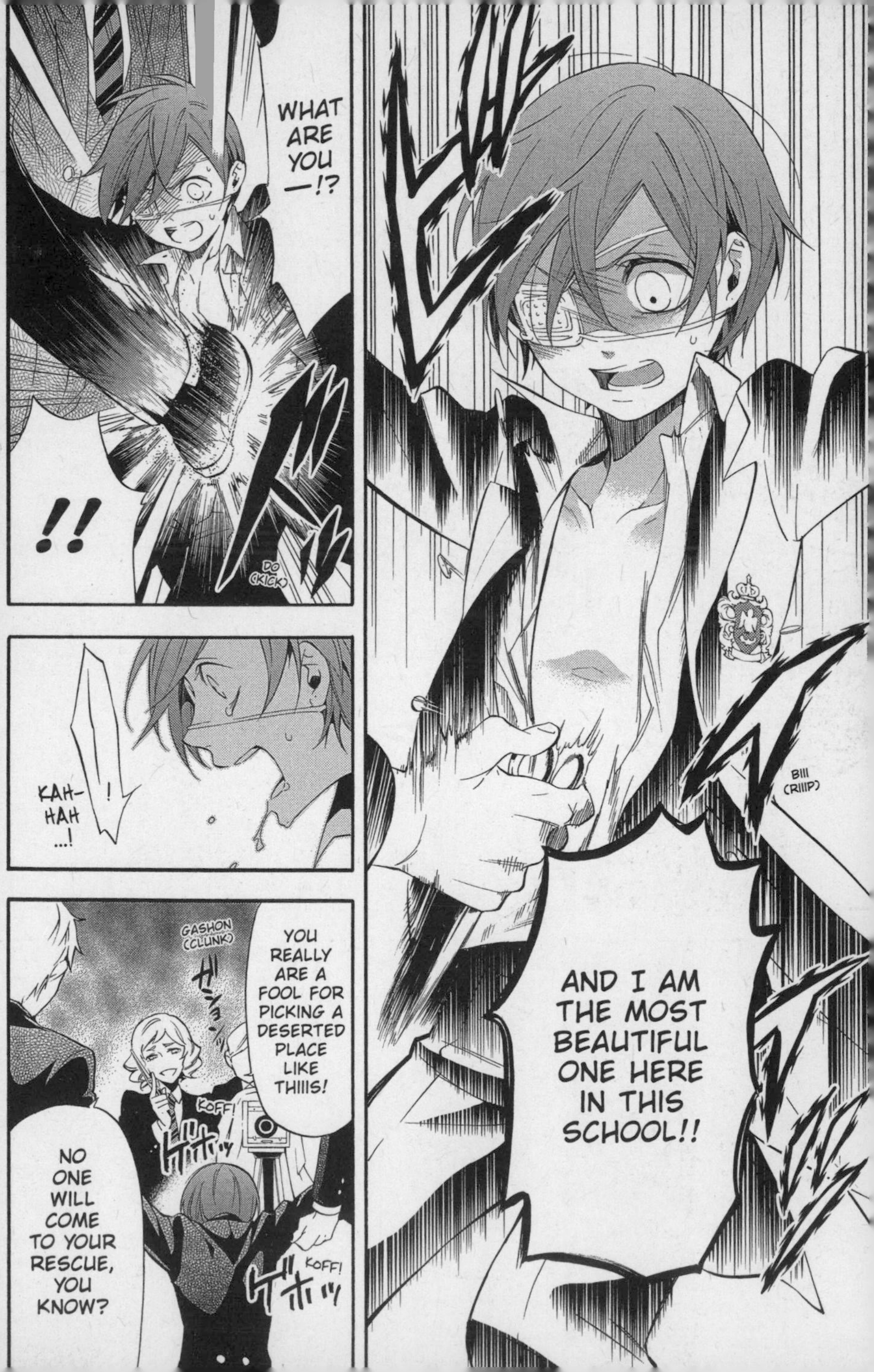

BIII (RIIIP)
AND I AM THE MOST BEAUTIFUL ONE HERE IN THIS SCHOOL!!
WHAT ARE YOU—!?
!!
DO (KICK)
!
KAH-HAH ...!
GASHON (CLUNK)
YOU REALLY ARE A FOOL FOR PICKING A DESERTED PLACE LIKE THIIIS!
KOFF!
KOFF!
NO ONE WILL COME TO YOUR RESCUE, YOU KNOW?

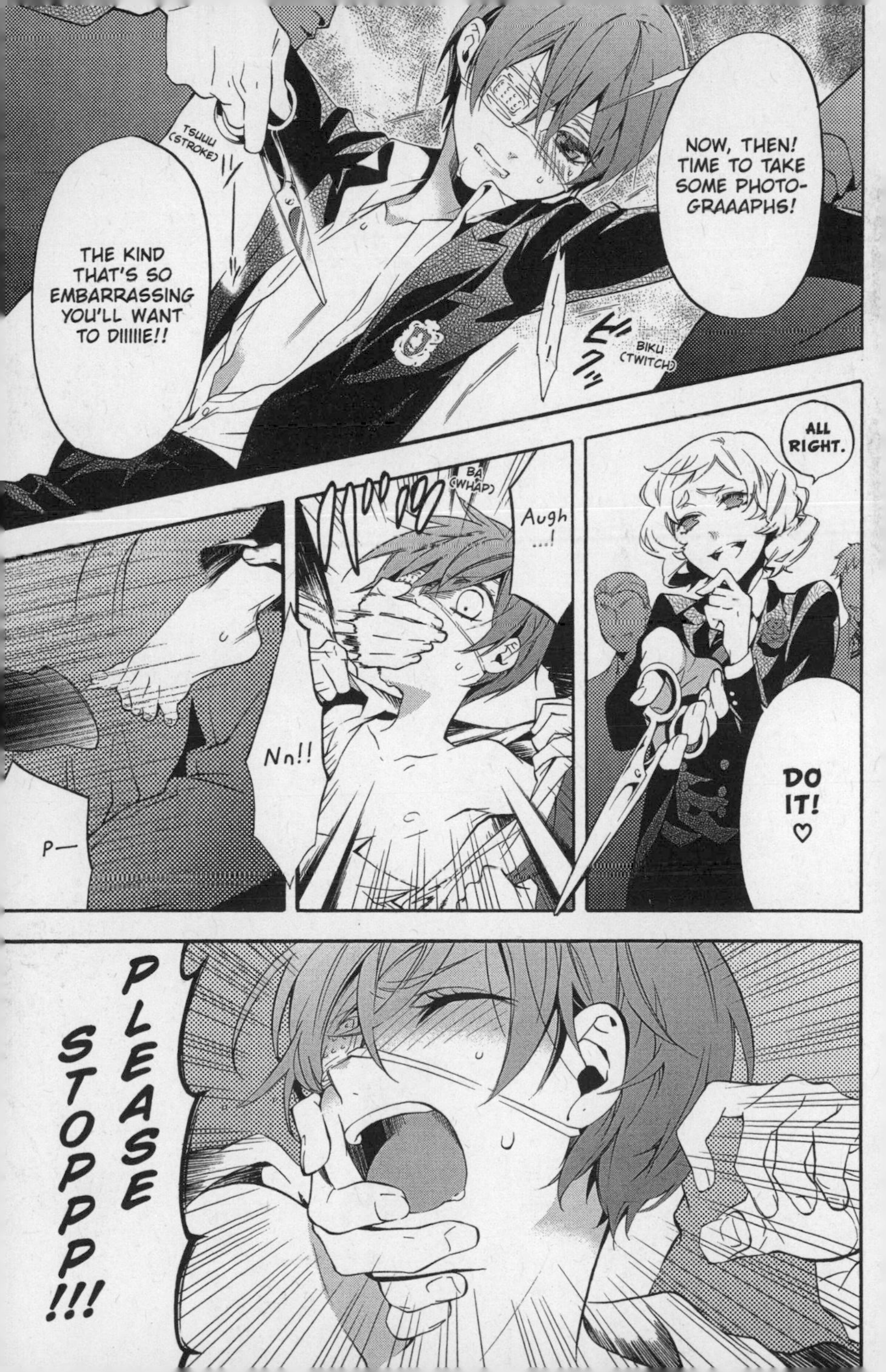

NOW, THEN! TIME TO TAKE SOME PHOTO-GRAAAPHS!
TSUUU (STROKE)
THE KIND THAT'S SO EMBARRASSING YOU'LL WANT TO DIIIIIE!!
BIKU (TWITCH)
ALL RIGHT.
DO IT! ♡
BA (WHAP)
Augh ...!
Nn!!
P—
PLEASE STOPPP!!!

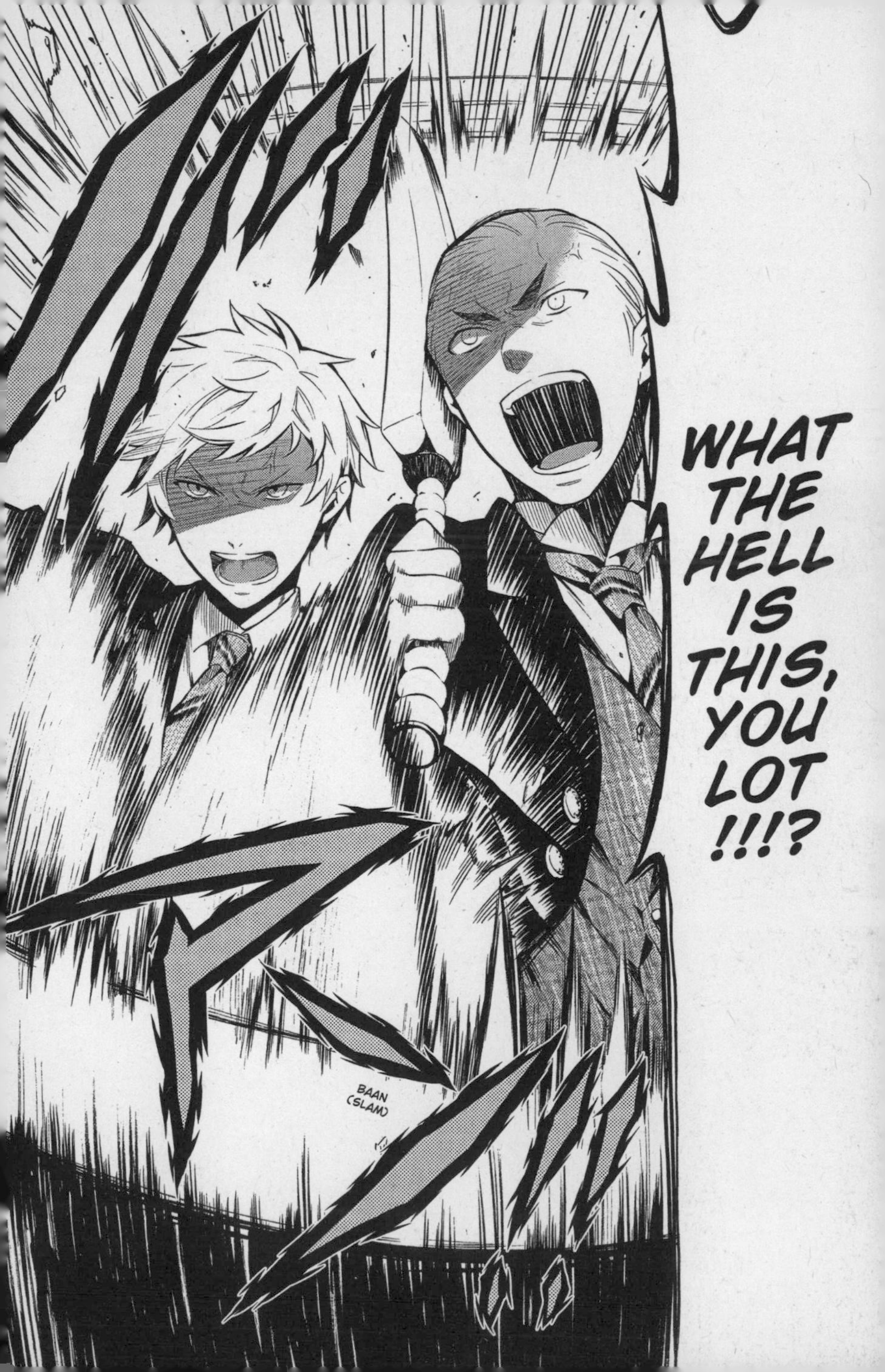
WHAT THE HELL IS THIS, YOU LOT !!!?
BAAN (SLAM)

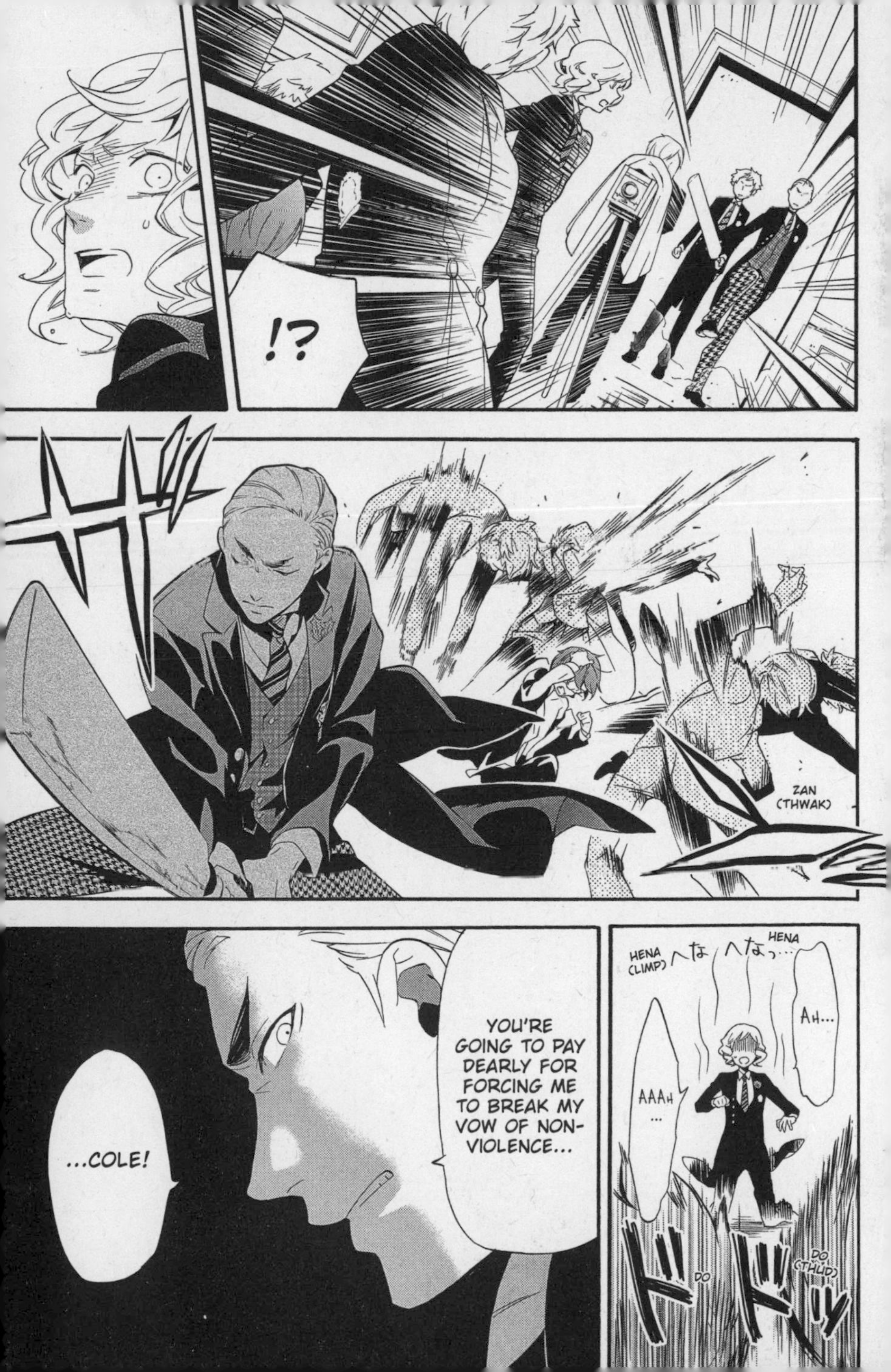

!?
ZAN (THWAK)
HENA へなっ…
HENA (LIMP) へな
AH...
AAAH ...
DO (THUD)
DO
YOU'RE GOING TO PAY DEARLY FOR FORCING ME TO BREAK MY VOW OF NON-VIOLENCE...
...COLE!

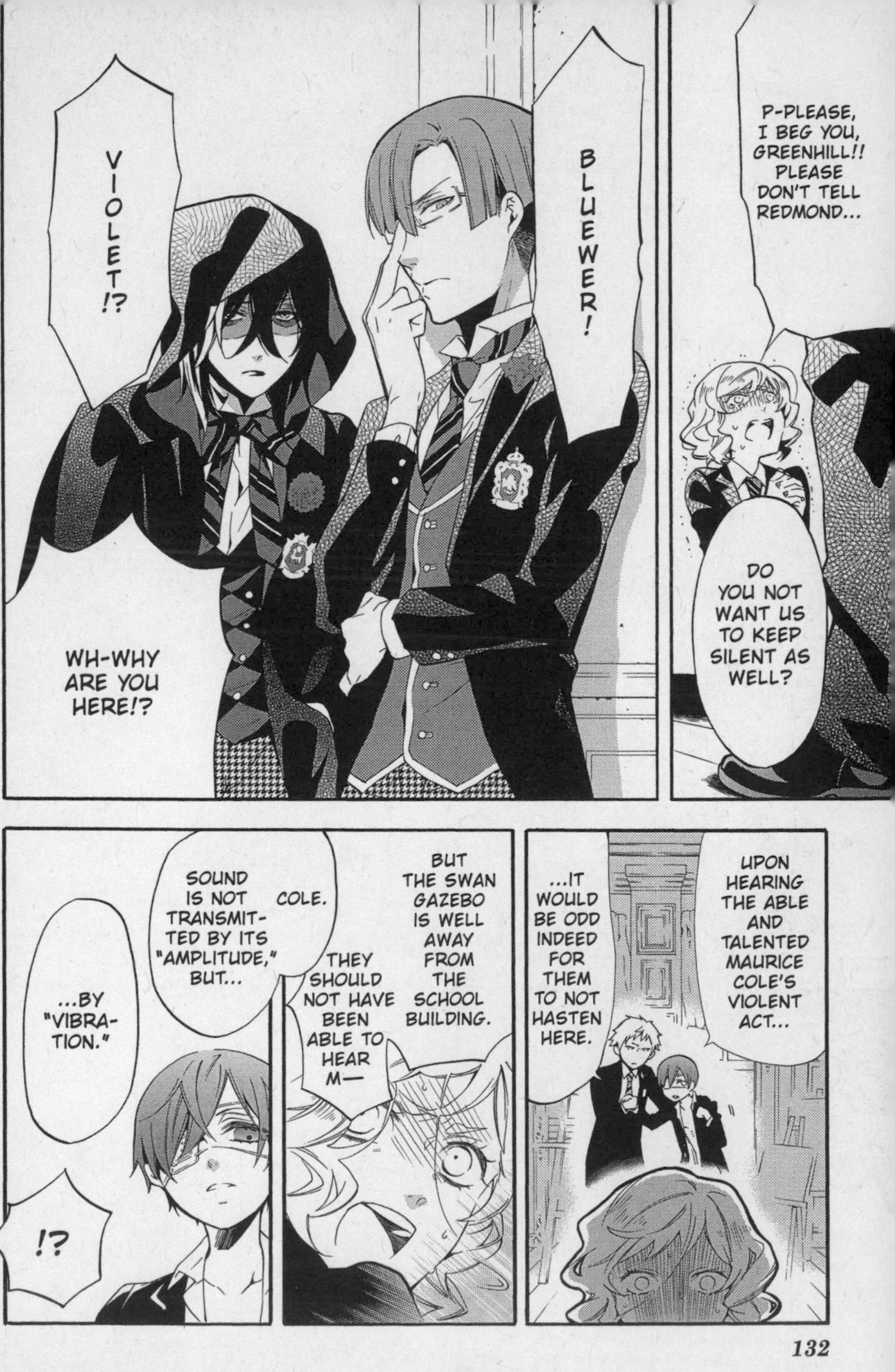
P-PLEASE, I BEG YOU, GREENHILL!! PLEASE DON'T TELL REDMOND...
DO YOU NOT WANT US TO KEEP SILENT AS WELL?
BLUEWER!
VIOLET!?
WH-WHY ARE YOU HERE!?
UPON HEARING THE ABLE AND TALENTED MAURICE COLE'S VIOLENT ACT...
...IT WOULD BE ODD INDEED FOR THEM TO NOT HASTEN HERE.
BUT THE SWAN GAZEBO IS WELL AWAY FROM THE SCHOOL BUILDING.
THEY SHOULD NOT HAVE BEEN ABLE TO HEAR M—
COLE.
SOUND IS NOT TRANSMIT-TED BY ITS "AMPLITUDE," BUT...
...BY "VIBRA-TION."
!?

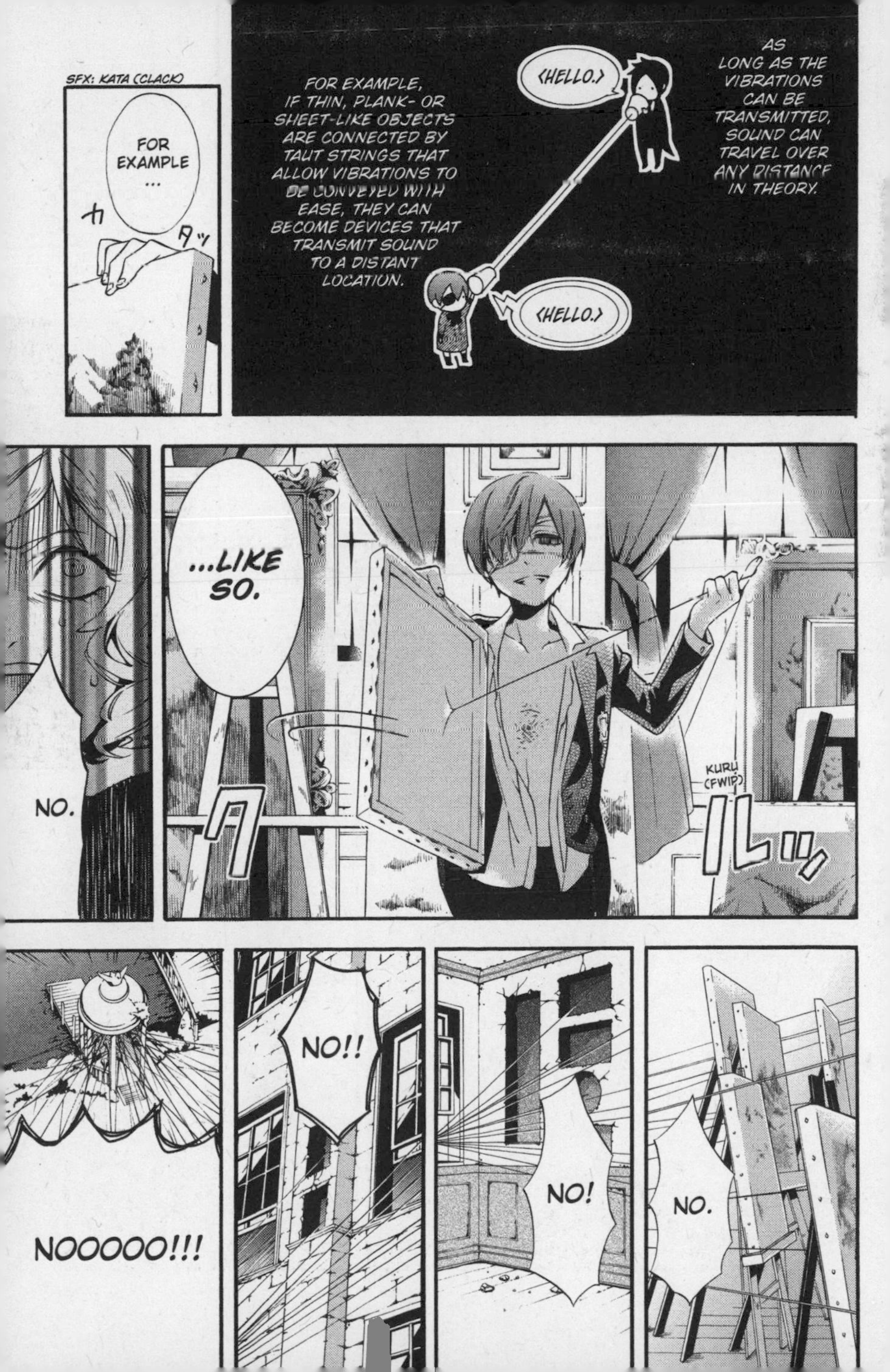
AS LONG AS THE VIBRATIONS CAN BE TRANSMITTED, SOUND CAN TRAVEL OVER ANY DISTANCE IN THEORY.
‹HELLO.›
FOR EXAMPLE, IF THIN, PLANK- OR SHEET-LIKE OBJECTS ARE CONNECTED BY TAUT STRINGS THAT ALLOW VIBRATIONS TO BE CONVEYED WITH EASE, THEY CAN BECOME DEVICES THAT TRANSMIT SOUND TO A DISTANT LOCATION.
‹HELLO.›
SFX: KATA (CLACK)
FOR EXAMPLE ...
...LIKE SO.
KURU (FWIP)
NO.
NO.
NO!
NO!!
NOOOOO!!!

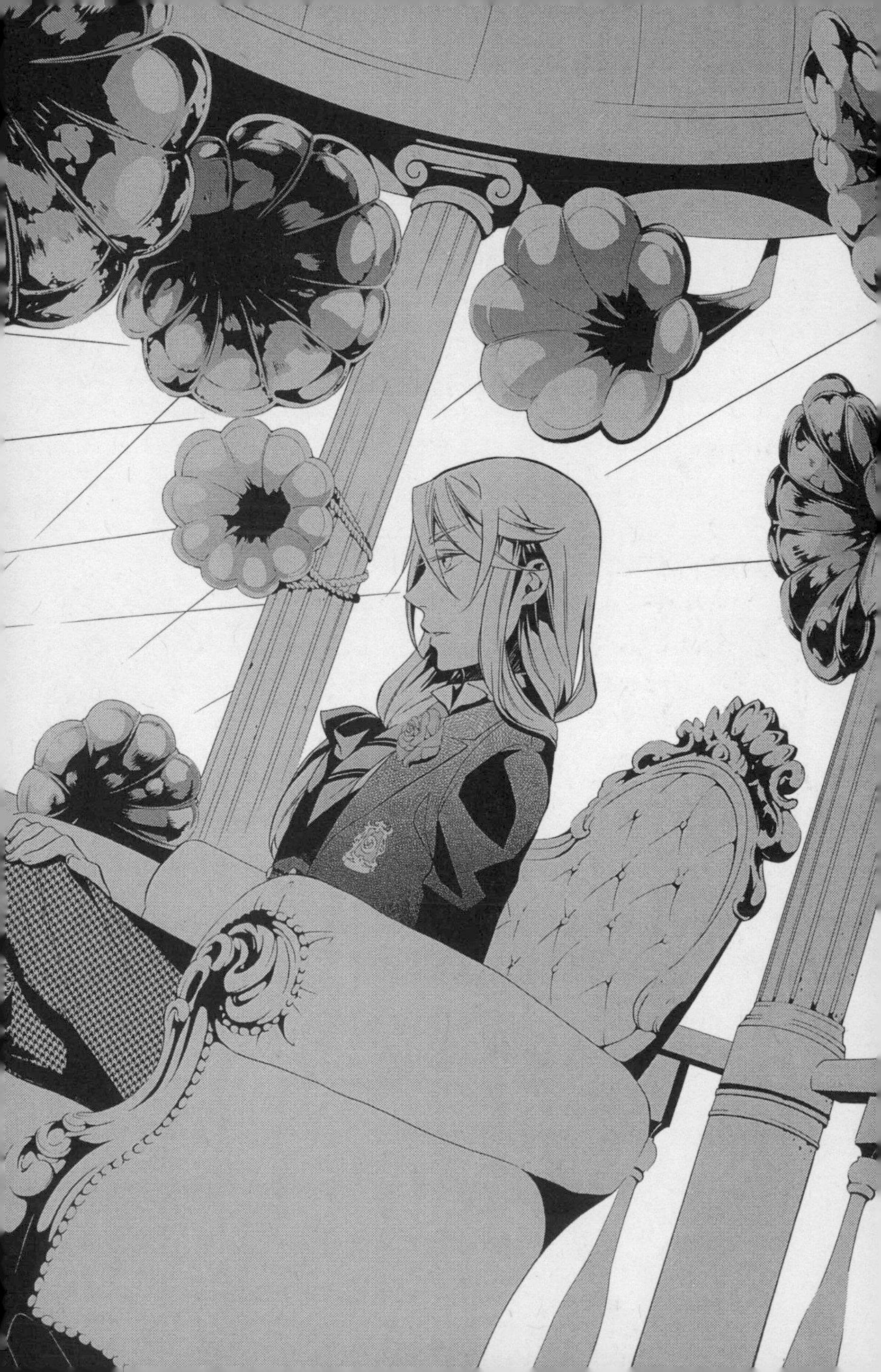

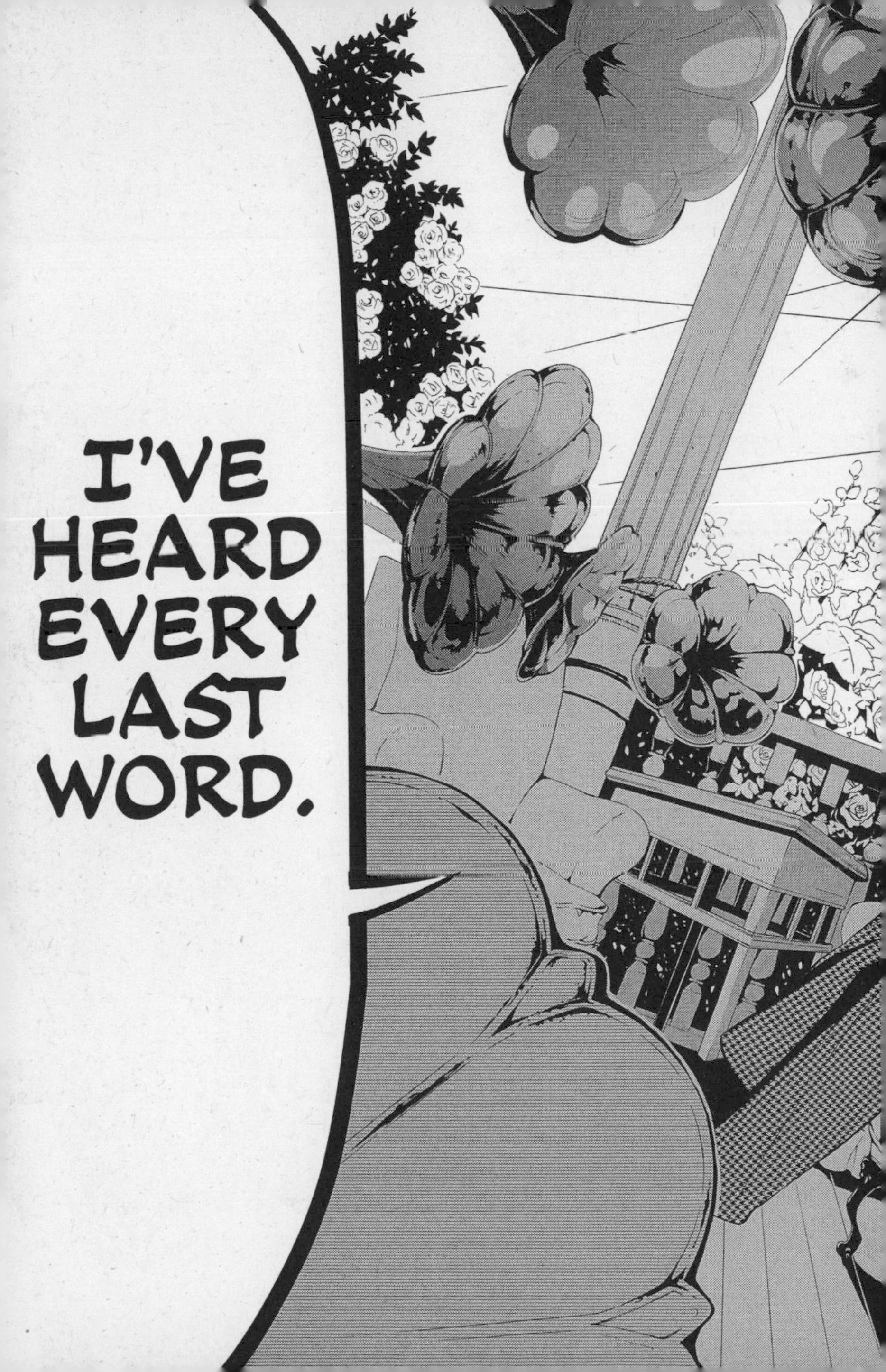
I'VE HEARD EVERY LAST WORD.

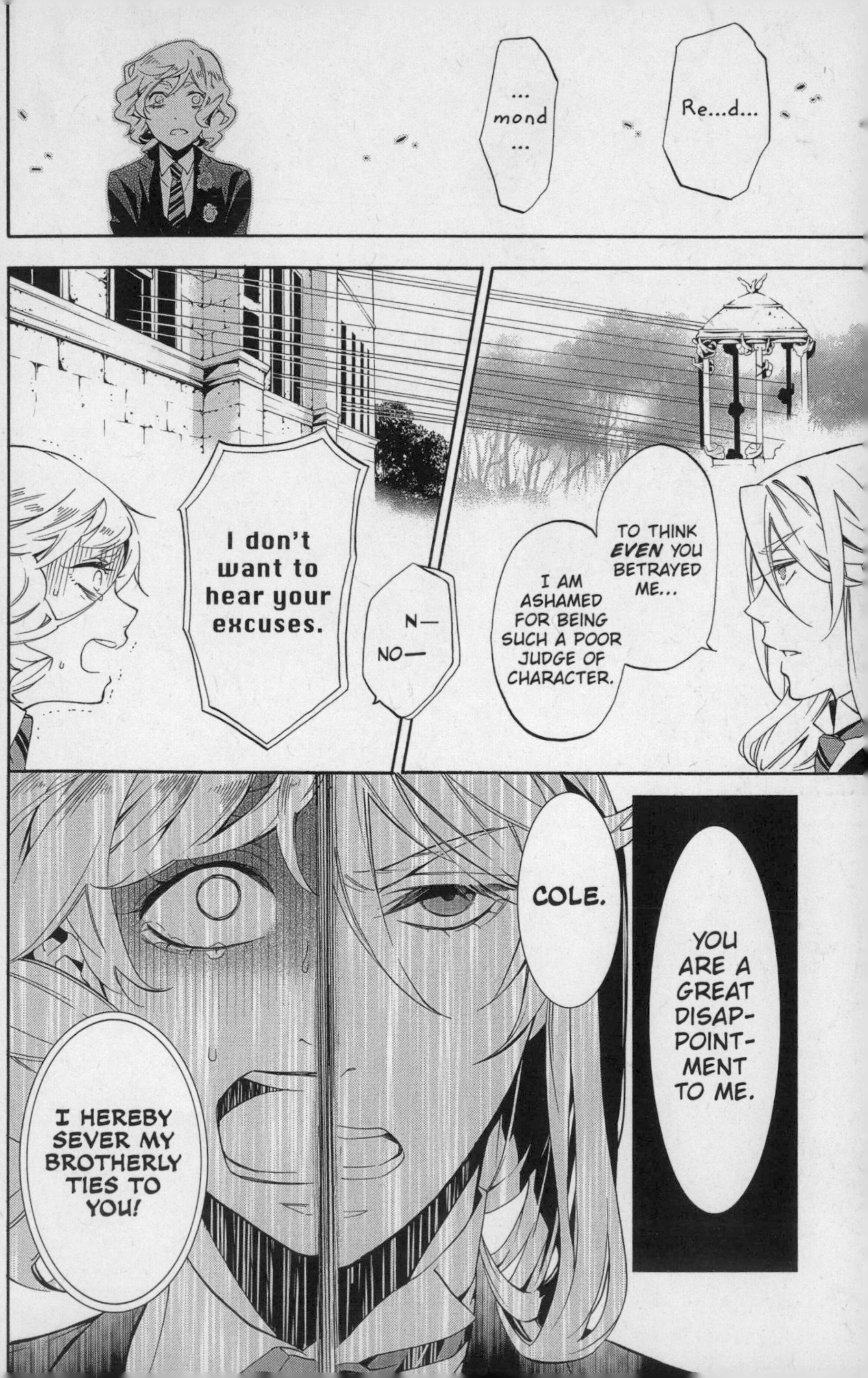
Re...d...
... mond ...
TO THINK EVEN YOU BETRAYED ME...
I AM ASHAMED FOR BEING SUCH A POOR JUDGE OF CHARACTER.
N— NO—
I don't want to hear your excuses.
YOU ARE A GREAT DISAPPOINTMENT TO ME.
COLE.
I HEREBY SEVER MY BROTHERLY TIES TO YOU!

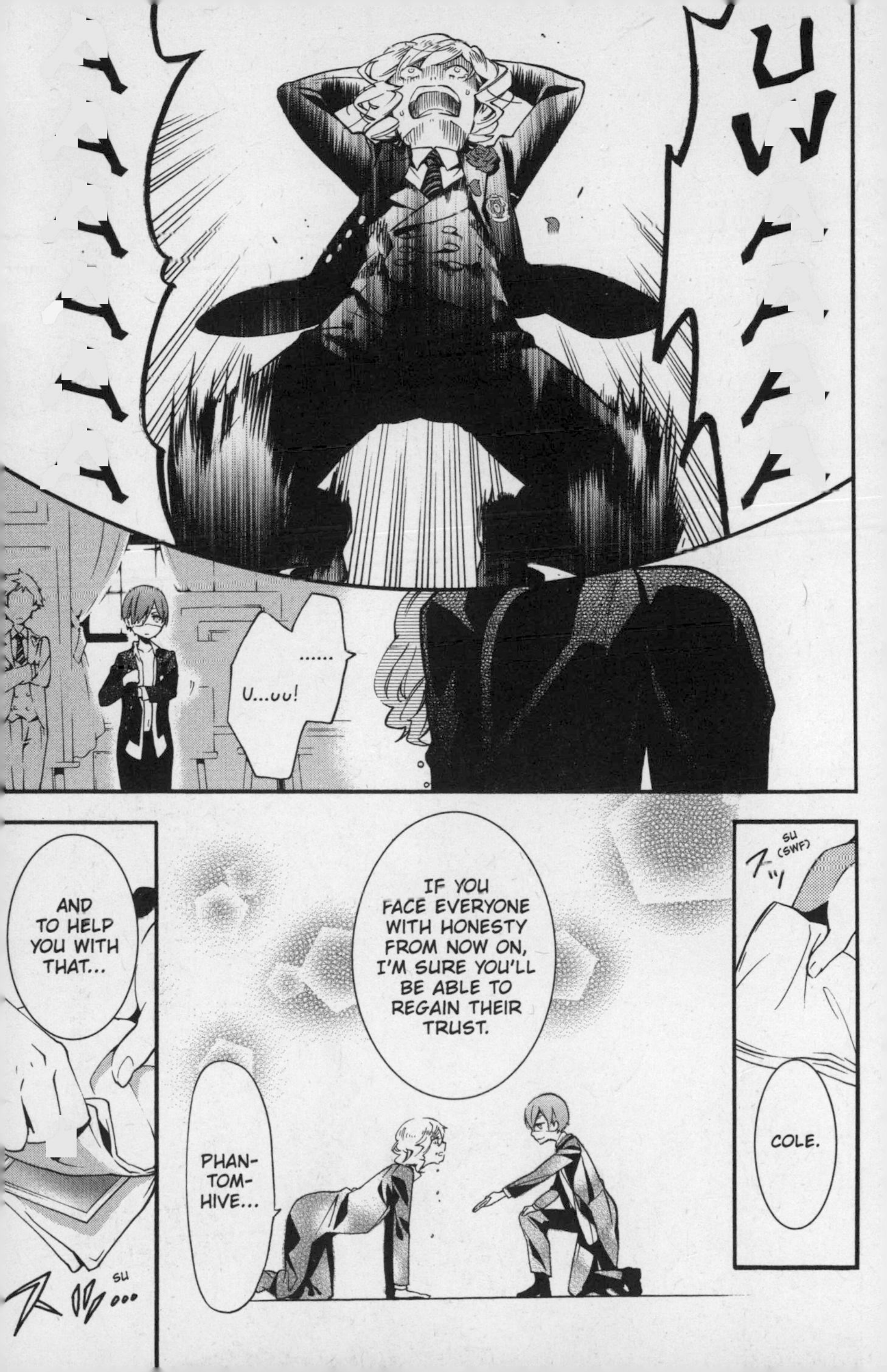
......
U...uu!
SU (SWF)
COLE.
IF YOU FACE EVERYONE WITH HONESTY FROM NOW ON, I'M SURE YOU'LL BE ABLE TO REGAIN THEIR TRUST.
PHAN-TOM-HIVE...
AND TO HELP YOU WITH THAT...
SU

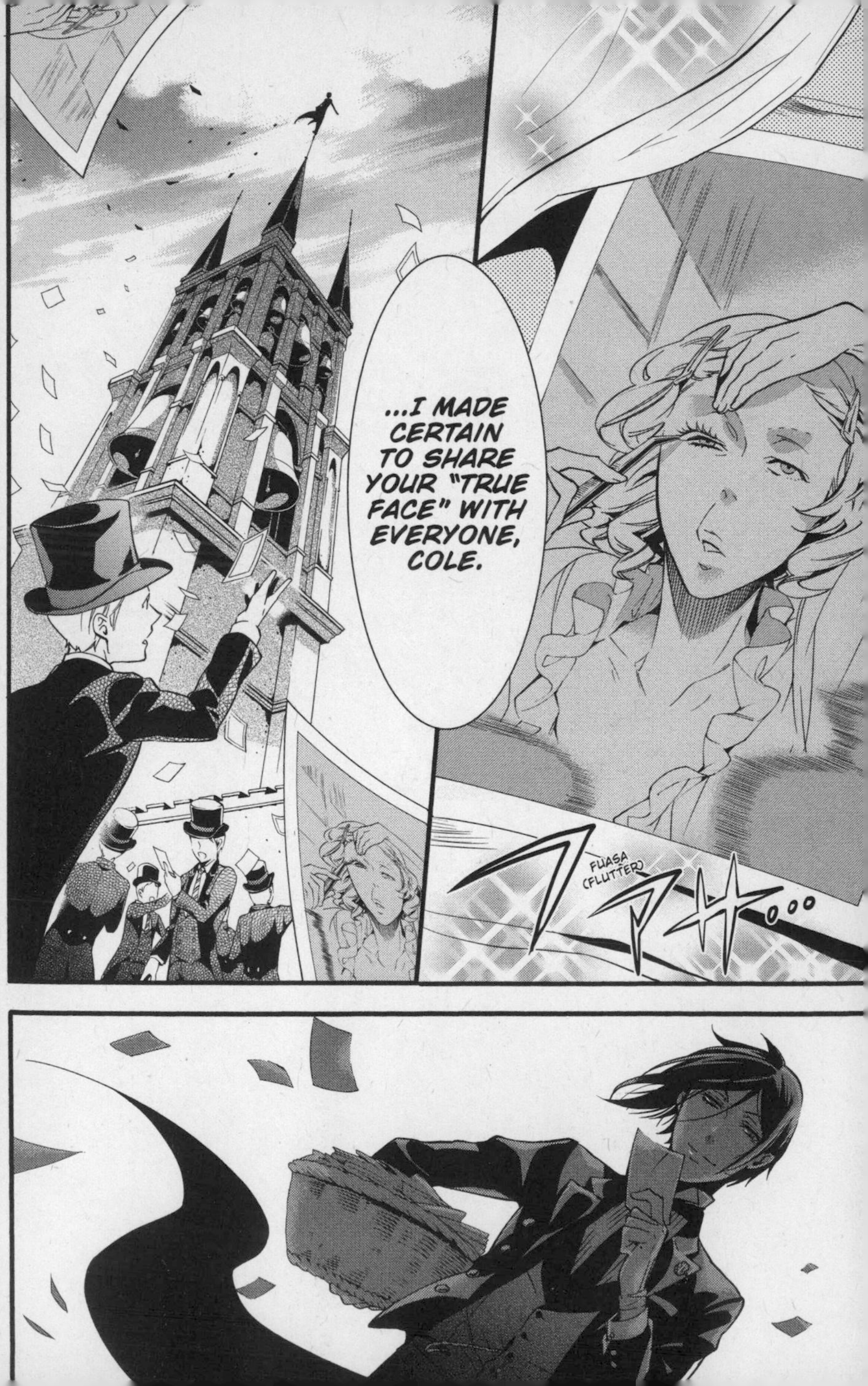
...I MADE CERTAIN TO SHARE YOUR "TRUE FACE" WITH EVERYONE, COLE.
FUASA (FLUTTER)

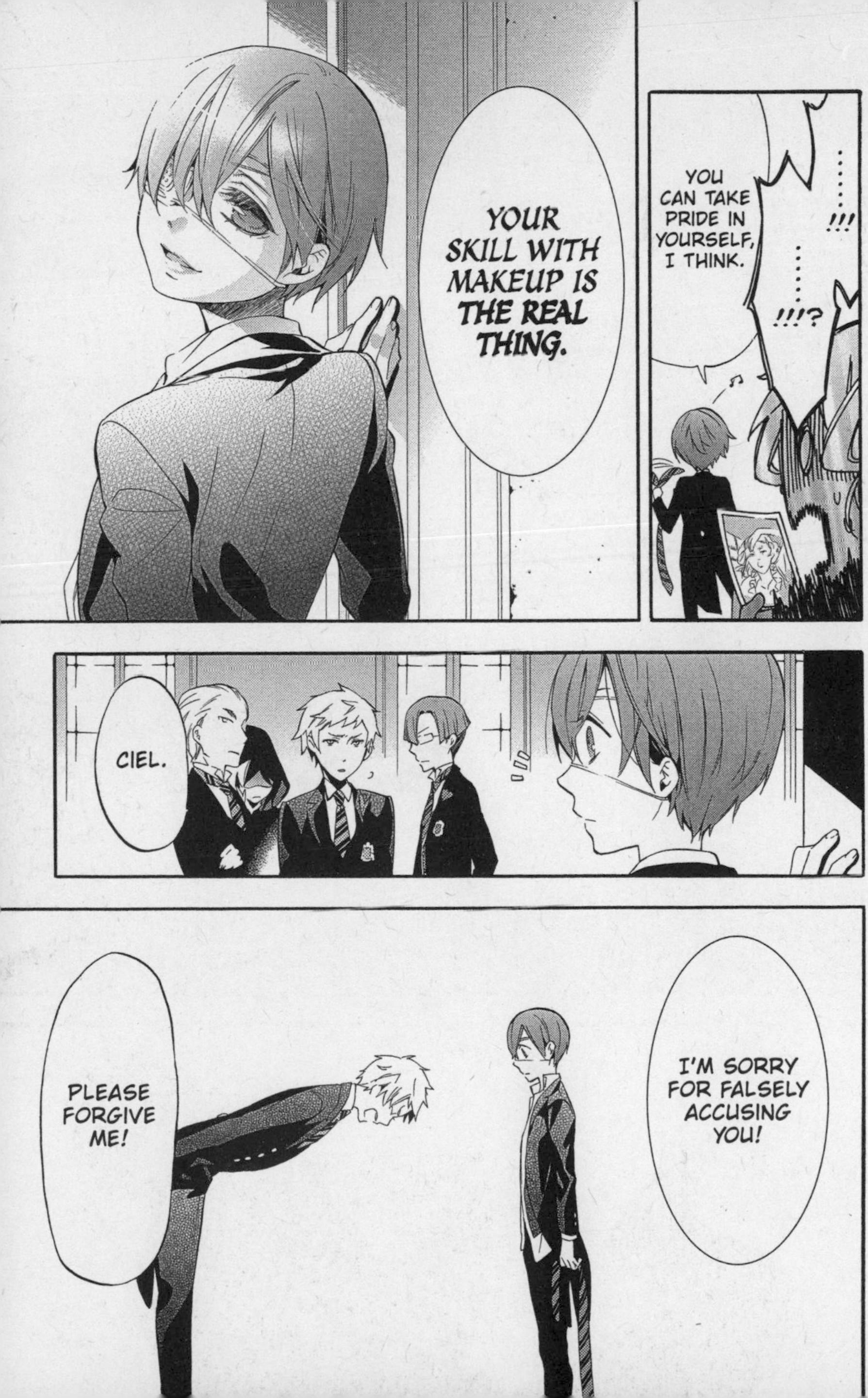
......!!!
......!!!?
YOU CAN TAKE PRIDE IN YOURSELF, I THINK.
YOUR SKILL WITH MAKEUP IS THE REAL THING.
CIEL.
I'M SORRY FOR FALSELY ACCUSING YOU!
PLEASE FORGIVE ME!

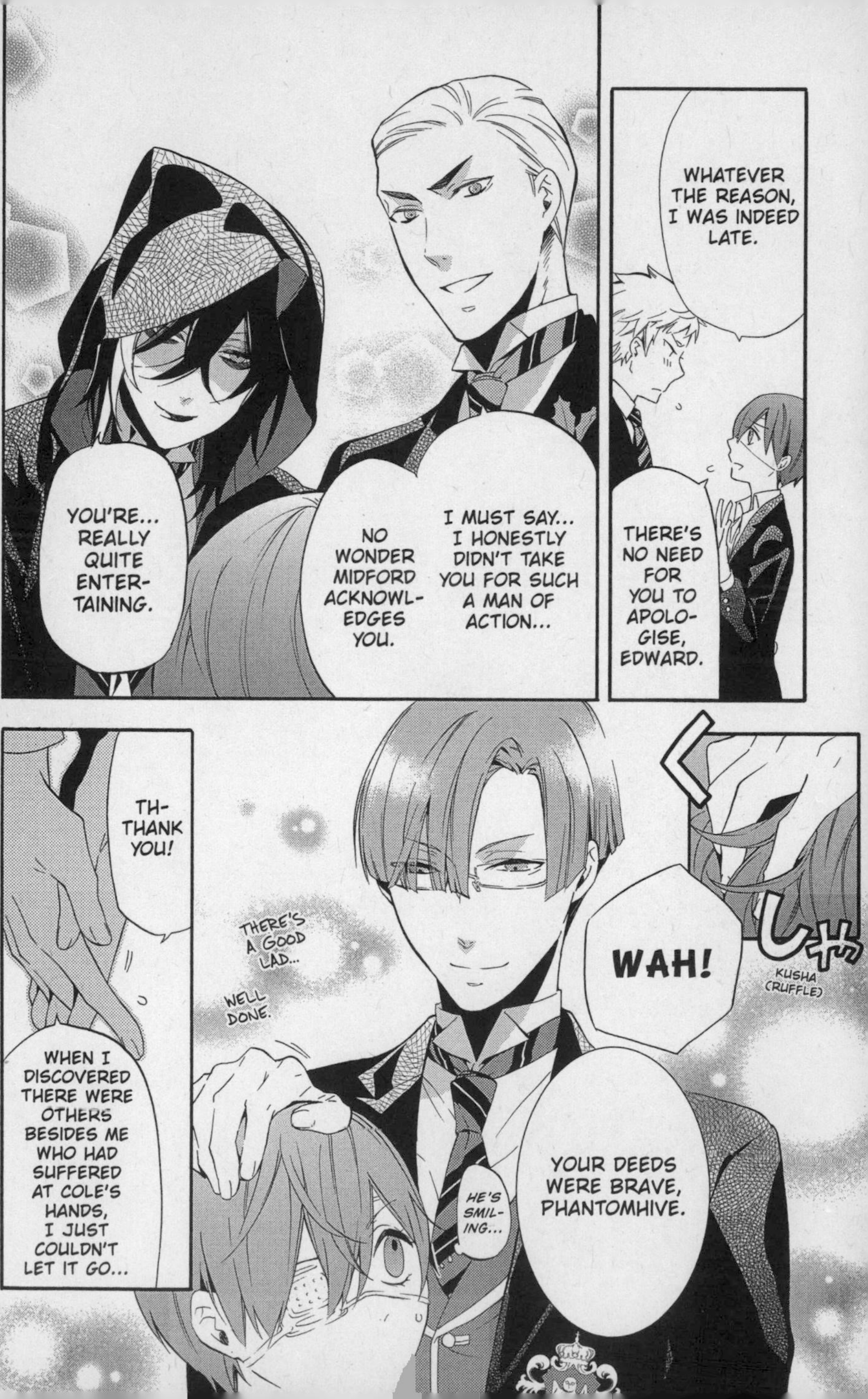
WHATEVER THE REASON, I WAS INDEED LATE.
THERE'S NO NEED FOR YOU TO APOLOGISE, EDWARD.
I MUST SAY... I HONESTLY DIDN'T TAKE YOU FOR SUCH A MAN OF ACTION...
NO WONDER MIDFORD ACKNOWLEDGES YOU.
YOU'RE... REALLY QUITE ENTERTAINING.
くしゃ
KUSHA (RUFFLE)
WAH!
YOUR DEEDS WERE BRAVE, PHANTOMHIVE.
HE'S SMILING...
THERE'S A GOOD LAD...
WELL DONE.
TH-THANK YOU!
WHEN I DISCOVERED THERE WERE OTHERS BESIDES ME WHO HAD SUFFERED AT COLE'S HANDS, I JUST COULDN'T LET IT GO...

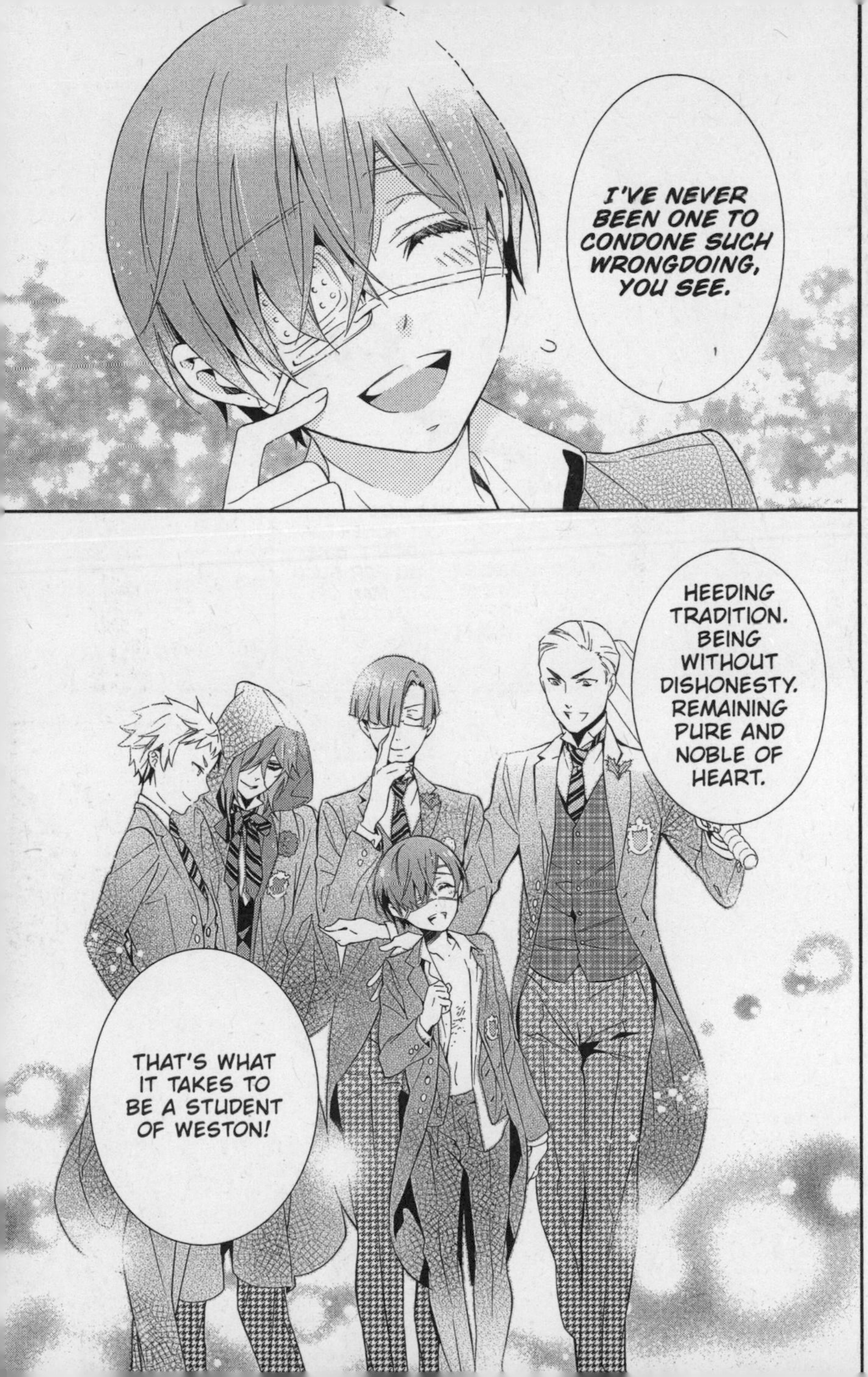
I'VE NEVER BEEN ONE TO CONDONE SUCH WRONGDOING, YOU SEE.
HEEDING TRADITION. BEING WITHOUT DISHONESTY. REMAINING PURE AND NOBLE OF HEART.
THAT'S WHAT IT TAKES TO BE A STUDENT OF WESTON!

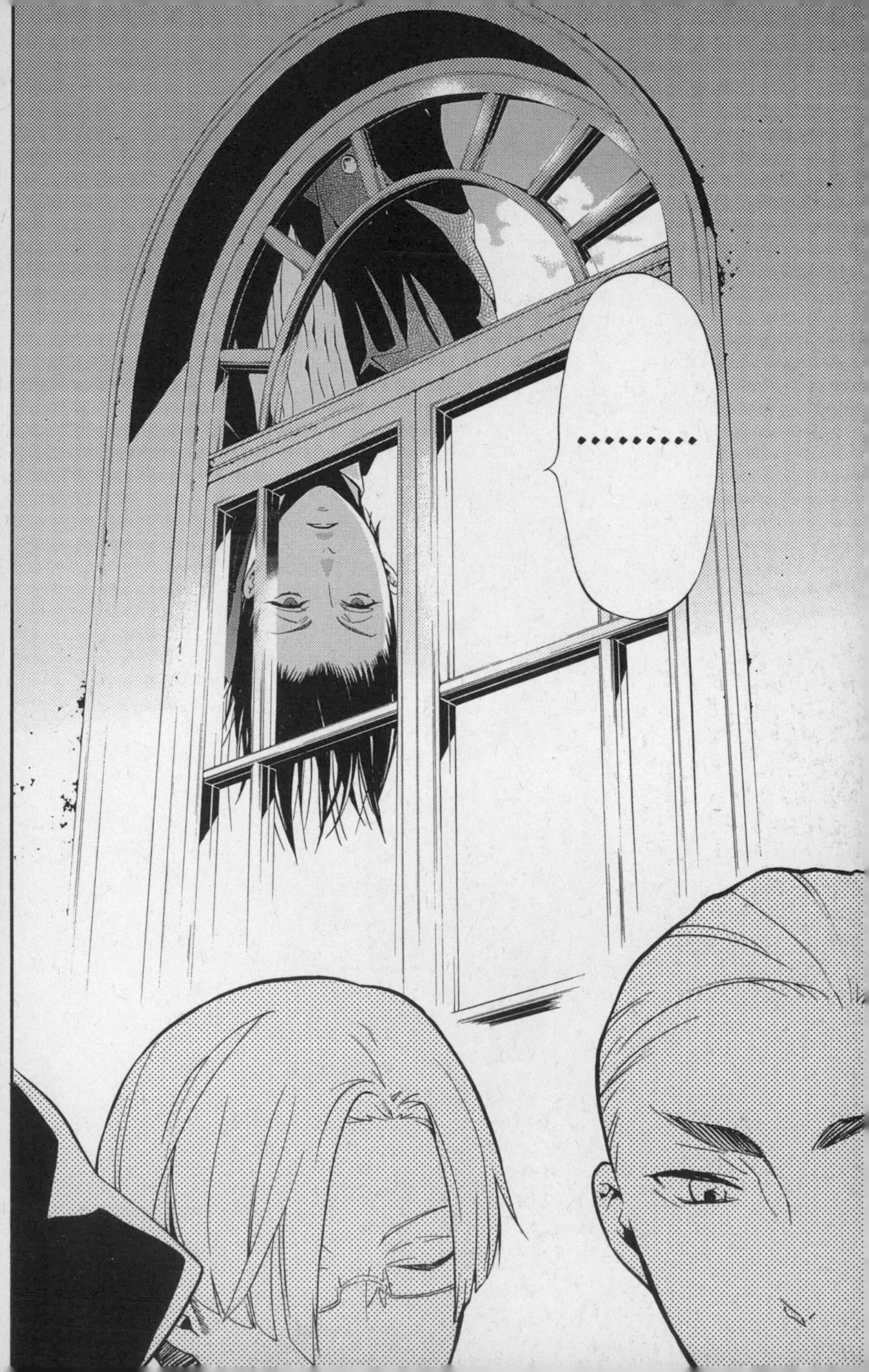
....

Black Butler

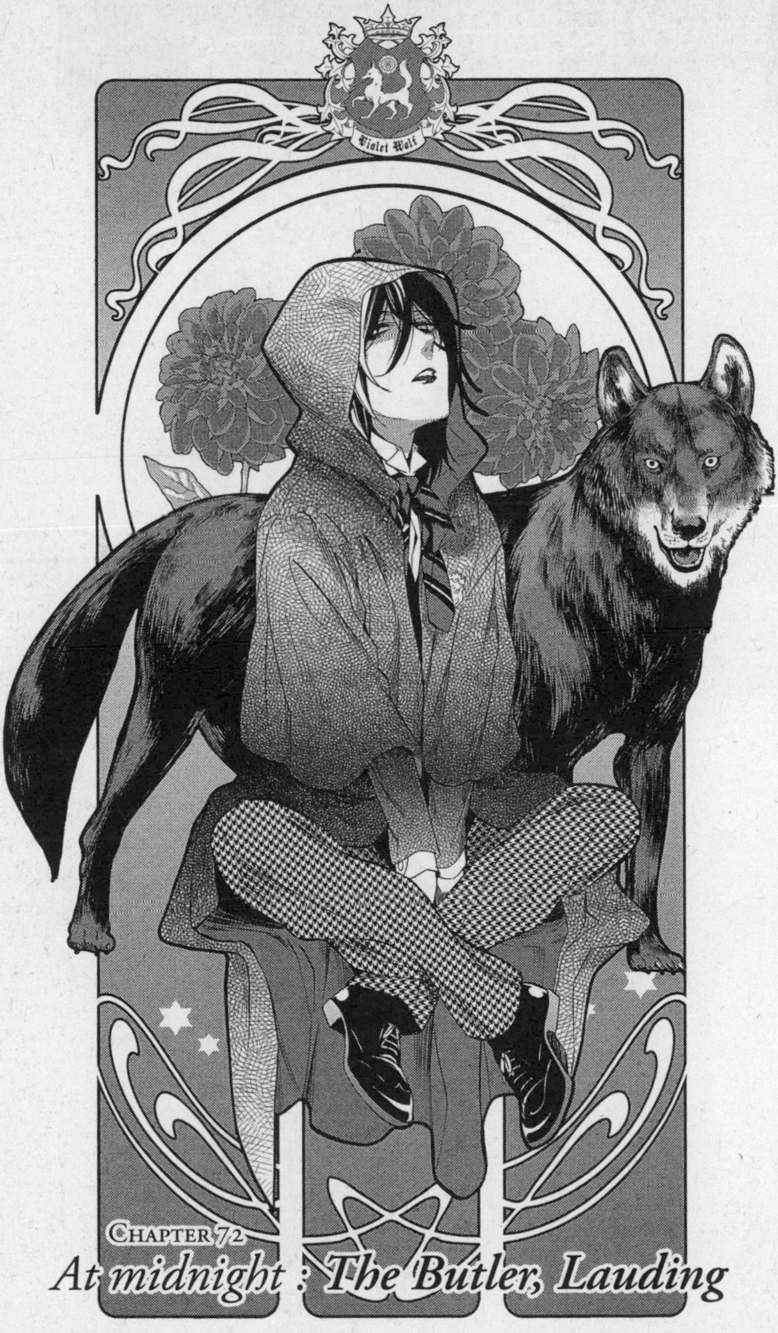
Violet Wolf

CHAPTER 72

At midnight : The Butler, Lauding

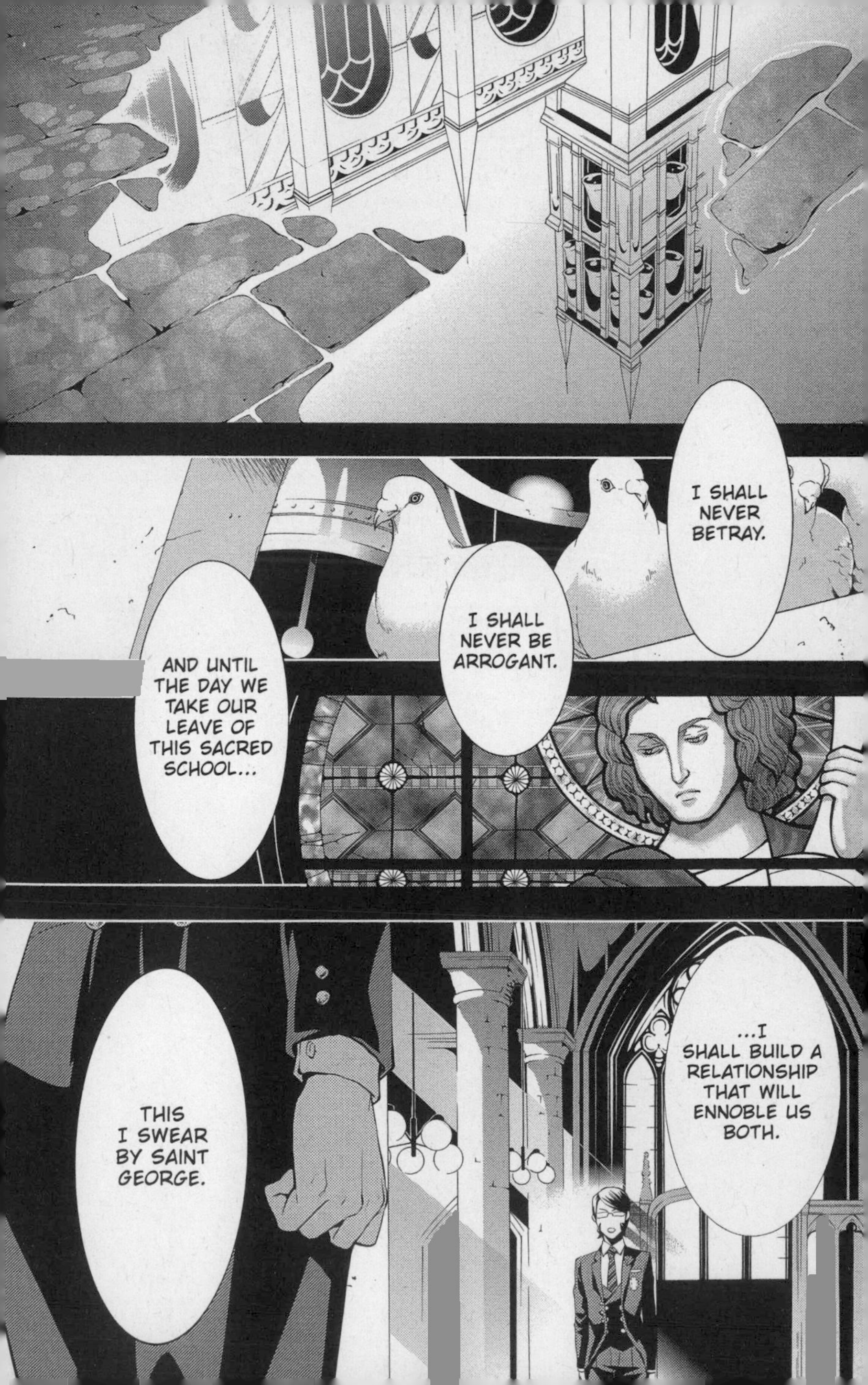
I SHALL NEVER BETRAY.
I SHALL NEVER BE ARROGANT.
AND UNTIL THE DAY WE TAKE OUR LEAVE OF THIS SACRED SCHOOL...
...I SHALL BUILD A RELATIONSHIP THAT WILL ENNOBLE US BOTH.
THIS I SWEAR BY SAINT GEORGE.

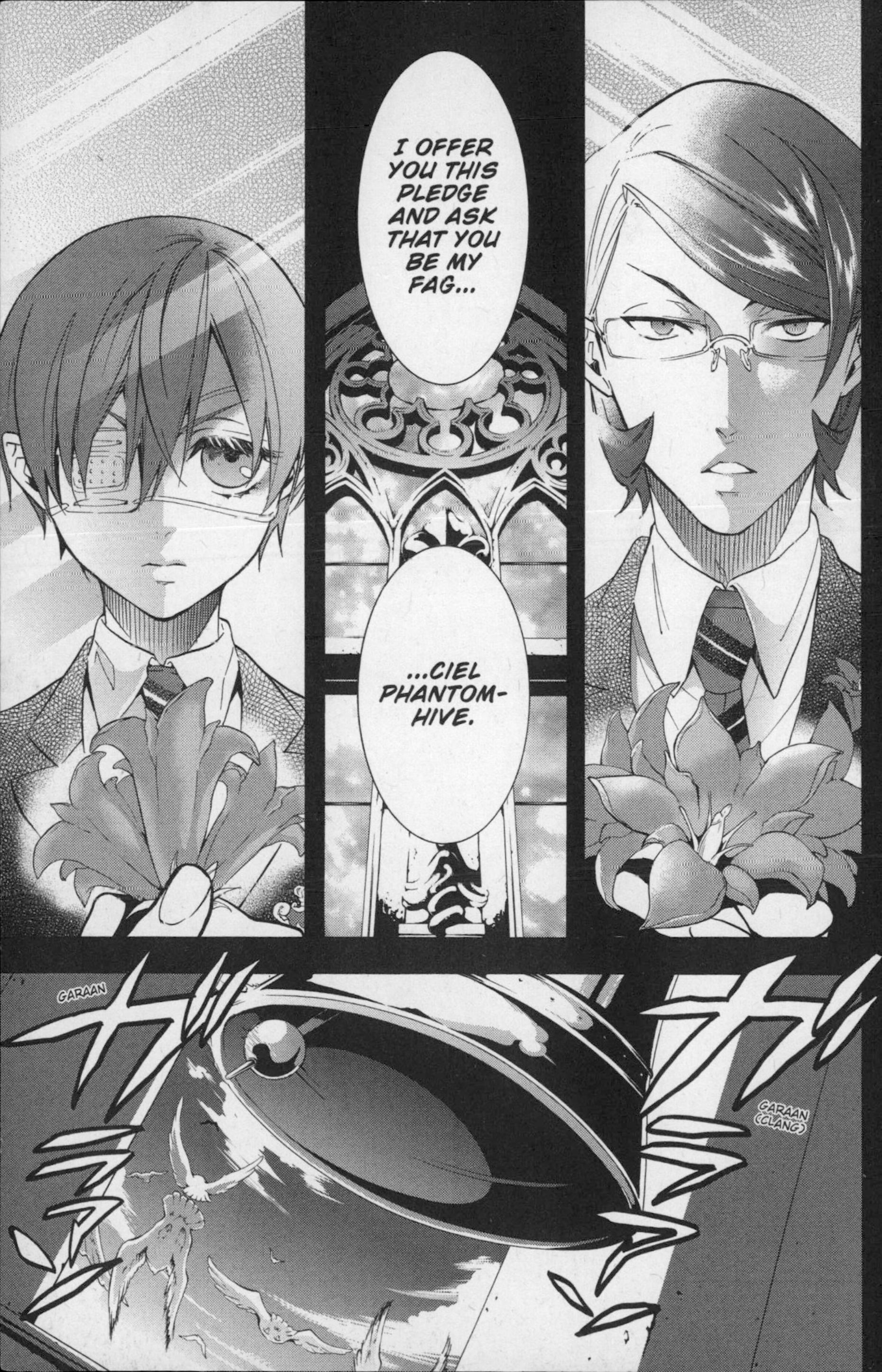
I OFFER YOU THIS PLEDGE AND ASK THAT YOU BE MY FAG...
...CIEL PHANTOMHIVE.
GARAAN (CLANG)
GARAAN

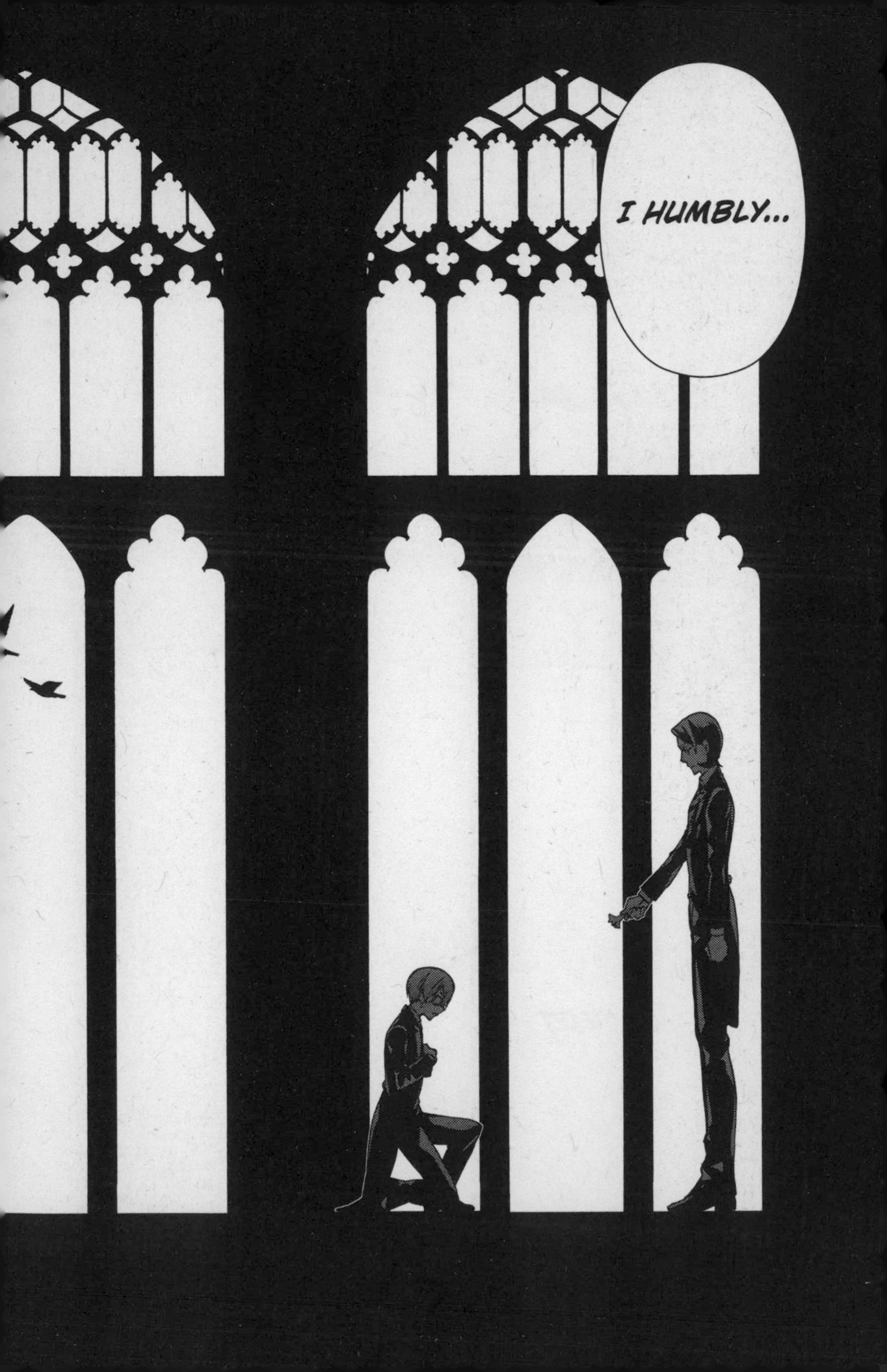
I HUMBLY...

...ACCEPT.

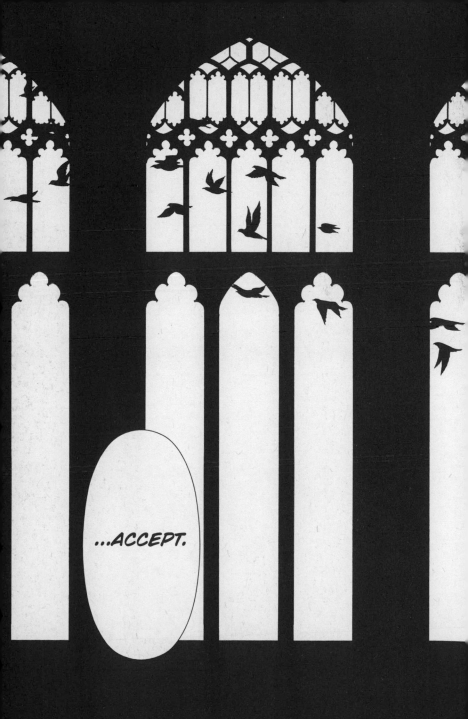

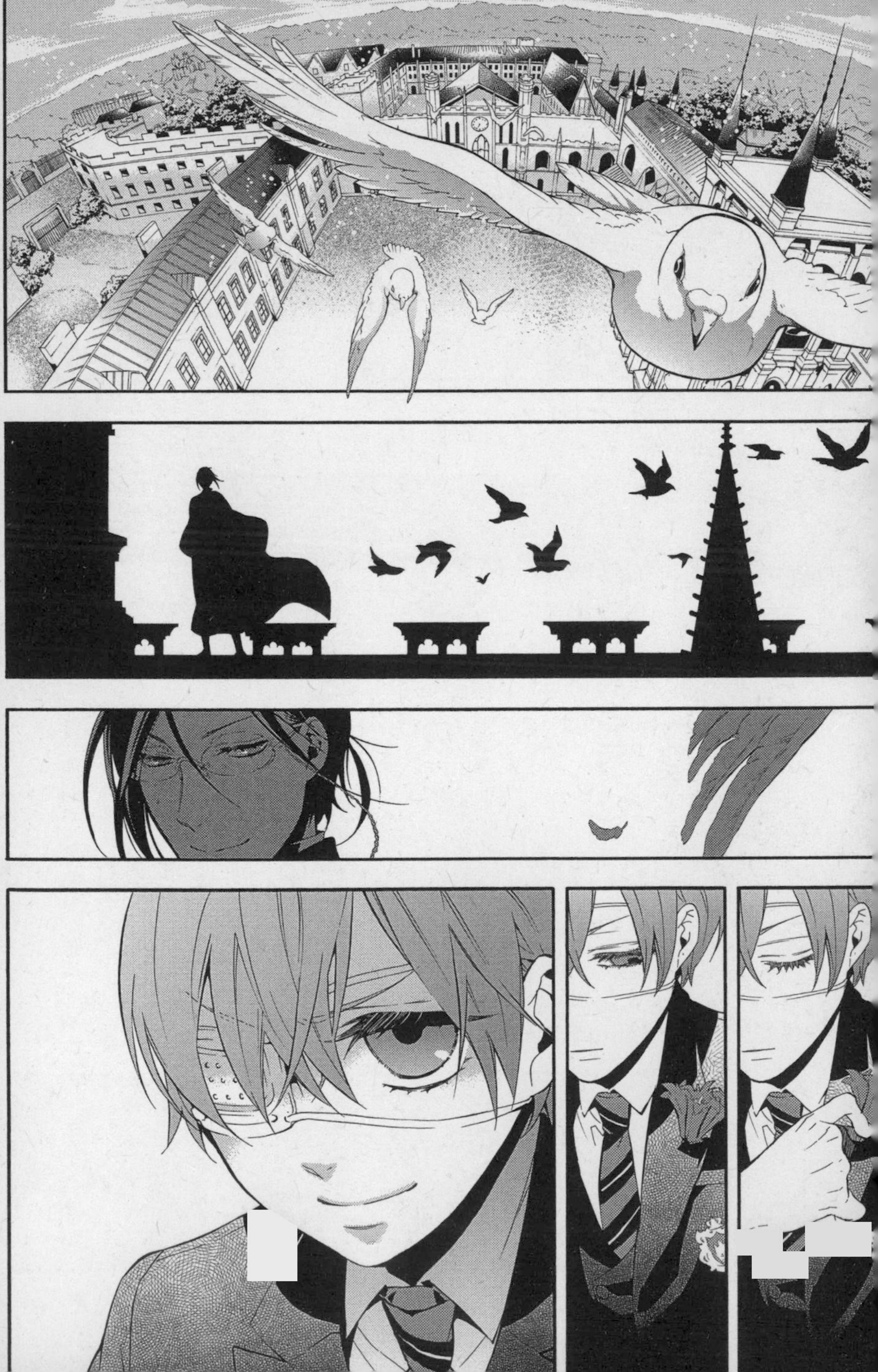

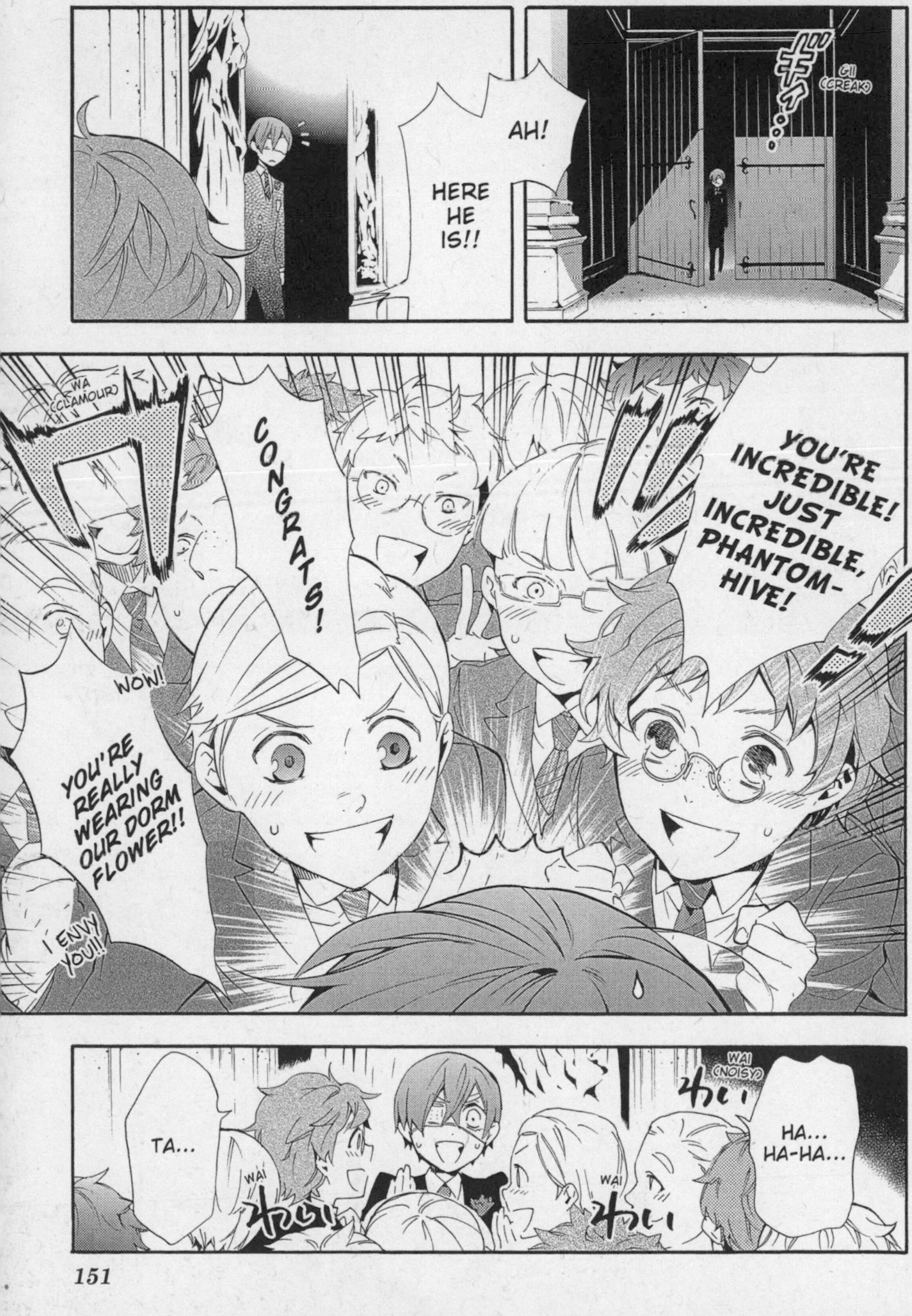
ギィ…
GII (CREAK)
AH!
HERE HE IS!!
YOU'RE INCREDIBLE! JUST INCREDIBLE, PHANTOM-HIVE!
CONGRATS!
WA (CLAMOUR)
WOW!
YOU'RE REALLY WEARING OUR DORM FLOWER!!
I ENVY YOU!!
WAI (NOISY)
わい
HA... HA-HA...
WAI
わい
WAI
わい!
TA...

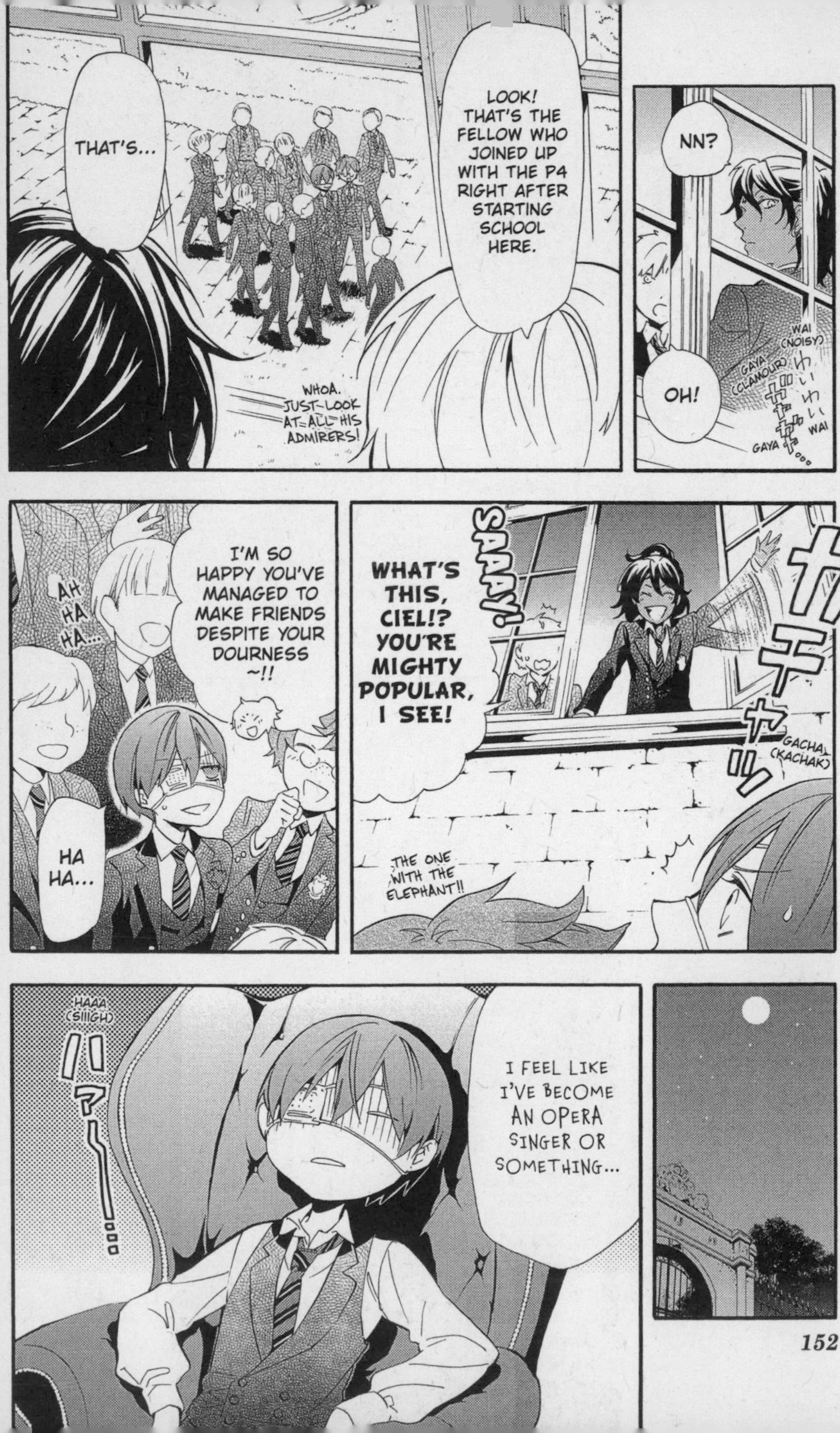
NN?
OH!
WAI (NOISY)
GAYA (CLAMOUR)
わいわい
ガヤガヤ...
WAI
GAYA
LOOK! THAT'S THE FELLOW WHO JOINED UP WITH THE P4 RIGHT AFTER STARTING SCHOOL HERE.
THAT'S...
WHOA. JUST LOOK AT ALL HIS ADMIRERS!
ガチャッ
GACHA (KACHAK)
SAAAY!
WHAT'S THIS, CIEL!? YOU'RE MIGHTY POPULAR, I SEE!
THE ONE WITH THE ELEPHANT!!
I'M SO HAPPY YOU'VE MANAGED TO MAKE FRIENDS DESPITE YOUR DOURNESS ~!!
AH HA HA...
HA HA...
I FEEL LIKE I'VE BECOME AN OPERA SINGER OR SOMETHING...
HAAA (SIIIGH)
はぁ〜...

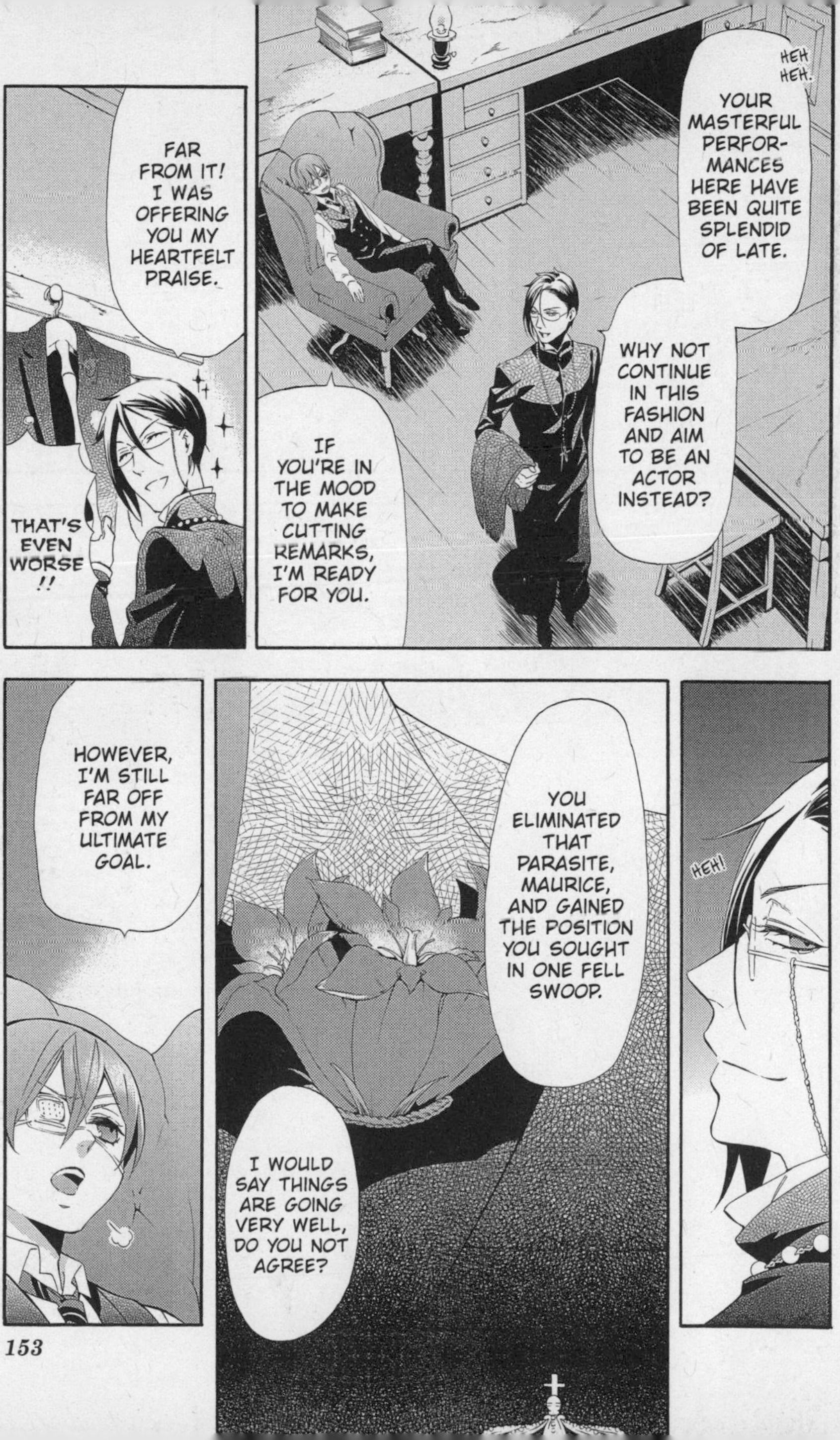
HEH HEH.
YOUR MASTERFUL PERFORMANCES HERE HAVE BEEN QUITE SPLENDID OF LATE.
WHY NOT CONTINUE IN THIS FASHION AND AIM TO BE AN ACTOR INSTEAD?
IF YOU'RE IN THE MOOD TO MAKE CUTTING REMARKS, I'M READY FOR YOU.
FAR FROM IT! I WAS OFFERING YOU MY HEARTFELT PRAISE.
THAT'S EVEN WORSE!!
HEH!
YOU ELIMINATED THAT PARASITE, MAURICE, AND GAINED THE POSITION YOU SOUGHT IN ONE FELL SWOOP.
I WOULD SAY THINGS ARE GOING VERY WELL, DO YOU NOT AGREE?
HOWEVER, I'M STILL FAR OFF FROM MY ULTIMATE GOAL.

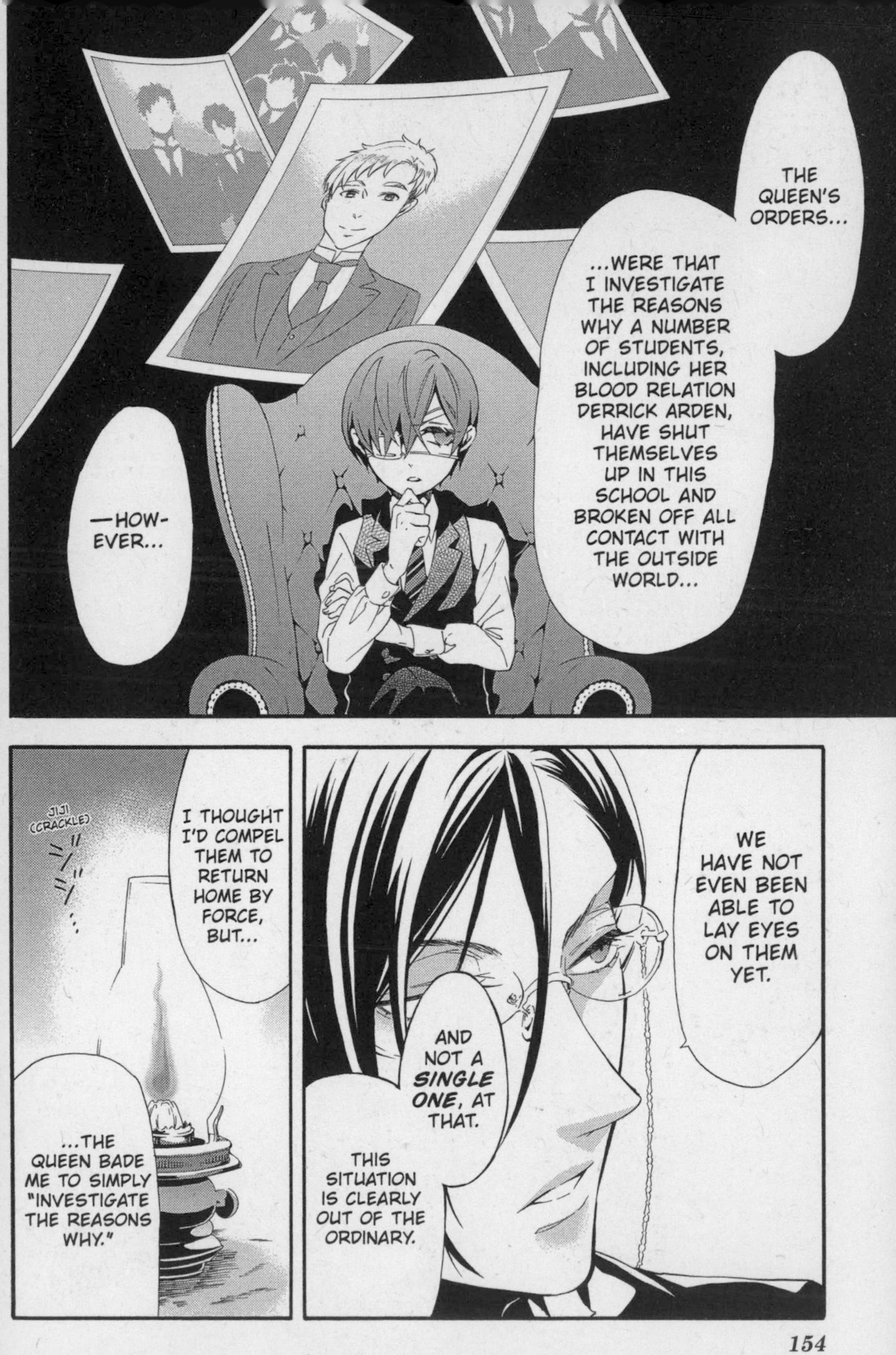
THE QUEEN'S ORDERS...
...WERE THAT I INVESTIGATE THE REASONS WHY A NUMBER OF STUDENTS, INCLUDING HER BLOOD RELATION DERRICK ARDEN, HAVE SHUT THEMSELVES UP IN THIS SCHOOL AND BROKEN OFF ALL CONTACT WITH THE OUTSIDE WORLD...
—HOW-EVER...
WE HAVE NOT EVEN BEEN ABLE TO LAY EYES ON THEM YET.
AND NOT A *SINGLE ONE*, AT THAT.
THIS SITUATION IS CLEARLY OUT OF THE ORDINARY.
I THOUGHT I'D COMPEL THEM TO RETURN HOME BY FORCE, BUT...
JIJI (CRACKLE)
...THE QUEEN BADE ME TO SIMPLY "INVESTIGATE THE REASONS WHY."

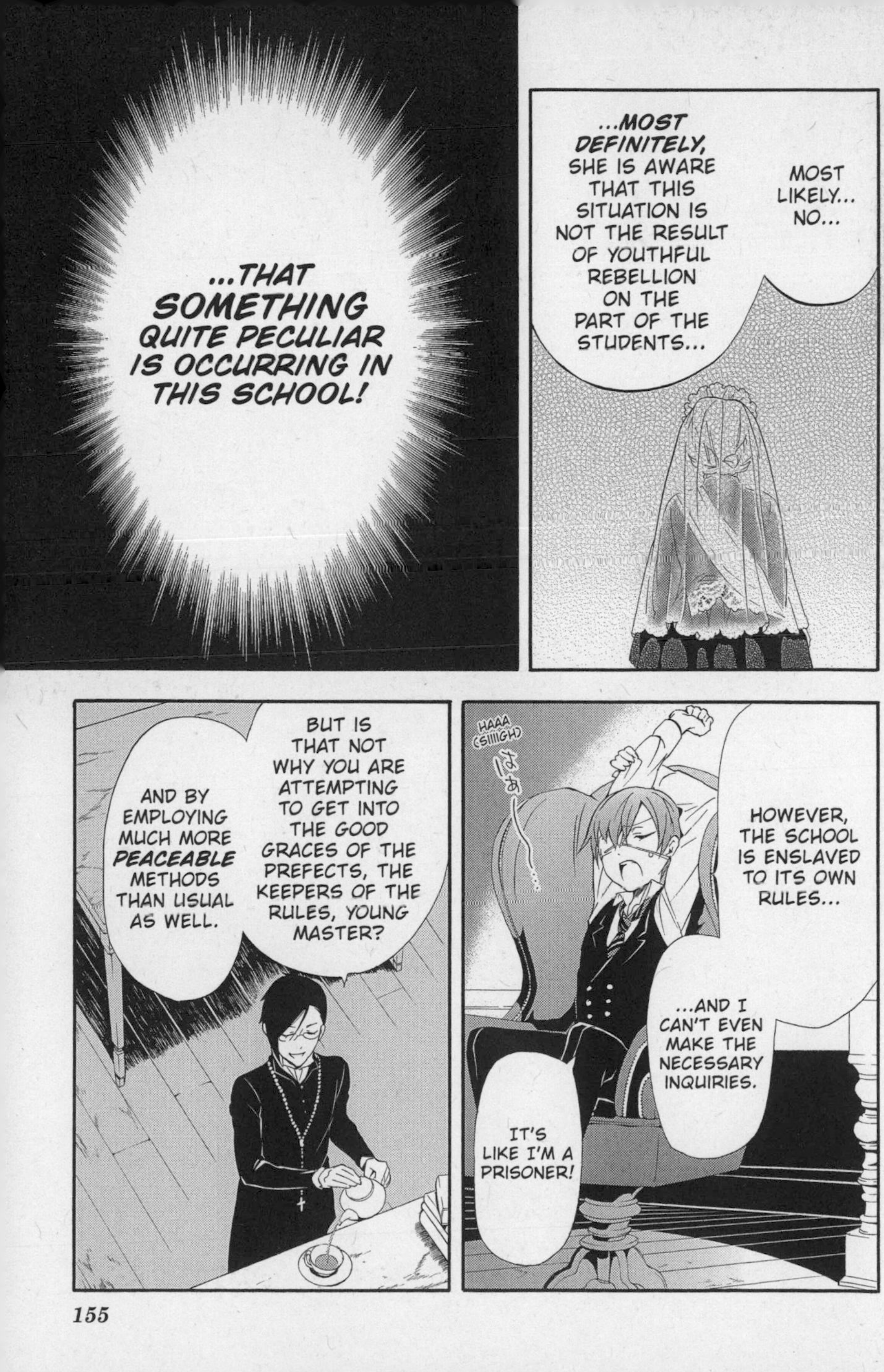
MOST LIKELY... NO...
...MOST DEFINITELY, SHE IS AWARE THAT THIS SITUATION IS NOT THE RESULT OF YOUTHFUL REBELLION ON THE PART OF THE STUDENTS...
...THAT SOMETHING QUITE PECULIAR IS OCCURRING IN THIS SCHOOL!
HAAA (SIIIGH)
はぁ
HOWEVER, THE SCHOOL IS ENSLAVED TO ITS OWN RULES...
...AND I CAN'T EVEN MAKE THE NECESSARY INQUIRIES.
IT'S LIKE I'M A PRISONER!
BUT IS THAT NOT WHY YOU ARE ATTEMPTING TO GET INTO THE GOOD GRACES OF THE PREFECTS, THE KEEPERS OF THE RULES, YOUNG MASTER?
AND BY EMPLOYING MUCH MORE PEACEABLE METHODS THAN USUAL AS WELL.

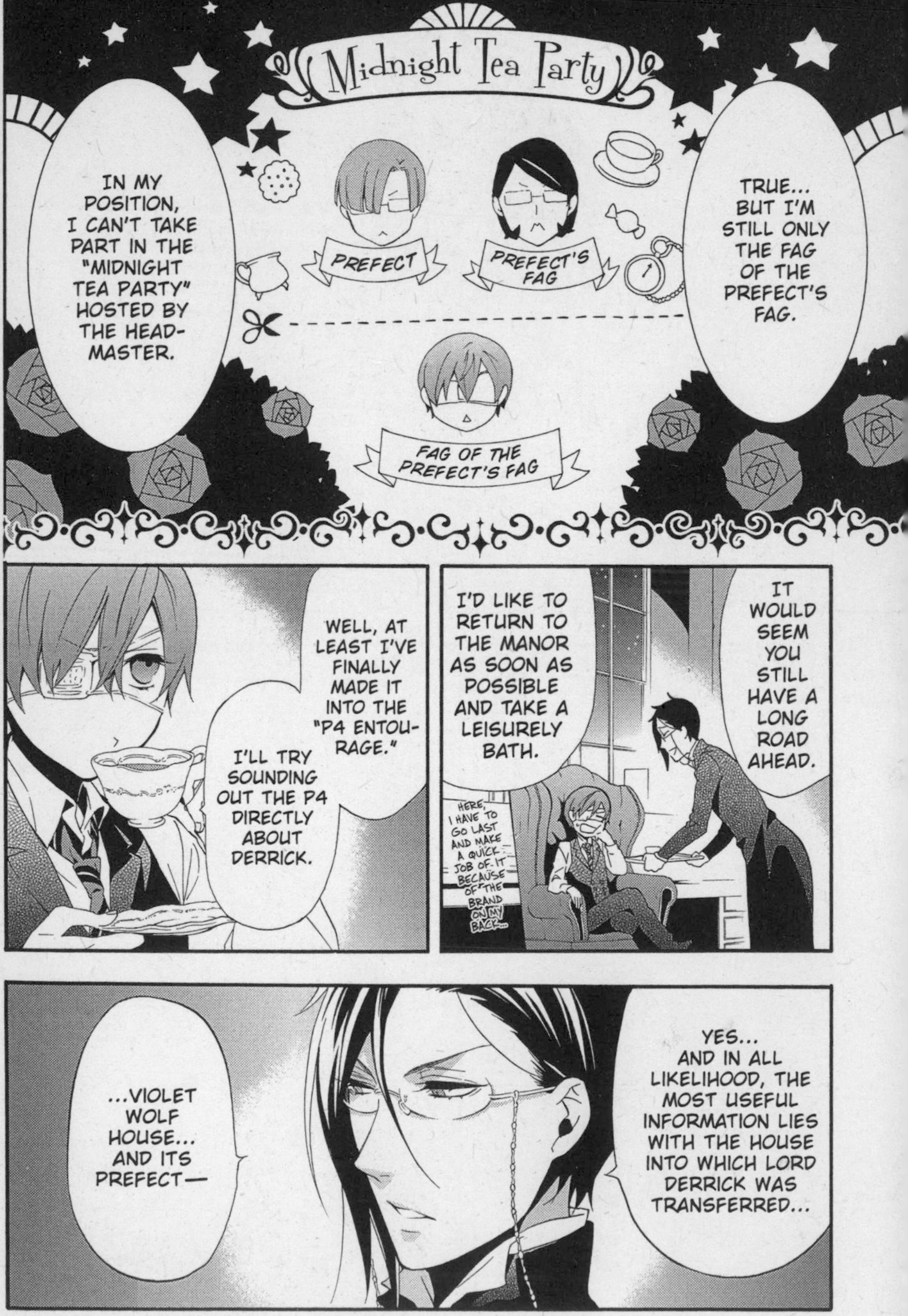
Midnight Tea Party
TRUE... BUT I'M STILL ONLY THE FAG OF THE PREFECT'S FAG.
PREFECT'S FAG
PREFECT
IN MY POSITION, I CAN'T TAKE PART IN THE "MIDNIGHT TEA PARTY" HOSTED BY THE HEAD-MASTER.
FAG OF THE PREFECT'S FAG
IT WOULD SEEM YOU STILL HAVE A LONG ROAD AHEAD.
I'D LIKE TO RETURN TO THE MANOR AS SOON AS POSSIBLE AND TAKE A LEISURELY BATH.
HERE, I HAVE TO GO LAST AND MAKE A QUICK JOB OF IT BECAUSE OF THE BRAND ON MY BACK...
WELL, AT LEAST I'VE FINALLY MADE IT INTO THE "P4 ENTOURAGE."
I'LL TRY SOUNDING OUT THE P4 DIRECTLY ABOUT DERRICK.
YES... AND IN ALL LIKELIHOOD, THE MOST USEFUL INFORMATION LIES WITH THE HOUSE INTO WHICH LORD DERRICK WAS TRANSFERRED...
...VIOLET WOLF HOUSE... AND ITS PREFECT—

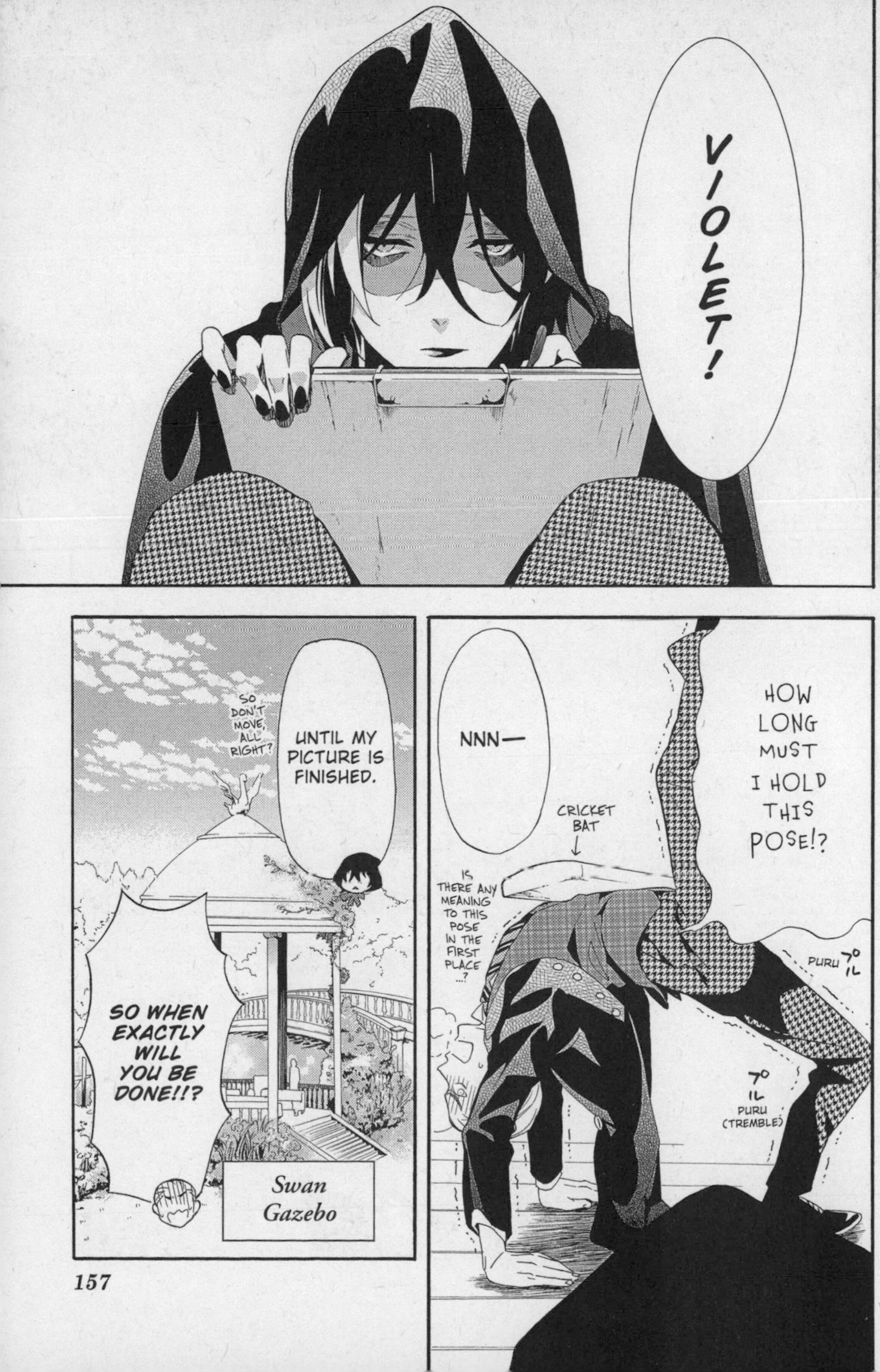
VIOLET!
HOW LONG MUST I HOLD THIS POSE!?
NNN—
CRICKET BAT
IS THERE ANY MEANING TO THIS POSE IN THE FIRST PLACE...?
プル PURU
プル PURU (TREMBLE)
UNTIL MY PICTURE IS FINISHED.
SO DON'T MOVE, ALL RIGHT?
SO WHEN EXACTLY WILL YOU BE DONE!!?
Swan Gazebo

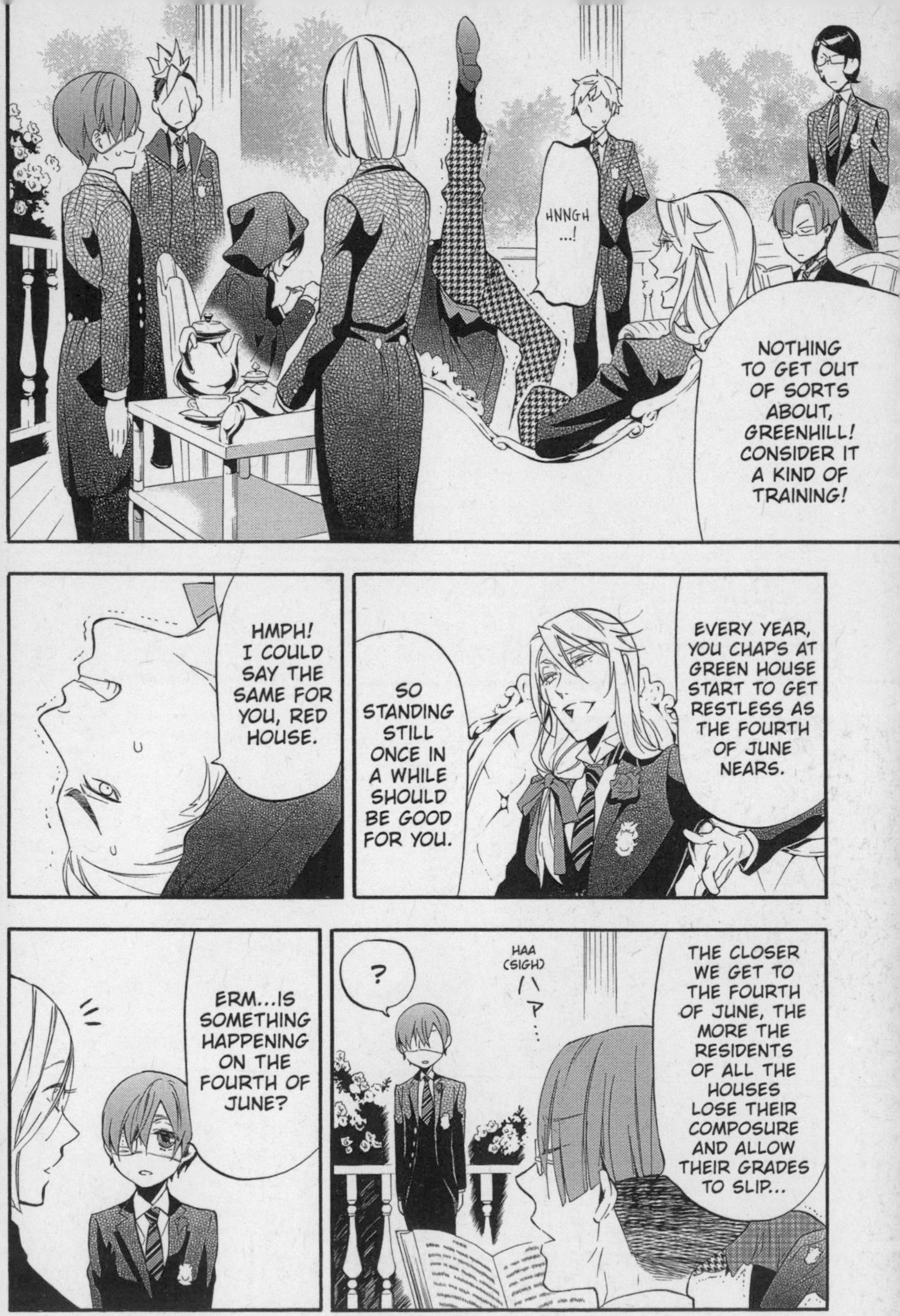
HNNGH ...!
NOTHING TO GET OUT OF SORTS ABOUT, GREENHILL! CONSIDER IT A KIND OF TRAINING!
EVERY YEAR, YOU CHAPS AT GREEN HOUSE START TO GET RESTLESS AS THE FOURTH OF JUNE NEARS.
SO STANDING STILL ONCE IN A WHILE SHOULD BE GOOD FOR YOU.
HMPH! I COULD SAY THE SAME FOR YOU, RED HOUSE.
THE CLOSER WE GET TO THE FOURTH OF JUNE, THE MORE THE RESIDENTS OF ALL THE HOUSES LOSE THEIR COMPOSURE AND ALLOW THEIR GRADES TO SLIP...
HAA (SIGH)
?
ERM...IS SOMETHING HAPPENING ON THE FOURTH OF JUNE?

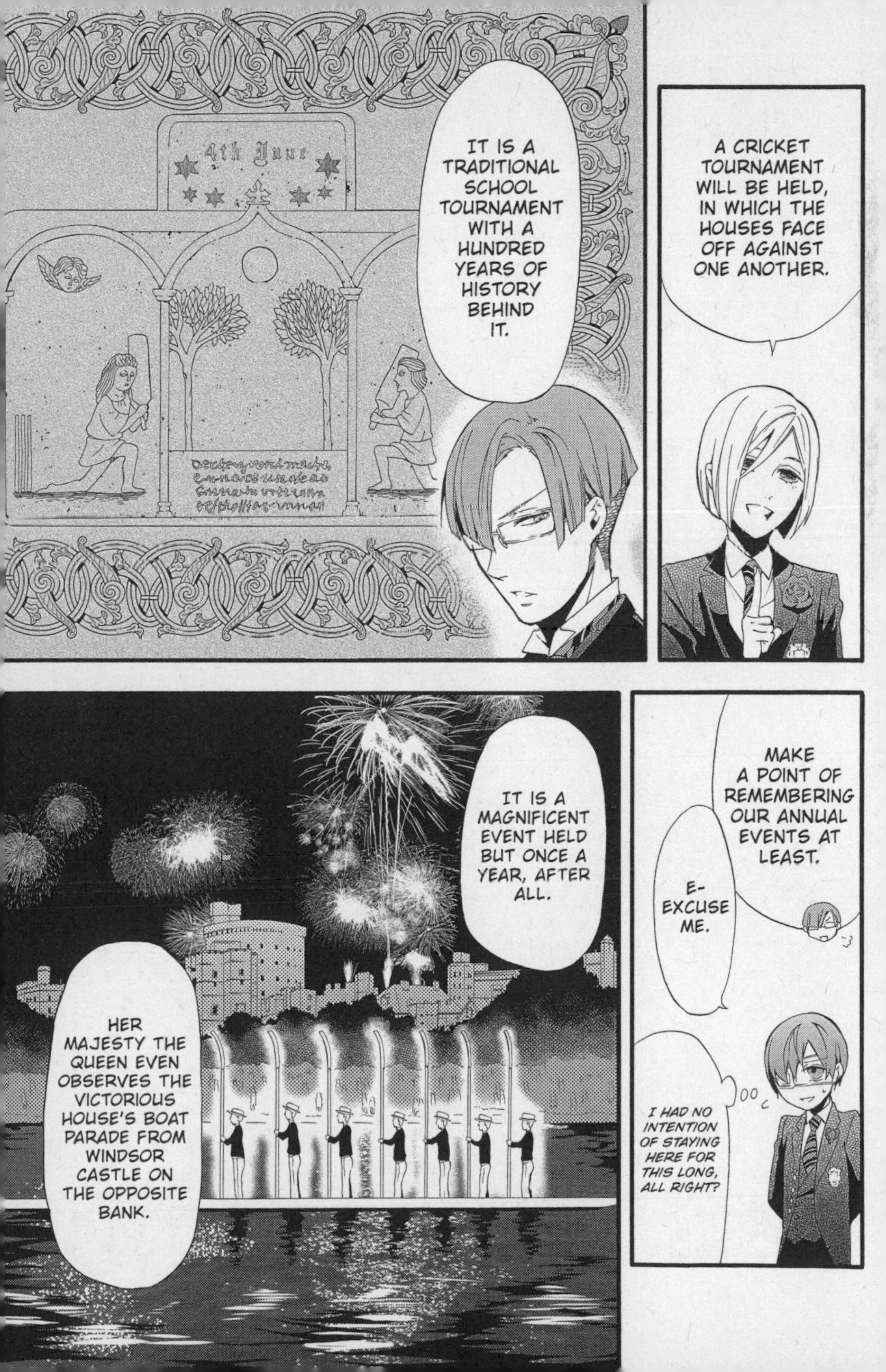
A CRICKET TOURNAMENT WILL BE HELD, IN WHICH THE HOUSES FACE OFF AGAINST ONE ANOTHER.
IT IS A TRADITIONAL SCHOOL TOURNAMENT WITH A HUNDRED YEARS OF HISTORY BEHIND IT.
4th June
MAKE A POINT OF REMEMBERING OUR ANNUAL EVENTS AT LEAST.
E-EXCUSE ME.
I HAD NO INTENTION OF STAYING HERE FOR THIS LONG, ALL RIGHT?
IT IS A MAGNIFICENT EVENT HELD BUT ONCE A YEAR, AFTER ALL.
HER MAJESTY THE QUEEN EVEN OBSERVES THE VICTORIOUS HOUSE'S BOAT PARADE FROM WINDSOR CASTLE ON THE OPPOSITE BANK.

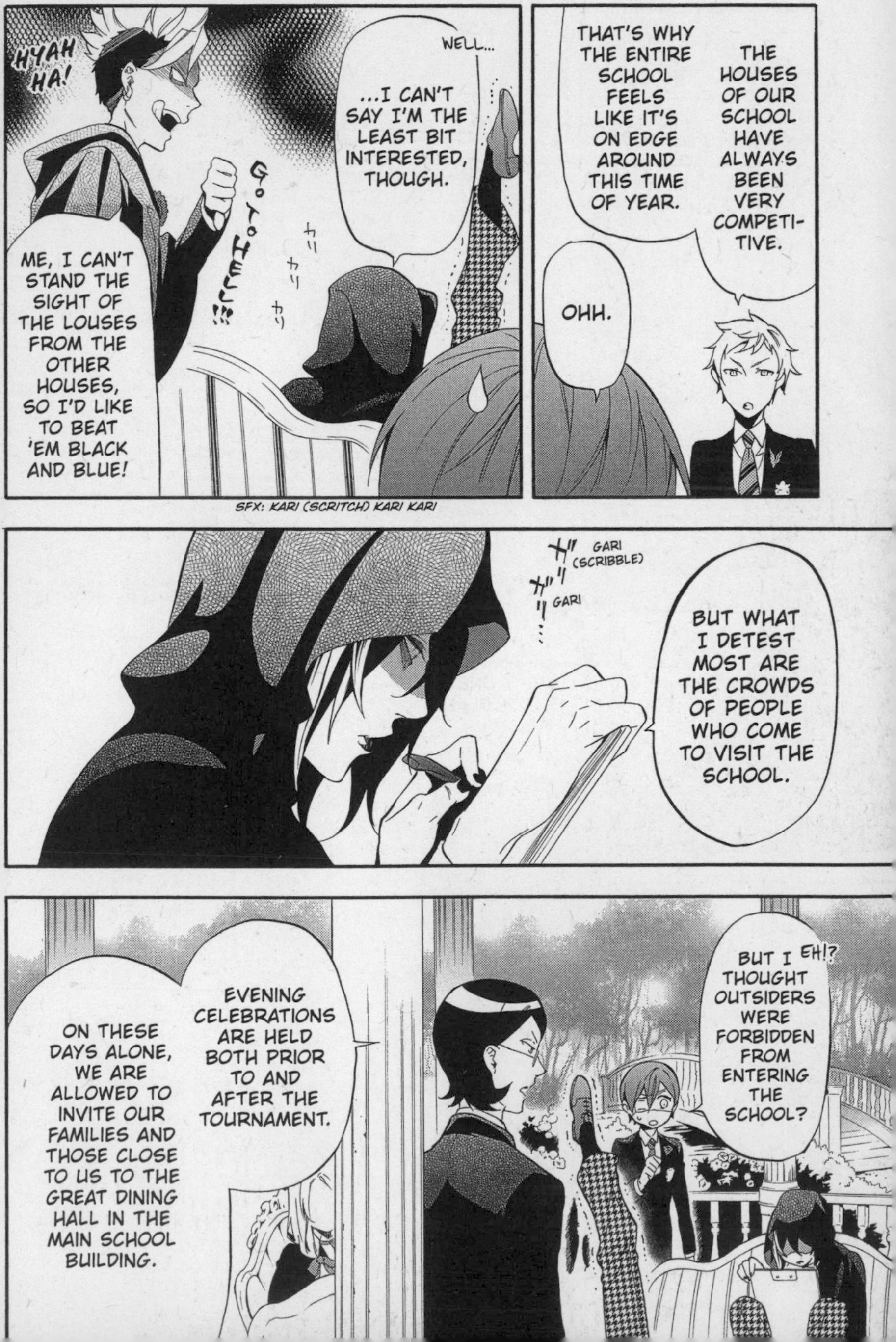
THE HOUSES OF OUR SCHOOL HAVE ALWAYS BEEN VERY COMPETI-TIVE.
THAT'S WHY THE ENTIRE SCHOOL FEELS LIKE IT'S ON EDGE AROUND THIS TIME OF YEAR.
OHH.
WELL...
...I CAN'T SAY I'M THE LEAST BIT INTERESTED, THOUGH.
HYAH HA!
GO TO HELL!!!
ME, I CAN'T STAND THE SIGHT OF THE LOUSES FROM THE OTHER HOUSES, SO I'D LIKE TO BEAT 'EM BLACK AND BLUE!
カリ
カリ
カリ
SFX: KARI (SCRITCH) KARI KARI
ガリ
GARI (SCRIBBLE)
ガリ
GARI
BUT WHAT I DETEST MOST ARE THE CROWDS OF PEOPLE WHO COME TO VISIT THE SCHOOL.
BUT I THOUGHT OUTSIDERS WERE FORBIDDEN FROM ENTERING THE SCHOOL?
EH!?
EVENING CELEBRATIONS ARE HELD BOTH PRIOR TO AND AFTER THE TOURNAMENT.
ON THESE DAYS ALONE, WE ARE ALLOWED TO INVITE OUR FAMILIES AND THOSE CLOSE TO US TO THE GREAT DINING HALL IN THE MAIN SCHOOL BUILDING.

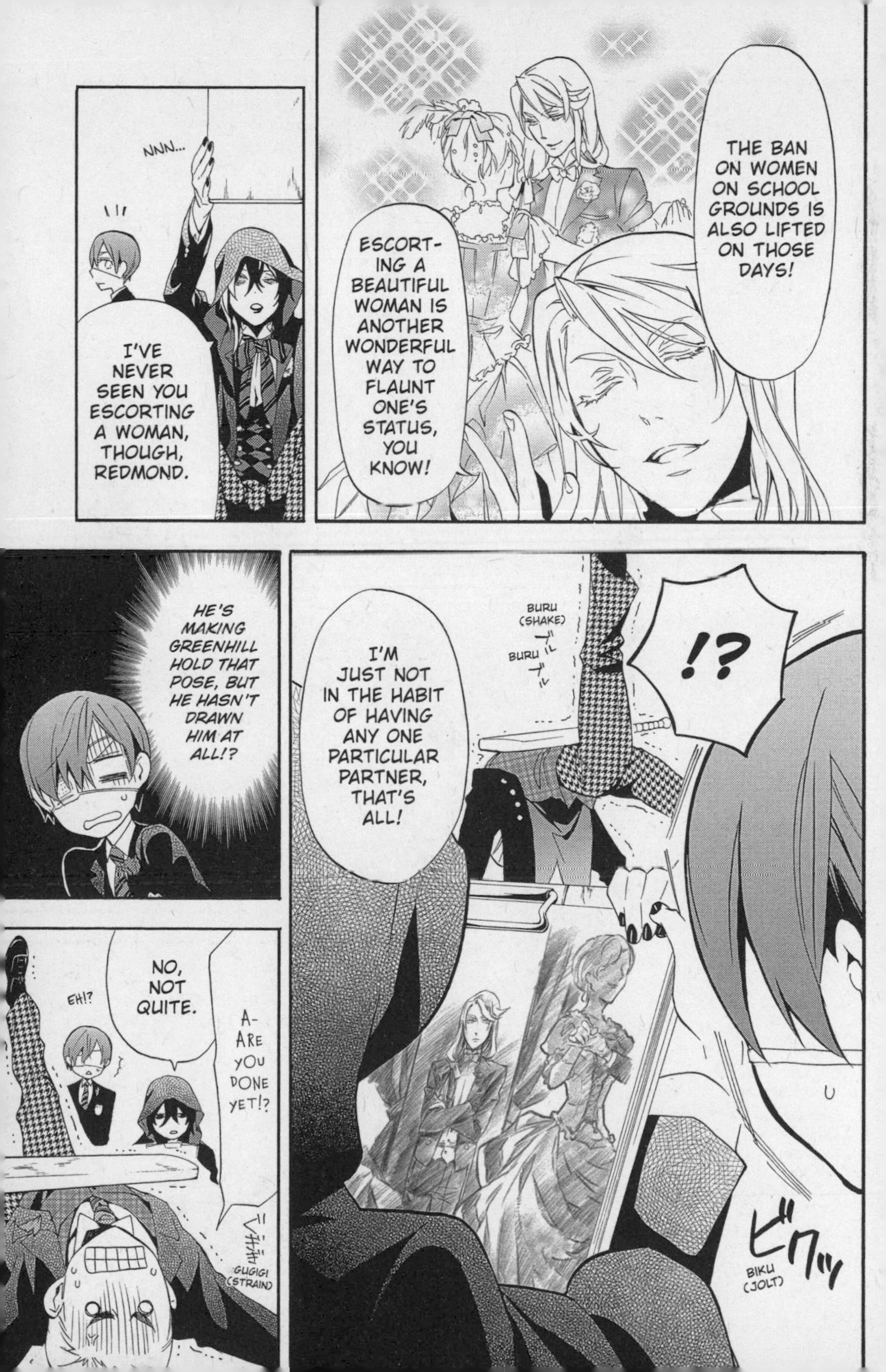
THE BAN ON WOMEN ON SCHOOL GROUNDS IS ALSO LIFTED ON THOSE DAYS!
ESCORT-ING A BEAUTIFUL WOMAN IS ANOTHER WONDERFUL WAY TO FLAUNT ONE'S STATUS, YOU KNOW!
NNN...
ılı
I'VE NEVER SEEN YOU ESCORTING A WOMAN, THOUGH, REDMOND.
!?
BURU (SHAKE)
ブル
BURU
ブル
I'M JUST NOT IN THE HABIT OF HAVING ANY ONE PARTICULAR PARTNER, THAT'S ALL!
ビクッ
BIKU (JOLT)
HE'S MAKING GREENHILL HOLD THAT POSE, BUT HE HASN'T DRAWN HIM AT ALL!?
NO, NOT QUITE.
EH!?
A- ARE YOU DONE YET!?
ぐぎぎ
GUGIGI (STRAIN)

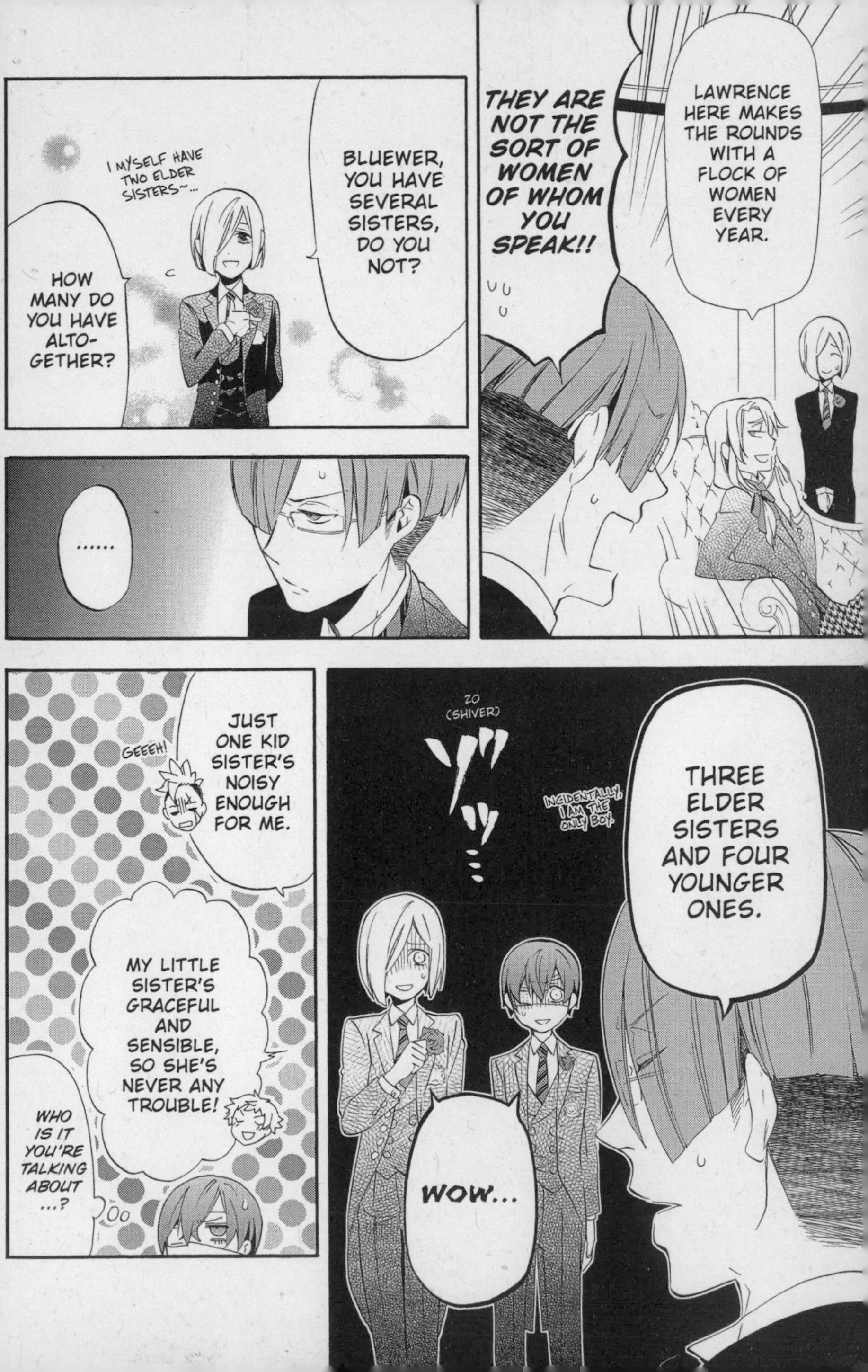
LAWRENCE HERE MAKES THE ROUNDS WITH A FLOCK OF WOMEN EVERY YEAR.
THEY ARE NOT THE SORT OF WOMEN OF WHOM YOU SPEAK!!
BLUEWER, YOU HAVE SEVERAL SISTERS, DO YOU NOT?
I MYSELF HAVE TWO ELDER SISTERS~...
HOW MANY DO YOU HAVE ALTOGETHER?
......
THREE ELDER SISTERS AND FOUR YOUNGER ONES.
INCIDENTALLY, I AM THE ONLY BOY.
ZO (SHIVER)
WOW...
JUST ONE KID SISTER'S NOISY ENOUGH FOR ME.
GEEEH!
MY LITTLE SISTER'S GRACEFUL AND SENSIBLE, SO SHE'S NEVER ANY TROUBLE!
WHO IS IT YOU'RE TALKING ABOUT...?

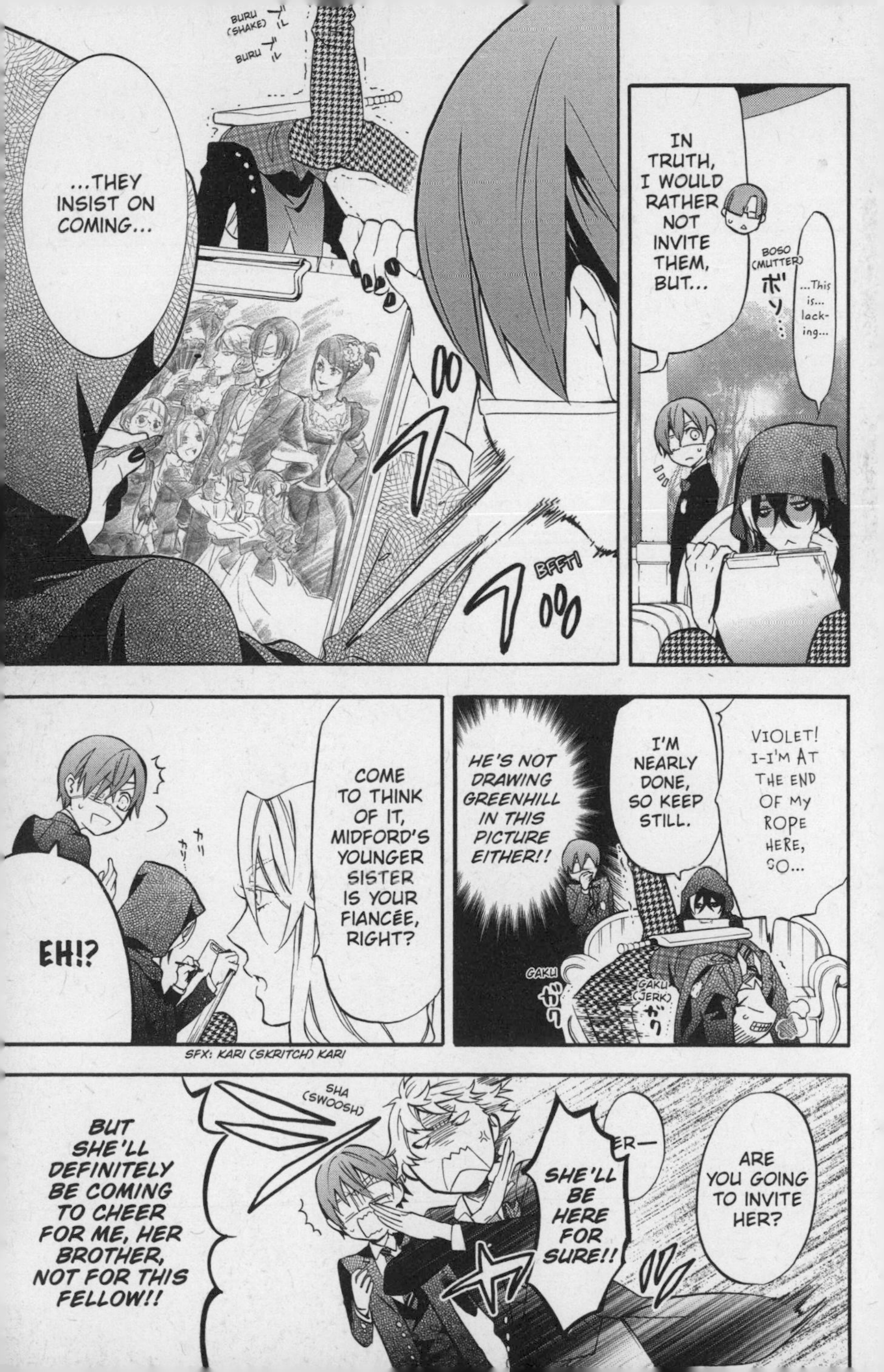
IN TRUTH, I WOULD RATHER NOT INVITE THEM, BUT...
BOSO (MUTTER)
...This is... lacking...
BURU (SHAKE)
BURU
...THEY INSIST ON COMING...
BFFT!
VIOLET! I-I'M AT THE END OF MY ROPE HERE, SO...
I'M NEARLY DONE, SO KEEP STILL.
HE'S NOT DRAWING GREENHILL IN THIS PICTURE EITHER!!
GAKU (JERK)
GAKU
COME TO THINK OF IT, MIDFORD'S YOUNGER SISTER IS YOUR FIANCÉE, RIGHT?
EH!?
SFX: KARI (SKRITCH) KARI
ARE YOU GOING TO INVITE HER?
ER—
SHE'LL BE HERE FOR SURE!!
SHA (SWOOSH)
BUT SHE'LL DEFINITELY BE COMING TO CHEER FOR ME, HER BROTHER, NOT FOR THIS FELLOW!!

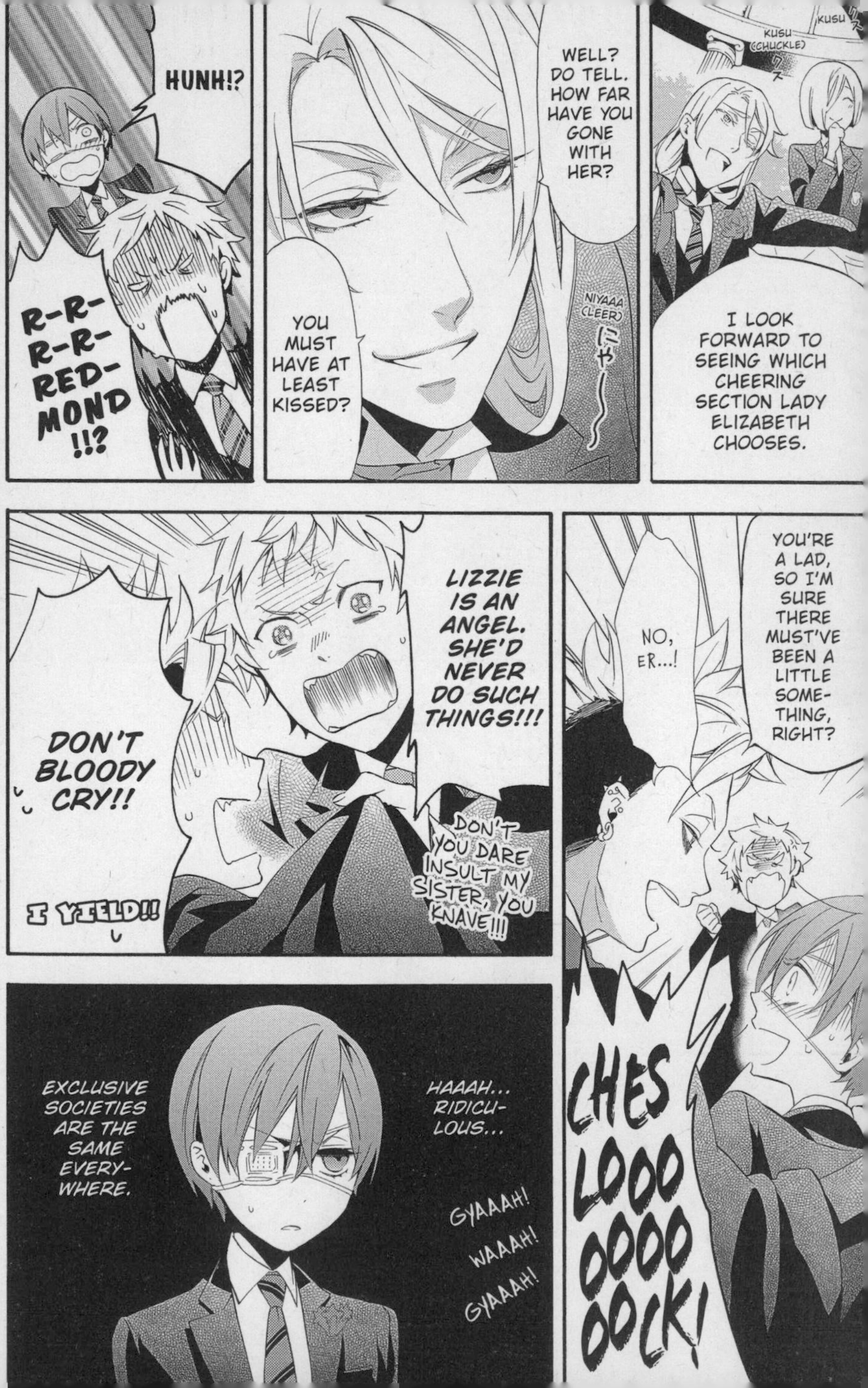
KUSU
KUSU (CHUCKLE)
I LOOK FORWARD TO SEEING WHICH CHEERING SECTION LADY ELIZABETH CHOOSES.
WELL? DO TELL. HOW FAR HAVE YOU GONE WITH HER?
NIYAAA (LEER)
YOU MUST HAVE AT LEAST KISSED?
HUNH!?
R-R-R-R-RED-MOND!!?
YOU'RE A LAD, SO I'M SURE THERE MUST'VE BEEN A LITTLE SOME-THING, RIGHT?
NO, ER...!
CHES LOOO OOOO OOOO OOCK!
LIZZIE IS AN ANGEL. SHE'D NEVER DO SUCH THINGS!!!
DON'T YOU DARE INSULT MY SISTER, YOU KNAVE!!!
DON'T BLOODY CRY!!
I YIELD!!
HAAAH... RIDICU-LOUS...
EXCLUSIVE SOCIETIES ARE THE SAME EVERY-WHERE.
GYAAAH!
WAAAH!
GYAAAH!

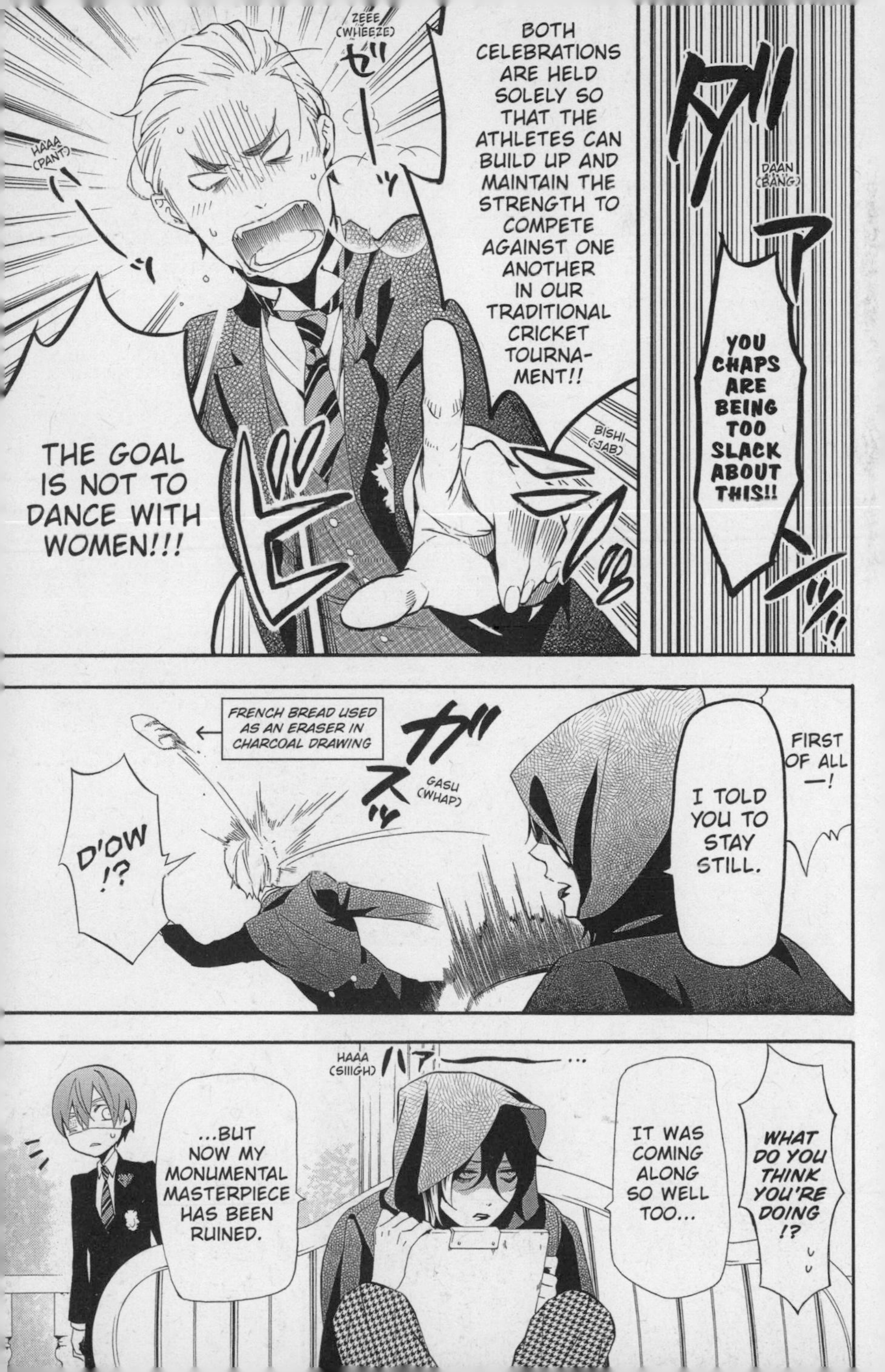
DAAN (BANG)
YOU CHAPS ARE BEING TOO SLACK ABOUT THIS!!
ZEEE (WHEEZE)
BOTH CELEBRATIONS ARE HELD SOLELY SO THAT THE ATHLETES CAN BUILD UP AND MAINTAIN THE STRENGTH TO COMPETE AGAINST ONE ANOTHER IN OUR TRADITIONAL CRICKET TOURNAMENT!!
HAAA (PANT)
BISHI (JAB)
THE GOAL IS NOT TO DANCE WITH WOMEN!!!
FIRST OF ALL —!
I TOLD YOU TO STAY STILL.
GASU (WHAP)
FRENCH BREAD USED AS AN ERASER IN CHARCOAL DRAWING
D'OW !?
WHAT DO YOU THINK YOU'RE DOING !?
IT WAS COMING ALONG SO WELL TOO...
HAAA (SIIIGH)
...BUT NOW MY MONUMENTAL MASTERPIECE HAS BEEN RUINED.

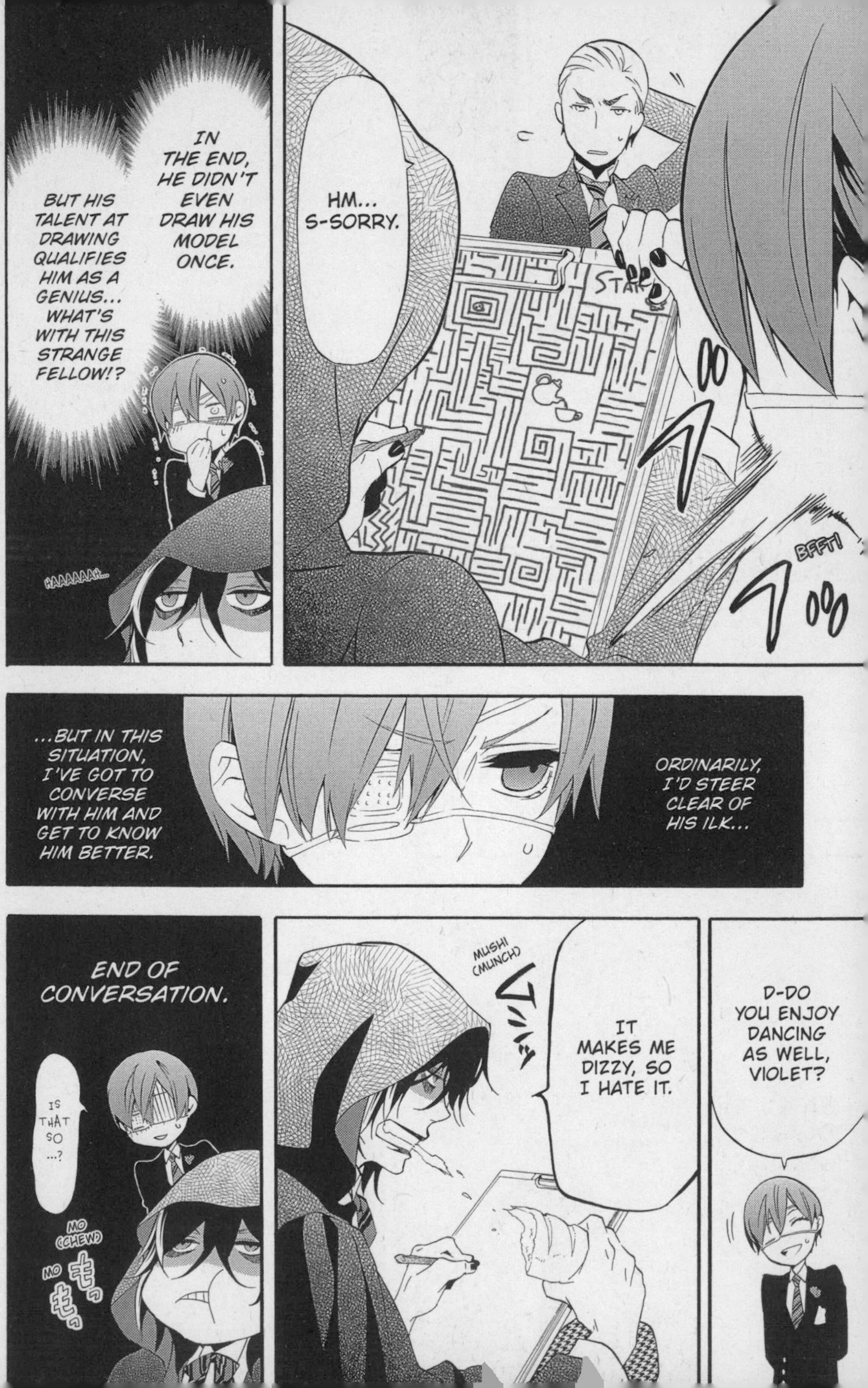
HM... S-SORRY.
BFFT!
IN THE END, HE DIDN'T EVEN DRAW HIS MODEL ONCE.
BUT HIS TALENT AT DRAWING QUALIFIES HIM AS A GENIUS... WHAT'S WITH THIS STRANGE FELLOW!?
HAAAAAAH...
ORDINARILY, I'D STEER CLEAR OF HIS ILK...
...BUT IN THIS SITUATION, I'VE GOT TO CONVERSE WITH HIM AND GET TO KNOW HIM BETTER.
D-DO YOU ENJOY DANCING AS WELL, VIOLET?
MUSHI (MUNCH)
IT MAKES ME DIZZY, SO I HATE IT.
END OF CONVERSATION.
IS THAT SO ...?
MO (CHEW) MO

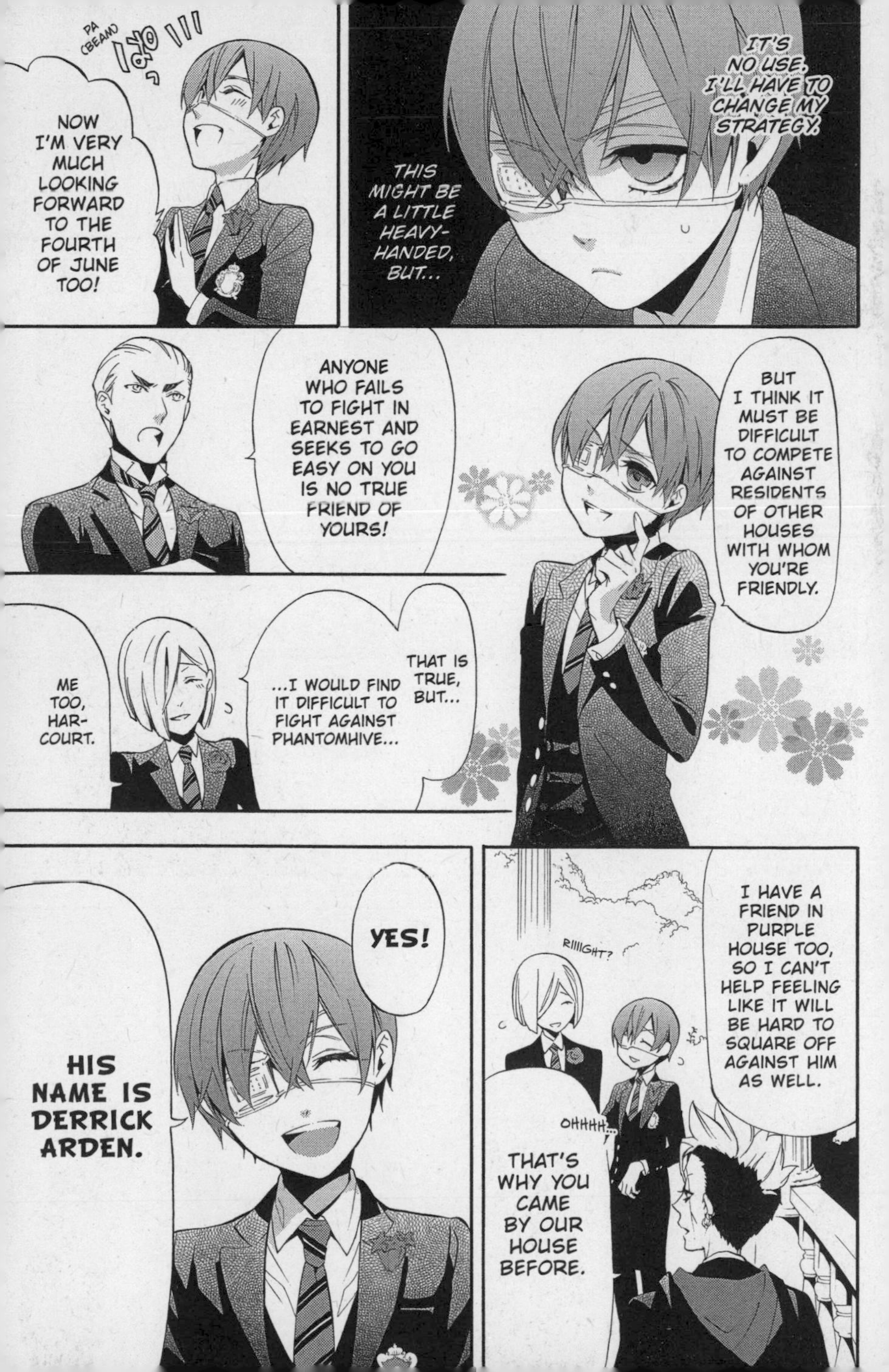
IT'S NO USE. I'LL HAVE TO CHANGE MY STRATEGY.
THIS MIGHT BE A LITTLE HEAVY-HANDED, BUT...
PA (BEAM)
NOW I'M VERY MUCH LOOKING FORWARD TO THE FOURTH OF JUNE TOO!
BUT I THINK IT MUST BE DIFFICULT TO COMPETE AGAINST RESIDENTS OF OTHER HOUSES WITH WHOM YOU'RE FRIENDLY.
ANYONE WHO FAILS TO FIGHT IN EARNEST AND SEEKS TO GO EASY ON YOU IS NO TRUE FRIEND OF YOURS!
THAT IS TRUE, BUT...
...I WOULD FIND IT DIFFICULT TO FIGHT AGAINST PHANTOMHIVE...
ME TOO, HARCOURT.
I HAVE A FRIEND IN PURPLE HOUSE TOO, SO I CAN'T HELP FEELING LIKE IT WILL BE HARD TO SQUARE OFF AGAINST HIM AS WELL.
RIIIIGHT?
OHHHH...
THAT'S WHY YOU CAME BY OUR HOUSE BEFORE.
YES!
HIS NAME IS DERRICK ARDEN.

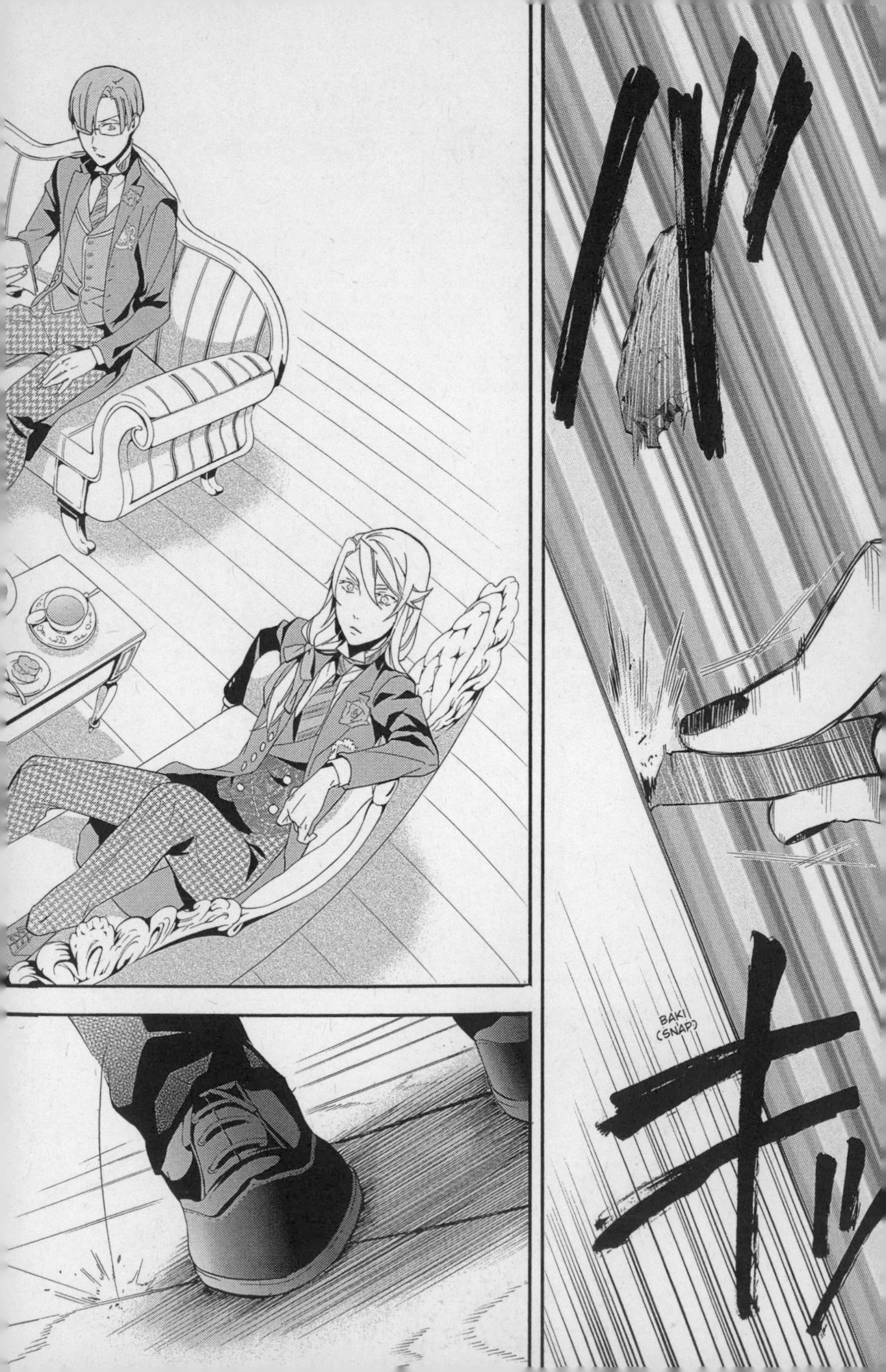
BAKI
(SNAP)

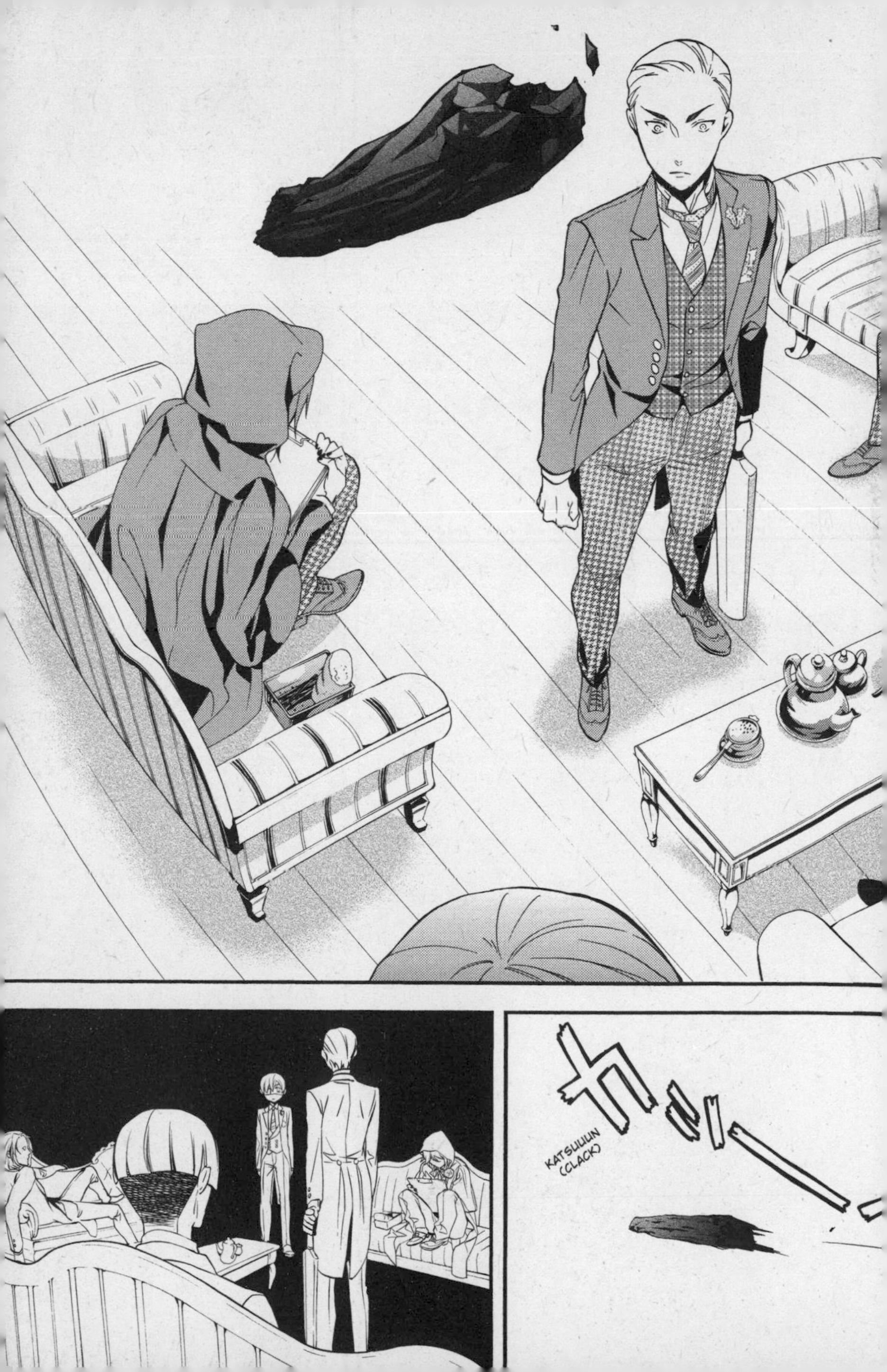
KATSUUUN
(CLACK)

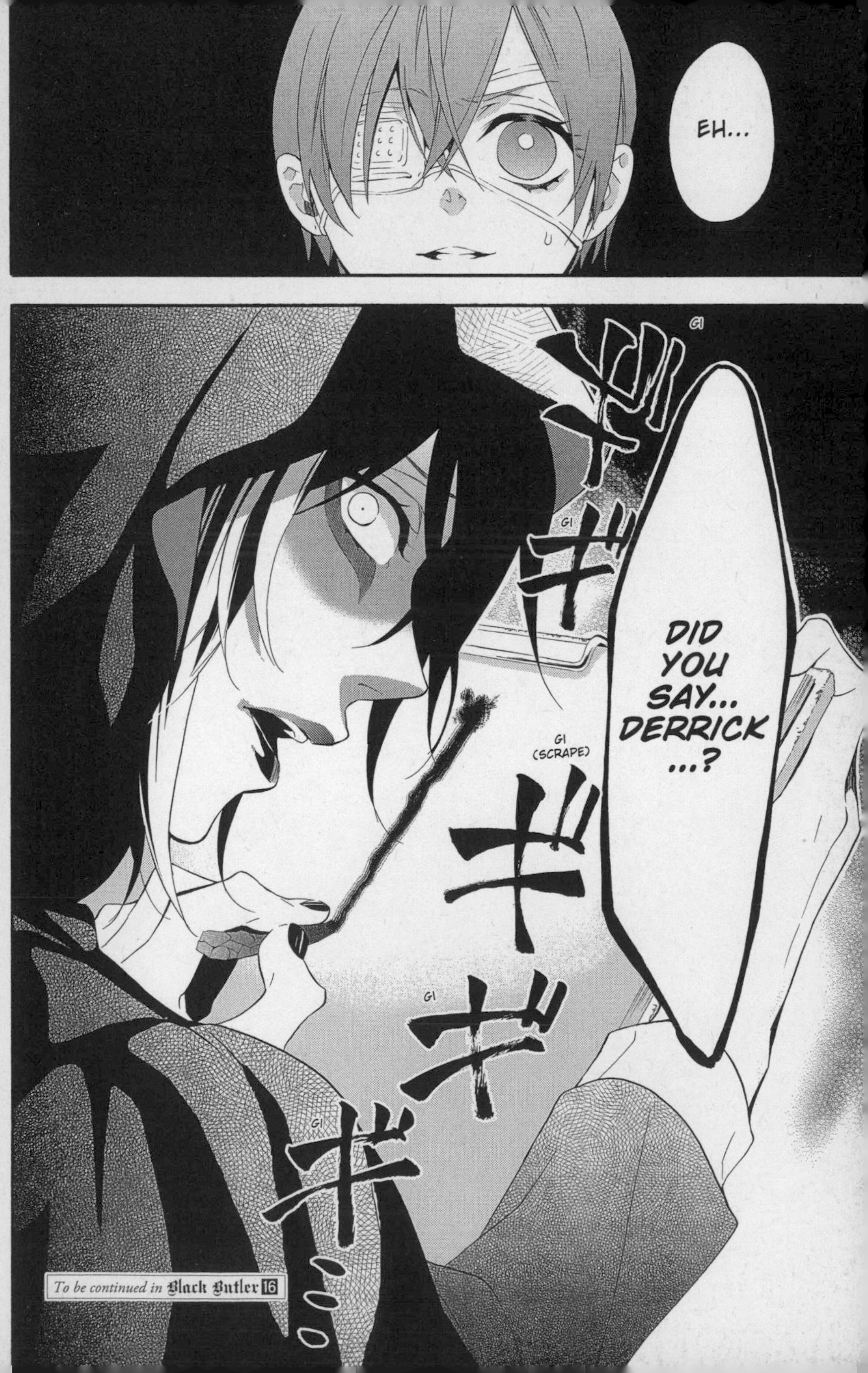
EH...
GI
GI
DID YOU SAY... DERRICK ...?
GI (SCRAPE)
GI
GI

To be continued in Black Butler 16

Black Butler

黒執事

Downstairs

Wakana Haduki
7
Saito Torino
Tsuki Sorano
Hashimoto
Asakura
Chiaki Nagaoka
*
Takeshi Kuma
*
Yana Toboso

Adviser

Rico Murakami

Special thanks for You!

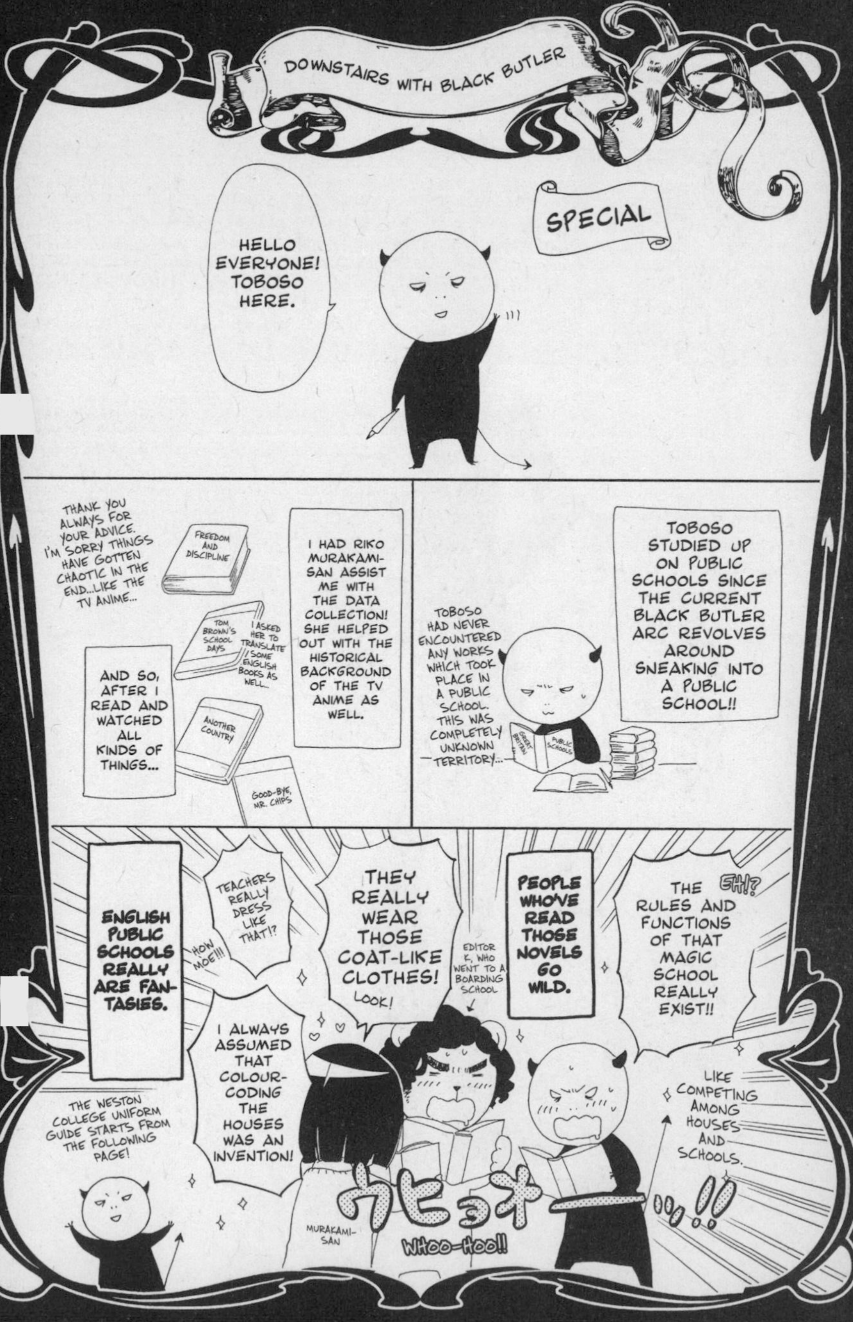
DOWNSTAIRS WITH BLACK BUTLER
SPECIAL
HELLO EVERYONE! TOBOSO HERE.
TOBOSO STUDIED UP ON PUBLIC SCHOOLS SINCE THE CURRENT BLACK BUTLER ARC REVOLVES AROUND SNEAKING INTO A PUBLIC SCHOOL!!
TOBOSO HAD NEVER ENCOUNTERED ANY WORKS WHICH TOOK PLACE IN A PUBLIC SCHOOL. THIS WAS COMPLETELY UNKNOWN TERRITORY...
GREAT BRITAIN
PUBLIC SCHOOLS
I HAD RIKO MURAKAMI-SAN ASSIST ME WITH THE DATA COLLECTION! SHE HELPED OUT WITH THE HISTORICAL BACKGROUND OF THE TV ANIME AS WELL.
THANK YOU ALWAYS FOR YOUR ADVICE. I'M SORRY THINGS HAVE GOTTEN CHAOTIC IN THE END...LIKE THE TV ANIME...
FREEDOM AND DISCIPLINE
I ASKED HER TO TRANSLATE SOME ENGLISH BOOKS AS WELL...
TOM BROWN'S SCHOOL DAYS
AND SO, AFTER I READ AND WATCHED ALL KINDS OF THINGS...
ANOTHER COUNTRY
GOOD-BYE, MR. CHIPS
THE RULES AND FUNCTIONS OF THAT MAGIC SCHOOL REALLY EXIST!!
EH!?
PEOPLE WHO'VE READ THOSE NOVELS GO WILD.
EDITOR K, WHO WENT TO A BOARDING SCHOOL
THEY REALLY WEAR THOSE COAT-LIKE CLOTHES!
LOOK!
TEACHERS REALLY DRESS LIKE THAT!?
HOW MOE!!!
ENGLISH PUBLIC SCHOOLS REALLY ARE FANTASIES.
LIKE COMPETING AMONG HOUSES AND SCHOOLS.
I ALWAYS ASSUMED THAT COLOUR-CODING THE HOUSES WAS AN INVENTION!
ウヒョオ!!
WHOO-HOO!!
MURAKAMI-SAN
THE WESTON COLLEGE UNIFORM GUIDE STARTS FROM THE FOLLOWING PAGE!

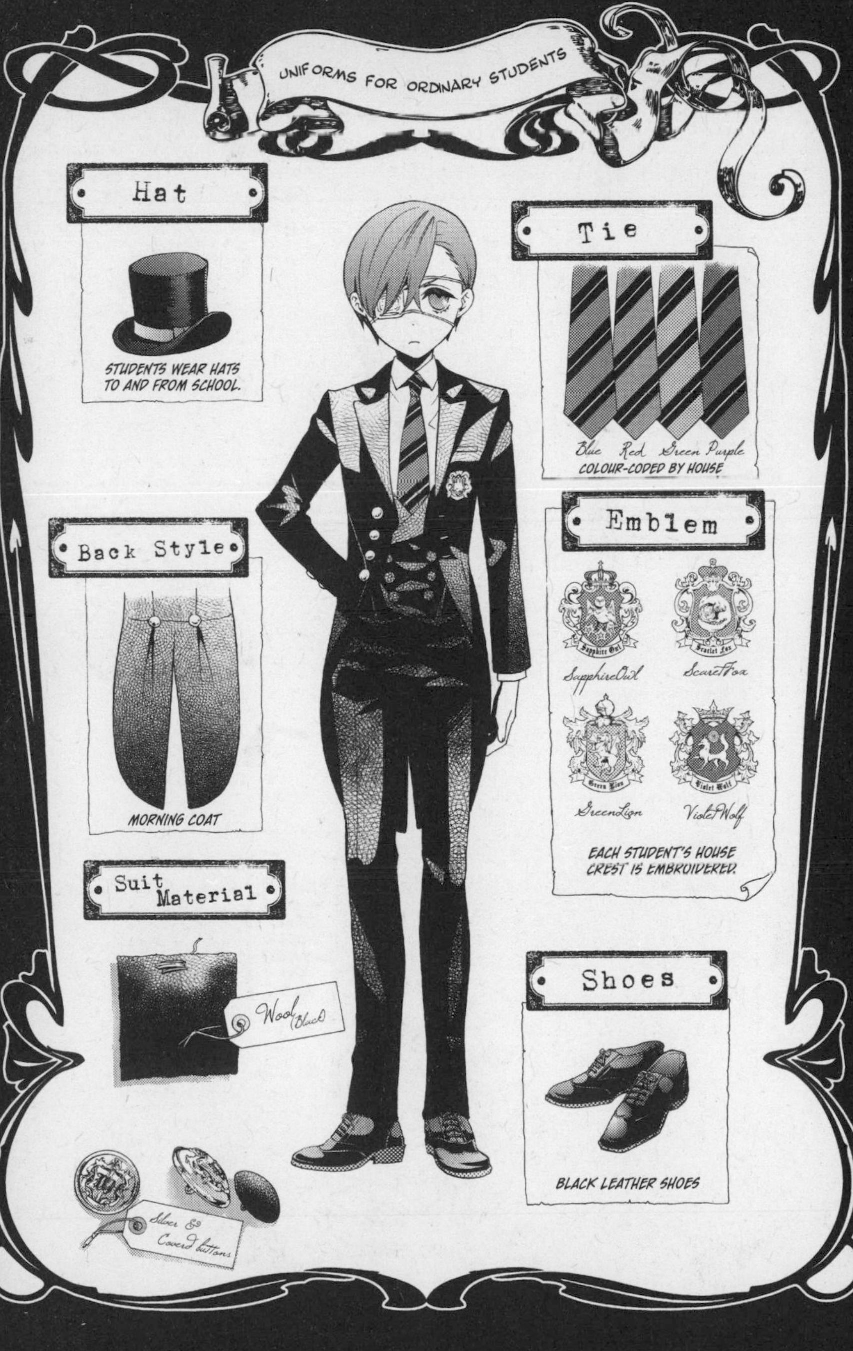
UNIFORMS FOR ORDINARY STUDENTS
Hat
STUDENTS WEAR HATS TO AND FROM SCHOOL.
Tie
Blue Red Green Purple
COLOUR-CODED BY HOUSE
Back Style
MORNING COAT
Emblem
SapphireOwl
ScarletFox
GreenLion
VioletWolf
EACH STUDENT'S HOUSE CREST IS EMBROIDERED.
Suit Material
Wool (Black)
Shoes
BLACK LEATHER SHOES
Silver & Covered buttons

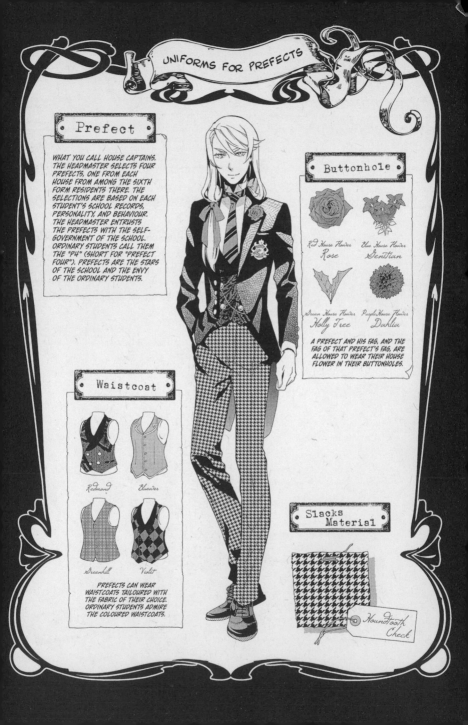

UNIFORMS FOR PREFECTS

Prefect

WHAT YOU CALL HOUSE CAPTAINS. THE HEADMASTER SELECTS FOUR PREFECTS, ONE FROM EACH HOUSE FROM AMONG THE SIXTH FORM RESIDENTS THERE. THE SELECTIONS ARE BASED ON EACH STUDENT'S SCHOOL RECORDS, PERSONALITY, AND BEHAVIOUR. THE HEADMASTER ENTRUSTS THE PREFECTS WITH THE SELF-GOVERNMENT OF THE SCHOOL. ORDINARY STUDENTS CALL THEM THE "P4" (SHORT FOR "PREFECT FOUR"). PREFECTS ARE THE STARS OF THE SCHOOL AND THE ENVY OF THE ORDINARY STUDENTS.

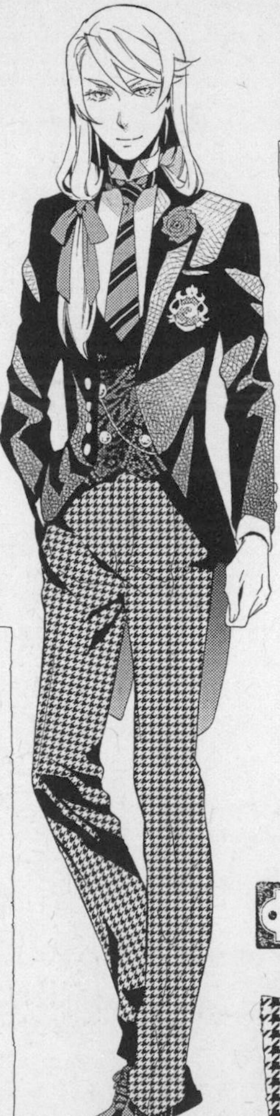

Buttonhole

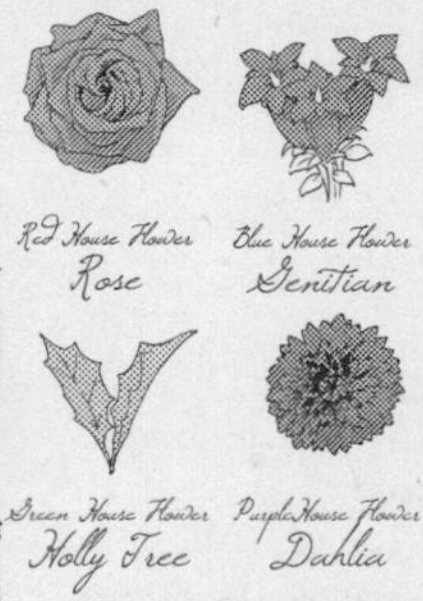
Red House Flower
Rose
Blue House Flower
Genitian
Green House Flower
Holly Tree
Purple House Flower
Dahlia

A PREFECT AND HIS FAG, AND THE FAG OF THAT PREFECT'S FAG, ARE ALLOWED TO WEAR THEIR HOUSE FLOWER IN THEIR BUTTONHOLES.

Waistcoat

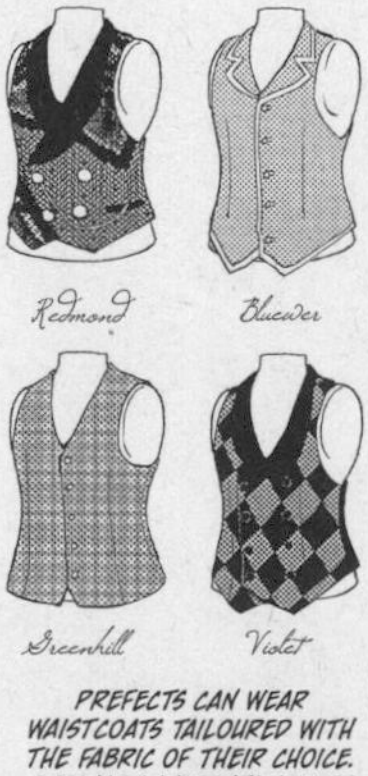
Redmond
Bluewer
Greenhill
Violet

PREFECTS CAN WEAR WAISTCOATS TAILOURED WITH THE FABRIC OF THEIR CHOICE. ORDINARY STUDENTS ADMIRE THE COLOURED WAISTCOATS.

Slacks Material

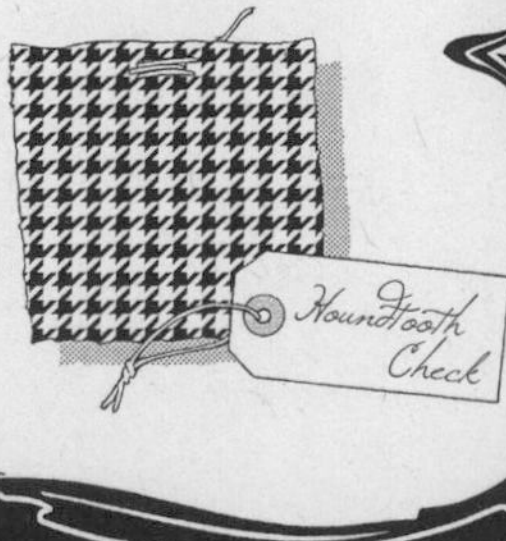
Houndtooth Check

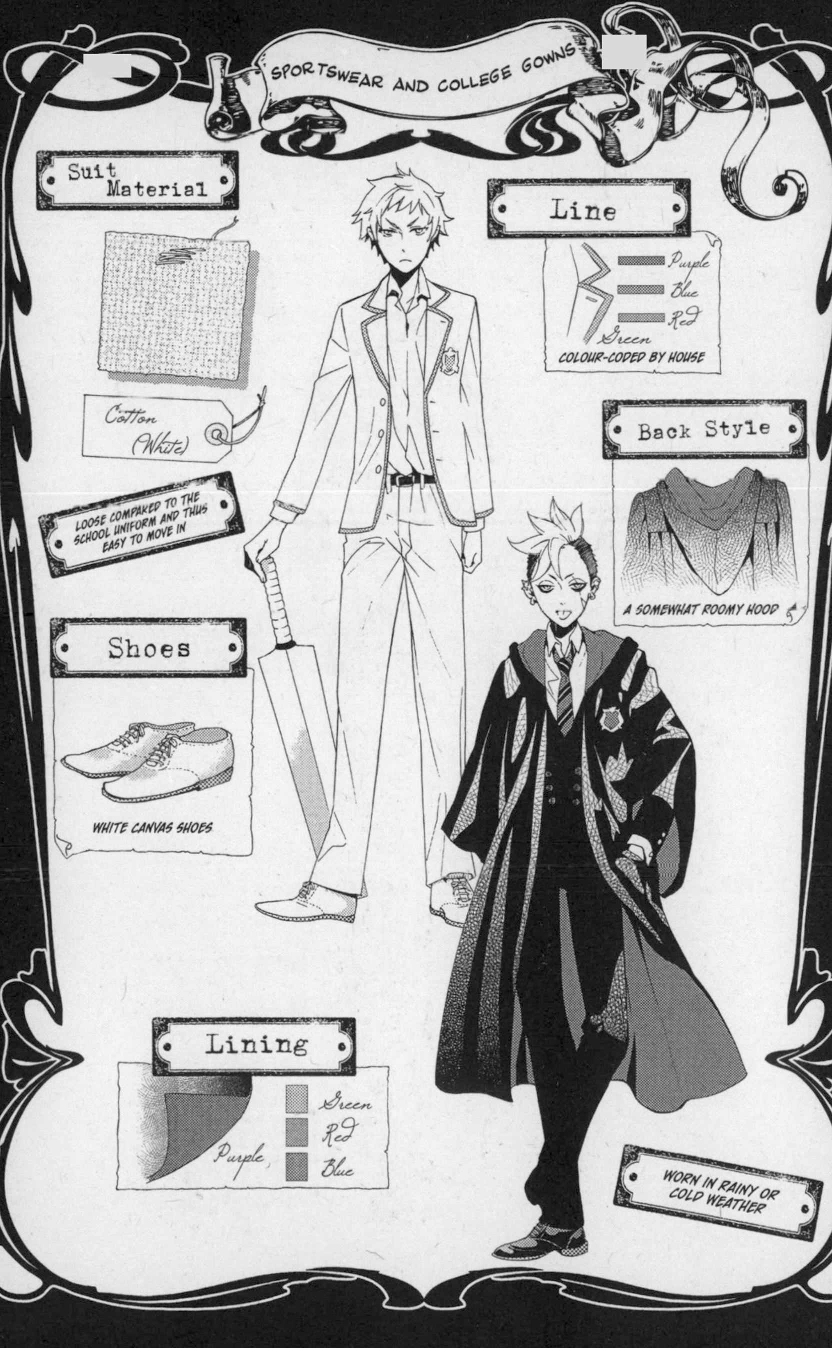
SPORTSWEAR AND COLLEGE GOWNS
Suit Material
Cotton (White)
LOOSE COMPARED TO THE SCHOOL UNIFORM AND THUS EASY TO MOVE IN
Shoes
WHITE CANVAS SHOES
Line
Purple
Blue
Red
Green
COLOUR-CODED BY HOUSE
Back Style
A SOMEWHAT ROOMY HOOD
Lining
Green
Red
Blue
Purple
WORN IN RAINY OR COLD WEATHER

Translation Notes

INSIDE BACK COVERS
Tanaka Brian
A Japanese racehorse named Narita Brian was voted Japanese Horse of the Year in 1994.

96
96 can be read *ku-ro*, like the start of *Kuroshitsuji*, the Japanese title of *Black Butler*.

Prix de l'Arc de Triomphe
One of the most distinguished French thoroughbred horse races run annually at Longchamp.

PAGE 4
Weston College
This illustrious learning establishment shares its name with an actual English college located in Weston-super-Mare in the southwest of England. The college was established in 1859 and attributes its earliest roots to art classes held by Henry Stacy in the historic Oriel Terrace building.

PAGE 8
Johann Agares
In demonology, Agares is a fallen angel and Great Duke who rules over the eastern regions of Hell. He is known as an expert linguist and is said to make humans dance.

PAGE 16
Fagging
Fagging was a long-running, if controversial, tradition in British public schools that was prevalent until the late twentieth century. While proponents of the practice believed that it taught responsibility and discipline to lower boys, it also lead to bullying and abuse in some cases. To this day, vestiges of the practice can still be found in aspects of British public school life.

PAGE 17
P4
The Prefect Four, and its acronym, bears a resemblance to the F4, or "Flower Four," a group of four elite boys who rule their private school in Yoko Kamio's classic shoujo manga, *Boys Over Flowers*.

PAGE 43
Golden syrup pudding
Golden syrup pudding, or golden syrup sponge pudding as it is sometimes called, is a sticky English dessert that is often associated with school life and cold weather. It is a sponge cake, steamed in a pudding basin filled with golden syrup, which is a pale amber-coloured treacle (the uncrystallised syrup left behind when sugar is refined). When the pudding is turned out, it is often drizzled with additional golden syrup on top.

PAGE 82
Lemon myrtle soufflé glacé
Soufflé glacé is a kind of French-style ice cream or frozen mousse made from a custard mixture that contains whipped egg and/or cream. The name derives from the dessert's appearance; it is frozen with a paper collar around the top, so that it resembles a soufflé risen out of its dish when served. Lemon myrtle is a flowering plant that has a culinary use as a replacement for lemon flavouring without the citric acidity of actual lemons.

PAGE 85
Uva tea leaves
Uva is a region on the eastern slopes of the central mountains of Sri Lanka (formerly known as Ceylon) that produces black tea of very high quality that takes well to milk. The unique geography of the region yields tea leaves with low moisture content, which in turn produces full, but balanced, flavour.

PAGE 87
The Logic of Hegel
A book of the same title was published in 1874 by Scottish philosopher and Oxford tutor William Wallace. In it, Wallace translated German philosopher Georg Wilhelm Friedrich Hegel's *Encyclopaedia of the Philosophical Sciences in Outline*.

PAGE 176
Freedom and Discipline
A book written by Kiyoshi Ikeda (a scholar of English Literature) that explains the British public school system based on his experiences attending the Leys School and the University of Cambridge.

Yana Toboso

Author's Note

When I began this series, I thought Great Britain was a magnificent and fantastic place, but now I feel it's actually pretty modest and conservative as a country.

That said, incredibly fantastic things do exist, and they continue to surprise me.

Both Sebastian's tutor outfit and Ciel's uniform actually exist; I've only slightly modified them. I find it wonderful that a school similar to that magic one currently exists, and students stride around leisurely in top hats and tails. I think it's about time I set foot in that country, don't you? And that's how I'm feeling with Volume 15.

BLACK BUTLER ⑮

YANA TOBOSO

Translation: Tomo Kimura • Lettering: Alexis Eckerman

KUROSHITSUJI Vol. 15 © 2012 Yana Toboso / SQUARE ENIX CO., LTD. All rights reserved. First published in Japan in 2012 by SQUARE ENIX CO., LTD. English translation rights arranged with SQUARE ENIX CO., LTD. and Hachette Book Group through Tuttle-Mori Agency, Inc.

Translation © 2013 by SQUARE ENIX CO., LTD.

Yen Press
Hachette Book Group
237 Park Avenue, New York, NY 10017

www.HachetteBookGroup.com
www.YenPress.com

Yen Press is an imprint of Hachette Book Group, Inc. The Yen Press name and logo are trademarks of Hachette Book Group, Inc.

First Yen Press Edition: October 2013

ISBN: 978-0-316-25419-9

10 9 8 7 6 5 4 3 2 1

BVG

Printed in the United States of America